THE FALL OF
CHRISTENDOM

THE FALL OF
CHRISTENDOM

The Road to Acre
1291

W. B. Bartlett

AMBERLEY

For Lauren

First published 2021

Amberley Publishing
The Hill, Stroud
Gloucestershire, GL5 4EP

www.amberley-books.com

British Library Cataloguing in Publication Data.
A catalogue record for this book is available from the British Library.

ISBN 978 1 4456 8417 8 (hardback)
ISBN 978 1 4456 8418 5 (ebook)

1 2 3 4 5 6 7 8 9 10

Typesetting by SJmagic DESIGN SERVICES, India.
Printed in the UK.

Contents

Acknowledgements

My sincere thanks are due to those who have helped with the writing of this book, in particular my Research Assistant, Deyna Bartlett-Williams. Her help and research skills have been most appreciated. Thanks also to my wife Angela who not for the first – nor probably the last – time has tolerated my absences on research or accompanied me uncomplainingly around some historically significant church, castle or other building on what is supposed to be a family holiday. This is not to mention the hours at home when my head has been stuck in a book or I have been hiding away in the study.

I am also grateful to Shaun Barrington and Connor Stait and their colleagues at Amberley Publishing, especially during the period of great uncertainty during the peak of the coronavirus pandemic. They have been unstintingly helpful, supportive and understanding. It has been a pleasure to work with them.

Introduction

The fall of Acre in 1291, which was then by far the most important remaining vestige of the Crusader lands in Outremer – 'The Land Beyond the Sea' or, more simply, 'Overseas' – was the apocalyptic conclusion to two centuries of intervention in the Levant by the Christian states of Western Europe. It was a harrowing finale, an end-of-the-world moment that would not be out of place in the Book of Revelation. Researching the last moments of Acre, one is made aware of the sense of terror as thousands of citizens realised that the denouement was nigh and that they were powerless to avoid it. For those without money to purchase an overinflated ticket to freedom on one of the last ships to leave the port, the unbearable realisation dawned that there was no escape.

But these events took place hundreds of years ago and the distance imposed by the passing of time makes it difficult to associate directly with what those doomed souls felt. Perhaps a more contemporary analogy would help. In April 1975, several decades of war in Vietnam were coming to an end. As triumphant North Vietnamese forces converged on Saigon, thousands of trapped South Vietnamese and Americans who wanted to escape frantically sought a way out. On 29 and 30 April, helicopters swooped into the city to carry evacuees to safety in the dramatically named Operation *Frequent Wind*. As an evacuation it was largely successful but not everyone who wanted to get out did. Iconic photos captured the moment as crowds of South Vietnamese desperately sought to escape and moved in on the last helicopters before they left.

Those images stay in the mind, and they powerfully capture the terror of those who want to flee and are unable to do so. We have no photos of course for Acre in 1291 but those more recent scenes may help us to understand something of the panic-induced fear facing thousands of men, women and children all those centuries ago. But for those trapped in Acre in many ways it was much worse. They had far less chance to escape and were about to come face to face with an enemy determined to avenge the wrongs of 200 years in a bloodbath of retribution and violent catharsis. In the process many lives were lost whilst those who survived the slaughter faced a half-existence of slavery and exploitation for the rest of their days.

It is important, however, to remember that there were two sides in this battle. For the victors, very different emotions were present. The Islamic inhabitants of the Levant had suffered much at the hands of the Crusaders. Whilst there may have been times of peaceful coexistence and even cooperation, they were interspersed with frightening outbreaks of violence. Terrible atrocities besmirched the story of the Crusades at places whose names resonated amongst the Islamic inhabitants of the region and haunted collective memory; for example Antioch and Jerusalem during the First Crusade – or most pertinently perhaps, Acre during the Third. There was certainly a strong sense of revenge motivating elements of the army that took Acre in 1291.

Although this violent denouement at Acre is perhaps a suitable symbolic conclusion to mark the ultimate destruction of the Crusader states in Outremer, its demise had been some time coming. The premise underpinning this book is that the loss of Acre was no out-of-the-blue cataclysm but the result of a long, slow-burning escalation between many different power blocs, not just Crusaders and Muslims. The demise of the Kingdom of Jerusalem as it was called (even though Jerusalem was lost half a century before Acre) was not like the sudden death of a favourite middle-aged relative, shocking and unexpected. It resembled that of a neglected aged aunt or uncle, slow, drawn-out and anticipated, the passing of a relative who had been ignored and virtually forgotten. Along the road to its final demise, there were disturbing and violent events. As interesting as the final fall of Acre were the events of preceding decades, when the inhabitants of the rump of a much bigger bloc of Crusader territories were eyewitnesses to some of the most significant events of the Middle Ages. Two great powers collided in a fight to the death which, if it had gone another way, could have changed the course of world history. The Crusaders were only a third force in this battle for supremacy between Mongols and Mamluks. But Outremer was no dispassionate bystander to these events. Her citizens played a role in them, even enjoying for a short time the sweet taste of success. It was not to last and a far bitterer taste would follow. Some in Outremer had chosen a side in these massive events; and in the end they had opted for the wrong one.

The great battle of the thirteenth century in the Levant was not that between Islam and Crusader Christendom. It was the conflict between Islam and the seemingly unstoppable Mongol khanate that defined the period in the Middle East. As the century progressed, it seemed that nothing could stop the Mongol deluge. Ever since the imperial expansionism of Genghis Khan the two worlds had been rivals. After his death the confrontation became even more ferocious. Islam suffered catastrophic defeat at the hands of the Mongols; Baghdad, one of its greatest cities, was obliterated by them. The Muslim religion tottered on the edge of an abyss into which it might fall, perhaps never to climb out again. It was almost literally under the noses of the Crusader states that the decisive battle in this vicious war was fought. Within a short march of Acre, the Muslim and Mongol world would fight for supremacy. In the aftermath, a new great power would be born, one which would sign the death warrant of Crusader Outremer.

Jerusalem, captured by the First Crusade in 1099, was lost to Christendom in 1187. Acre then became the seat of power for the rump of the Crusader states that survived. It largely remained so for another century (though Jerusalem was regained for a few years in the thirteenth century). It became the heart of a kingdom where mutating and unlikely alliances became the norm, when a Muslim power could combine with a Crusader force against a common Muslim enemy; or when two different Christian factions could be far more concerned about getting one over each other than in uniting against an Islamic rival. At the same time, the lure of crusading to the Levant became less attractive as other prizes closer to home became more available to aspiring Crusaders. The religious advantages that a pilgrim could once only gain by completing the perilous journey to the Church of the Holy Sepulchre in Jerusalem could now be obtained by taking part in an expedition against Cathar heretics in the south of France, or a heretic emperor in Italy. Why then bother to travel across the hostile Mediterranean and into Muslim-held territory when a much more convenient alternative was at hand? Vows could also be redeemed more quickly in the process. As the thirteenth century progressed, this had a major impact on the Kingdom of Jerusalem.

I have been subconsciously writing this book for many years. My first publication, *God Wills It!,* was released in 1998. I had been drawn into writing it by the magnificent crusade trilogy that was penned by Sir Steven Runciman, a work that was even then four decades old and perhaps with some of its conclusions overtaken by subsequent research but with breathtaking prose nonetheless. Runciman's magnum opus (in my eyes at least) had been a strange source of solace – the sublime eloquence of the writing rather than the events it covered – during a terrible low moment in my life after the loss of someone very close and very young. Since writing *God Wills It!* there has been a distant thought at the back of my mind that I should one day research and write on those momentous events that brought an effective end to the enterprise of Outremer. For me, this book's subtitle, *The Road to Acre,* has a dual and somewhat personal nature; it has taken me twenty years to get here.

As a result, I have been, until quite recently unknowingly, researching this subject ever since my first book was published. Many of the places I am writing about I have been fortunate enough to visit, in some cases not specifically for research for this book. The best example of the serendipitous nature of my travels would undoubtedly be when I visited Syria in 2007 when it was still safe to go there. Spending time in historic places like Damascus, Aleppo and Crac des Chevaliers was, I now appreciate, a special opportunity which should not be taken for granted, one which might quite possibly not come again in my lifetime. The serendipity has continued through my work, which has taken me to countries that play a big part in the story that follows, including Mongolia, Uzbekistan, Azerbaijan, Turkey and Egypt. This has been backed up by visits to parts of the Middle East more predicated on research than work. And many visits to *La Serenissima* (Venice), Rome, Pisa, Sicily and other parts of Italy have also helped. Even in a very indirect way, working in Vietnam has given me a little glimpse of what it feels like to be in a country that is living through those turbulent times when war is coming inexorably closer to its destructive conclusion and an epoch is about to end. The widespread locations of the countries that played a part in a period in history that ends in one very specific spot on the coast of modern Israel reminds us that what took place there was part of a much bigger story. To understand history properly, we need to appreciate the wider context in which great events take place to make sense of them. History is rarely decided by one-offs.

This hopefully helps to explain the context of what follows. *The Fall of Christendom* looks at the build-up to the loss of Acre as well as its final obliteration. Its main premise is that, riveting and dramatic as the final act of the drama was, it makes more sense if one looks at it as an event that did not happen in isolation. With the priceless gift of hindsight, it can be seen that the end of Acre became almost inevitable as a series of events conspired to make the slimmed-down, eventually emaciated, Kingdom of Jerusalem a potential source of danger that its neighbours, the Mamluk land of Egypt in particular, felt they could not ignore, even though by the end it was almost an irrelevance.

Jerusalem 1099, Acre 1291; the Crusader era in the Levant was neatly bookmarked by parallel instances of fanaticism which had little to do with the Christian concept of turning the other cheek or loving one's enemies. But the storyline is about far more than religion gone wrong. It is also a tale of political intrigue and miscalculation, of military brilliance and incompetence. It is an epic of emerging great powers, of Mongols and Mamluks, of conniving and scheming commercial rivals from Genoa, Venice and Pisa, of unscrupulous Holy Roman Emperors, Popes seeking to expand their powers and scheming Angevin princes. Above all, it is a plot line twisting and turning in unpredictable fashion until it reaches its terminus on a May day in 1291 when at last the sun set on the Kingdom of Jerusalem, never to shine down on it again.

1

In the Beginning

'The race of perdition, unjust and criminal'
Muslim chronicler Imad al-Din commenting
on the Franks

Triumph and Disaster: The First Crusades and the
Evolution of Outremer
On 15 July 1099, the streets of Jerusalem ran red with blood. A ragtag
army composed of a hotchpotch of different nationalities which had
travelled across Europe and Asia Minor (modern Turkey), suffering
appalling hardships along the way, at last achieved what seemed to
be an impossible dream by taking the Holy City. The apocalyptic
words of Revelation 14:20 resonated: during the Last Days, the Angel
of the Lord would stalk the earth and grapes would be 'trampled in
the winepress … and blood [flow] out of the press, rising as high as
the horses' bridles'. The defenders of Jerusalem were beheaded on the
spot, pierced with arrows, lances and swords, thrown to their deaths
from high towers or burned alive. The stench of death was said to be
unbearable.

After over four centuries under Muslim rule, the First Crusade had
reclaimed for Christendom the city where Christ died and had, for
three days, been buried in a rock-cut tomb before His resurrection.
Alongside the death and devastation, there was joy, as eloquently
expressed by the cleric Fulcher of Chartres:

The clergy and laity, going to the Lord's Sepulcher [*sic*] and His most
glorious temple, singing a new canticle to the Lord in a resounding voice

of exultation, and making offerings and most humble supplications, joyously visited the holy places as they had long desired to do.[1]

So sacred was the city to the Crusaders that its first Western ruler, Godfrey of Bouillon, had refused to take the title of King of Jerusalem. There could only be one monarch in God's City, and that was God Himself. Godfrey instead took the title of Advocate of the Holy Sepulchre. It was a moving and pious gesture on Godfrey's part, but such fine intentions did not survive his death in 1100. From then on, his successors unashamedly took up the title of King of Jerusalem. But it became apparent that military strength on its own would not ensure the survival of this vulnerable new kingdom. As the realities of co-existence with Muslim neighbours hit home, a once unthinkable maxim, live and let live, eventually became the order of the day.

The crusading movement had been formally launched by Pope Urban II in 1095 when, responding to appeals for military help from the Byzantine Emperor Alexius Comnenus, he had summoned the West to arms. Although this was a deliberate clarion call on Urban's part, it had a number of inadvertent and drastic consequences. For one thing, Urban probably had in mind the assembling of a force of professional warriors marching across Europe to Constantinople's aid; what he got was a mass movement of an ill-assorted variety of people with many non-combatants, including those too old to fight, those too young to fight, those (by the general mores of the time) of the wrong gender to fight and many others who were just inadequately equipped to fight. The various expeditions (for despite the simplistic title generically given to these events as 'the First Crusade', there were many poorly coordinated groups involved) suffered terrible hardships on their way east. They took Jerusalem after an awful rate of attrition brought about by disease, exposure, malnutrition, combat loss or plain exhaustion. At the same time they also heralded what was arguably 'the largest scale military mobilizations of the medieval age'.[2]

The newly won Kingdom of Jerusalem needed a port. Acre, about 100 miles (160 km) to the north of Jerusalem, offered comparatively good harbour facilities, as the Muslims who still held it fully appreciated. It was not perfect as large ships could not enter the harbour and had to offload outside it but it was the best available in a region that suffered from a major shortage of decent ports.[3] It was also located at a key point on the road network. As such it was a natural place for a Crusader emporium to form. It was initially a tough nut for the Crusaders to crack. They bypassed it on the march to Jerusalem in 1099 and it only fell to them in 1104 after several years of siege warfare. An important lesson learned from these events was that the siege was unsuccessful until the Franks obtained command of the sea with the help of seventy Genoese (and possibly Pisan) ships. There was, according to the account of Albert of Aachen (though not some others), a massacre instigated by the Genoese (and, again, possibly Pisans) after the city fell as its treasures proved too hard to resist, even though an honourable surrender had been negotiated.[4] But, regardless of the motivations, behind the actions of the Italian maritime powers – driven by commerce rather than religion – it showed that the sea power that they brought with them swung matters decisively in favour of the Franks as far as the capture of coastal cities was concerned. It gave them a position of maritime supremacy that they never lost.

Acre soon proved its value as a point of entry into the Crusader states, particularly after land routes across Asia Minor became increasingly perilous with the emergence of a resurgent Seljuk Turk power. It was soon established as the main port of the new kingdom. It had the best available harbour in the region and a good infrastructure, offering obvious commercial attractions. Although Jerusalem was the undoubted *primus intra pares* among the Crusader states, others developed centred on Edessa, Antioch (taken with great bloodshed whilst the First Crusade was on its way to Jerusalem) and Tripoli. The relationship between these various polities was often a complex one. Each of them had its own ruler who might recognise some kind of nominal subservience to the King of Jerusalem but they could often also function as quasi-autonomous entities. Over time internal tensions were going to increase rather than decrease. The name 'Outremer' is a useful shorthand to adopt but might erroneously suggest a kind of unity of purpose and cooperation that did not always exist among the Frankish states in the region.

Edessa, an outlier in the north-east quadrant of these Frankish territories, was always the most vulnerable. It was a day's ride beyond the Euphrates and formed a salient. It was a symbolically important city containing relics of St Thomas, the doubting disciple of Christ. It was attacked by a formidable Muslim warrior, Imad al-Din Zengi, at Christmas 1144. The walls were undermined and collapsed and the city was soon once more in Islamic hands. There was a widespread massacre of the citizens after Edessa fell, and of those people of European descent who survived the slaughter, most were taken off into a life of captivity. It was personally terrifying for them but also harrowing for Christendom as a whole. After the euphoria of capturing Jerusalem nearly half a century before, it was a salutary reminder that the Franks were strangers in a foreign land, and as such vulnerable.

Despite this, throughout much of the twelfth century, the Kingdom of Jerusalem was able to consolidate its position. It was, it is true, sometimes a roller-coaster ride. For example, after the loss of Edessa a great expedition was sent from the West with vague plans to recover the city. Led by Louis VII, King of France, and his German counterpart Conrad III, the Second Crusade was badly cut up in Asia Minor. (Although this was in theory one crusade, the two armies arrived at different times in Constantinople in 1147 and marched separately across Asia Minor.) Those who did survive the dreadful crossing of the region then failed in their final objective of taking Damascus, which had been deemed a more viable target than Edessa. It was a foolish decision to attack Damascus in the first place as the ruler of the city, although a Muslim, was friendly towards the Franks. The decision to do so had been made at Acre in 1148, with some of the local leaders noticeably absent from the decision-making process. It was an early example of how short-term visitors from the West did not understand, or at least did not agree with, the realities of *realpolitik* in Outremer. Strategically, the attack on Damascus was short-sighted; tactically it was a fiasco in its execution, with too few troops to surround the city.

There were other disturbing undercurrents that became apparent during the course of the ill-fated Second Crusade. Those who commanded the crusade and the local leaders from Outremer were soon at odds with each other, a situation no doubt fed in part by the spectacular lack of success arising from the attack on Damascus. Neither were the leaders of the Western forces happy that the Byzantines in Constantinople had entered into a truce with the Seljuk Turks who attacked them vigorously as they crossed their territory – another example of a lack of shared understanding within Christendom. Nevertheless, despite the failure of the crusade to achieve its major objectives, Christendom was at least still on the front foot and eager to expand and the outcome of the expedition, negative though it was, did not immediately jeopardise the viability of Outremer. In addition, the decision of Conrad III to participate in the crusade marked an increase in German involvement in the movement that would continue into the thirteenth century.

With much of Palestine under Crusader rule, targets further afield were considered. One was Egypt. The Franks saw an attractive target in the country.[5] Ascalon, a crucial frontier town between Outremer and Egypt, was taken by them after several abortive attempts, opening up the latter to the threat of invasion. Egypt's situation was not helped by the sometimes vicious factionalism that characterised its rule. The Franks later attempted several failed interventions in Egypt during the reign of Amalric, King of Jerusalem (b. 1136; reigned 1163–74). The country was both wealthy and vulnerable, a fatally attractive combination. Expeditions from Outremer in 1166 and 1168 pushed right up to the gates of Fustat (Old Cairo). Yet, though it seemed for a short time that they would be successful, ultimately the Franks were outmanoeuvred. This had, for them, a most unfortunate side effect. Egypt shifted from Shi'a control into the Sunni camp when the last Fatimid caliph of the country died, helping to unite it with Syria, a potentially lethal combination for the Kingdom of Jerusalem. Outremer was now surrounded by a unified Muslim domain (in theory at least) whereas before this the Franks had been able to play off one neighbouring Islamic state against the other. A new Muslim power emerged from these events. This was in the form of a Kurd by the name of An-Nasir Salah ad-Din Yusuf ibn Ayyub, 'righteousness of the faith, Joseph, son of Ayyub'. The last part of his name gave rise to that of the dynasty, the Ayyubids, that he formed part of. He is best known to the West in abbreviated form: Saladin.

Egypt rather than Syria was the point of origin of Saladin's power. Now best known for his war against Richard I of England, most of his early career involved fighting against other Muslims, actions which made some of his co-religionists suspicious of his claims to be a pious protector of the faith. At one time a protégé of Nur ad-Din, himself a fearsome foe of the Franks, Saladin later struck a disconcertingly independent course, which threatened to put him into direct conflict with his erstwhile master; but the death of Nur ad-Din means that we will never know whether they would have come to blows or how such a confrontation might have ended. When Nur ad-Din died in 1174, Saladin was effectively the governor of Egypt, and he spent much of the next few years bringing together that country and Syria. When he finally succeeded in doing so, Outremer was now much more seriously threatened as the Frankish territories were surrounded by a hostile and more united Muslim region. To make matters worse, in the year of Nur ad-Din's death a thirteen-year-old boy became King Baldwin IV of Jerusalem; and as if his age were not obstacle enough, the new King was suffering from leprosy.

Hattin and the First Great Siege of Acre

Saladin proceeded to launch several campaigns against Outremer after he came to power, though he did not always meet with success. Nevertheless, the ruling Frankish caste began to realise the full extent of the danger facing them. Delegations were sent from the Kingdom of Jerusalem to the West, visiting the courts of France and England for example, in an attempt to drum up practical support to face the growing threat. They succeeded in raising funds but not men, who were a far greater priority. Saladin launched a massive invasion of Galilee, following a near-death experience in 1186 when his days appeared numbered. After his recovery he resolved to retake Jerusalem. The opposing Crusader forces were also vast – probably the biggest ever army raised by the Kingdom of Jerusalem – but they were lured into a carefully set trap in the parched hinterland. The unfortunate King Baldwin had died, as had his child heir, and the kingdom was now led by Guy of Lusignan, King through his marriage to the person legitimately next in line to the throne, Queen Sibylla. Short of water, surrounded and out-generalled, Guy's army was annihilated at the Battle of Hattin on 4 July 1187.

This was one of those rare battles in history that was truly decisive. In the aftermath of Hattin, the Kingdom of Jerusalem collapsed. Everything had been gambled on one throw of the dice, an atypical variation from the normal strategy of the Kingdom of Jerusalem in recent times, which was to act cautiously and avoid being drawn into pitched battles whose outcome was uncertain. Many of the garrisons of the major fortresses of Outremer had been denuded to strengthen the army. A general levy – an *arrière ban* – had been ordered and virtually every available fighting man had been required to take part in the Hattin campaign. Military orders such as the Hospitallers and Templars lost the vast majority of their men in the cataclysmic battle and its immediate aftermath; aware of the threat they posed, Saladin had ordered that most of those captured should be beheaded after Hattin. Imad al-Din, Saladin's secretary, told how religious scholars with the army 'each begged to be allowed to kill one of them, and drew his sword and rolled back his sleeve'.[6] It was a botched job by amateur and consequently inefficient executioners, an act of butchery more than execution, and it fits uncomfortably with the image of Saladin as a paragon of chivalric virtue. Few members of the military orders escaped the carnage. One who did, Terricus – Grand Commander of the Templars – spoke of 290 Templar knights being lost here and at the smaller-scale disaster at the Springs of Cresson shortly before, out of a probable 300 in the Kingdom of Jerusalem.[7]

Although the cities of the north such as Antioch and Tripoli were left alone, Frankish territories to the south were almost without exception lost. Acre, with virtually no troops to defend it, was assaulted days after Hattin and fell without the semblance of a fight. Frankish prisoners were put to work restoring the main church in the city to the mosque it had once been. Christian wall paintings were concealed beneath lashings of whitewash so that the building was again purified for Muslim use. Soon after, Saladin took to strengthening the city's defences and heightening its towers. And then came the most painful loss of all, when after a more difficult siege Jerusalem was retaken by Saladin on 2 October 1187, the anniversary of the day on which Muhammed had been transported to Heaven from the city. In contrast to the bloodbath that had followed the city's capture by the First Crusade in 1099, there was no massacre when Jerusalem fell on this occasion. Suggestions have been made that this was because its commander, Balian of Ibelin, threatened to destroy the city rather than hand it over intact unless the lives of the Franks there were spared, terms that Saladin agreed to. Nevertheless, thousands who could not afford to pay the required ransom were taken off into a life of slavery. The 'race of perdition, unjust and criminal' as it was described by the Muslim chronicler Imad al-Din, was ejected from Jerusalem, or Al-Quts – 'The Holy' – as it was known to his co-religionists.[8]

There was an overwhelming sense of shock, accompanied by guilt, when news of the fall of Jerusalem reached Western Europe; so horrified was Pope Urban III that he promptly had a heart attack and died. Pope Gregory VII, his successor, was consecrated on 25 October 1187 and just two days later he issued a bull, *Audita Tremendi*, demanding that the competing Western powers, currently at odds in Europe, put aside their rivalries and unite in a common effort against the enemy. He reminded his audience that the loss of Edessa over forty years before should have acted as a warning. One of the first to respond was Richard, son of Henry II of England, who soon afterwards became king on the death of his father. The Holy Roman Emperor, Frederick Barbarossa ('Red Beard'), also pledged to take part, as did King Philip II ('Augustus') of France. Once more, the Third Crusade promised much; this time it would also not deliver the required results, though the outcome was less disastrous than that of the Second as some tangible gains were made at least. The three armies made their way east separately with Frederick opting to take the land route across Europe and through Asia Minor whilst the French and the English armies sailed in two separate fleets across the Mediterranean.

Richard sailed across the Mediterranean, practising his fighting skills as he went. He put Tancred, King of Sicily, in his place with a show of force after his sister, Joanna, the former Queen of Sicily, had been shabbily treated following the death of her husband, King William 'the Good'. However, much more significant for the future of Outremer was the capture of Cyprus. The island was at the time ruled by a self-proclaimed Byzantine Emperor, the usurper Isaac Comnenus. When Richard's bride-to-be Berengaria, who had only just joined him in Sicily, was shipwrecked and threatened with captivity on Cyprus, he reacted with fury. His forces overwhelmed those of the Emperor and Cyprus quickly became a Crusader territory. Its crucial strategic position off the coast of the Levant was a priceless asset, given the naval superiority of Crusader forces. It meant that supplies and reinforcements could be shipped to the mainland in times of trouble. Over the century that remained for the Crusader states in Outremer, the island was to play a vital role. It would stay in Western hands until 1571.[9]

Whilst the Crusader armies journeyed east, an unlikely fightback had started amongst the Franks still in Outremer. The deposed King of Jerusalem, Guy de Lusignan, laid siege to Acre. This was a desperate move partly prompted by the refusal of the last major town held by the Franks in the Kingdom of Jerusalem, Tyre, to let him enter as it was under the control of his rival, Conrad of Montferrat. Guy did not have sufficient men to take Acre but neither were his opponents able to dislodge him. Fierce counter-attacks launched by Saladin from the landward side behind Frankish lines could not drive Guy off. He became a symbol of defiance in marked contrast to his image after Hattin, when he had ultimately been responsible for the disastrous campaign. Guy had acted with boldness, putting himself between the hammer and the anvil as one contemporary put it by placing his forces between Muslim-held Acre on the one hand and Saladin's relieving force on the other. With the large reinforcements heading for Acre from France and England (the German army on the land route to Outremer was badly depleted after large-scale desertions following the death of Frederick Barbarossa en route) there was every hope that Acre might be retaken.

This particular siege of Acre was one of the great set-piece examples of this type of warfare during the Middle Ages. The defenders were bottled up in the city but could be resupplied by sea, as it was not until Richard and Philip arrived that the balance of naval power shifted against Saladin. The besieging Franks suffered enormous losses, from disease as well as combat, but hung on stoically. The besiegers were repeatedly attacked and effectively trapped in a vice. They had to withstand hunger, extreme weather conditions and the persistence of their opponents. That their morale survived these blows bears witness to the determination of the men and women there. It testifies to the motivational impact of an ideal that they believed in so strongly that they were prepared to risk, and often lose, their lives for it. Attacks by Saladin on their rear were heroically repulsed with chroniclers noting that even women took part and perished in the fighting. The siege started in 1189 and lasted until 1191. But the arrival of Richard and Philip (both a year late in leaving their respective kingdoms) tipped the scales and at last the garrison surrendered, to the despair of Saladin who was powerless to intervene. Acre now passed back into Crusader hands. Philip soon after returned to France and left the army under the effective command of Richard, though the French contingent that remained stubbornly resisted his attempt to be the sole decider of strategy.

After the capture of the city, Richard was left with the problem of what to do with 3,000 Muslim prisoners. An agreement was made to exchange them for Frankish captives and the payment of a ransom along with the return of a sacred and highly prized relic, a fragment of the True Cross; a relic so highly regarded that for once the normally hyperbolic word of 'priceless' could be ascribed to it. However, there were delays in complying with the agreement on Saladin's part and Richard, possessed of that famously volatile Plantagenet temper, exploded. On 20 August 1191, most of the Muslim prisoners taken at Acre (the exceptions being the rich and powerful who would command a large individual ransom) were led outside the city to a small hill called Ayyadieh. Here they were butchered. Some it was said were disembowelled, as it was believed that they had swallowed their gold rather than let it be taken from them. The massacre took place in full view of onlooking Muslim scouts, who rushed to tell Saladin what was happening. He was powerless to intervene. It was a brutal act, though it should be noted that there were no Christian commentators criticising Richard for it at the time. Almost exactly a century later another massacre took place at Acre, this time in very different circumstances. It is hard not to assume that for at least some of the Muslim warriors involved in that later event an element of retribution for the events of 1191 was a motivation.

A Diversion to Constantinople – Then 'trapped like a fish in a net'

The Third Crusade continued its efforts to try to recover Jerusalem; but despite winning several major battles at Arsūf and Jaffa, Richard was unable to win the war. Eventually a truce was agreed – a *hudna* as it was known in the Islamic world – and Richard returned home with his quest to recapture Jerusalem unfulfilled. His journey back to England was forcibly interrupted when he was incarcerated by the Holy Roman Emperor, Henry VI, and only released after payment of a massive ransom.[10] Some of the gains made by the Franks were retained as part of the *hudna* but Jerusalem remained elusive; the reality was that what now remained to them was a disjointed rump of what they had once held. There were three main territorial segments that the Franks hung onto, which did not form a contiguous land mass. In the north was one region centred on Antioch, in the south another based on Acre and between the two a third around Tripoli. They were divided by Muslim-held territories. It remained to be seen if this abbreviated version of Outremer was viable in the longer term.

Some strategic rethinking was necessary. The unification of Syria and Egypt was the nightmare scenario for the Franks. For centuries the two had been divided but that had now changed and they had been united under Saladin, though that unity was still fragile. The Frankish states potentially formed a wedge between the two, which gave them some strategic significance to counteract the fact that they were surrounded. It made sense for the Franks to take advantage of this situation and try and push them apart again. Richard himself saw this and considered a campaign against Egypt. It did not happen, partly because for many rank-and-file Crusaders it was Jerusalem or nothing. But the idea of Egypt as a primary objective had been seeded and would slowly germinate. Increasingly, Egypt became the preferred target for expeditions from the West. Jerusalem still mattered for many Crusaders, but the leaders of most of the major crusades of the thirteenth century came to see Egypt as an increasingly important goal. There was a hope that if Egypt fell then the whole of the region would be affected as a result; the situation of Outremer would be greatly strengthened and Jerusalem itself might even be recovered. But rather than a means to an end, the capture of Egypt came to be seen as an end in its own right. The great wealth of Egypt and its significant strategic position in terms of Mediterranean commerce only added to its attraction.

There was one other decision made by Richard before returning home that was to have long-term repercussions for the shrunken Kingdom of Jerusalem. Richard had sold off Cyprus to the Templars, but their rule was not a success. Guy de Lusignan, once King of Jerusalem, was now without a realm. His kingship was owed to his marriage to Sibylla, the rightful Queen of Jerusalem, and she was now dead. Attempts to reinstate him as King had failed despite Richard's support. Richard therefore arranged for the Templars to transfer Cyprus to Guy (for a fee). As a result a Lusignan ruling dynasty was established on the island that would play a part in the remaining years of the Kingdom of Acre, as it should perhaps now properly be called, until the end of its days. The dynasty would rule on in Cyprus for several hundred years after the eventual fall of Acre.

Early in the thirteenth century, another crusade from Europe was launched. There would be no kings involved but a number of important nobles from Champagne and other parts of France as well as further afield took part. The Doge of Venice was persuaded to provide a large fleet for which, in true Venetian fashion, he would extort a large price. But when the Crusaders duly arrived in Venice to take ship, the numbers who assembled there were far short of what had been expected. There was therefore a substantial shortfall in the funds required to pay for the crusade, an opportunity that entrepreneurial Venetians proceeded to take full advantage of. If sufficient funds were not available, then the Crusaders could work off their debt to Venice through services rendered. What followed was an extraordinary deviation from the objectives of the planned crusade and one of the most controversial episodes in medieval history.

Initially it was announced that Egypt was to be the target of the expedition. For some Crusaders, this was bad enough. The lure of Jerusalem was still strong for the pilgrim and Egypt was to many not an acceptable substitute. But then the plot thickened. The wily octogenarian Doge, Enrico Dandolo – who had accompanied the expedition – persuaded and cajoled its leadership to help recover the port of Zara, on the Dalmatian coast of the Adriatic, for Venice. Once this was achieved, an even greater deviation from the plan followed. The crusade was persuaded to help reinstate the ousted Byzantine Emperor on his throne in Constantinople, something for which in return they would receive a vast payment. The aim of reinstalling the Emperor was achieved but when the fortune that had been promised to them did not subsequently materialise, they stormed the city.

On 12 April 1204, the forces of the Fourth Crusade broke in through the great walls of Constantinople that had resisted all attempts to breach them for nearly a thousand years. Several days of rape and pillage followed, not unleashed against a Muslim opponent but targeted at fellow Christians, albeit ones of the Greek Orthodox rather than Roman Catholic persuasion. The Orthodox and Catholic churches had been in formal schism since 1054 and tensions that had been barely concealed below the surface now erupted with violent intensity. It was a horrific and shameful interlude, which also impacted on the geopolitical situation in the Levant significantly. A new 'Latin' Empire was set up in Constantinople, though several remnants of the Byzantine Empire struggled on in parts of Asia Minor and Greece. The Crusaders in Outremer theoretically had a new ally in Constantinople – relations with the Byzantine Empire had often been strained since the first Crusaders failed to return reconquered lands to the Emperor to whom they had historically belonged. The capture of Constantinople introduced a new and as yet uncertain dimension to the politics of the region. Yet whilst the original plan to attack Egypt was not without its merits, as Saladin's Ayyubid confederation had begun to unravel after his death (in fact Damascus and Egypt were at war with each other in 1194, just a year after), the country itself was never threatened by this expedition. This suited the Venetians – who placed a high value on trading relationships with Egypt – very well.

Pope Innocent III strongly disapproved of the diversion of the Fourth Crusade but in true Innocent style resolved to make the most of a bad job. He quickly came to terms with the existence of the newly acquired territory, which was given the name of Romania (not to be confused with the modern country of the same name) and did his best to exploit the unexpected addition of the largest city in Christendom to the Latin fold. Indeed, by the 1230s the Papacy was encouraging Crusaders to go to the aid of the new and vulnerable Latin Empire now based on Constantinople. That said, in the short-term Innocent continued to preach the need for another crusade to the Levant, which he formally summoned in 1213. By the time it set off he had been called to meet his Maker. A substantial force was nevertheless recruited from across large parts of France, England, Germany, Austria, Hungary and elsewhere. Ironically, there are suggestions that it was not altogether welcome in Acre, where food was in short supply and the arrival of so many extra mouths to feed compounded the problem. Some residents convinced groups of Crusaders to return home and Pope Honorius III, forewarned of the food shortages, encouraged the Crusaders travelling east to take adequate supplies with them.[11] A war council was nevertheless held in Acre in 1217 to decide on its target. During this meeting it was argued that Damietta, an important port on the Nile Delta, should be the first objective. The Ayyubid territories continued to fracture and Damietta was a great prize in its own right; its capture would help widen the fissure apparent in the ruling regime. This time, the crusade would arrive at its intended destination at the mouth of the Nile.

The invasion fleet set off from Atlit, to the south of Haifa, where a great fortification (also known as Chastel Pèlerin) was about to be built that was so impressive that eight centuries on in modern Israel it is out of bounds to the general public as it is still being used as a military base. It was constructed during the winter of 1217-18 through the efforts of a Flemish Crusader, Walter of Avesnes, and contingents of Templars and Teutonic Knights. It would be surrounded by the sea on three sides and the eastern wall, on the landward side, would never be breached. An attack on it by forces from Damascus in 1220 was resisted even though the castle was not then complete. The curtain walls were so enormous that armed horsemen could ride inside them whilst there was a moat that could be flooded by water from the sea on demand. The regent of the Kingdom of Acre, John of Brienne, led the army to Egypt from here.

Despite the Franks assembling a strong force, Damietta proved difficult to capture. The siege went on for over a year with the besiegers suffering greatly both from the attrition caused by their opponents and disease, often a far deadlier enemy in medieval warfare than any human foe. The military orders played a prominent part in the battle including a relatively new body, the Teutonic Knights, who had been established during the siege of Acre in 1190–91.

Eventually (after eighteen months) Damietta fell. Cut off from the rest of Egypt, malnutrition and disease took their toll on the defending garrison. When the Crusaders finally breached the walls, they found something like a city of the dead. Damietta was then transformed into a Frankish city, the Great Mosque became a cathedral and a Christian bishop was installed. This was a great success. However, the next move made by the expedition was anything but.

The crusade suffered from a divided leadership with ideas diametrically opposed to each other; on the one hand its secular leader, John of Brienne, argued for one course of action, on the other its religious figurehead, the papal legate Cardinal Pelagius, for something quite different. Eventually, the Crusaders resolved to push on towards Cairo. Unfortunately the move was made just as the Nile was about to flood, assisted by the strategic opening of sluices behind the Frankish lines by knowledgeable local forces who developed a carefully laid trap into which the crusade helpfully blundered. Stopped from going any further at Manṣūra, the Crusaders found that they could also not retreat; the army was, as one contemporary put it, 'trapped like a fish in a net'.[12] It was faced with the prospect of surrender or starvation. The former option was chosen. Damietta was handed back as the price of freedom and an eight-year truce was agreed. In return for great expense and loss of life no benefit had accrued; in comparison, the Third Crusade was a military triumph.

This delivered a painful lesson but unfortunately it was one that was not learned, if later events are any guide. Egypt was tempting bait but its conquest presented many challenges, such as coping with and understanding the Nile. There were wider strategic problems too. Whilst the crusade had been busy invading Egypt, Muslim forces from Syria were raiding Outremer, threatening Acre and Antioch. Some Muslim gains had indeed been made, such as the capture of Caesarea. Outremer was surrounded and outnumbered and therefore vulnerable to moves such as these. In the long run, all the attacks on Egypt would do was to create a determination amongst the rulers of that country that the Frankish enclaves must be eliminated. Attacking Egypt offered illusory prospects of gain that the Crusaders were simply unable to achieve. After other attempts on Egypt had failed, such expeditions helped hasten the demise of Outremer. The rulers of Egypt ultimately decided that they had had enough of being attacked and resolved to remove the threat from Outremer for once and for all.

The Wonder of the World

A remarkable figure was about to enter the world of Levantine Crusader politics. Since the time of the Second Crusade the Germans had been key players in crusading activities but that involvement was about to move up several notches. In 1225, the Holy Roman Emperor Frederick II, *stupor mundi* ('the wonder of the world'), married Isabella II (also known as Yolande), heiress to the Kingdom of Jerusalem, in Brindisi. This introduced a claim to the Kingdom of Jerusalem into the Hohenstaufen bloodline. Frederick was an immense personality capable of inspiring both admiration from his friends and disdain from his enemies in equal measure. One of his prized possessions was Sicily, where a culture had developed that was an amazing fusion of Latin Catholic, Greek Orthodox and Muslim elements. It was also in a prime strategic location, keeping a close eye on the traffic between the East and West Mediterranean and from Europe in the north to Africa in the south. To some, Frederick's court was a ray of light in a dark world. To others, it was a disgrace to the dictates of Christianity. Frederick's religious tolerance disgusted Pope Gregory IX so much that he labelled him *preambulus Antichristi* – 'The Predecessor of the Antichrist'. He was a man who certainly divided opinions, yet his brilliance is almost dazzling nearly a millennium later. Here was a 'polymath, intellectual, linguist, scholar, falconry expert and politician of imagination, arrogance, ambition and energy'.[13] But because of this brilliance much (perhaps too much) was expected of him and to some, including historians centuries after the event, he was ultimately a disappointment.[14]

Frederick's direct involvement in Outremer was to be brief but important. One of his first steps after the celebration of his marriage was to have the rights to govern the kingdom, formerly the remit of his father-in-law John of Brienne who was acting as regent for his daughter, transferred to him before he even left for the East.

The reason why John had such rights at all is an interesting case study concerning the complex succession processes in place in Outremer. There had been a series of situations in the kingdom when a king died without leaving a son to replace him but where there was a female heir. In such cases, she would become queen and her husband would then become *de facto* king.[15] However, when the queen died, if her husband outlived her then his kingship was annulled. Such was the case with John. He had married a granddaughter of King Amalric of Jerusalem, Maria, who eventually became queen. They produced a daughter, Isabella, but Maria later died, leaving John a widower. His daughter then became queen but was too young to rule so her father became her regent. Now access to this lucrative and powerful position had been summarily removed by Frederick. John was predictably furious. A few years later, Frederick would find himself fighting against papal forces in Italy. Prominent amongst those leading the army arrayed against him was John of Brienne, his father-in-law.

Isabella, who had been born in Sicily, was only in her early teens when she was married. Frederick was around thirty and already a widower. Her age though did not enter into Frederick's thinking. Much more significant was that Isabella, as the daughter of the last holder of the title, Isabella I, was Queen of Jerusalem. Whoever married her was effectively King of Jerusalem, *de facto* if not *de jure*. Frederick allegedly treated his young bride shamefully. He had an almost countless stream of mistresses and children, both legitimate and illegitimate. But in her tragically short life (she died on 4 May 1228, at the age of sixteen and possibly not even that) Isabella fulfilled one of the core functions of a medieval queen. On 25 April, less than a fortnight before her premature demise, she gave birth to a son and heir, Conrad. He was her second child – the first (a daughter) had died when a few months old two years previously. But in giving birth to Conrad she lost her own life. Just a week old, he duly became King of Jerusalem, *de jure* but certainly not *de facto*.

The production of a son and heir for the Kingdom of Jerusalem gave Frederick and the Hohenstaufen dynasty of which he was part a legal foothold in Outremer. Intending to take full advantage of this, he arrived in Acre in September 1228, in fulfilment of Crusader vows he had made some years before. But he had been so dilatory in setting out on his mission (it was twelve years since he had undertaken to do so) that he had by now been excommunicated by Pope Gregory IX.

After his extended period of prevarication, his latest excuse that he was ill and incapable of travelling was ironically probably true (several of his leading lieutenants died of an illness at this time) but Gregory's patience had run out. As it happened, the timing of Frederick's arrival in Acre was immaculate (apart from the fact that he received news of his excommunication whilst he was there). He could involve himself in the internecine struggles that were being fought by Saladin's successors in the region and by a deal with one of them, al-Kāmil, was able to negotiate for Jerusalem to be handed back into Crusader hands. A ten-year truce was also agreed by which most of Jerusalem as well as the other two holiest sites in Christian Outremer, Bethlehem and Nazareth, were handed over to him. However, problems were evident from the outset. Aware of his excommunication, the Templars and Hospitallers refused to collaborate with him. Only the Teutonic Knights and the Genoese could be prevailed upon to do so. The former in particular were not unnaturally closely aligned to Frederick II, given their connections to Germany; and their current master, Hermann von Salza, proved a strong ally of the Emperor in the negotiations with the Egyptian ruler al-Kāmil.

Frederick entered Jerusalem on 18 March 1229. He ostentatiously placed the imperial crown on his head in a ceremony in the Holy Sepulchre (he was not crowning himself King of Jerusalem but reminding his audience that he was an Emperor as well as the regent for his infant son). The Treaty of Jaffa, which agreed terms between the Emperor and al-Kāmil, incensed both Christians and Muslims. The Patriarch of Jerusalem, Gerold, was furious at Frederick's actions and Peter, the Bishop of Caesarea, was instructed to put the entire city of Jerusalem under interdict, a truly extraordinary state of affairs given its importance and the fact that it was now back in Christian hands, as were other places such as Bethlehem, Nazareth and the hinterland around Sidon. But the opprobrium Frederick suffered was an ominous foretaste of how myopic Christendom was becoming. The anonymous chronicler whose words can be found in what is known as the Rothelin Continuation of the works of William of Tyre was particularly scathing. Leaving spiritually important sites in Muslim hands (they retained their holy places in Jerusalem) was in his eyes particularly worthy of fierce criticism. Frederick's close relationships with Muslims created a great deal of angst. The chronicler claimed that 'the Pope and all Christians who knew of this were very much afraid he [Frederick] had fallen into the unbelief of Muhammad's law... He [the Emperor] also said, they alleged, that Moses had fooled the Jews, Jesus Christ the Christians and Muhammad the Saracens.'[16]

Frederick did not stay in the East for long. As ruler of an extended empire, he had other duties to attend to elsewhere. Nevertheless, his sojourn in Outremer was short but divisive and had a long-term impact out of all proportion to the time he spent there. He claimed to be the rightful regent of Cyprus as its infant king, Henry I, was only a minor and nominally his vassal, but his attempts to claim Beirut, Tripoli and Antioch were fiercely resisted by barons such as John of Ibelin in Outremer who had formerly been regent in Cyprus.[17] The Emperor anyway had bigger fish to fry. Frederick was constantly threatened in his lands in Italy and he needed to give priority to dealing with this situation. One eyewitness said that the butchers of Acre pelted him with offal as he left. Frederick left behind him an ongoing Hohenstaufen interest in the Kingdom of Jerusalem. It added a complication to Frankish politics that would create issues in the future. When Conrad, Frederick's son, wrote to the leaders in Outremer in 1241, reminding them that he was now of age and asserting his right to be king, his claim was resisted. There was little support from elements in the kingdom who felt that an absentee king would contribute nothing but in return take what he could for his own self-interests. In Acre itself, a Commune formed of baronial elements who were determined to protect their rights against the imperial power.

The military orders were caught up in the ensuing tension. As a 'German' Emperor, Frederick naturally favoured the Teutonic Knights over orders such as the Templars, who had little reason to support him.[18] The Templars were no doubt furious that their old headquarters in Jerusalem, the site of the al-Aqsa Mosque, was one of those areas in the city that remained in Muslim hands after the deal with al-Kāmil, and also that the terms of the truce prevented them and the Hospitallers from strengthening their major castles in the region. They were presumably equally incensed when Frederick had earlier demanded that they hand over the new super-fortress of Atlit to him, an order they totally rejected in no uncertain manner when they barred its gates against him. In contrast, the Teutonic Knights found their position greatly strengthened by Frederick's time in Outremer. But their nearby castle of Montfort ('Starkenburg' in German) that was taking shape with Frederick's help almost looked like more of a threat to dissenting elements in Acre than it was to Muslims. Ultimately, the right to be King of Jerusalem would be fiercely contested between claimants from competing European factions hundreds of miles to the west. Outremer, although distinct from Europe in some ways, especially in terms of its unique culture, would in others become an extension of it.

Frederick left behind him a fractured state in Outremer, imperialists on the one hand and anti-imperialists on the other, a problem that would fester for the next four decades. Whilst his policies might have appeared to have achieved a great deal, he singularly failed to understand the realities of life in Outremer. The Hospitallers later took his part whilst the Templars were dead against him. He nearly came to blows with the Templars in Acre, posting crossbowmen in key positions to disrupt communications between them, using violence if necessary. Matthew Paris paints a different picture, suggesting that the Templars were involved in a plot to assassinate Frederick.[19] A symbolic affirmation of the Emperor's resentment towards the Templars occurred when he arrived back in Sicily and pillaged all their wealth there. In the meantime, what was effectively a civil war in Outremer, known as the 'Lombard War', was fought between Frederick's representatives such as Marshal Richard Filangieri and the supporters of barons like John of Ibelin between 1229 and 1243. The Hohenstaufens only ever had firm control of Tyre and Jerusalem in the main and even that would soon be challenged. The Hospitallers (with the Teutonic Knights) and Templars found themselves allied to different parties in the dispute and in 1241 the former were attacked by the latter in Acre.[20]

But Frederick did at least leave behind him a kingdom governed from Acre that was benefitting from a truce with the Muslim powers. This generally held even after Frederick's departure, primarily because surrounding Muslim powers were at odds with each other and were happy to avoid the unnecessary distractions that a war with the Franks would bring. The coastal strip was largely restored to Outremer once more, strengthening its position as a viable entity. But a truce does not equate to permanent peace and when it expired in 1239 Pope Gregory IX encouraged the formation of a crusade from England and France. It arrived in Acre in September, led by Theobald, count of Champagne and King of Navarre, and Richard of Cornwall, brother of King Henry III of England. It succeeded in making significant territorial gains including the castles of Beaufort, Safad and Belvoir, and retook Tiberias, by the Sea of Galilee, plus the key frontier town of Ascalon in the south. Whatever else might be said of Frederick in a negative sense – and there was certainly a lot that could be and was said – he laid the foundations for a revived state which was more extensive than it had been at any time since 1187. Further, its position had strengthened because the Muslim territories in the Levant had continued to fragment. In contrast, the era of Saladin appeared to be something of a rapidly disappearing Golden Age from the Islamic viewpoint. But before long the world of Outremer would be turned on its head.

2

A New Equilibrium

'One obedient slave is better than three hundred sons.'

Islamic poet Nizām al-Mulk

The coming of the Mamluks

The situation was about to change radically with the formation of a new balance of power in the Levant. The Muslim position in Egypt and Syria was about to undergo a sea change with the emergence of the Mamluks (the word means literally 'property' but as this was of the human variety 'slave' might be a better way of describing them). They would play a crucial, indeed the decisive, role in the final destruction of Outremer. The idea of a strong force of slaves being established as an elite corps of warriors went back a long way in Muslim society. The Caliph al-Mu'tasim is known to have used such men as long ago as the mid-ninth century and for many centuries the selling-off of surplus children had been a staple part of life in areas such as the Central Asian steppes – Mamluk soldiers generally came from here. This of course appears cold, even cruel, to us, but there were limited resources available to feed a surplus population on the steppes and this helps to explain why such practices were adopted.[1] And back then slavery was widely practised and did not in many places attract the opprobrium that it did later.

Traditionally, such men had been Turkic, often of pagan stock, though on their induction into the Mamluk system they would be converted to Islam. The Caucasus and the steppes of Central Asia were favoured regions in which to seek recruits. Those enlisted were subjected to rigorous training. They lived in barracks (*tibaq*), effectively as a professional army available to   (or his emirs who recruited their own bodies of Mamluks) to use as and when they saw fit. Al-Mu'tasim used them as an alternative to Arab forces whose loyalty he had come to suspect. By the thirteenth century, Mamluk warriors had proved themselves indispensable to the Sultans. They were a formidable body and were the foundation on which Sultans built their rule, though their power could also undo such a man should they plot against him as a number of rulers would find out to their cost. When al-Sālih Ayyub became Sultan in 1240, he was grateful for Mamluk support. They were established as his guard in his palace quarters on al-Rawda, an island in the Nile at Cairo. An elite regiment of about 1,000 men was formed, known as the Bahriyya ('of the river') after the location of their barracks. We may find it ironic that slaves were believed to be more loyal than those who were freemen. A Muslim statesman of the period, Nizām al-Mulk, wrote a poem in explanation:

One obedient slave is better than three hundred sons;

For the latter desire their father's death, the former long life for their master.[2]

Mamluk loyalty to their masters could be almost incredible. There are stories of Mamluks urged by their masters to flee when a battle was lost refusing to do so; instead they hamstrung their horses and perished to a man fighting in support of him.[3] Such loyalty is more understandable when the wider context is considered. The slaves were acquired during puberty when their physical attributes were starting to develop but when their personalities had not yet been fully shaped and could therefore be moulded as required. Whilst for many the master would remain a more or less distant figure, for the chosen (or perhaps more pertinently the talented) few, very close bonds might be forged and the master might almost become a surrogate father figure. Training in the barracks was harsh however, and the death penalty was handed out for various offences including sodomy, perhaps as a result of which those in charge of the barracks on a day-to-day basis were normally eunuchs. At the end of several years training the Mamluk warrior was given his freedom, but his personal ties to the man who freed him remained intensely strong. This contrasted favourably, for example, with Arab soldiers whose tribal loyalties always remained largely unbreakable. However, it also meant that being a Mamluk was a one-generation vocation, for any children they sired would be free-born and therefore ineligible to become Mamluks themselves.

Mamluks were also vulnerable, for when a Sultan died his replacement would bring his own followers with him as he could trust them more. They could be immensely powerful and would occasionally take on the role of kingmaker. As we shall see, they could even become king themselves. Ayyub took the recruitment of Mamluks to unprecedented levels, giving them a political and military significance that had not been seen before. He needed them, for internecine rivalry with other Muslim elements, particularly with al-Sālih Ismā'il of Damascus, remained fierce. The Franks were able to take advantage of this. They skilfully played off one party against the other, acquiring important lands and rebuilding the Kingdom of Jerusalem for a time.

Amongst the Bahriyya was a Mamluk called Baybars. There is uncertainty as to the date of his birth and a range from 1220 to 1229 has been suggested.[4] There is more agreement about his region of origin, probably among the Qipchāk Turks, known to the West as the Cumans and in Russian as the *Polovtzi*. Having been driven westwards by nomadic movements further east that are now largely invisible to us, they had arrived on the fringes of Europe by about 1050. They then settled in the southern Russian steppe. This brought them into the line of fire of several later Mongol advances in the region. The first of these in 1222 was led by Subedei and the second in 1238 by Batū. Batū's campaign had longer-lasting effects as the Qipchāk were absorbed into what became part of the territory of the famous Golden Horde. The Qipchāk were known to the West but not highly regarded by it. A report on them by a Dominican observer in around 1236 noted sniffily that 'they do not cultivate the land, they eat the flesh of mares, wolves and the like, and they drink mare's milk and blood'.[5] Much of this may well have been true, as similar practices were known among other nomadic groups such as the Mongols, but nevertheless such details came as a shock to the West where such things were virtually unknown.

Disturbed by the Mongol advance, Baybars' people sought sanctuary with Anās Khan, a Turcoman chief. It was a grave error of judgment. He betrayed the refugees, falling on them in a surprise attack, killing some and selling others into slavery. Baybars was among the latter group. They were taken through Sivas in Anatolia into Syria where Baybars was purchased by an emir, Aydakin al-Bunduqdār. Baybars was a striking figure. In one of his eyes was a white speck, which put off some potential purchasers as being some kind of deformity that they were suspicious of. Baybars found his way through various hands into an elite Mamluk regiment where he rose to prominence due to his outstanding abilities and his impressive physical and intellectual presence; he was described as being a tall man with a powerful voice, swarthy skin and blue eyes.[6]

In 1244 Jerusalem was lost once more to the Crusaders when Khwarazmian forces – refugees from Mongol incursions in Persia – swept down on the city. It had been left without walls after they were dismantled in 1219 and the treaty of 1229 forbade their reconstruction so it was an easy target.[7] Pilgrims were slaughtered in churches and the notoriously unruly Khwarazmians 'cut the throats of nuns and aged and infirm men like sheep'.[8] Among the dead was the Hospitaller Grand Commander William of Senlis. A trail of refugees tried to escape the slaughter but they were persistently attacked by bandits in actions so fierce that their blood 'ran down the sides of the mountains like water'. A small garrison fought on for several weeks around the Tower of David but eventually surrendered in return for a safe conduct. Jerusalem was lost yet again to the Crusaders, this time for good; although some of Crusader Jerusalem's architecture lives on, as fragments of it were subsequently built into Islamic sites such as the al-Aqsa Mosque, which had once been home to the Templars in the city.[9] It was a grievous blow. In stark contrast to Saladin's capture of Jerusalem in 1187, the Holy Sepulchre was pillaged and damaged and the tombs of the Frankish kings buried there were desecrated and their bones scattered. However, the battle for supremacy between Saladin's successors in the Muslim Levant continued; in fact, when Jerusalem was lost the Franks were still in alliance with Damascus. The Islamic states in the region remained disunited, a situation that bought the Franks of Outremer breathing space even after these damaging reverses.

But an even greater disaster loomed for the Franks. They raised their largest army since Hattin, composed of perhaps 1,500 cavalry and 10,000 foot soldiers. They marched with their ally al-Mansur Ibrahim of Homs, who led a force of troops from his city and Damascus.

They came up against a strong enemy force at La Forbie near Gaza on 17 October 1244 (the battle that followed was called Harbiyya by Muslim sources). Al-Mansur wanted to proceed with caution. The Franks did not. To compound the difficulties that the Franks found themselves in, they were politically divided and the leader of one of the divisions, Gautier of Brienne, count of Jaffa, had been excommunicated by the Patriarch of Jerusalem in a dispute between the two men over property that they both claimed in Jaffa. In the end it was the Franks' arguments that won out and a precipitous attack was launched. It was a catastrophe; the Frankish army was largely destroyed and many irreplaceable men were lost.

The men of Homs were also massacred, with only 280 men surviving out of the 2,000 who had started the battle. A member of the Muslim element of this allied force, Sibt ibn al-Jawzi, was concerned when he saw that 'crosses were above their heads and priests with the battalions were making the sign of the cross over the Muslims and offering them the sacrament. In their hands were chalices and drinking vessels from which they gave them to drink.' The lord of Homs remarked that 'I knew when we departed under the crosses of the Franks that we would not prosper.'[10] Ironically, from a distance Frederick II offered the same argument but in reverse; the Franks had lost because Christians had entered into an accommodation with Muslims.[11] Gautier was captured whilst many of his men drowned in a vain attempt to escape the battlefield. After being used in an attempt to force Jaffa to surrender – tied on a pole in front of the city, he told his men inside that he would kill them with his own hands if they handed it over – Gautier was eventually taken to Cairo where he died in prison.[12] The effect of the battle on the military orders was particularly disastrous; only 36 out of 348 Templars, 26 out of 351 Hospitallers and 3 out of 400 Teutonic Knights escaped alive.[13] Losses of this magnitude were totally unsustainable and required the shipment of massive reinforcements from the military orders' resources in Europe.

This great victory allowed Ayyub for the time being to ignore the Franks as a viable fighting force and he turned his attentions instead to his Ayyubid opponents. He duly took Damascus, in many ways almost as crippling a blow for the Franks as the loss of so many men at La Forbie, as it reunited the region under one Muslim ruler again. Al-Mansur, in theory a rival, did Ayyub a favour by destroying the Khwarazmians, until recently his allies; they were unruly and difficult to control and in the long run the elimination of their threat was of great potential benefit to almost everyone. Ayyub secured his position in the south of Syria and then turned once more on the Franks, taking Tiberias and Ascalon from them. But his health was about to deteriorate alarmingly; and two great challenges now loomed for the Islamic Levant. There was news of a large crusade about to set out from Western Europe. This was alarming in its own right, but in the long run it would prove much less terrifying than the tempest that was about to blow in from the East.

Another Debacle in Egypt

Just after the disaster near Gaza, Galeran, the Bishop of Beirut, sailed from Acre to tell the West of the terrible news, demanding that reinforcements be sent urgently. So great was the danger that the delegation set out in November, outside the normal sailing season, and as a result it took six months to reach Venice.[14] The loss of the Frankish army at La Forbie came as a hammer blow to the West in a way that caused a similar, if perhaps slightly less fevered, reaction to that which occurred following the arrival of news of Hattin and the loss of Jerusalem in 1187. Pope Innocent IV held discussions at the Council of Lyons that led to the development of plans for another expedition to the Levant in an attempt to restore much-diminished Frankish fortunes there. The gauntlet was thrown down to the rulers of Western Europe; the most significant man to pick it up was Louis IX, King of France. Louis had anticipated Innocent and declared his intention to go on crusade beforehand when he recovered, as if by a miracle, from a malady that threatened to take him off before his time.[15]

Louis was a striking figure, marked by his extreme religious devotion but also by determination and no little organisational ability. He put the full resources of his blossoming nation at the disposal of the expedition. These resources included his own personal qualities: indefatigable energy, even if diminished through his illness, and a single-minded sense of purpose. A period of meticulous planning followed, during which time Louis made detailed preparations for the fleet that was due to set out from Aigues-Mortes on the Mediterranean coast. It made for Cyprus, with Louis announcing that the crusade's ultimate objective would again be Egypt. The expedition cost a fortune, with the Church in France being cajoled into picking up a significant part of the tab and the banking resources of Genoa also proving invaluable.[16]

Louis IX launched his crusade against Egypt with a noisy fanfare declaring his intentions. The omens looked promising: Islam was still divided despite recent events and Egypt was once more at war with Syria. Louis wrote imperiously to the government in Egypt: 'I have already warned you many times but you have paid no heed. Henceforth my decision is made: I will assault your territory and even were you to swear allegiance to the Cross, my mind would not be changed.'[17] He was backed by a sizeable force, so big, he said, that it covered mountains and plains, and with so many men that they were like the pebbles of the earth. It was a proud and defiant statement of intent, designed to make the rulers of Egypt quake in their boots; but within a short space of time these boastful proclamations came to have a very hollow ring. Sultan Ayyub was equally defiant: 'Soon you will bitterly regret the adventure on which you have embarked.'[18] But Louis had the better of things initially. Damietta fell quickly shortly after the crusade arrived there on 4 June 1249, in triumphant contrast to what had happened during the previous expedition to Egypt. William of Sonnac, Master of the Temple, wrote to Robert of Sandford in England that just one man had been lost in taking it.[19] God was apparently on Louis' side in this particular campaign, though representatives of the Kingdom of Jerusalem may have been concerned at Louis' imperialist ambitions as he showed every sign of turning Egypt into a French-governed territory rather than an extension of Outremer.[20]

There was palpable shock in Egypt at the fall of Damietta. This comes across in the words of Ibn Wasil:

> The behaviour of the people, of Fakhr ad-Din [notionally in charge of the defence] and of the troops was shameful: if Fakhr ad-Din Yusuf had prevented their flight and stood firm Damietta would have been able to defend itself, for when the Franks attacked it the first time, in the reign of al-Malik al-Kamil, it was even worse provisioned and armed, yet the enemy failed to take it for a whole year.[21]

Ayyub's ill health then played into Louis' hands. Suffering from tuberculosis, his heart was not in the fight and his soldiers knew it. To him, Jerusalem was now little more than a battered bauble and he offered to exchange Damietta for it. In reality, whatever Jerusalem's status as a holy city, Damietta was a far greater strategic prize. If the Franks were to hold it – and God forbid turn their attention to Alexandria too – they could control the Delta and access to the Mediterranean, depriving Cairo of oxygen and slowly suffocating it. Louis, elated and overconfident because of his initial easy triumph, refused to entertain the proposal; 'victory disease' had already started to kick in.[22] In response Ayyub summoned up the last reserves from his depleted stores of energy and had himself carried on a litter to Manṣūra, 'the Victorious', on the road to Cairo. It was too much for him and he fell into a coma from which he never emerged, dying on 23 November. Ayyub's son and successor, Turän-Shäh, was several weeks' march away in Mesopotamia and just at this precise moment Louis' expedition left Damietta for Cairo. The news of Ayyub's demise was kept from his men for some time, a strategy in which the Mamluk regiments played an important part, even though Louis got wind of it and was suitably buoyant as a result.

However, the way ahead was not straightforward for the crusade. Manṣūra was protected by a network of canals hampering the onward movement of the army and the River Tanis, a tributary of the Nile, provided an even greater obstacle. A face-off followed, one which helped the defending forces rediscover their equilibrium. They were aided by Louis' indecision following the capture of Damietta. His rapid success there had caught him unprepared with no clear strategy as to what should be done next. Six months were wasted whilst this important issue was resolved and the crusade finally set out for Cairo before arriving at Manṣūra, downriver from the city. It took some time to find a way over to the far bank on which the town was situated but eventually a crossing was found and some of the Crusader force made their way across. Louis, a cautious commander, had issued orders that no further onward movement should be made until he gave his approval. He intended to consolidate his forces and move them *en bloc* against his Muslim enemy. Unfortunately, there were impetuous elements in his army who could not, or would not, wait. An advanced contingent led by the King's brother, Robert of Artois, headed over on 9 February 1250. They refused to halt and then descended on Manṣūra, which seemed to be undefended as far as they could see.

Despite the rashness of this move, at first it seemed destined to succeed. The Muslim forces inside Manṣūra were taken by surprise.

Their commander, the emir Fakhr al-Dīn, was not in the front line when the attack came as he was taking a bath. He reacted instantly, rushing outside to find out what was happening without his armour. Commendably prompt though these actions were, they were personally disastrous for he was unable to defend himself when he ran into the Crusader force and was cut down. Unstoppable, or so it seemed, the Crusaders charged through the gates of Manşūra, confident now of their success. The Muslim defence quickly disintegrated and everywhere men started to fall. God was once more supporting the Crusaders.

But God's support, if such it was, proved ephemeral. The defenders recovered their poise and started to fight back. The Mamluk regiments inside kept their discipline and stayed calm whilst all around them were losing their heads (in some cases, one would assume literally). The streets were narrow, a labyrinth that was hard for the Crusaders to navigate, and they were on unfamiliar territory. Here and there at first, isolated pockets of defenders started to fight back. They climbed up on the rooftops where their mounted enemy could not follow and bombarded them with bricks, rubble, anything solid that was to hand. The momentum of the Crusader onslaught slowed and then faltered altogether. Emboldened by the first signs of success, more and more of the defenders started to fight back. At the same time the confidence of the attackers started to ebb away as they saw that the result was not quite so certain after all. They were eventually overwhelmed and their force was decimated. Robert of Artois, Louis' brother, was among the dead. The Templars, too, were badly cut up with allegedly 280 men lost. Given their normal capacity of 300 knights in Outremer, this was a crippling blow, especially as only a few years before they had been forced to replenish their fighting power after the disaster at La Forbie.

The residents of Cairo were on tenterhooks as to the outcome of the battle at Manşūra. According to the contemporary Islamic writer Ibn Wasil, news had been received by carrier pigeon that a fight had started but for a while no further information arrived. Whilst Ibn Wasil may possibly be exaggerating for effect, he says that the citizens feared the worst. Then, at last the welcome tidings reached the city; news of a glorious triumph for Islam in which many of the leading Crusader warriors had been slaughtered in the streets of Manşūra. Cairo erupted in a carnival of joy and thanksgiving. It was a significant moment in history, for it marked the turning point of the crusade. More than that, it marked the moment when the Mamluks rose to power in Egypt and ushered in the end of the Crusader states in Outremer.

On eventually arriving in Egypt, Turän-Shäh threw himself energetically into the important task of driving Louis and his crusade back. The intricate network of canals running off the Nile played into his hands. It meant that his forces could encircle those of Louis, trapping him in a vice-like arrangement from which he would find it very difficult to extricate himself. Louis planned to hold a defensive position but Egyptian ships blockaded the river route down from Damietta behind him and began to starve him out. Disease is a close relation of malnutrition and soon followed. Louis now saw that his only option was to withdraw back to Damietta and rebuild so that another attack could be launched when the time was right. But he appeared to have forgotten that Egypt was the land of the Nile. Its level rose with the seasons with the effect of closing off escape routes to him. The country was at the mercy of the flood. If it rose too little there would be drought; if it rose too much, there would be inundation. Now Egypt was in flood. Louis, worn down by both defeat and disease, tried desperately to break out but to no avail. They were trapped in a tightening noose. He and thousands of his men were taken prisoner (though many of those who were sick were slaughtered by their captors in cold blood). Louis was forced to negotiate a massive ransom whilst his personal entourage was reduced to just his chaplain and his cook. He had such a bad bout of dysentery that a hole was cut in his breeches so that he could defecate quickly as the need arose. His crusade, which had promised so much, had ended in debacle and humiliation.

But now, at the moment of supreme triumph, Turän-Shäh's world came crashing down around him. He sought to advance the interests of his supporters at the expense of the Mamluk leadership that had done so much to bring about the resurgence in his fortunes. This was understandable but unwise; the Mamluks were dangerous people to make enemies of. Prominent among them was Baybars, who was behind the plot that now unfolded. The plan was simple: assassinate Turän-Shäh and replace him with someone more pliable. On 2 May 1250, Turän-Shäh hosted a banquet. He suddenly found himself under attack. Wounded by Baybars, he made it back to the wooden tower he had ordered to be erected for his security – a sure sign of how vulnerable he already felt – but the attacking Mamluks set fire to it. He tried to make it to the Nile where he hoped to get a boat to safety but was overtaken. He pleaded for his life but in vain. With the attackers led by Baybars, he was killed there and then. So ruthless was the act that his servants had to enter into special pleading to be allowed to bury his remains with some kind of dignity. It marked the effective end of the Ayyubid dynasty in Egypt and the conclusion of a line of succession that flowed from Saladin, though it lived on still in Syria.

Despite this violent coup, the Mamluks did not yet feel confident enough to assume power in their own right; in fact, some of them were far from happy with Turän-Shäh's assassination and may even have plotted to kill Baybars in revenge.[23] Appearances mattered and they clearly did not believe they possessed the legitimacy to govern – not yet at least. Their next step was nevertheless remarkably bold. They passed the reins of government to Shajar al-Durr, a wife of Ayyub. She took the name of 'Umm Kalil, 'mother of Kalil', a deceased son of Ayyub. Friday prayers were offered up in her name in the Great Mosque at Cairo. It was a sham. Shortly afterwards she married Aybak, a Mamluk commander, who took the royal name of al-Malik al-Muizz. Aybak worked with an entourage of close Mamluk advisers. There were four who stood out: Faris ad-Din Aktii, Bilban as-Rashidi, Qutuz and Baybars. The last two would play a particularly significant role in the development of the Mamluk dynasty and the ultimate destruction of Outremer.

The new regime ultimately proved itself far more hard-line with respect to Outremer, though they did not immediately show their hand. The deal to release Louis and the remains of his army which had been brokered with Turän-Shäh was honoured; there was after all the massive ransom of one million dinars, some of which was as yet unpaid, to consider. But apart from his life and the lives of the surviving prisoners with him, Louis had nothing to show for his extravagant efforts. Worse than that, the outcome had hammered another nail into the coffin of the crusading ideal. It was a blow from which it would never recover.

Louis in Outremer

Despite the debacle in Egypt, Louis' crusade was not yet over. On 8 May 1250, shortly after he had delivered the down payment on his huge ransom, he arrived in Acre. He considered he was still on crusade. His brother Charles of Anjou on the other hand thought it was over, so he returned to his gambling, which had been prohibited for the duration. So angry was the French king that he threw the die Charles had been playing with over the side of the ship. However, Charles' opponent, Gauthier de Nemours, profited from this situation as he managed to grab all the money that was on the table – we are told that there was 'plenty of it' – before it went overboard.[24] The totality of Louis' defeat was evidenced by the fact that he journeyed to Acre without his own clothes, wearing some given to him by the Sultan. They were opulent enough, made of black satin lined with miniver fur with a 'vast quantity' of gold buttons.[25] Despite the appalling setback he had suffered in Egypt, Acre was elated to see him. An eyewitness described his arrival:

> Knights, citizens, sergeants, ladies, girls and everyone else were all as splendidly dressed and adorned as they could manage. All the bells in the town were rung ... many tears were shed in compassion and joy that the king, his brothers and companions, had been saved from the great blow Christendom had suffered. Then they escorted the king to his residence and all the great men of Acre gave him handsome gifts, rich and pleasant.[26]

There was pressure on Louis to return to France immediately after his release, but he resisted it. Many of his army were still in captivity – and the evidence of the King's companion and chronicler, Jean de Joinville, was that their fate weighed heavily on his conscience – and it would be devastating to go home having achieved nothing in return for an enormous outlay of money and men. In our world it is all too easy to be cynical about the actions of politicians and rulers, but Louis appears to have been inspired by genuine crusading motives. He only had 1,200 men left with him and of the 2,800 knights who had sailed to Egypt from Cyprus with him barely 100 remained; but he believed that this rump was sufficient to make something of a difference. He also feared a mass exodus from Acre should he leave, leading to the final collapse of what remained of the Kingdom of Jerusalem. His brother Charles remained with him for a short time, gaming as much as ever; he was particularly generous with gifts to those around him when he won, giving us an insight into the winning ways (in more than one sense of the word) that made him a charismatic personality. After a short time Louis ordered him back to France, perhaps to govern the country should he not return from Outremer.

Louis' mother (and his regent in France whilst he was absent), Blanche of Castile, sent him letters urging his return from Acre but he stayed in Outremer for four years (from May 1250 to the spring of 1254) and in that time became its *de facto* ruler. He worked energetically to rebuild the defences of the realm during this time; fortifications were strengthened at Acre, Jaffa, Sidon and Caesarea. At the last ramparts, ditches and sixteen towers were added. Acre particularly needed work. The suburb of Montmusard had developed on the northern side of Acre in recent decades, increasing the size of the city by about 50 per cent. Currently it was only surrounded by one set of walls, to which Louis now added a second, which was integrated with the rest of the fortifications of the city. Satisfied with his work, Louis took himself off on a pilgrimage to Nazareth, then in Crusader hands, where he attended a service in the Church of the Incarnation. At Jaffa, Louis happily carried loads of earth around as this act would qualify him for extra spiritual benefits under the terms of the papal indulgences in force. He even exiled the Master of the Temple, something he had no legal right to do, because he had been negotiating secretly with the Syrian Ayyubids. Indeed, Louis was frequently very assertive with regard to the Templars, despite the fact that they were notionally not answerable to any secular power. It was a sign that over the coming years the Templars were going to increasingly come under French influence, but this was by no means a unique phenomenon; in practice, at least seven of the twenty-two Templar Masters were appointed in part at the instigation of a secular ruler.[27]

The dominance of Louis whilst he was in Outremer emphasised its political weakness by this stage. The loss of Jerusalem in 1187 may have been sixty years in the past, but more recent events had served to emphasise the increasingly perilous situation of the Kingdom of Jerusalem. Louis may only have been a visitor but he was an extremely important and powerful one. He was still the best hope for a restoration of the Frankish position in the region, given the vast resources at his disposal. This is emphasised by the reaction from the Masters of the Temple and Hospital and the local barons when Louis announced his intention to attack Nablus. They all agreed it was a good idea, but cautioned the King that he should not take part in person, because 'if anything happened to him, the whole land would be lost'.[28] These words may have been written up with the benefit of hindsight – Joinville, Louis' chronicler, tells us that his book was assembled in 1309, long after the final fall of Acre – but they also suggest that, decades before it was finally lost, Outremer was already seen to be in serious trouble.

The divided nature of Outremer was emphasised during Louis' time there. He was approached by Prince Bohemond of Antioch for help in regaining what he saw as his rightful place as ruler of the city. Being only sixteen years of age, he was not old enough to rule in his own right and his mother was acting as regent. Bohemond sought Louis' help in ignoring convention. He was currently living in Tripoli but wanted to return to Antioch with men and money to improve his position there. He succeeded in winning Louis' support; by way of payback, he henceforth quartered his arms with those of France. This strengthening of relationships between the French crown and some of the key factions in Outremer would assume added importance as French-Hohenstaufen friction increased in Europe and the worsening political situation that resulted was played out in surrogate fashion in the Levant.

Louis played off the competing Muslim rulers in Cairo and Damascus in an attempt to improve his position through negotiation. The Egyptians were persuaded to return the heads of the fallen Crusaders that had previously decorated the walls of Cairo so that they could be given a Christian burial. Young Frankish slaves were sent back to Louis, to the disappointment of some in Egypt as many of them had converted to Islam. Louis also received an exotic gift in the form of an elephant.

Louis was also attracted by the idea of a Mongol alliance as their power continued to expand. Smbat, the brother of King Het'um of Armenia, had journeyed to the Mongols as his envoy. He wrote back of what he had found to his sisters from Samarkand in 1248. He had come across many Christians in the Mongol khanate and had even seen portable chapels near the great khagan's tent. The significance of Smbat's report was that he was the brother of two sisters married to the King of Cyprus and the Count of Jaffa. This information had been fed to Louis IX when he arrived in Cyprus on his way to his disastrous rendezvous with destiny in Egypt. The King took this as a sign that some kind of deal with the Mongols might be possible. At around the same time, Louis had received an envoy from the khagan. This ambassador, whose name was Eljigidei, did his best to assure Louis that his master was ripe for conversion. It was no more than an act of diplomatic subterfuge but, coinciding as it did with reports of Smbat's mission, it touched a chord inside the French King.[29]

But the death of Blanche of Castile in 1252 was a painful reminder that Louis could not stay in Outremer forever. He remained for a short while longer but ran out of money in 1253 and had to take out a large loan from Italian bankers to continue to finance his stay. He had spent the vast sum of 120,000 *livres tournois* on rebuilding fortifications in Outremer, which came to two-thirds of the amount paid on his ransom. This equated to half the annual revenue of the French Crown.[30] Now that he was out of money the barons of Outremer quickly advised him to return home, perhaps not wanting to be too long in the shadow of a French king, however pious he was, especially when he was effectively bankrupt. Louis had much to divert him elsewhere anyway and his reputation had survived the buffeting it received after the fiasco in Egypt, helped when the larger-than-life Frederick II died in 1250. The removal of Frederick from the international stage was gleefully responded to by the Papacy; Innocent IV was almost obsessive with regard to the Emperor and trying to get the better of him. He wrote of Frederick's death in the following ecstatic terms with any sign of Christian charity sadly lacking: 'Let the heavens rejoice. Let the earth be filled with gladness. For the fall of the tyrant has changed the thunderbolts and tempests that God Almighty held over your heads into gentle zephyrs and fecund dews.'[31]

These caustic if elegant words suggest that Innocent was far more interested in the ongoing dispute between himself and the Empire – reflected in the frequent outbreaks of violence between his Guelph supporters in Italy and those supporting the Emperor, the Ghibellines – than he was in the affairs of Outremer at the time. But the reality was, however justified the Papacy might have been in its distrust of Frederick, its policy towards him helped create a long-running disaster. When half a century later Pope Nicholas IV entered into negotiations with opponents in Italy offering a truce if they would crusade to the East, they came to nothing because the recipients of the offer were reminded that in Frederick's time the Pope's ancestors had taken advantage of his absence in Outremer to invade his Italian lands.[32] The actions taken against Frederick were seen by the Papacy as being as crucial as those taken to protect the Holy Land. This had been formally recognised when in 1246 Pope Innocent IV had issued an indulgence, a tangible spiritual reward which gave the recipient a ticket to bypass purgatory into Heaven, which stated that those who earned it by crusading against Frederick would receive the same benefits as an indulgence 'which has been granted generally to those who go to aid the Holy Land'.[33] The long-running and rancorous Italian wars, which continued into the fourteenth century, became a debilitating ulcer eating away at the body of Christendom without respite. They also had a critical impact on affairs in Outremer as scarce resources, both manpower and financial, were tied up in Italy rather than the Holy Land on a long-term basis at a time when they might have made an impact on the survival prospects of the Crusader states there.

Louis began his journey home on 24 April 1254, leaving behind a French regiment with 100 knights under the command of Geoffrey de Sergines that he would continue to pay for after he returned to France. He had strengthened the defences of the coastal cities significantly and these, it was hoped, would provide a springboard for future expeditions from the West to push inland and regain some of the lost hinterland of Outremer. His departure from Outremer came at a complicated moment politically for the Crusader states. With the death of Conrad IV, the Hohenstaufen King of Jerusalem, in May 1254 the throne passed to his son, also Conrad ('Conradin') – the second consecutive infant succession at a time when the Empire could perhaps least afford it. Conradin was two years old and his main sphere of interest even if he had been an adult would have been Western Europe, particularly Germany and Italy. Whilst the Hohenstaufens might nominally be Kings of Jerusalem, they were in effect absentee rulers.

The fact that the Pope refused to recognise Hohenstaufen claims to Jerusalem created tensions; in 1245 for example, Innocent IV had granted commercial privileges in the kingdom to the city of Ancona, ignoring the Hohenstaufen claim to rule (though as this was at a time when he had been driven from Italy by the Emperor Frederick, this stance was not particularly surprising).[34] However, the barons in Acre took little notice of this and Conradin was duly recognised as king, though probably with a realisation that he was unlikely ever to set foot in Outremer. A regent would be needed anyway given his age, whether Conradin came or not. The role would be exercised over the next few years by the house of Ibelin, by John of Arsūf and John of Jaffa at different times. Powerful local men were quite happy to pay nominal allegiance to the Hohenstaufens when it meant little in practice in terms of life in Outremer.

The various pieces were now on the chessboard: Mamluks and Mongols, Byzantines and Franks. There were many nuances to take into account. The Franks were often at odds with each other. Angevins were scheming against Hohenstaufens, Pisans and Venetians against the Genoese, Frankish settlers in the region held views that often differed from occasional crusading visitors from the West, whilst Templars, Hospitallers and Teutonic Knights were frequently taking up opposing positions. At the same time, the Muslim powers were still to a significant extent divided between the successors of the Ayyubids in Syria and the Mamluks, whilst an increasingly irrelevant religious head, the caliph in Baghdad, did his best to retain some measure of authority (the term 'caliph' means 'Commander of the Faithful' – the political heir of the Prophet). Even different Mongol factions would soon be at each other's throats. A series of sometimes bewildering alliances took shape, which moved the pieces around the board in puzzling patterns. But for the Franks of Outremer, the game would ultimately end in checkmate.

3

Rising Powers

'Probably not until the end of time will a catastrophe of such
magnitude be seen again'

The Muslim chronicler Ibn al-Athīr
concerning the Mongol assault on Islam

The Emergence of the Mongol Khanate

The Mongol khanate was vast, by some measures the biggest empire
in history. Its genesis lay in the emergence of a visionary leader, the
infamous Genghis *Khan* (Temūjin). He was born the son of the chief
of an insignificant tribe in Mongolia in around 1167 and after his
father was poisoned whilst he was still a child, Temūjin went through
the adolescence from hell. This involved exile, aimless nomadic
wanderings and ultimately imprisonment and the threat of execution.
After his escape, he married the beautiful Börte but his suffering was
far from over. She was captured and forced to become the concubine
of a rival. Some months later Temūjin succeeded in rescuing her but
by this time she was pregnant and it was unclear who the father of her
unborn child was. This inevitably led to doubts as to the parenthood of
Temūjin's eldest 'son', Jochi. If the future khan developed a harrowing
violent streak, perhaps it is not completely surprising.

It was an unpromising start to life which made his subsequent
achievements all the more remarkable. Temūjin was adept at forging
alliances, allowing him to increase the fighting power available to him
significantly. By 1194, he was recognised as khan of the Mongols.
A brutally effective fighting force was developed that relied on its

speed and manoeuvrability through its fleet-footed cavalry for its success. Allied to the flexibility this gave him, Genghis, as he became known, honed a tactical approach that left his enemies leaden-footed in response. His tactics made generous use of horse archers weaving their way in and out of the ranks of his opponents as if his warriors were a swarm of bees, impossible to swat off and moving rapidly around, probing for weaknesses until they managed to find one. Heavy cavalry using spears added brute battering force to the subtler manoeuvres of his archers; not for nothing were Second World War German tank commanders keen students of Mongol tactics. World domination was the simple aim; this might seem like some cliché from a Hollywood B movie plot, but the concept of 'one sun in the sky, one lord on the earth', the Mongols' maxim, suggests that in this case the cliché is appropriate.[1] As a result of this incredible ambition and a combination of military and political factors, the Mongol khanate grew at a remarkable rate.

The thirteenth-century writer and Muslim observer Ata-Malik Juvaini told how before Genghis, the Mongols had no chief or ruler. 'Each one or two tribes lived separately; they were not united with one another, and there was constant fighting and hostility between them. Some of them regarded robbery and violence, immorality and debauchery as deeds of manliness and excellence.' They even, according to him, dressed in the skins of dogs and dormice.[2] Unity and discipline were instilled by Genghis who turned the Mongol army into a terrifying, well-oiled fighting machine. The Mongols employed subterfuge as well as offensive power on the battlefield. They would feign retreat, bamboozling their less-disciplined opponents into breaking ranks and launching an uncoordinated pursuit after them, assuming that the Mongols were retreating in panic. Then when the cohesion of their pursuers was fatally broken the fleeing Mongols would re-form as if by magic. They would roll back against their enemy like the waves of an inrushing tide running up a beach. They would swamp them, leaving in their wake the tsunami-damage of masses of dead men and horses who had been overwhelmed by the human flood. It was a devastatingly effective approach, honed in an annual 'Great Hunt' when Mongol cavalry assembled to chase, trap and ultimately kill all the wildlife across a vast area in perfect coordination with each other. The hunt itself was organised with military precision, involving thousands of men combining their movements across the area, forming a massive circle miles across and ultimately closing it, leaving any living thing unfortunate enough to be caught in the trap with no means of escape. It led to similar precision on the field of battle.

Effective as the Mongols were, there was no doubting their savagery. Life was taken on a whim. Sometimes Genghis defeated an enemy and enlisted most of the conquered soldiers in his own army; on other occasions whole cities would be slaughtered with none left alive. Yet brutal though this was, it was made more chillingly so because there was a warped rationality behind the mass killing; slaughtering all and sundry in one city would encourage the next to surrender without a fight due to the horrific example that had been set. Such was the ruthlessness and cold calculation of the man who was given the name of Genghis Khan, the 'Universal Ruler'.

His reign saw an impressive number of conquests. China was his initial target once Mongolia had been subdued, an immensely wealthy civilisation close to home. Superficially, China enjoyed huge material advantages over the Mongols. Impressive walls had been built to keep invaders out. Genghis neutralised them by simply going around them. A terrifying period of conquest followed and by 1215 Peking/Beijing was in Mongol hands. The material advantages held by the Chinese were more than offset by the military machine that Genghis had created. Whilst many sedentary populations such as those in China suffered greatly, not all conquered peoples were obliterated. In some cases, troops from Turkic tribes were absorbed into the Mongol army. Eventually, the Mongols became a kind of racial confederation with many different strains represented.[3] Those who might prove useful even if they were not combatants – engineers or artisans for example – were often allowed to live for the skills they possessed.

Much further to the west in Central Asia the powerful Khwarazmian state dominated Transoxiana and Khorasan at the time. Genghis sent a trade mission there in 1218 but it was brutally handled by the governor of Otrar, a frontier town, who suspected the merchants of being spies. The envoys were executed, perhaps one of the greatest blunders in diplomatic history. Genghis was incensed and demanded reparations from the Khwarazmian Shah, which were not forthcoming. As a result Genghis and his Mongols invaded with devastating effect. Some of the greatest cities in the contemporary world such as Samarkand and Bukhara suffered appalling damage. A brutal seven-year campaign of death and destruction followed that obliterated the Khwarazmian kingdom. The Khwarazmians were powerful in their own right; Pope Gregory IX wrote of them in 1231, warning that the rise of a man he vaguely called 'king of the Persians', who was in fact the Khwarazmian ruler, was creating a threat. Ironically, the very destruction of this power created a catastrophic overspill. There were repercussions from these events much further afield as a domino effect worked itself out with what seemed to be a terrible logic of its own. The Khwarazmians were made homeless and some found service as mercenaries in Syria, leading eventually to their fatal collision with the Franks in the Kingdom of Jerusalem. Ultimately the attentions of the Mongols moved westwards, eventually exposing the wider Middle East to events so terrible that they were beyond imagining. The poorly advised governor of Otrar has a lot to answer for.

Genghis Khan was the initial driving force behind the rapid rate of expansion of the Mongol khanate; yet after his death in 1227 it continued to grow because of the ruthless military principles which he had inculcated into his generals and his successors, not to mention his creed that the world belonged to the Mongols. For a time, they appeared unstoppable as Genghis' successor, his son Ogodai, picked up the baton of conquest that had been handed down to him. Between 1230 and 1233, Persia fell victim to the Mongol advance. Conquests continued elsewhere in the next decade ranging from Korea in the east to Russia in the west. By 1241 the Mongols had breached the outer defences of Europe. European armies that took them on in battle in Poland and Hungary were annihilated at Liegnitz and Mohi respectively. The rulers of Western Europe were terrified that they would not survive the onslaught, as indeed was Pope Gregory IX, who urged the formation of a European alliance to face up to the threat. They were, according to some, only saved by the timely (from the perspective of the West) death of the khan Ogodai at Karakorum on 11 December 1241, which removed the momentum from the Mongol advance.[4] The Hohenstaufens assembled a crusading force to meet the threat but it was not needed because the Mongols had by then retreated of their own accord.

As the Mongol khanate continued to expand, the seeds of its own destruction had already been planted; like Rome before it, it overextended its boundaries and in the process the fabric that held it together began to tear. Eventually it fragmented, no longer a viable proposition for one man alone to manage. Though one individual might be deemed the khagan, the Supreme Khan, the wiser holders of this esteemed position cultivated good relations with others in order to rule over their vast territories. It did not always work and there were frequently tensions, especially around the time of the death of a khagan, which was almost inevitably a fraught moment as would-be successors jostled for position, a period of interregnum that could sometimes take several years to resolve.

An important Mongol acquisition was Georgia in 1232. This was effectively a land bridge between Central Asia and the Russian steppes. Armenia too came under pressure, bringing the Mongols ever closer to the lands of Syria and beyond.[5] Armenia in its contemporary form was a relatively young state formed as a result of mass migrations largely brought about by Islamic incursions into Asia Minor, firstly Arabs and later Seljuk Turks. Georgia was also forcibly added to the khanate and was cajoled into supplying military aid to the Mongols, though there were ongoing signs of dissent in the country. Armenia, however, was more pliable and adopted a subtler policy. One king in particular, the long-lived Het'um I (reigned 1227–70), was astute enough to see that the Mongol tempest was likely to overwhelm his kingdom unless he threw in his lot with them. So he offered subservience to the Mongols, an offer that they promptly took up, whilst at the same time he strengthened his ties with Antioch and Cyprus. For a time, the alliance with the Mongols served him well. He was able to call on Mongol help when he needed it and his position appeared secure. However, he and his people were in the long run to pay a heavy price for their friendly relations with the Mongols. But before that point was reached, both the Armenians and the Georgians would be involved in military affairs in Syria as allies of the Mongols.

The Mongols now launched raids into Syria, though this was not yet a full-scale invasion. But the rise to power of the Mongols was so rapid that for a while the Muslim world in particular seemed to underestimate it. In 1242, Mongols from the Caucasus launched an attack on the Seljuk Turks in Rūm (Asia Minor). The following year, the Mongols overcame them at Köse Dagh near Sivas, defeating their Sultan, Kay-Khusraw II, and effectively making Rūm a Mongol protectorate with a subservient client ruler. The Seljuks, for several centuries the pre-eminent Turkic group in the region, were now in terminal decline. They left a vacuum into which later on the Mamluks and then the Ottomans would step, but for now their demise seemed to leave the way open for the Mongols to tighten their already powerful grip on power. In the meantime, Het'um I further ingratiated himself with the Mongols through the morally dubious step of handing over the Sultan's fugitive mother and sister to them. Het'um was vastly outmatched by the Mongols and had little choice but to reach an accommodation with them given the horrific consequences should he choose not to do so. But he was very good at making a virtue out of necessity and would for many years manage to make the arrangements with the Mongols work to his own advantage as well as theirs.

The man who threatened to be Islam's ultimate nemesis was Möngke, who became khagan in 1251. His election – for succession to the khaganate was not strictly based on primogeniture – followed an interregnum of three years after the death of his predecessor Güyüg. Güyüg himself only became khagan after a five-year gap. These breaks in rule did not totally stop Mongol campaigning but they inevitably had an impact on the vigour or coordination with which campaigns were conducted; and they frequently led to, or were caused by, intense rivalry between competing claimants. But the Mongol infighting was now reduced, for a few years at least, and Möngke was determined to leave his mark on the world by continuing Genghis Khan's efforts to achieve global domination. He unleashed forces that threatened to have terrifying repercussions for the Islamic world in particular. And he also, as a very useful by-product for himself, helped to keep the great men of Mongolia, many of whom had been at each other's throats in recent years, fully occupied and distracted.

Möngke could not keep this massive territory – stretching from Europe to South-East Asia – under his control without delegating responsibility. Two of his brothers, Kublai and Hūlegū, were the main beneficiaries of this policy. Kublai's area of responsibility was China, where he eventually achieved lasting fame, partly – in the West at least – because of the works of Marco Polo who journeyed there from Venice; some Venetians would even use distortions of Mongol names for their children such as Can Grande ('Great Khan') or Alaone (Hūlegū).[6] The support of Möngke's brothers was necessary but it sometimes proved difficult to keep them under control. Whilst Möngke ruled in the traditional Mongol heartlands from Karakorum, it was Hūlegū, based in Persia, who played the key role from a Mongol perspective in the Levant and who would in an indirect way initiate the events that, with others, spelt the end for Outremer. The defeat of

Louis' expedition in Egypt, with its disastrous conclusion, had already dealt a more direct blow to the hopes of the Crusader kingdom. The Mongols were about to add another ingredient to the cocktail of dangerous developments that had been mixed.

Collision Course

The events that led to the catastrophic Mongol attack on the Islamic Middle East were instigated when Hūlegū held discussions with his brother Möngke concerning the strategy for further conquest. Baghdad and Syria were his designated targets. Hūlegū moved to Samarkand where he was received with great honours by the city (it would have been unwise to do anything else). Warriors from other parts of the widely dispersed Mongol khanate now started to converge on the region. Hūlegū had not previously been repressive in his approach towards Islam in Persia, where it was the religion of the majority of his subjects. Indeed, Mongol religious policies were generally tolerant; both churches and mosques were exempt from paying taxes in the Mongol khanate. Genghis Khan had issued an edict, a *yasa,* ordering that all faiths were to be treated equally and this was still largely official Mongol policy. This led Juvaini to suggest that Genghis Khan had been 'the adherent of no religion and the follower of no creed'[7] though that appears to be an interpretation that misunderstands Genghis's personal beliefs based on the traditional shamanistic lore of the steppe. That said, Hūlegū's religious attitudes were complicated; both his mother and his favourite wife, Doquz Khatan, were Nestorian Christians, as were some of his closest advisers. Some Mongol envoys even claimed that Doquz Khatan was the daughter of the legendary Prester John (of whom more later), whilst the Syriac writer Bar Hebraeus referred to her as 'a believing queen and lover of Christ'.[8] Hūlegū did not share these Christian beliefs though; he continued to practise the shamanistic rituals that had been adopted by many of his ancestors. However, there was no doubting his ambition and the territories which bordered his – in Mesopotamia, Syria and beyond to Egypt – were in the main Muslim. They were to feel the full brunt of his ferocity, and it probably mattered not to his many victims that the brutal campaign that followed owed little to religious zealotry and was the result of political ambition. Despite this, Hūlegū was content to let European powers believe that he was ripe for conversion to Christianity. Dissimulation was just another weapon in the Mongol armoury, and when, soon after, he sought alliances with the West he was happy to employ it.

Even after the crushing success that the Mamluks enjoyed against Louis IX in Egypt, the Islamic powers were still divided in the Levant. In the aftermath of that stunning victory there had been a dispute between Muslims in Syria and Egypt as to who should be dominant going forward. The Mamluks, given their role as kingmakers, thought they should control the political agenda, but other factions in Syria, the power base of the Ayyubid successors of Saladin, did not concur. Over time the Mamluks began to gain the upper hand through a combination of military vigour and more subtle political means such as the recognition of the caliph in Baghdad as the supreme spiritual overlord of Islam. This was a clever move; the caliph had no military power so posed little threat to the Mamluks but still had a strong symbolic role in the eyes of orthodox Muslims, who might therefore be won over to support them. The Mamluks, however, threatened to overreach themselves. They began to dominate the political landscape of Egypt and seemed to be largely outside the law, indulging in acts of indiscriminate rapine, violence and thuggery against the civilian population. Further, they were both divided and divisive; there were many different Mamluk factions who were in opposition to each other. The Bahriyya were on the wrong end of a coup in 1254. Their commander Aqtāy was seized and beheaded and strikes were made against other Mamluks in Egypt. Those who could, fled, some to Syria, others to Rūm. Baybars was in the former group, offering his services to al-Nasir Yusuf in Damascus, a man described by the great French Crusader historian Grousset as 'a mediocre person without courage'.[9] In the meantime, Egypt continued to fracture into different Mamluk groups.

Baybars regularly lobbied al-Nasir to attack Egypt, hoping to restore the Bahriyya there, but with limited success. Even the elimination of the Egyptian ruler Aybak – murdered in his bath in a plot involving his wife in 1257 – failed to persuade al-Nasir to intervene (Shajar, the woman behind the murder, did not survive the month herself). Baybars and his Bahriyya compatriots grew frustrated. Unnerved by Baybars, al-Nasir launched a pre-emptive attack on his men at Nablus in November 1257. He was successful in the battle that followed, though Baybars managed to escape to Karak, a key position in the south of Jordan whose ruler was prepared to welcome him as it would enable him to operate a policy that was separate from both Cairo and Damascus. Subsequent attempts to defeat the Egyptians by forces from Karak were, however, unsuccessful, though the Bahriyya under Baybars won a morale-boosting victory against Damascene forces at Gaza, enhancing the military reputations of both the Mamluks and their leader. Given the growing Mongol threat, this disunity could not have come at a worse time. In an age renowned for its brutality, the looming confrontation between Mongol and Mamluk stood out for its savagery. It seemed for a time that the entire Islamic power in the region was threatened with annihilation. The Muslim chronicler Ibn al-Athīr may have been guilty of an element of hyperbole, but from what we can tell, not by very much. He told the readers of his *Perfect History* that what was about to happen made biblical catastrophes such as Nebuchadnezzar's massacres of the children of Israel and his destruction of Jerusalem pale into insignificance. He concluded that 'probably not until the end of time will a catastrophe of such magnitude be seen again'.[10]

Baghdad was one of the most sacred cities in Islam outside of Mecca and Medina. It was the home of the caliph, the leader of the faith, or at least the Sunni version of it. Its best days were behind it now; its Golden Age had been in the ninth and tenth centuries and it had been in decline since then. By now, the caliph ruled over a much-reduced area. Yet his and Baghdad's name still had lustre and symbolic significance and presented a great prize to any would-be conqueror. Mesopotamia and Syria were already under the shadow of the Mongols. When Möngke called a *kurultai*, a great assembly of the Mongols, at the start of his reign in 1251, it was attended by Ayyubid representatives from Mayyafariqin and Aleppo in Syria and the Sultanate of Rüm in Anatolia, as well as Mosul in Mesopotamia. Given their latest conquests, Baghdad was the obvious next target for the Mongols. That would then leave Syria as the next stage in their itinerary.

The Abbasid caliph, al-Musta'sim, described by one Islamic commentator as 'a man of poor judgement, irresolute, and neglectful of what is needed for the conduct of government',[11] attempted to placate the Mongols without formally submitting to them. Envoys were sent from him to Möngke's enthronement.[12] This was not good enough for the khagan who demanded that the caliph meet him in person, an occasion which he would probably exploit to demand the formal submission of Baghdad. This would not necessarily mean a full Mongol takeover, lock, stock and barrel; Mongol policy relied on governing the vast khanate through subject rulers as well as by out-and-out conquest. But the meeting never took place and Möngke ordered Hūlegū to force the issue. 1,000 siege engineers were sent from China by him to supplement the already substantial forces available to his brother. The army appears to have been enormous, perhaps as many as 300,000 men strong, and even if these numbers are dubious there can be no doubting the vast scale of the force.[13] It would be a long-term and methodical plan of conquest, launched in 1252 under the command of a Nestorian Christian, Kitbughā. Not until September 1255 did the army enter Samarkand and push on into Persia.

When the Mongols then demanded that al-Musta'sim should surrender Baghdad to them they were scornfully rebuffed. He reminded them that no foe had taken the city before. It was a foolish, defiant answer, guaranteed to generate a Mongol response; it is not a good idea to pick a fight with a much more powerful enemy. From then on, it was only a matter of time before the Mongols advanced on Baghdad to make good on their claim to it. En route, they stopped off to deal with some unfinished business. In the remote fastnesses of the mountains north of Tehran in Persia was the headquarters of a small but influential Islamic sect, the Nizaris. They are better known to the West by the derogatory nickname given to them by their Muslim enemies: the 'hashish-takers' or 'hashshāshīn', westernised as 'Assassins'. As their name suggests, their stock in trade was the murder of their opponents and, whilst they are best known in the West for isolated attacks on men of European descent, most notably Conrad of Montferrat, King of Jerusalem, in 1192, the vast majority of their victims were Muslim.

A sect within the Shia branch of Islam, the Nizaris were despised by Sunnis for their religious unorthodoxy as well as their terror tactics. The Mongols were unconcerned with religious scruples; but they were angered at the temerity the Nizaris had shown to them in the recent past. They had allegedly sent assassins to eliminate Möngke, though without success. William of Rubruck wrote that 400 assassins were sent to despatch the khagan whilst he was in Karakorum and that he himself was questioned closely, so there was presumably a suspicion that even he might be one of the would-be killers.[14] The best days of the Nizaris were in the past now and they were weakened and vulnerable. Their then leader, Rukn ad-Dīn, when he heard that a vast

Mongol army was headed his way, tried to dissimulate. He asked for a year to arrange for his people's submission (although not possessing a vast territory, Nizari settlements were dispersed over a wide area). Hūlegū had no intention of agreeing to this request. Outlying Nizari fortresses were then given up, though they were considered relatively unimportant in the scheme of things, but others resisted.

The headquarters of the sect was at a mountaintop eyrie called Alamut, 'the Eagle's Nest'. No name could have been more appropriate. Alamut was perched at the top of a 200-metre-high rock at an altitude of over 2,000 metres above sea level. The approach to it was vertiginous; the castle appeared impervious to attack and had indeed been so thus far in its long history. Such locations were classic spots in which to build Nizari castles, another of which was Maymun-Diz. Contemporary Islamic poets waxed lyrical about the latter: 'Men cannot reach its highest peaks, nor can the birds, not even the vulture and the eagle. And the wishes of a seeker have not desired it, and its dogs have barked only at the stars.'[15] But Alamut was powerless in the face of the Mongol tidal wave. The castle fell on 22 November 1256 and was destroyed. As the Mongols moved on, they left behind them Alamut's magnificent library, stuffed with priceless texts and manuscripts, a blazing wreck. After the fall of Alamut, Rukn ad-Dīn was initially kept in benevolent captivity, even taking a Mongol bride. But it was not to last. After a time he was sent to Karakorum to present himself to Möngke where he was not well received. On his return he was assassinated by his Mongol escort on the khagan's orders, being kicked to a pulp and then run through with a sword. Neither was the fate of his people any kinder; many of them were summoned to assemble, ostensibly as part of a tax-collecting exercise, but it was a ruse. When they arrived, 12,000 of them were slaughtered.[16]

Several decades later, Marco Polo travelled through the region on his remarkable journey east. Memories of the Nizaris lived on enough for him to register some details. In particular, their most famous leader, the Sheikh of the Mountain (whose name was Alaodin), was renowned for the way that he recruited and trained his assassins, the *fida'is* as they were known. They were drugged and when they woke from their stupor were told that they were in Paradise. There were four fountains there, one flowing with milk, another with wine, another with honey and the last with water. There were beautiful women at their beck and call to administer to their every need; all a taster of what was to come if they died in the service of their lord. They would then be given some suicidal mission to undertake involving the assassination of a chosen target, an enterprise from which it was unlikely that they would return alive; but given the promise of Paradise, this was of no great concern to them.

Now that world had gone, consigned to oblivion by Hūlegū. The Sheikh of the Nizaris had, according to Marco Polo, two deputies, one in Damascus, the other in Kurdistan; there were certainly two separate Nizari groups, one in Syria, the other in Persia. Hūlegū had obliterated the Persian group after a three-year campaign. In Marco Polo's words, 'From that time to this there have been no more of these Sheikhs and no more Assassins; but with him there came an end to all the power that had been wielded of old by the Sheiks of the Mountain and all the evil they had done.' It was true in part but not completely so – the Nizaris in Persia had largely been destroyed but the group in Syria was still alive, if not in robust health, and they would yet have a say in the final decades of life that remained to Outremer.[17]

Whilst conventional Sunni Muslims regarded the Nizaris as heretics, Baghdad was something altogether different. Hūlegū pushed on relentlessly towards the city. As he moved on it, messages were sent to the caliph which unambiguously made clear what he could look forward to:

> When I lead my army against Baghdad in anger, whether you hide in heaven or on earth, I will bring you down from the spinning spheres; I will toss you in the air like a lion. I will leave no one alive in your realm; I will burn your city, your land, your self.[18]

It was a terrifying and unequivocal message. Too late al-Musta'sim realised the extent of the threat facing him. Full of bravado when he first received the Mongol demands to surrender, now he performed a complete *volte face,* offering to mention Hūlegū in Friday prayers, a mark of great respect. But the moment had passed. Al-Musta'sim had stirred the mighty Mongol war machine into motion and it would take more than a few symbolic gestures to halt it now. The day of reckoning loomed on 18 January 1258, when the Mongols appeared before Baghdad.

They had made a three-pronged move on the city. The central force led by Hūlegū crossed the plain of the Tigris from the direction of

Kermanshah, the left wing moved up through Luristan and the right came from Azerbaijan and down through Erbil. To ensure that no one could escape, Hūlegū placed a force to the west of Baghdad to complete its encirclement. The forces defending Baghdad were hugely outmatched. The meagre resources available to al-Musta'sim largely consisted of a non-professional civilian militia supplemented by a few Mamluks and Arab tribesmen from the south of Mesopotamia. Despite this, initially the defenders put up a heroic resistance. But they were then trapped in marshy ground outside the city. The Mongols destroyed some dams in the area, cutting the caliph's army off. Only a few men escaped, either back into the city – a dubious deliverance as it turned out – or south into the desert, which on this occasion proved to be very much the lesser of two evils.

Helped by the contingent of Chinese siege engineers sent to him from Möngke, Hūlegū put in place a tight siege. The final assault began on 29 January 1258. It took a few days for breaches in the defensive walls to appear but by 4 February one was opened in the south-eastern corner of the city. By the following day, the Mongols controlled a significant stretch of the walls. It was now only a matter of time before the city was taken. It fell on 10 February and a terrible retribution followed. At the request of the Nestorians with Hūlegū, Christian churches and those seeking shelter in them were spared but for the rest of the population the end was nightmarish. Baghdad drowned in a sea of blood. Al-Musta'sim was taken captive. The details of his end are blurred and contradictory; in one version he was either tied in a sack or rolled up in carpets and then kicked to death or trampled to a pulp by stampeding horses (other versions of his end suggest that he was beheaded by Hūlegū in person).[19] 3,000 of his leading advisers and nobles perished before him, killed in cold blood after the capture of the city.

Marco Polo gives the caliph a slightly more exotic end. When Hūlegū's army took Baghdad, they found a tower crammed with gold. They were amazed at how the caliph had failed to use these massive resources to hire extra soldiers to face them. Clearly, the caliph valued money more than anything else and as a salutary lesson he was locked inside the tower with nothing to eat or drink. If he wished to live, let him eat gold. Within four days, he was dead. It savours of a tall tale written by a man who wished to emphasise the enormous wealth of the countries through which he had travelled (though whether this is an invention of Marco himself or his ghostwriter, Rustichello of Pisa, is a moot point).[20] Whatever the caliph's final fate, the caliphate which he governed was now effectively extinct after half a millennium. It was perhaps 'the greatest disaster ever sustained by the Islamic world'.[21] As the chronicler Ibn Kathir remarked, 'Baghdad, which had been the most civilised of all cities, became a ruin with only a few inhabitants, and they were in fear and hunger and wretchedness and insignificance.'[22]

The Mongols and Christendom: The Unlikely Alliance

A legend developed in the West about a mighty Christian ruler in the little-known lands of the East. He was first mentioned in a forged letter that started to circulate in around 1160. His name was 'Prester John'. Otto of Freising, the first Western writer to mention him, said that he was a direct lineal descendant of the Magi, or Three Kings, who visited the Christ Child.[23] Whilst there was little to suggest that he truly existed, to some optimistic Christians he offered the prospect of a devastating alliance against Islam. By 1217, Jacques de Vitry, made Bishop of Acre in 1214 and a prominent theologian of his time, was writing that 'the numerous Christian monarchs who dwell in the East as far as the territory of Prester John' would hopefully join the rest of Christendom in their joint struggle against religious enemies.[24] To some, the Mongols, who came from the region that Prester John was believed to inhabit, were not so much a power to be feared as a potential partner to be cultivated in the fight against Islam.[25] This impression, however, soon started to wear off. William of Rubruck, who journeyed through the lands where this semi-mythical figure was believed to live, reported that the Nestorian Christians there spoke of a 'King John and ... say things of him ten times more than was true'.[26] Despite this, in some quarters the prospect of an alliance took some time to be revealed as the illusion it really was.

Superficially, the Mongols did seem to offer Christendom some hope of an alliance against Islam. Among their number were many Nestorian Christians, some holding senior positions. Tentative approaches were made to the Mongols to see if there was any possibility of uniting in a common cause. Initially Louis IX hoped to exploit the potential of a Mongol alliance; but his hopes were delusional. What Louis foresaw was a partnership of equals, failing totally to understand the Mongol desire for world domination. Louis sent gifts to the Mongols as a way of oiling the wheels of an alliance; they included a scarlet tent decked out with reminders of the key elements of Christian ritual such as baptism, the Annunciation, the Nativity, the Passion and the Coming of the Holy Ghost, symbols of both Louis' piety and his naiveté.[27] Nevertheless, hopes of an alliance showed themselves in some extraordinary ways. An icon from an iconostasis beam in St Catherine's Monastery in Sinai (but possibly intended for a church in Damascus) that may have been crafted by an artist from Venice or Acre in the 1250s or 1260s (both the identity of the artist and the precise dating are unclear) shows one of the Magi visiting the Christ Child dressed in a costume that makes him look distinctly Mongol. Such images hint at hopes amongst the Christian community responsible for producing them of an alliance with the Mongols.[28]

The Mongols interpreted these gifts as tribute and asked Louis to repeat the gesture annually. A chilling realisation slowly dawned on the West that the price of alliance with the Mongols was subservience. As one historian remarked, 'The Mongols were the only people in the second half of the thirteenth century who were capable of destroying Islam, though in the event the Christians would have had to face the very real danger that they would be their allies' next victims.'[29] The hope of a Mongol alliance was based primarily on wishful thinking. It is true that the Nestorian branch of Christianity, which had existed for many centuries, had influenced some of the Mongols, though their practices and doctrines were very different than those of the Latin church. But the Nestorians had since the fifth century lived in isolation from the West where they would have been regarded as heretics. Western visitors continued to regard them as such: one, William of Rubruck, was totally dismissive of their priests and their practices, particularly their non-celibate lifestyles and their excessive consumption of alcohol. He left one of their services in disgust, commenting that 'the priests [were] singing in great howling in their drunkenness, which in those parts is not reprehensible in man or in woman'.[30] Several popes and some of the secular rulers of Western Europe believed that the Nestorians could be converted to the 'true' doctrines of Christianity. This optimistic view failed to consider the fierce ambition of Mongol khagans to rule the globe and kowtow to nobody, including the papacy.

Louis' envoys to the Mongols must have been made increasingly aware of their impact on the region even when journeying to meet them.

After passing through Antioch, it took a full year to arrive at their final destination. As they moved east, they passed devastated cities and piles of human bones. When news of Mongol triumphs against Christian nations such as Georgia, Poland and Hungary reached the ears of the Cistercian analyst Aubry of Trois-Fontaines, he was convinced that there had been a revolt and that Prester John had been killed by his own people.[31] Marco Polo on the other hand later suggested that he had been killed in battle fighting against Genghis Khan.[32]

Several European delegations made their way to the home of the Great khagan, pre-dating the more famous journeys of Marco Polo by decades. One of them included a Franciscan friar, John of Plano del Carpini, despatched by Innocent IV and away from 1245 to 1247. In fact, three delegations set out at around this time, possibly reflecting the belief that three different Mongol armies were in place: one to attack Egypt, a second the Seljuk Turks and the third Eastern Europe.[33] Another envoy, Ascelin of Lombardy, also reached the Mongols but his stubborn and disrespectful behaviour in the presence of the Mongol general, Baiju, ensured that his mission achieved little and may indeed have endangered his life. Carpini achieved much more. He was no spring chicken, being around sixty years of age and not in the best of physical condition. He was, on his own admission, something of a spy; he made the journey 'so that we might help the Christians ... to know the Tartars' [a pseudonym for the Mongols] attitude and intent'.[34]

Carpini did manage to obtain some very useful information which he recorded in what we might think of as a 'Manual of the Mongols', alongside other snippets that are beyond bizarre, such as stories of forest dwellers born without knees, of the Parossitai whose stomachs and mouths were so small that they could not eat meat but instead cooked it and breathed in its fumes for nutrition, and of a race who lived under the ground because they could not stand the noise of the sun. There were also tales of monsters with a human head and shape but with the feet of cattle and the face of a dog. When they spoke, they uttered two human words followed by a bark.[35] But alongside these fantastical accounts came more believable and therefore disquieting news. After being sent to the *khagan* Güyüg in Karakorum (which he did not actually see though he journeyed to within half a day of it), Carpini returned home with the far-from-reassuring message from the *khagan* that he looked forward to receiving the formal submission of the Pope and recognition of his claims as supreme world leader. Further details from Carpini, such as the fact that he had travelled through the region of Kiev and found countless skulls and bones scattered around and barely 200 houses left standing, would have done nothing to ease the nerves of his audience.

In 1249, Louis IX despatched Andrew of Longjumeau on a mission from Cyprus. Andrew, a Dominican friar, was no more successful than his predecessors had been, though whilst away he met a cleric from Acre, Theodolus (alias Raymond), who was presenting himself as an envoy but in fact was a hoaxer.[36] The fact that these men were friars was no coincidence. They were part of a recent phenomenon, having only emerged in the early years of the thirteenth century. The friars lived simple and austere lives and were more than capable of what we might now colloquially call 'slumming it'. They were pioneer adventurers, cut out for rough and potentially dangerous missions. These early initiatives were more diplomatic than proselytising in nature.[37] Not just the Mongols were on their itinerary at this time. Andrew, for example, may have been the delegate who visited Cairo in 1245, trying to break the Mamluk Sultan, Ayyub, away from his alliance with Emperor Frederick, a task in which he was singularly unsuccessful. Ayyub did though declaim all responsibility for the Khwarazmian attack on Jerusalem in the previous year, presumably hoping to diminish the chances of a retaliatory strike heading in Egypt's direction from Europe.

Another visitor from the West (his journey lasted from 1253 to 1256) was William of Rubruck. Like Carpini, he wrote up a wealth of detail about Mongol life, much of which is beyond the scope of our consideration here. These works form a treasure trove of detail, capturing everyday life in Mongol lands in a way that at the time must have enthralled a Western audience. William also does not seem to have been in peak physical condition; he told his readers that his escort always gave him a strong horse to ride, 'on account of my great weight'.[38] He was purely and simply a missionary (a Flemish Franciscan friar) but he journeyed with a letter of support from Louis IX. This was misunderstood to be a request for an alliance from the French king, as a result of which William was escorted to the Mongol capital of Karakorum, where the *khagan's* palace impressed him greatly. When he eventually arrived there, he was in for a surprise when he met a captive Parisian goldsmith, Guillame Boucher, who had designed a magnificent silver tree in Karakorum complete with lions of silver at its foot and with conduits that poured forth wine and other refreshment on special occasions. He also met a woman from Metz, Basil, the son of an Englishman, and a nephew of a Bishop of Normandy, possibly captured when the Mongols invaded Hungary.[39]

William was shocked when he saw for himself the suspect doctrines of the Nestorians at work. The doctrinal abuses (as he saw them) that he witnessed included the practice of polygamy, the mass ordination by bishops of untrained and unindoctrinated adolescents as priests and the imitation of the Islamic custom of the washing of feet before entering a sacred building. When he returned to the West in 1255, it was with the understanding that Möngke regarded Louis as his potential vassal, which was certainly not the impression that the French king had intended to give. William, like other would-be proselytisers to the Mongols, soon hit a wall when he reached them. He was at first thrown off guard when he was frequently asked if he had come to offer peace from Louis, not realising that to the Mongols peace and submission were the same thing, though the realisation gradually dawned on him. Christendom's insistence that their God was omnipotent and that the Church was His only legitimate representative directly contradicted the Mongols' view that the descendants of Genghis Khan were destined to rule the world, a difficulty compounded by the aversion of Christianity to the practice of magic, which was significant in shamanistic Mongol religion. Ultimately, other more inclusive religions such as some strands of Buddhism or Taoism appeared preferable to the Mongols; even Islam seemed less dogmatic.[40] William, after an epic journey, eventually made his way back to Outremer, traversing much of Asia before passing through Armenia and then Tripoli and finally arriving at Acre. By the time he arrived there he found that Louis IX had returned to France, which was good news for historians, for it forced him to write up an account of his mission and despatch it to the French king. It is this account that has survived into modern times, giving us an exceptional insight into the world of the mid-thirteenth century.

Those up close to the Mongols were less likely to be taken in by the hopes of a Mongol alliance. In 1260, the Master of the Templars in Outremer was Thomas Bérard. He was more enlightened than some of his contemporaries and saw that the Templars, Hospitallers and Teutonic Knights should be cooperating rather than competing with each other. He was even concerned at the ease with which the Mongols had been able to destroy the caliph in Baghdad, 'the Pope of the Saracens' as he called him. He was closer to the front line than most and appreciated how vast the resources available to the Mongols were. Ominously, he wrote to King Henry III of England and Amadeus, commander of the English Templars: '…nor will Christendom be able to resist them unless supported by the powerful hand of God'. He predicted that unless help came quickly, 'a horrible annihilation will swiftly be visited upon the world'.[41]

So Bérard for one was not seduced by the mirage of a Mongol alliance. Neither was Peter des Roches, Bishop of Winchester (d. 1238), who was an early pessimist; according to Matthew Paris he expressed the hope that the Mongols and Muslims would destroy each other.[42] The number of sceptics in the West grew over time. Thomas of Spalato recorded that several commentators saw the Mongols as the forerunners of Antichrist. Some asserted that the Mongols' ultimate objective was Rome.[43] Louis IX was certainly taken aback when he understood that the Mongols expected subservience rather than alliance; his adviser and chronicler Joinville told his readers 'His Majesty, I can assure you, bitterly regretted that he had ever sent his envoys to the great King of the Tartars.'[44]

Concerns about the Mongol threat in Outremer became very real as it drew closer, a threatening shadow looming over the kingdom from out of the darkness and growing in size as it moved westwards. Matthew Paris wrote that Acre received an ultimatum from the Mongols in 1257. So serious was the threat that soon after the Templars, Hospitallers and Teutonic Knights resolved to stop squabbling with each other and start cooperating instead.[45] In the same year, the Patriarch of Jerusalem, Jacques Pantaléon (later to become Pope Urban IV), told Pope Alexander IV that a Mongol attack on the kingdom was imminent. The receptor of the Temple wrote in similar terms at around the same time. Nor was it just Outremer that was concerned. Béla IV, King of Hungary, had expressed his astonishment in writing about a decade earlier to Innocent IV that the Pope was allowing Louis IX to lead a crusade to Egypt when the heart of Europe was threatened by the Mongol advance. As if to prove the point, there had been a devastating Mongol raid on Poland in 1259. Attacks on neighbouring Lithuania and Prussia had involved the Teutonic Knights and led to heavy losses amongst them.[46] Pope Alexander appealed for unity in the light of the danger in his bull *Clamat in auribus* ('listen to the cries'), issued in 1261, in apocalyptic tones:

> There rings in the ears of all, and rouses to vigilant alertness those who are not befuddled by mental torpor, a terrible trumpet of dire forewarning which, corroborated by the evidence of events, proclaims with so unmistakable a sound the wars of universal destruction wherewith the scourge of Heaven's wrath in the hands of the inhuman Tartars, erupting as it were from the secret confines of Hell, oppresses and crushes the earth...[47]

In Outremer, concerns about the intentions of the Mongols went back further. Antioch, more exposed than other parts of the Crusader states in the region due to its location, had been put on notice as far back as 1244 when, after a victorious campaign against the Seljuks of Anatolia, the Mongol general Baiju approached the city and ordered its then Prince, Bohemond V, to demolish its walls, hand over its gold and silver and supply 3,000 maidens for the benefit of his army. Bohemond refused, but within two years he was a tributary of the Mongols. Papal embassies from Innocent IV to the region in 1247–48 reported back that the extent of the territory now dominated by the Mongols extended two days to the south of Antioch.[48] However, despite the weakening of the Frankish position in the region, Bohemond appeared to do well out of the deal he made with the Mongols with various territories in the Orontes Valley being handed over to him that had previously been in Muslim hands.[49] But though it was only over-optimistic dreamers in the West who believed in the possibility of a Mongol alliance in these early years, events in the Middle East were about to reignite such hopes. This came about in the aftermath of a battle between the Mongols and the Mamluks that was significant in terms of world history and potentially decisive with regard to the future of Outremer.

4

The Turning of the Tide

'You cannot escape from the terror of our armies. Where can you flee?'
The Mongol message to Sultan Qutuz

Egypt under Threat

The decimation of Baghdad was a link in a chain of horrific events. Hūlegū now prepared to push his campaign further west though not before taking an extended break in Azerbaijan so that the army could reinvigorate itself for the next stage of the campaign. Then he moved into the Jazira (which means 'island' in Arabic, a reference to its position between the Tigris and Euphrates), a land of plains, deserts and high mountains. Mayyafariqin, a key strategic point, resisted stoutly. Al-Kamil Mohammed, the emir of the city, had known for some time that he was exposed, being in the line of the Mongols' advance. He had sent envoys to them to try to negotiate a better position for himself but finally lost patience. Hūlegū sent a Christian priest to Mayyafariqin, demanding its surrender. In response, al-Kamil had the envoy crucified. Al-Kamil Mohammed, who had previously submitted to the Mongols, had now defied them, something that was inevitably interpreted as an unforgivable act of rebellion. When Mayyafariqin finally fell to the Mongols, al-Kamil's fate was brutal. He was forced to gorge on his own flesh until he mercifully died.[1]

The Mongol army was, as mentioned, huge – according to the Templar of Tyre, the anonymous chronicler to whom we owe much regarding the Western perspective of the events that led up to the final fall of Acre, there were 120,000 Mongol horsemen alone – and there was also a range of allies including Turks, Georgians and Armenians.[2] The 'Templar' wrote by far the most complete surviving account of the final decades of Outremer, but we know little about him. That he was connected to the order, and especially one of its last Masters, William of Beaujeu, is clear from his writings;[3] but despite the title he has been given, there is no evidence that he was actually a full member of the order. He describes the Mongols and their allies in some detail, talking of the Georgians for example as 'a handsome race of doughty warriors, good archers and good fighters on the battlefield. They are Christians and observe the rule of the Greek church. They wear their hair cropped in clerical fashion' – small details that illuminate the period.[4] A number of towns fell to the Mongols as they advanced, again creating a domino effect. One of the jewels of Syria was Aleppo, replete with its magnificent citadel. It was one of the oldest continuously inhabited cities in the world with a history dating back millennia. Its wealth and position as a hub in a valuable trading network in the region had made it a magnet for invaders over the centuries including Alexander the Great, Romans, Arabs and Crusaders, though the latter had attempted to take the city several times without success.

Aleppo was ruled by al-Nasir Yusuf who had a chequered relationship with the Mamluks in Egypt. The region was politically volatile and Baybars and Qalāwūn, another prominent Mamluk, had fled to Al-Nasir persuading him to attempt an invasion of Egypt, but when he followed through with this plan, he was defeated. Such disunity in the region was potentially disastrous. When the Mongols approached Syria, al-Nasir Yusuf at one stage thought to enter into an alliance with them and jointly attack Egypt. However, as the horror stories of the Mongol advance reached him, he realised he had badly misjudged the situation. His approaches to Hūlegū, designed to prevaricate, had been disdainfully received with the response that he should submit unconditionally and level his fortresses. He was also to surrender himself to Hūlegū in person; as he was a man lacking in personal courage, this was a terrifying prospect. Belatedly, seeing that prevarication was an ineffective tactic, al-Nasir Yusuf changed tack, seeking support from Egypt to protect him from the huge army now headed towards him. The power behind the throne in Egypt was now the Vice-Sultan Saif ad-Din Qutuz. Theoretically, the ruler of the country was the Sultan al-Mansir Ali, but he was a fifteen-year old figurehead. Faced with the Mongol threat, Qutuz removed the Sultan from power, though he claimed that this was merely a temporary expedient until the moment of danger had passed. In reality it was no such thing.

Aleppo was next in the Mongol firing line. Al-Nasir Yusuf's advisers recommended that he should seek terms with them; or at least one group of them, labelled the 'defeatists', did so. Their attitude inflamed Baybars who considered assassinating al-Nasir Yusuf, though this plan came to nothing. Instead, al-Nasir Yusuf fled to Damascus. The forces defending Aleppo were defeated outside the city and shortly after it fell, though there was a gallant if doomed defence led by al-Mu'azzam Turānshāh, an elderly son of Saladin. The Christian Armenian contingent with the army took great pleasure in setting fire to the Great Mosque whilst the citadel garrison fought desperately but futilely on, being overwhelmed a month later. Unusually, they were allowed to live, though the citadel was destroyed. Both Het'um of Armenia and Bohemond of Antioch were richly rewarded for their part in the fall of the city, including the granting of land to them that had previously been held by Muslims. The fall of the city on 24 January 1260 created a sense of panic throughout Muslim Syria.[5] But soon after Hūlegū returned north-east to Tabriz, possibly disturbed by news of the death of Möngke and the imminent threat of civil war between his would-be successors. He left Kitbughā in charge in Syria.

For various possible reasons, the bulk of the Mongol army also retreated from Syria with him. One explanation indeed may be the death of Möngke, which occurred at around this time; the leaders of the army needed to be closer to home when the election of a successor *khagan* took place. There were also logistical challenges for the Mongols when campaigning in Syria. Their horses, used to foraging on the steppes, suffered greatly because of the lack of sufficient grasslands. It was tough, stony terrain that damaged the hooves of animals unconditioned to it. The desiccating intensity of the Syrian summer heat added further to the potential toll taken of the Mongols' horse stock. Anyone who has travelled through the wide ribbon of desert that acts as a kind of natural shield against would-be nomadic invaders in parts of Syria can appreciate just how tough the terrain could be for the Mongols' horses. Mongol forces that attacked Syria again at the end of the thirteenth century came accompanied by large numbers of camels carrying fodder for the horses, in contrast to earlier campaigns.[6] With even fairly humble Mongol troopers bringing up to five horses with them, plus the vast flocks of sheep, goats and camels that the army relied on for provisions, the pressure on local resources must have been huge.

After Baghdad, the most important Muslim city in Mesopotamia and Syria was Damascus. Once Aleppo fell it was clear that this was the most likely major target for the Mongols. En route to attack the city, the Mongols took Hama and Homs, but Damascus was the main objective. It fell, apparently without much of a fight; al-Nasir escaped to Nablus before the attack, cursed by the citizens he abandoned as he ran for cover. Many of the inhabitants fled too, including those Christians in the city who did not trust the Mongols to distinguish friend from foe should Damascus fall. The account of one such man, Ibn al-'Amid, tells us that he and other scribes went to Tyre. The weather was hostile, bitterly cold and wet, a suitable metaphor for the state of Damascus and the Muslim territories in the region. The roads were flooded and the retreat hellish; the column with al-Nasir was frequently raided by bandits who plundered their baggage and harems without mercy.[7] In the aftermath of the city's fall a former Byzantine church which had been converted to a mosque was returned to its original use. The Latin mass was sung in the city and church bells were rung, something that was forbidden under Muslim rule. Some accounts suggest that the walls of mosques were daubed with wine and pork fat and donkeys were stabled in them.[8] The important desert castle of Karak soon after submitted to the Mongols too.

Palestine was the next target. During the spring, Kitbughā, leading the Mongol army, sent detachments to occupy Nablus and Gaza and probed the approaches to Jerusalem, possibly even taking and holding it for a time. Ascalon, on the southern borders of Outremer, also fell. The Mongols fell on the straggling rearguard of al-Nasir's bedraggled force and annihilated it. Nablus was thoroughly pillaged with great slaughter unleashed on the townsfolk. The Mongols then returned to Damascus loaded with booty and slaves. The Franks were uncomfortably aware of how close the Mongols now were and received an ultimatum from them in February 1260. This demanded that the Franks destroy the fortifications of their cities. The Papal Legate, Thomas Agni, Bishop of Bethlehem, thought this blasphemous, understandably when it came accompanied with a bold statement that the Mongols had a divine right to rule the world. The situation of the Franks appeared dire for other reasons. Tensions between competing Italian factions in the region which led to the War of St Sabas had taken a toll of already limited manpower and had adversely affected the availability of ready cash due to the resultant economic fallout. The Templar Master, Thomas Bérard, sent appeals to the West in March with the drastic warning that, apart from Acre and Tyre, only two Templar castles (probably Atlit and Safad) and one held by the Teutonic Knights (presumably Montfort) were in a strong enough position to hold out if attacked by the Mongols. The price of mercenaries had also gone up and to compound the difficulties the withdrawal of Genoese and other Italian moneylenders from Acre had reduced the supply of available loans to close any budgetary gaps. The receptor of the Temple in England was instructed to raise a loan of 10,000 silver marks from King Henry III.[9]

Egypt was also alarmed by this string of Mongol successes, which to some must have seemed like an unstoppable victory procession. At one stage, al-Nasir Yusuf appeared to be heading there but then suffered a predictable loss of nerve and turned about. Instead, he headed across the desert, a disastrous decision for him personally as he was captured by a Mongol patrol near Karak. Some of his men, however, carried on to Egypt where they were assimilated into the Sultan's army. In Cairo, Qutuz stayed calm. He received a request for safe conduct into Egypt from a recent opponent, no less a person than Baybars, who was in Palestine and threatened by Mongol patrols. The safe conduct was duly given. On arrival Baybars, who had an implacable hatred of the Mongols, urged Qutuz to fight fire with fire.

Six Mongol envoys arrived soon after, demanding the surrender of Egypt. The demand was couched in formal terms but nevertheless contained a barely concealed jibe at Qutuz: 'He is of the race of Mamluks who fled before our sword into this country [a reference to the Mamluks' Qipchāk origins], who enjoyed its comforts and then killed its rulers.'[10] It was a message full of bombast and threat:

> You should think of what happened to other countries and submit to us. You have heard how we have conquered a vast empire and have purified the earth of the disorders that tainted it. We have conquered vast areas, massacring all the people. You cannot escape from the terror of our armies. Where can you flee? What road will you use to escape us? Our horses are swift, our arrows sharp, our swords like thunderbolts,

our hearts as hard as the mountains, our soldiers are numerous as the sand ... your prayers will not avail against us. We are not moved by tears nor touched by lamentations. Only those who beg our protection will be safe. Hasten your reply before the fire of war is kindled. Resist and you will suffer the most terrible catastrophes. We will shatter your mosques and reveal the weakness of your God and then we will kill your children and your old men together.

It was a message couched in the most imperious terms, giving a vivid insight into the mentality of the Mongols and their unshaken vision of world conquest. It generated an unequivocal response. In a cold fury, Qutuz had the envoys executed; they were sliced in half at the waist and their heads stuck up above one of the Cairo city gates, the Zuweila. This was a response that the Mongols could not possibly misinterpret.

Ain Jalut: The Fork in the Road

Qutuz decided that the best means of defence was attack. He assembled a large force with Syrian, Turcoman and Arab contingents and the core of his Egyptian army and marched out of Cairo. However, many of his soldiers wished to stay on the defensive and wait for the Mongols to come to them. Qutuz harangued them, making appeals to their religious fervour and at one point telling them that he would cross into Syria on his own if they would not come with him. In the end, they were shamed into action. Reluctantly, they headed east into Palestine. Baybars was sent on ahead leading an advance contingent. When it reached Gaza, they were spotted by Mongol sentries who sent news back to Syria. Gaza was soon taken by the Mamluks and Qutuz moved in with the bulk of his army. He then sent a delegation to Acre asking for safe passage across Frank-held lands. This presented Acre with a quandary. Unlike Bohemond in Antioch, the rulers of the city were no allies of the Mongols and had recently suffered from raids they had launched. Some city officials even argued that they should enter into a formal alliance with Qutuz, but the objections of the Teutonic Knights under their Master, Anno of Sangerhausen, proved decisive in preventing this (they were more embroiled in the affairs of Armenia than the other orders and may have felt that it was politically unwise to support the Mamluks in their campaign against the Mongols). Acre therefore agreed to Qutuz's request for safe passage whilst deciding to remain neutral. This was the Franks of Acre hedging their bets.

On the one hand, it was in their interests for the Mongols to be ejected from the region, thereby removing the threat to the city. On the other, should the Mongols be successful in the coming campaign, the fact that Acre had remained neutral might take the edge off their wrath. Otherwise the Franks might find themselves in line for fierce retribution for their support of the Mamluk cause.

The Mamluks were allowed to set up camp outside Acre unmolested, waiting for news of the Mongol advance into Palestine that was expected imminently. They could also trade for provisions and some members of the army were given permission to enter the city. Baybars was one of those who took advantage of the offer to enter, and so many others did that eventually the citizens grew fearful that they might launch a coup whilst in the city and conditions of entry were tightened. Despite this, a deal was struck with Qutuz that, should he defeat the Mongols, any horses captured would be sold to Acre for an agreed price (evidencing a shortage of such stock amongst the Franks), though in the end no such thing happened.[11] Aware that a potentially decisive confrontation might not be far away, Qutuz took advantage of the time available to give an inspirational speech to his army. He appealed to their sensibilities, both religious and material. He reminded his men that they must fight to protect their families and their property with a coded message to his officers that should the coming fight be lost, even if they escaped with their lives, their power would be broken.

Qutuz did not have long to wait. Messengers arrived with news that the Mongols had crossed the Jordan and headed into Galilee. Qutuz responded decisively, soon after leading his men forward through Nazareth. They came up to Ain Jalut, the Pools of Goliath, in the Jezreel Valley. For those who believed in omens this was not encouraging as Saladin had been successfully resisted by a Crusader army there in 1183. The Mongols were led by Kitbughā, described by a contemporary Syrian writer, al-Yūnīnī, as 'an old man reaching back to the time of Chinggis [sic] Khan', probably putting him in his sixties.[12] He was a man of great military experience.

On 3 September 1260 (25 Ramadan) the scene was set for a crucial battle. The Mongols were at a disadvantage in several respects. For one, they did not know the territory and were poorly supplied with scouts. The Mamluks on the other hand were on 'home turf'. Qutuz probably also enjoyed a numerical advantage over his opponent. It has been suggested that by the time that the Battle of Ain Jalut was fought, out of an original force of 120,000 men fewer than 20,000 Mongols remained, the rest having retreated to Azerbaijan.[13] At the time of facing its greatest challenge in Syria, the Mongol army was at its minimum size, a very unfortunate coincidence. Despite frequently quoted suggestions that Qutuz hid his force in the hills and laid a trap for his enemy, it has been cogently argued that the Mongols arrived on the battlefield before the Mamluks did.[14] An advance Mamluk force under the command of Baybars made its way to the top of a hill overlooking the Mongols, who again were something of a cosmopolitan group including Armenians and Georgians. When Kitbughā saw Baybars, he ordered his men to charge. Baybars and his men retreated into the hills with the Mongols in hot pursuit. They were presumably confident in themselves given their recent successes in the region. But hubris is a powerful and dangerous narcotic and the recent triumphal procession of the Mongols through Syria had lulled them into a false sense of superiority.

The Mongols regrouped and formed a line that roughly ran from north to south with its southern flank guarded by the slopes of Mount Gilboa. Despite their supposed numerical advantage (though not every historian concurs that this was the case and some suggest instead that the size of the two armies was approximately equal), the Mamluks did not immediately gain the upper hand when battle commenced. Instead, the Mamluk left started to crack under the pressure of a fierce Mongol onslaught. Qutuz was forced to charge into the thick of the fray several times, urging his men on to greater efforts, crying for the help of Allah. His exhortations began to take effect. Slowly, the Mamluks began to take control of the battlefield, pushing forward inch by inch. It was now the turn of the Mongols to feel the pressure and they started to give way. Among their number were Muslim allies who at the decisive moment suddenly changed sides. Some of Kitbughā's force managed to fight their way out as the Mongols were gradually pushed back. Kitbughā was not one of them. Fighting until overwhelmed, he was taken alive and led before Qutuz. He was defiant to the end. When Qutuz mocked him, Kitbughā responded with some truth that at least he had remained true to his master, which is more than could be said for Qutuz. Irritated by his braggadocio, Qutuz ordered him to be beheaded there and then. His head was soon after sent back to Cairo as grisly evidence of the Mamluks' success.[15]

As the battle drew towards its dire close, Mongol units who had not managed to escape the scene were attacked piecemeal and mostly slaughtered. Even local villagers joined in the massacre. Some Mongols sought safety by hiding in nearby reed beds but they were flushed out when the Mamluks set fire to them. The Mongol camp was taken and some of the camp followers taken prisoner, among them Mongol families including that of Kitbughā. The surviving Mongols made another stand about 8 miles away at Baysān but were again bested and those that remained made their way back across the Jordan and out of Galilee.[16]

On 8 September, Qutuz entered Damascus at the head of his conquering army. The Mongol governor of the city knew what was coming and fled. The Muslim citizens, also sensing the way the wind was blowing, rose in revolt and took their revenge on the Christian population and possibly on the Jews there too. Those fleeing Mongols who were not quick enough were overtaken and butchered. Churches were burned and some Christian houses were ransacked and residents killed. The arrival of Qutuz brought an end to the rioting and Syria was absorbed into the expanding Mamluk territories. There was little else in the way of retribution though, and those who had collaborated with the Mongols during the time of their rule went largely unpunished with the exception of a few officials who had supported them, who were duly executed. Perhaps for political reasons, Qutuz generally acted with discretion and restaint.[17] The Mongols also abandoned Hama and Aleppo whilst Baybars chased them north, giving them another beating at Homs. The Mongol invasion of Syria had been decisively rebuffed, though they had as yet not completely abandoned their ambitions in the country.

The Fall of Qutuz

Qutuz spent the night after the battle at Tiberias. It may, or may not, have been coincidence but this was just a short ride from the battlefield of Hattin. But there was no time for gloating. From his perspective, an awful lot remained to be done. One important step forward came when the leader of the north Syrian Bedouin, Īsā ibn Muhannā, presented himself before Qutuz and offered his support. He could be an invaluable ally in the region given his power and influence among a tough group of fighters. With their superb scouting abilities and their capacity for guerrilla warfare they had a significance out of all proportion to their numbers, as more recently T. E. Lawrence appreciated. In time, these attacks not only took the form of forays against Mongol warriors in Syria but were also sometimes offensive in nature when forces crossed the Euphrates and took the fight to the enemy in their own territory. Some accounts mention the ingenious if cruel tactic of releasing wild foxes in Mongol territory in Mesopotamia with flaming torches tied to their tails. Hungry dogs were then released to increase their panic. The result was that grasslands went up in flames, depriving the Mongols of a critical way of feeding their horses. The men responsible for arranging these unorthodox activities were known descriptively as 'burners' (*al-munawwirūn*).[18] Such tactics were typical of those used to interfere with the logistics of the Mongol army, its Achilles' heel. They also included the spoiling of watercourses, the overall aim being to ensure that a buffer zone was created, with the intention that land covering at least ten days' of travel on the Mongol side of the border was effectively transformed into a desert.

The outcome of Ain Jalut was bad news for the Ayyubid prisoners held by Hūlegū, a long way from the action in Azerbaijan, as he had them put to death. Those killed included the inconstant Al-Nasir Yusuf who had been sent to him by Kitbughā after his capture near Karak. But there was no overwhelming Mongol response to this great reverse (though Aleppo was retaken for a few months at the end of the year) for one very good reason. The *khagan* Möngke had died on 11 August 1259. He was buried, in accordance with Mongol custom, in a secret location in the Altai Mountains. Marco Polo noted that on the death of a *khagan,* any bystanders who witnessed his funeral procession would be killed on the spot so that they could serve their lord in the next life. Similarly, the finest horses in the kingdom would be slaughtered. Following the demise of Möngke, Marco recorded that 20,000 people who had had the misfortune to witness the burial party were killed.[19]

Möngke's death exposed weaknesses in the Mongol khanate. Its huge extent made it hard to rule and the death of a *khagan* almost inevitably led to a succession dispute as would-be replacements jockeyed for position. Prospective successors and their key supporters needed to be present at the *kurultai* in Mongolia where these great matters would be decided. So, just at this decisive moment, the attention of the Mongols was focused on events 4,000 miles to the east. Worse still from their perspective, the feared succession dispute duly took place, leading to four years of civil war between two rival claimants, Kublai and Ariq Böke. By 1264, although the war had come to an end with Kublai the decisive winner, the unity of the Mongol *khanate* was shattered. There were effectively by then four distinct Mongol power blocs in place: one centred on China and Mongolia; another on the *Ilkhanate* in Persia and the surrounding lands;[20] a third, that of the Golden Horde in Russia and the fringes of eastern Europe; and a fourth, the Chaghatays, in Central Asia. The last branch were particularly opposed to Kublai and the *Ilkhanate,* whilst the latter were in bitter opposition to the Golden Horde.

Just as Christendom and Islam were divided by internal tensions, then so too were the Mongols. That part of the Mongol *khanate* known as the lands of the Golden Horde held territories that are now in southern Russia and around the Black Sea and included many Muslims. The leader of the Golden Horde, Berke, was – according to Muslim chroniclers writing a few years later – far from happy at the brutal intervention of his fellow Mongols in Mesopotamia and Syria. Despite this the Golden Horde had provided troops who took part in the sack of Baghdad; indeed, they had little choice for this had been at the express order of Möngke. But with Möngke's death, Berke was increasingly at odds with Hūlegū and when the moment was right plotted against him, aligning himself with the party of Ariq Böke.[21] This would help the Muslim cause in the Levant no end.

Ain Jalut was a critically important battle though it was the internal disputes among the Mongols themselves that were ultimately the decisive factor in diminishing their threat. Ain Jalut did not lead to the overnight elimination of the Mongol threat in the Levant. But it marked a turning of the tide. The Mongols, who had steamrollered their way through Mesopotamia and Syria, had been stopped in their tracks. They had been shown to be beatable. On the other hand, the ascendancy of the Mamluks was forcefully confirmed. In some eyes, they had saved Islam from extinction. The Mamluk dynasty would survive and for a time thrive, leading to the establishment of a ruling power in Egypt that would retain its place there for the next three centuries.

An important by-product of the triumph of the Mamluks at Ain Jalut was that it also increased the threat against the Crusader states in Outremer exponentially.[22] In the long term, the Mamluk victory spelt danger for Acre, both politically and economically. The hinterland of Palestine became a war zone and it was difficult for trade as a result, with consequent economic repercussions. In addition, the Mamluks did not encourage Latin commerce in the region and Acre became increasingly isolated as trade routes moved north and east. The Genoese and Venetians did well out of this as their ships carried trade to the Black Sea, the Caspian and beyond. In contrast, Outremer became a less significant and more vulnerable Frankish enclave.

At a personal level, Qutuz's triumph served to prove just how chimerical the high points in life can be. He and Baybars had enjoyed a volatile relationship in the years preceding the battle and only the Mongol threat had brought them together. Once the threat had been dealt with, old tensions soon bubbled to the surface again. Baybars felt that he had been promised more in the way of reward than he subsequently received, including the governorship of Aleppo. But in all probability Qutuz felt that this was too great a prize, which Baybars might exploit to use against him. The anticipated governorship did not follow. Contemporary Muslim chroniclers wrote that mutual distrust could be read in the eyes and faces of the two men.[23]

The Mamluk army turned around to make its way back to Egypt. On 22 October 1260, Qutuz was out hunting; he was an enthusiastic lover of the chase. A hare broke cover and he rode after it, accompanied by a small retinue. But the hare was not the real prey; when the opportunity presented itself, the men with Qutuz – who included Baybars – set about him and struck him down. This was no spontaneous act, though the opportunity may have arisen unexpectedly; it is clear that a plot had been hatched in advance, of which Baybars would be the main beneficiary. Different chroniclers give varying details of these events but all have Baybars as a key participant in the assassination, possibly because he feared that if he did not remove Qutuz, Qutuz would remove him. One account suggests that Baybars asked Qutuz for a favour. When it was granted, Baybars took the Sultan's hand to kiss it in gratitude. Whilst he gripped it firmly, an attendant stabbed Qutuz in the neck. The Sultan perished beneath a frenzied flurry of blows.[24]

Baybars was now made Sultan, having promised to be generous to the emirs who made him so. Baybars – a convenient (indeed merciful) abbreviation of his full name, al-Malik al-Zahir Rukn al-Din Baybars al-Banduqdari al-Salihi – would prove himself a formidable opponent of the Franks. He was mighty in war and sagacious as a statesman. He was also Machiavellian and unpredictable, a great opportunist, quick to take advantage when an unexpected chance presented itself. The Franks were soon put on their guard that any improvement in relationships with the Mamluks due to their tacit support during the Ain Jalut campaign was at an end with the change in regime, as evidenced shortly afterwards when Baybars' lieutenant in Jerusalem closed the city to Christian pilgrim traffic.[25]

The new Sultan also took measures to ingratiate himself with his subjects in Cairo. As an alien interloper, he needed to emphasise his credentials as a ruler, especially as there had recently been a revolt by black slaves in the city. In January 1261 he was the leading actor in a magnificent inauguration ceremony in Cairo. A riderless horse went ahead of him, draped in a golden saddle cloth. Over Baybars' head was a parasol, adorned with the image of a golden bird, the emblem of the ancient Fatimid sultans who had once ruled in Egypt. He wore a black turban, the symbol of the Abbasid caliphs, and carried a sword that was once the property of Umar, the second Caliph.[26] He was going out of his way to establish his legitimacy and signal his intention to rule as a great but suitably pious head of state. The stage was set for a spectacular sultanate, marked both by great ambition and no little achievement.

The Involvement of the Franks

Among those probably present when the Mongol forces entered Damascus was Bohemond VI, prince of Antioch, along with Het'um of Armenia – Antioch and Armenia were historically close allies (in recent times at least) and were now both collaborating with the Mongols.[27] In mitigation of their stance, owing to their geographical location and the enormous military disadvantages that they suffered, they had very little choice but to submit to the previously all-conquering Mongol power. William of Rubruck had passed through Antioch five years before and noted the dilapidated condition of the defences there and that particular issue had come to the fore when faced with a significant Mongol force outside those extended walls, leaving the Antiochians with little choice but to submit.

It must nevertheless have been a proud moment for the Christian rulers entering Damascus as part of a conquering army, even if it was the Mongols who were ultimately responsible for the victory; no Frankish army had entered the city in triumph before.[28] The outrages against Islam alleged during the conquest of Damascus, such as the defiling of the mosques there, were supposedly ordered by Bohemond. But this was to be a fleeting moment of triumph for which there would ultimately be drastic consequences. Not that Bohemond's stance was altogether welcome in Outremer; Thomas Agni de Lentino, the bishop of Bethlehem, excommunicated him for his support of the Mongols.

A truce had been agreed between the Franks and Damascus in 1254, and with Egypt in 1255. It was in both cases supposed to last for ten years. However, the involvement of Bohemond in the Syrian campaign against the Muslims there would encourage an adverse response in retaliation. The situation was also complicated because Outremer was at the time divided and, whilst some Franks were allies of the Mongols, others were targets. Nowhere evidenced this better than Sidon, on the Mediterranean coast, which had a castle that was said to be 'very strong and surrounded on all sides by sea'.[29] Despite this, the port had been sacked by forces from Damascus whilst Louis IX was in the Levant. Those residents present at the time sought safety in the castle, but it was simply not big enough to shelter them all. The town was not then surrounded by walls and several thousand people were killed. Some work had taken place there in 1227–28 but it was clearly insufficient. Louis had as a result of the decimation of Sidon been persuaded to strengthen the defences, adding high walls and towers and clearing the moat of mud.

Whilst Kitbughā was campaigning in Syria before the battle of Ain Jalut, a Mongol force moved on Sidon in 1260. The town was defended by its lord, Julian Grenier. But although he fought bravely he was greatly outnumbered and the Mongols took the city. Some of the citizens of Sidon were killed and others enslaved – though a few found refuge in several castles nearby that the Mongols were unable to take. Two passing Crusader galleys were able to take yet more to safety. But the final outcome was a catastrophe for Sidon. The defences were destroyed so thoroughly that the port was left totally vulnerable and sold to the Templars because Julian, who survived, did not have the funds to repair it. Panic gripped the land and reached as far as Acre, where trees were cut down in orchards outside the city and stones were even removed from cemeteries in case they could be used to feed Mongol siege artillery.[30]

The Templar of Tyre portrays Julian as a heroic figure who fought determinedly against heavy odds, but the same writer also suggested he was reckless and 'light-headed'. He is also painted as a wastrel seduced by the pleasures of gambling and whoring.[31] In addition, he was a man who did not choose his enemies too carefully. These included his own uncle when he attacked his lands around Tyre. More dangerously, he had also led raids into the Beqaa valley, in modern Lebanon. These territories were by then in Mongol hands. This had inevitably led to Mongol reprisals. Kitbughā initially sent his nephew to Sidon with a small force to bring Julian back into line but this was ambushed and defeated and the nephew was killed. This of course then made the grudge personal and Kitbughā had reacted by sending a much stronger force to obtain redress and it duly devastated Sidon. However much Julian had gained from his raiding activities it is doubtful that his loot compensated for the great losses he sustained by the fall of this important settlement.

Further weakening the Franks, they also suffered a bad defeat at Tiberias against 'Turkish' forces in the same year. The Frankish army was composed of Templars and forces of secular knights from elsewhere in the region. The latter included contingents from John II of Ibelin, lord of Beirut, John of Jubail, the Marshall of the Kingdom of Jerusalem, and men from Acre. It was a disaster. Many sergeants were captured or killed and the Templars lost most of their equipment, which would be difficult and expensive to replace. John of Ibelin was one of those taken prisoner along with John of Jubail and William of Beaujeu who would later on become the 21st Master of the Templars. A large ransom of 20,000 'Saracen' bezants was paid for their release, though pitifully few captives remained alive.[32]

There were clear signs of division in the Frankish camp then. The lack of a firm hand on the tiller giving overall direction to Outremer as a whole was shockingly apparent. This was by no means a new phenomenon, but it was a potentially fatal flaw given the inferior resources available to the Crusader states in the region. It meant that a powerful and well-organised enemy could pick off the separate elements of Outremer one by one.

Division in Christendom was also apparent further afield. When Pope Alexander IV summoned a council in July 1261, crusading focus was not just on Outremer but also the increasingly fragile security of the Latin Empire in Constantinople and on the Hohenstaufens in Sicily. Ever since the first days of Norman rule of the island in the eleventh century, Sicily had essentially been awarded to her kings as a papal gift and the pontiffs saw it as being under their secular as well as their spiritual authority. The fallout between the papacy and the Hohenstaufens therefore became a prominent issue. Attention was increasingly pulled in several different directions and the effectiveness of individual strategies was therefore compromised. Meanwhile, Louis IX had been receiving Mongol delegations in Paris. One came from Hūlegū seeking an alliance. Another source suggests that a quite different delegation came from Berke of the Golden Horde. This again sought not alliance but submission. Given Mongol advances elsewhere in Europe, this must have caused alarm.[33]

This situation was about to be further complicated given the unpredictable nature of two things in particular: the changing policy of Acre towards the Mamluks and the rise to power of Baybars. In the years that followed, raids would be launched on Mamluk territory from Acre. It is not clear whether this was in response to the actions of Baybars and whether it caused him to respond in kind; as is often the case, it is hard to discern whether the chicken or the egg came first. But the end result was clear enough: a serious weakening in the position of the Franks in Outremer. However, violent confrontation was not always the case and there were short-term truces between the Franks and the Mamluks. For example, in 1263 Baybars entered into an agreement with John of Ibelin, the ruler of Jaffa. The Ibelins were one of those settler families who had risen to prominence in the region and had a dynastic history there which stretched back for many decades. As part of the understanding between John and Baybars, the latter could use Jaffa as a harbour through which to transport grain from Damietta in Egypt to Syria, which was at the time experiencing serious famine; a plague of rats there was adding to the damage.[34]

At around the same time, Baybars also agreed a truce with Acre which allowed for the exchange of prisoners, though the Franks were not quick to follow through with the terms agreed.[35] The Templar of Tyre explains why this prisoner exchange plan did not come to anything. Baybars had proposed a rate of exchange of two 'Saracens' for one Christian. But the Templar and Hospitaller knights, crucial political and military players in the Kingdom of Jerusalem, were reluctant to go along with the scheme. Many of the prisoners they held were artisans, difficult and expensive to replace and making an important economic contribution. Eventually, John of Ibelin did take part in the prisoner exchange but Acre did not. Baybars also sent a messenger to Hugh Revel, the Master of the Hospital. Through him, he complained that the fortifications of Arsūf had been strengthened contrary to agreements that had been made not to do so. However, he still received envoys from Arsūf and Jaffa warmly enough in the same year, but in retrospect this was more than anything to buy time. He saw the re-fortification of Arsūf as a sign that the word of the Franks did not count for much and resolved to repay their bad faith back in kind when an opportunity presented itself not long after.

5

Acre and the Crusader States in the Mid-thirteenth Century

'For we who were Occidentals have now become Orientals'
The twelfth-century Crusader chronicler Fulcher of Chartres

Acre: The New 'Capital'

When the Spanish Muslim traveller Ibn Jubayr saw Acre in 1184, three years before it fell to Saladin, he described it as 'the unloading place of ships reared aloft in the sea like mountains'. Whilst he did not think much of the filth and ordure that caused the streets to stink and he naturally deplored the fact that ancient mosques had been converted to churches, he was nevertheless impressed by some aspects of it, causing him to compare it to Constantinople.[1] Acre was a bustling, busy port, effectively an *entrepot* to the commerce of Syria and beyond. There had historically been a long road, the *Via Maris* ('the way of the sea') which linked the east, from India and China through Mesopotamia and Persia, to the Mediterranean. Through a series of middlemen, goods moved to and fro along the *Via Maris*, making it a huge wealth generator for merchants and nobles alike. Acre, with its crucial position as a link between East and West, was a key part of this network. It made the city a prime piece of real estate. Even the Frankish currency of the region reflected these commercial realities; by the thirteenth century coins in Acre were largely modelled on similar Islamic styles whilst the gold *bezants* of Antioch were also based on those used by Muslim powers in the region.

What was also notable to Ibn Jubayr was the way in which secular authorities generally acted with tolerance towards Muslims living under their jurisdiction. He remarked that both Acre and Tyre housed mosques, though they tended to be kept away from Christian churches. He did, however, see columns of Muslim slaves being led into captivity during his journey. He witnessed everyday activities being undertaken in Acre too, such as the collection of taxes near the gates of the port. Unsurprisingly, he spoke with disgust of seeing pigs roaming the streets; they were apparently extremely widespread, which probably added significantly both to the ordure and the noise in the city. But the general tolerance he found made a favourable impression. Such was also the case in other parts of Christendom where Christianity and Islam were being forced by events to co-exist; the Christian victory at Las Navas de Toledo in Spain in 1212 was marked by dissension when Spanish elements wished to act with mercy towards their defeated Muslim enemy, a stance that allied French troops simply could not understand. Such toleration testified to the realities of living in a frontier region where overbearing fanaticism could have an entirely negative outcome in the longer term.[2]

Whilst Acre traded with the hinterland of Syria, it was also reliant on supplies from Christian Europe. Imports came in from Italy and the south of France in particular. The military orders, deprived of their estates in Outremer as the century went on, were particularly significant importers.[3] Joinville noted whilst he was in Outremer that he would stock up on supplies before the winter came because prices would rise then as no ships were arriving with provisions. He would replenish his pigsties and his sheepfolds. He would buy as much flour and wine as he could. As a good Frenchman, he was particularly keen to ensure that he was well provided with wine, buying 100 barrels of it and making sure that the best was drunk first. When eating, his knights were provided with both wine and water at table so that they could mix them as they so desired. The need to rely on shipped-in supplies is a reminder that Acre was in some ways still a frontier town, still needing provisions from 'back home' as they were not available locally in sufficient quantity.[4]

Acre was a cosmopolitan city, where east met west. It is worth remembering the well-known words of Fulcher of Chartres, written in about 1127:

For we who were Occidentals have now become Orientals. He who was a Roman or a Frank has in this land been made into a Galilean or a

Palestinian. He who was of Rheims has now become a citizen of Tyre or Antioch. We have already forgotten the places of our birth.[5]

If that was true of Tyre or Antioch in 1127, it was even more so of Acre a century later. There were many long-standing settler families here by now going back a number of generations. That said, there were occasional injections from the West which disturbed the equilibrium from time to time, be it ships from Italian city states or arrivals of Crusaders, short-term visitors who sometimes had little time for the live-and-let-live attitudes of the local Franks. Jacques de Vitry, Bishop of Acre, was scathing in his criticism of the city as 'a beast with nine heads fighting against each other'. As far as the Church was concerned, levels of intolerance increased during the thirteenth century as under the pontificate of Innocent III in particular it truly became a Church Militant. Hard-line attitudes were apparent through extraordinarily violent episodes such as the crusade against the Cathars. But the situation was very different amongst the indigenous population in Acre, where settlers of West European origin freely mingled with what were known as Oriental Christians, who were part of the local Syriac churches that were particularly prominent in the suburb of Montmusard. There was also a Jewish community in the city throughout the life of Frankish Outremer.

As a trading emporium the cosmopolitan nature of Acre is demonstrated by the variety of languages spoken in its markets, with evidence that alongside French – the primary language of the city – Arabic, Coptic, Provencal, Hebrew, Greek, German, English and Italian was also in use.[6] One thing that is readily apparent is that, during the first half of the thirteenth century in particular, Acre was wealthy. Matthew Paris asserted that the Templars and Hospitallers had told Richard of Cornwall, who was in Outremer in 1240–1, that the royal revenue of Acre was 50,000 pounds of silver per annum, which exceeded that of the king of England.[7] Given the crucial situation of Acre as a key point of exchange for goods flowing from east to west and vice-versa, the Crown was in an excellent position to levy duties to boost its income. The situation of Acre economically was elevated after the fall of Jerusalem. With the loss of much of the rural hinterland many basic foodstuffs needed to be imported, with items such as wine, grain and chicken having to be brought in, especially when a large crusade expedition was in the region. The production of sugar cane – one of Outremer's major exports as it was the principal supplier of sugar to Europe – was relocated nearer Acre and olives were also an important crop. Timber, iron, furs, copper, amber and textiles moved eastwards whilst gold, spices and silk went back the other way.[8] The export of local sand to Venice was also particularly significant for the Italian city state as it was used as part of its prestigious glass-making industry. Acre was also a key access point to the pilgrimage sites of the Holy Land and later developed a pilgrim status in its own right with around forty Latin Christian churches, monasteries and hospitals there by the middle of the thirteenth century.[9]

It is clear from looking at the development of art in the region that a degree of assimilation had been going on since the Franks first arrived and established themselves in the region. At first, it had been very Western in its inspiration and could be seen as a form of colonial art. Subsequently, this cultural colonialism was toned down. Local ideas started to reshape the art of the Franks, which, whilst still retaining strong Western influences, was also affected by both Levantine and Byzantine stylistic inputs. This, in a very elegant way, epitomises how Frankish culture in Outremer had developed a specific voice in response to the environment in which it existed. It was a culture that had different paradigms of the world from some short-term visitors from the West. These different world views could, and did, lead to unfortunate differences of opinion between the 'locals' and the 'visitors', with occasional violent repercussions.

Whatever the weakened political and military state that Acre was in during the second half of the thirteenth century, artistic production still continued there, perhaps ironically leading to a peak in such work even when the kingdom was living on borrowed time. With Jerusalem gone, the ateliers and *scriptoria* of the Holy City had relocated to Acre and some remarkable works were produced. Many have no doubt been destroyed owing to the ultimate loss of Acre but what survives is a tantalising glimpse into a lost world. One superb example is the so-called Arsenal Bible, a wonderfully illustrated manuscript commissioned by Louis IX in about 1250. Other works survive but this, with its scenes of Solomon and David for example, is exquisite. Whilst there are strong local elements in the artwork, the presence of a contemporary French Gothic influence is equally noticeable. Louis seems to have acted as a catalyst for some kind of artistic revival whilst he was in Acre. It is notable that not only religious subjects were produced but also some secular works, mirroring contemporary developments in France. Where the artists came from is a matter of debate, though one plausible suggestion is that they journeyed from Constantinople, which was at the time still part of a Latin Empire, though only for a few more years.[10] There is evidence too of first-class icon production in Acre, again with strong local influences. The use of icons was a feature of eastern (especially Byzantine) practices and the development of a Crusader style of iconography was another good example of the fusion of different cultural influences that took place in Outremer.[11]

Within Acre, the different 'quarters' held by the various Italian city states acted in a very autonomous fashion. Venice was particularly significant in this respect. It possessed mighty seapower; in a crisis it could produce 100 new ships in six months, making it the envy of just about every maritime state in the world. A contemporary inventory of the Venetian quarter in Acre at this time divides it into four districts. In one of them was the *fondaco,* a warehouse and retail complex with lodgings for rent. It included space for sixteen shops and living quarters for officials such as the parish priest and the court clerk. There were also palaces belonging to important individuals such as the *bailli.* Here there were also six shops clustered around it and more lodgings. The quarter also contained its own church – inevitably dedicated to San Marco – and there was room for stalls to be rented out to street traders. The Genoese quarter was also significant. Whether the effect of handing over control of these quarters to city states like Venice and Genoa was negative or positive has become a matter of debate between historians. On the one hand it inhibited the growth of a Frankish mercantile class, but on the other the flow of goods brought in significant income through taxes and levies.[12] But the presence of these rival powers in Outremer undoubtedly had a detrimental political impact, one which was ultimately to cause the kingdom significant difficulties.

The various quarters within the city became largely self-contained cells. Walls were erected to partition them off with their own gates and defences. Even sewers were often specific to a particular quarter, though they were not very effective and Acre became infamous for its levels of pollution. The harbour was known in French as 'Lordemer' – 'The Filthy Sea' – because of the levels of effluent that were regularly deposited in it. May–June and September–October were times of the year when risk levels for the spread of disease shot up. An unfortunate coincidence of unhelpful weather conditions, with the wind blowing from the east and temperatures rising, and the seasonal arrival of pilgrims during the twice-yearly passage across the Mediterranean (one before Easter, the other in late summer) sometimes led to outbreaks of epidemics fuelled by the high levels of pollution. Outside the city, however, the plains adjacent to it retained a rural character with fields, orchards, farms and vineyards and areas where horses and cattle could be grazed.

The addition of the suburb of Montmusard to Acre was a much-needed development providing valuable room for expansion as the Old City had become overcrowded; as the century went on any spare space in the latter was quickly gobbled up. As other Frankish settlements in Outremer were lost in the second half of the century, this capacity in Montmusard became increasingly important as refugees came in from elsewhere. However, even by the time that Acre was lost in 1291 there was still sufficient room left in the suburb to fit more people in if needed. Whilst refugees were coming in to Acre during the preceding decades, there is evidence that some others had decided to cut their losses and leave Outremer and return to their roots in Europe long before the final fall of the city.

The Military Orders in Outremer
Whether it be via the Crusades, the Inquisition, the forced conversion of non-Christians by colonial settlers or one of the many other examples where organised Christian religion has acted in a violent way, there is plenty of evidence that what is doctrinally in many ways a pacifist faith could tap into dangerous undercurrents with catastrophic results for those on the receiving end of them. Christianity is assuredly not the only religion that this could be said of, but there are inconsistencies in basic Christian doctrine that are hard to reconcile. For example, Christ told his followers to turn the other cheek when they were attacked but the Book of Revelation wrote in graphic terms of the last great battle between Good and Evil, liberally using imagery of a very violent nature. There was also the example of the Old Testament to refer to, full of wars and conflicts and great generals like Joshua and David who slaughtered their enemies on the battlefield. It was little wonder that defining when and how a 'just war' might be fought, as St Augustine of Hippo had tried to do as far back as the fifth century,

led theologians into the most complicated of moral mazes. But some have concluded that by the mid-thirteenth century 'remarkably few in the West questioned the tradition of sacred violence' that had by then become the norm.[13]

It is an irony that some of the military orders were initially set up with largely pacific activities in mind. The Hospitallers, for example, were originally established to run a hospital for ailing pilgrims in Jerusalem. They were set up even before the First Crusade was launched whilst the city was still in Muslim hands. Theirs was a tradition that continued on for centuries; for example, by the fourteenth century there were 600 hospitals run by them in England alone.[14] The great hospital in Jerusalem could accommodate 2,000 patients.[15] When the Teutonic Knights were founded during the Siege of Acre in 1190 their original function was similar to that initially performed by the Hospitallers. Initially they were known as the Teutonic Hospital of St Mary in Jerusalem, taking their name from a house in the city that had been acquired by a German couple and converted into a hospital at the beginning of the twelfth century and later run by Hospitallers. However, crusading was martial and militant and before long the orders took on a very different function, namely to escort pilgrims safely to their ultimate destination, primarily Jerusalem. Eventually they became something even more than this, taking up a key role as what was essentially a standing army for the Kingdom of Jerusalem, although the orders reported to a spiritual rather than a secular leadership. They also received many generous bequests and developed enormous wealth, especially in terms of land, in many parts of Europe as well as Outremer.

There was a violent reality behind this development. The crusading movement sanctioned warfare in the right environment and Crusaders fought fierce battles in the fulfilment of their vows as pilgrims journeying to the Holy Sepulchre in Jerusalem. But there were never enough fighters to go around. The fledgling Crusader states were surrounded by hostile Muslim polities with relatively unlimited access to fighting men. Occasional injections of new Crusader blood made little long-term difference to the balance of military power as many of those who came returned home again after fulfilling their pilgrim vows by worshipping at the Holy Sepulchre. Something was needed to even up the odds. This is how the great military orders developed. They started as small and relatively insignificant groups of fighting men who decided to stay in the Levant but at the same time live a holy, monk-like life. They attached themselves to holy men and kings alike, but they were soon transformed from small hotchpotch groups of warriors into brotherhoods of warrior-monks, subject to strict discipline and a stern and unforgiving way of life. There was no contradiction at all in these actions as far as many contemporary moralists were concerned; the Council of Nablus in 1120 even allowed churchmen to fight if the conditions were right, with Canon 20 saying unequivocally that 'if a cleric takes up arms in self-defence, he shall not bear any guilt'.[16] Recruits to the orders gave up everything, their property as well as their lives, to serve, seeing themselves as 'paupers for God'.

There were also practical reasons why military assistance of this type was needed. Great crusades with thousands of participants were the exception rather than the rule. Many pilgrims came in much smaller groups and were consequently very vulnerable. The local environment played into the hands of bandits (and also added to the risk by supporting significant numbers of wild Asiatic lions, which, sadly, have since become virtually extinct in most of Asia except for a tiny population in India). The borders of the Kingdom of Jerusalem were extremely porous and the rugged terrain meant that there were many places where ambushes could be set. River crossings were a site of particular vulnerability for the pilgrims. There were frequent attacks on them and contemporary commentators told how corpses could be seen unburied by the side of the road, partly because the soil was not deep enough to dig a grave and partly because someone who stopped to try and do so might be digging his own. In a time when funeral rites and a 'proper Christian burial' were extremely important, this was an outrage that could not be tolerated.

Although smaller groups were obviously the most vulnerable, even larger ones were at risk. One good example was the attack on a party of 700 pilgrims in 1118 when one half of the group was killed and the other half taken off into captivity, an event so shocking that it may well have led to the founding of the Knights Templar. Travelling, even in Europe, was a dangerous activity at the time, but it was especially so in this frontier country. Something needed to be done to protect these travellers. Fulcher of Chartres, who became a long-term resident of Outremer in the early decades of the twelfth century, spoke of how residents were subject to frequent attack when they were outside of

Jerusalem, whether formalised raids by Muslim neighbours or by plain old-fashioned bandits. He said that they were always listening out for the trumpet blast that warned them of danger.[17]

Hugh de Payns was one example of someone who decided to form a group of like-minded men tasked with the protection of pilgrims travelling to Jerusalem. He founded his small brotherhood in around 1119/1120.[18] They were soon given quarters in what had been the al-Aqsa Mosque and had been converted into a royal palace after the Crusader conquest in 1099. It was believed to be close to the site of Solomon's great temple, and from this belief the order would get its name, the Templars. There were already similar bodies in Jerusalem, in particular a group of Benedictine monks who ran the Hospital of St John of Jerusalem, initially founded by merchants from Amalfi to look after ill and wounded pilgrims. The importance and influence of the Templars soared when they came under the patronage of St Bernard of Clairvaux, a spiritual colossus of the twelfth century. This period saw an explosion in the number of monastic institutions in Europe. Fundamentally linked to this was the development of new religious orders, most of them adopting austere and stern forms of living in deliberate contrast to what was seen by their founding members as the lax and extravagant lifestyles that had developed in existing monastic institutions. Bernard was linked to one such new order, the Cistercians, named the 'white monks' after the colour of their habits. They lived simple lives, away from cities and the trappings of wealth. But however spiritually minded Bernard was, he still thought warriors were needed. As he sharply retorted when he heard that a Cistercian mission was planning to make its way to Outremer, what was needed were 'fighting knights, not singing and wailing monks'.[19]

The Templars were the military counterpoints of the Cistercians. They offered a new kind of knighthood, one where their martial skills were dedicated to the glory of God. When Hugh de Payns journeyed to the West to drum up support in 1127, he was enthusiastically received by many, including Bernard. His delegation visited England (mentioned in one of the later entries in the *Anglo-Saxon Chronicle*) and Scotland. The new knighthood touched a nerve somewhere deep: it brought together the growing spiritual awareness of the era and the military nature of knighthood. It allowed knights (and sergeants and other men-at-arms) to fight in what was regarded as a just cause. This visit was well-timed. There is some evidence that for much of the first decade of the Temple's existence it faced considerable difficulties and could well have expired before even reaching adolescence. The European mission gave it a new lease of life.

Other events at around the same time in Europe would also have significant long-term consequences for Outremer. Fulk, count of Anjou, was persuaded to hand over his large tracts of land in France to his son and seek his fortune in the Levant instead (he was also a supporter of the Temple, which helped their cause). Fulk duly departed and was later made King of Jerusalem as the husband of Queen Melisende, to whom the throne passed in the absence of a son for the late King Baldwin II. Angevin involvement in the region would remain strong right up until the ultimate demise of the kingdom.

A key development took place at the Council of Troyes, held in France in 1129. Here, a Primitive (or Latin) Rule was developed for the Templars. There are some suggestive clauses in it. One said unequivocally that 'this armed company of knights may kill the enemies of the cross without sinning'.[20] Another concerned the absolute authority of the Master of the order; his instructions were to be obeyed 'as though Christ Himself had commanded it'.[21] Bernard, a masterful orator and letter writer, gave further frightening clarity to the legitimisation of sanctified violence by distinguishing between homicide and malicide, the latter being the act of killing evil itself.[22] It was a subtle distinction that legitimised holy violence in certain circumstances. Bernard's treatise *De laude novae militiae* ('In praise of the new knighthood') was effectively a detailed manual for the Templars, still evolving their philosophy in the early decades of their existence. The Primitive Rule was based on monastic discipline but with appropriate flexibility taking into account the fact that these were fighting men. Some elements relaxed the normal rules of fasting during Christian festivals or attending mass every day, for example. But others were completely in line with monastic principles, such as rules on strict chastity and the rejection of earthly material trappings such as the wearing of extravagant clothes. The Templars were to wear robes of white, mirroring the colours of the Cistercian movement.

The military orders touched a nerve not just in the Levant but also in Europe. When a renowned king, Alfonso the Battler of Aragon, died in 1134 he bequeathed his entire kingdom to be divided between the canons of the Holy Sepulchre, the Hospitallers and the Templars. In the event the will was contested and not ultimately complied with;

even so, the Templars in particular still did well out of it – they were in a position to prove useful in the conquest of lands in Moorish Spain and their usefulness in this respect was sufficient to encourage patronage of them there.[23] A number of smaller orders also developed. There was even one specifically for lepers known as the Order of St Lazarus.[24] In 1139, Pope Innocent II issued a Papal bull, *omne datum optimum* ('every good gift') which granted the Templars an extraordinary range of privileges including the wearing of a red cross on their white robes, a symbol of the Templars' willingness to undergo martyrdom. Most significantly, the bull placed the order under the direct protection of the Pope; no secular power was to rule over them. Previously they had been answerable to the Patriarch of Jerusalem, but now their ultimate overlord was the Pope himself. They were exempted from paying tithes whilst retaining the right to receive them from those who earned a living from their land. The Hospitallers also evolved in the wake of these developments, though they did not receive their own Rule until 1153.

The Teutonic Knights were relative newcomers. Formed during the Siege of Acre in 1190–91 to minister to the needs of injured and sick German Crusaders, they also came to form an important part in the affairs of the Frankish states in the Levant. Initially established to support German Crusaders by providing a field hospital function – much needed given the brutality of the fighting outside the city's walls – by 1198 they had become militarised and took their place alongside the other orders in waging war against the enemies of Christendom (though it should be noted that this military aspect was in addition to their hospital function and not instead of it). This was a result of a major German expedition at around that time, although somehow this is one that has escaped the general (rather random) numbering system that has been established for the crusades.[25]

The orders were ultimately not answerable to the King of Jerusalem or any secular ruler but to the Pope, though the Templars became rather too close to the French crown – as early as 1150 the closeness of the Master Everard des Barres to Louis VII of France was creating tension within the order itself.[26] They evolved their own independent ways of thinking and often one order would have different practical policies and strategies than another. This meant that they were hard to coordinate, the military equivalent of trying to herd a group of cats. This would create difficulties on a number of occasions. Increasingly in the years ahead, Templars, Hospitallers, Teutonic Knights and others would find themselves on different sides in the power struggles that loomed.

Even at the time not everyone was happy that the orders were granted such generous religious benefits. The renowned theologian John of Salisbury was particularly concerned at what he saw as an unjustified granting of these privileges to the new knighthood.[27] His concerns came in the wake of a marked increase in power and influence of the Templars between 1129 and 1148 that built on the crucial role they played in helping to ensure that the Second Crusade did not completely disintegrate. Their contribution to this had been hugely significant both militarily and financially. On the other hand, the ultimate failure of the crusade exposed the Templars to criticism for their alleged part in its unsuccessful outcome.

One result of the favours granted to the orders is that they built up vast landholdings across Europe and became extremely wealthy. They were totally dependent on revenues from these for funding their operations in Outremer. Each year their various priories in Europe were required to send a third of their revenues to the east in what were known as *responsiones*. Whilst individual knights were poor, the orders as a whole were the polar opposite. Bequests of land, property and other wealth poured into their coffers from a range of benefactors. The orders also came to play an important role in non-military matters with the Templars especially developing a role as bankers in which capacity they came to be greatly trusted by French kings and nobles in particular.

In their role as effectively part of the standing army of the Kingdom of Jerusalem, the orders became vital to the affairs of Outremer. By the middle of the thirteenth century, there were possibly 600 Templar knights and 2,000 sergeants in the east.[28] The orders provided a reliable professional warrior force that offered many advantages compared to the feudal levies and volunteers who hitherto had been the main source of manpower. Increasingly, they developed a role in garrisoning the fortresses that provided the hard outer shell of the defences of the kingdom as secular lords were unable to do so; the famous Hospitaller fortress of Crac des Chevaliers was given to them in 1144 for this reason. All the orders were governed by a strict hierarchy. Supporting the Master of the Temple, for example, were his deputy, the Seneschal, then the Marshal, the head of the military establishment, the Commander who acted as Treasurer and the Draper who issued clothes and distributed gifts. There were also local Commanders in Outremer with responsibilities for Jerusalem, Tripoli and Antioch respectively. The other major orders had similar structures. There was also a geographical hierarchy in place. Local establishments, known as commanderies, were answerable to priories or provinces, which were responsible for regions across Christendom. The priories in turn reported in to Grand Chapters of the orders – 'HQ' as it were.

Increasingly though, some began to question the *raison d'être* of the orders. Walter Map, a late twelfth-century chronicler, even queried the fundamental principles on which they were based. Why, he wondered, were 'men allowed to take the sword to protect Christendom, when Peter was forbidden to defend Christ?' (which seems a very good theological question). Christ had taught Peter to use patience rather than violence and to sheath his sword when he drew it in the Garden of Gethsemane. Whilst Map's view was in a minority, there were others who noted the increasing influence of the orders with distaste. Isaac of L'Etoile, a Cistercian abbot from Poitou, remembering the description of the Templars as a 'new knighthood' renamed them 'a new monstrosity' and was also concerned that violence was being used to convert Muslims to Christianity.[29] Whilst the Templars seem to have attracted particular opprobrium – when Richard the Lionheart was accused of being excessively proud, he promised to bequeath his pride to the Templars – the other orders were also more than capable of looking after their own interests rather than those of their co-religionists. Even in the mid-twelfth century John of Salisbury was writing in fairly explicit terms criticising them and noting that the dangers of avarice and pride overtaking the military orders were already starting to become apparent.

The Italians Go to War

In the mid-thirteenth century several Italian city states were competing for commercial supremacy in the Mediterranean. The fiercest rivalry was that between Venice and Genoa, and a third power, Pisa, was also heavily involved. The existence of these rivalries is a reminder that the medieval world was more fragmented than today's. This was strongly evident in Italy, which beyond the city states was also split between papally controlled territories and those held by the Hohenstaufen emperors such as the Kingdom of Sicily (which then included not just the island but also the south of the Italian mainland too). Outside of the peninsula other powers were also involved in intense commercial competition in the Mediterranean, such as Barcelona and Marseille. These territories may have been a long way from Outremer – but the Frankish states were sucked into the wider struggle for power across the region.

The city states of Italy had been involved in the affairs of Outremer almost from the start. Given their extremely vulnerable position, surrounded on land by a bevy of hostile Muslim powers, the ships of Genoa, Venice and others acted as a vital link back to Europe for the fledgling Frankish states; a modern analogy would be that they were like the lifeline that tethers a space walker to a mothership. Supplies and reinforcements could be brought in to counteract the build-up of hostile powers around the isolated Kingdom of Jerusalem. Hints can be seen even in modern Acre, with thoroughfares like Pizan Street or the Amalfi district. Almost from the outset the Italian city states were quick to see opportunities to turn a profit from their involvement. When the Franks attacked Acre in 1104, the Genoese offered their support in return for being allowed part of the city for themselves as a commercial district and for tax exemptions. These were duly given when the city fell. When shortly afterwards Tyre was captured, the Venetians, who had signed up to a similar deal, also took up residence in Acre. Whilst Jerusalem was undoubtedly the spiritual highlight for pilgrims, for those of a more commercial bent Acre was crucial from the start.

Circumstances evolved to make these maritime powers even more important. From very early on, the land passage to Outremer across Asia Minor became untenable. The disastrous journey experienced by the Second Crusade had long-term ramifications for the way in which Crusaders made their way east. From the Third Crusade onwards, all the major expeditions took the sea route to Outremer via Acre (though during the Third Crusade they could not land in the port of the city when it was in Muslim hands). This made the city states even more crucial, especially as the final outcome of the post-Hattin crusade was to leave much of the hinterland in the hands of Islamic powers. The city states made substantial commercial gains as a result of this change in the mode of transportation, with Venice providing the most famous/ infamous example when she hijacked the Fourth Crusade to her own advantage. The taking of Constantinople provided huge material gains for Venice, as the famous bronze horses that are now in the Basilica of San Marco symbolise.

The importance of the various quarters held by the Italian city states in Acre grew, as did the rivalry between them. Inside the city was the monastery of St Sabas. The monastery owned some houses to which the representatives of both Venice and Genoa laid claim. It was located on the borders of the two quarters in the city. Claim and counter-claim went before the courts of Acre and the dispute dragged on for years. In 1256, in an unfortunate coincidence of timing, delegations from both cities arrived in Acre simultaneously. Each carried with them letters from the pope; the content of these letters was irreconcilably contradictory. The disputed houses were on the Montjoie hill. The Genoese seized the properties but did not stop at that, also attempting to take over the Venetian quarter. The Venetians fought back and drove them out. Philip de Montfort took advantage of the opportunity to expel the Venetians from Tyre, where they had held a third of the city since 1123. From a Venetian perspective, Tyre was as important as Acre and its loss could not be accepted as a *fait accompli*.

Resources needed to come from distant Venice to boost those available to her representatives in the Levant if her position was to be adequately defended. But the Doges and officials of *La Serenissima* were used to such challenges; the city's power and wealth was derived from its overseas territories. They duly responded, but the spark consequently ignited threatened to turn into an uncontrollable conflagration when what became known as the War of St Sabas broke out and the whole of Outremer was sucked into the dispute. The Venetians were supported by the Pisans, the Provençals, most of the house of Ibelin, the Templars and the Teutonic Knights. The Genoese were supported by John of Arsūf, who had just become regent, Philip de Montfort, the Hospitallers and the Catalans. In 1258, the fight reached the outskirts of Acre. But in that year the Genoese fleet was badly defeated off the city and Philip de Montfort failed in his landward attempts to break in. With greater threats ominously appearing on the horizon, the war was frankly foolish. It divided what were already inferior resources and played into the hands of the Franks' real opponents, the Mamluks. By 1261 a fragile truce had been brokered. Genoa was debarred from Acre though she was to have more than adequate revenge soon after. There was, however, one more positive outcome. The military orders agreed that in future any disputes between them should be resolved by arbitration.

Other serious challenges were about to emerge. The conquest of Constantinople in 1204 may have been an event of very doubtful moral validity but it marked an upturn of sorts in the fortunes of West European adventurers and of Venice in particular. But whilst great economic benefits accrued to the victors, they were never secure in their tenure. Remnants of the old Byzantine Empire stubbornly hung on and emperors in exile never stopped hoping that one day they might return to their lost capital. This dream was achieved in 1261 when Michael VIII Palaeologus, who was based in Nicaea (now Iznik) in Asia Minor, made the short crossing over the Bosporus and back into the city with the assistance of the Genoese. The latter were anxious to increase their power at the expense of their arch-rivals the Venetians, who played a prominent role in the government of Constantinople. The recapture of the city was surprisingly straightforward as many of the Latin garrison were away raiding when Michael's army approached and the Greeks inside the walls were more than happy to allow someone they saw as a legitimate emperor to enter in their absence. The short-lived Latin Empire in the city thus came to an end, though territories were retained by the westerners elsewhere, such as in the Peloponnese. Genoa had been amply compensated for her ejection from Acre. This turn of events emphasised how much the battle for supremacy between Italian city states was being fought in the Levant as well as further west.

Baybars was on good terms with the Genoese; indeed, he took advantage of the maritime resources of Genoa as the major provider of shipping to bring slaves (and potential Mamluk recruits) from the Russian steppes across the Black Sea and then on to Egypt. He also wanted good relations with the Byzantine Empire; if these could be forged, then the Byzantines could act as a buffer against any crusading reinforcements that might seek to take advantage of the land route across Asia Minor and down into the Levant. Baybars was quick to build positive diplomatic relationships with the new Emperor, Michael VIII, in Constantinople. This again helped foster closer relationships between Egypt and Genoa whilst inevitably leading to a contrary result vis-à-vis Venice. Michael was keen to strengthen his still fragile position; not only were the expelled Latins a threat but Michael was also a usurper at the expense of the more legitimate Byzantine Emperor, a young child whom he had imprisoned and then ordered to be blinded when the boy reached the age of ten. He therefore responded enthusiastically to Baybars' approaches and a treaty was agreed between them. There would now be an annual movement of ships out of the Black Sea and on to Egypt through the Bosporus and the Dardanelles without Byzantine intervention. The safe passage ensured that the flow of Mamluk reinforcements would be uninterrupted, thereby securing new recruits for Baybars' forces. Baybars was further delighted to learn that a mosque had been set up in Constantinople for which he subsequently sent gifts.

The Mediterranean became a battleground for the Genoese and Venetians and Outremer was not immune from the consequences. In 1264, a fleet of around twenty vessels set out from Genoa commanded by Simeone Grillo, a man who was 'wise and knowledgeable and very skilful in war'. Venetian spies informed the city of this, and Venice responded by sending out a large force of around fifty galleys. A false rumour was spread around that the Genoese were heading for Tyre, though in fact their destination was Malta. The Venetians accordingly headed for Tyre where the Genoese currently held the upper hand. The Venetians fell on the city one morning at around dawn and there was a hard fight as the Genoese inside, led by Milian of Marino, resisted them. Venetian ships with fighting platforms raised high up in the vessels moved alongside the walls. They towered above them, meaning that men inside could throw down rocks and spears onto the defenders, a tactic that the Venetians had used with great effect during the capture of Constantinople in 1204. Milian of Marino was struck by a spear but his helmet, underneath which he was wearing a padded coif, saved his life.

The Genoese responded by erecting their own fighting platforms on the walls which were even higher than those on the Venetian ships. This was enough to intimidate the attackers who backed off. Other Venetian galleys had come up from Acre but then the news came through that Simeone Grillo had launched a surprise attack on the Gulf of Venice from Malta, pillaging a number of Venetian merchant ships in the process, and the attack fizzled out. The Venetian attempt on Tyre ultimately came to nothing, but it epitomised how Outremer had become a surrogate battlefield for the major Italian city states. This did not augur well should the Muslim forces in the region combine more effectively than they had in the past. Hostilities between the Italian city states continued on and off until 1270, but by then the Levant was a very different place. The Genoese were finally allowed back into Acre, though their quarter was by now in ruins; and later the

Venetians returned to Tyre. Pisa stayed aloof from these developments and it was not until 1288 that peaceful relations between her and Genoa were restored. By then the Levant was unrecognisable when compared to the post-Hattin rump that remained of it in 1250.

Further Alliances

It was not only the Italian city states that were at odds with each other in the Levant. There were wider tensions too involving other great powers in Europe, most significantly the Holy Roman Empire on the one hand and the forces of the Angevins on the other. Europe as well as the Middle East was in a state of turmoil and grubby power politics normally trumped all other considerations. It is in this context that diplomatic exchanges between Baybars and Sicily should be seen. The Hohenstaufen emperors who ruled Sicily were embroiled in a long-standing dispute with the papacy that could be traced back to the reign of Frederick II. France was allied with the papacy in this confrontation and Charles of Anjou, brother of Louis IX, wanted Sicily for himself. In 1261 Frederick's successor, Manfred, received a delegation from Egypt accompanied by generous gifts including a giraffe. The giraffe came in the company of captured Mongols taken at Ain Jalut. The delegation was well received by Manfred who sent back envoys of his own by return. Good relations between the Hohenstaufens and the Muslims in Egypt went back a surprisingly long time. Frederick Barbarossa had sent a delegation to Cairo as long ago as 1172, looking for help in his face-off with the papacy. If Frederick rather undid these good intentions by leading an army to invade Saladin's kingdom fifteen years later – an enterprise that was for him a personal disaster as he drowned en route – such events showed that the idea of selective Christian-Muslim alliances in the region was nothing new. It was another example of that well-known maxim, my enemy's enemy is my friend, in action.

This maxim was also in evidence regarding relationships between Berke of the Golden Horde and Baybars. Mongol infighting became a very significant issue that threatened to rip apart the fabric of their vast *khanate*. Berke and Hūlegū came to blows with each other. Hūlegū was increasingly isolated in Persia, which helped the Mamluks in Syria considerably. Matters came to a head when he led his army across the River Terek in the north of the Caucasus with the intention of defeating Berke, who had been raiding his territories. Berke's army, led by his nephew Nogai, moved to meet them. It was winter, perishing cold in this part of the world, when the two armies clashed on 13 January 1263. Hūlegū's army was crushed in the battle that followed, many of his troops losing their lives when they fell through the ice that covered the river.

There had allegedly been a falling-out between Hūlegū and Berke after the capture of Baghdad a few years previously. There was disagreement over the division of the spoils from the city's capture, which ended according to some accounts with Hūlegū executing some of Berke's envoys. There were also disputed territories where Berke's lands bordered those of Hūlegū. When Berke's remaining men decided to return home from the Baghdad campaign, they felt that it was too dangerous to take the direct route back. Instead, they presented themselves at Damascus, then in Muslim hands again, and journeyed from there to Cairo where they were well received by Baybars. He was generous towards them, helping to foment further dissent between them and supporters of Hūlegū. The recruitment of men who were not of Mamluk stock into the Egyptian army, both Mongols and Turks, played an important role. There was even a specific name given to such, the *wāfidiyya*, or 'one who comes in a group'. The first such group was made up of 200 men, the next 1,300.[30] Baybars was generous in his reception of these men, which encouraged others who wished to escape Mongol domination to follow suit. There is a strong impression in reading the records that his sensible policy paid dividends. The Sultan also wrote to Berke, encouraging him as a fellow Muslim to fight Hūlegū, who he even suggested was now a Christian. Once more then, the political situation is more complicated than it appears to be at first glance. Just as Christendom and Islam were disunited and composed of competing factions, so too was the Mongol *khanate*.

In the wake of Ain Jalut, and the ongoing tensions affecting the unity of the Mongol *khanate*, Hūlegū opted to change tack with regard to the West. Whereas previously world domination had been the motivator, in which Christendom would be subjugated in the same way as every other world power would be, he instead (superficially at least) sought alliance. Diplomatic initiatives were launched involving the rulers of England, France, Aragon and Sicily. The Franks in Outremer were only peripheral now; a 'negligible quantity' as they have been described. But there was a bitter irony in this: peripheral they may have been but Hūlegū's overtures to Western rulers increased the determination of Baybars and his immediate successors that Outremer should not be allowed to survive.[31] In 1262, Hūlegū, describing himself as a 'kindly exalter of the Christian faith', sent an embassy to Louis IX suggesting that whilst he and his army attacked Egypt by land, Louis should despatch a fleet to blockade the country. This was an innovative offer to combine forces in an area where the Mongols were traditionally ill at ease. The Mongols were from a landlocked region and their experiments with naval warfare were sometimes disastrous including ill-fated attempts on Japan in 1274 and 1281. Their forces were destroyed by typhoons known to the Japanese as the divine winds – *kamikaze* – due to their timely appearance. Baybars was still concerned about rumours of a renewed Mongol attack but none came. Hūlegū was too busy with his conflict with Berke to consider a major new assault on Syria.[32]

Even if the Mongols toned down demands regarding their divine right to rule after Ain Jalut, they did not drop them completely. Hūlegū's generally politely phrased letter included some words that may well have been adapted from the Bible, possibly with the help of a Christian scribe. It mentioned the occasion when a shaman, Teb-Tenggeri ('The Heavenly One'), a remarkable figure who wandered naked through the freezing mountains and harsh deserts of Mongolia, met Genghis Khan and gave him a message from God, saying 'I am the one all-powerful God in the highest, and I have set thee to be lord over the nations and kingdoms and to be ruler of the whole earth.' The fact that Hūlegū still saw fit to include these words affirms that the ultimate dream of world domination had not gone away.[33]

There was also a messenger known as John the Hungarian who journeyed to Rome with the welcome news that Hūlegū was friendly towards Christianity and was even contemplating baptism for himself. Urban IV was not convinced of the sincerity of the approach – for one thing John came without formal credentials. However, his successor Pope Clement IV (1265–68) was more enthusiastic, possibly because the Franks in Outremer were by then under much greater threat than they had been due to the aggressive outlook of Baybars. But in reality the hoped-for conversion of Hūlegū was never more than a pipe dream. By the time of his death in 1265 he was in the thrall of Buddhist lamas, and he was the last known Mongol Ilkhan to be buried accompanied by live female slaves to serve him in the afterlife.

This hardly seems like the actions of a man who was on the verge of becoming a Christian, even if his mother was one.[34] Even at the time many remained unconvinced. Alfonso X of Castile warned his fellow ruler, Jaime of Aragon, in 1269 that the Mongols were 'a very deceitful people'.[35]

Hūlegū was anxious to reverse the outcome of Ain Jalut and continue the conquest of Syria and then Egypt. He needed to demonstrate to his Muslim subjects in the *Ilkhanate* that Ain Jalut was a temporary blip and that the Mongols remained an irresistible force and he hoped that an alliance with the Franks would assist him in achieving his objectives. This search for alliances by the various factions in the Mongol civil war was not limited to Hūlegū. Berke sent a delegation to Cairo in 1263. It arrived in May, along with a delegation from the Byzantines and another from the Genoese, giving the opportunity for a conference to be held. The parties had mutual interests. Baybars still relied on young Mamluk recruits being shipped (in Genoese vessels) from lands held by the Golden Horde to Egypt via the narrow Bosporus, which was controlled by Byzantium. The Sultan was delighted with the visit of Berke's ambassadors, loading them down with generous gifts. Berke was even prayed for in the Great Mosque on 7 July, a remarkable sign of acceptance given the fact that some of his men had participated in the massacres at Baghdad in 1258. A delegation was sent by Baybars in return, setting out to meet Berke in Sarāy on 25 July.

It made its way through Constantinople. Here though, a problem emerged. Michael VIII's position was so vulnerable that he was in negotiations with Hūlegū as well as Baybars, his arch-rival. Even as Baybars' delegation arrived, so too did one from Hūlegū. The Byzantine emperor strained every sinew to keep the two apart. The delegation to Sarāy was held up in Constantinople for a year. Open hostilities followed soon after when Mongol troops attacked the Empire and met with some success. Baybars was furious when he heard of the detention of his delegation but reacted with remarkable political acumen. He put pressure on Orthodox prelates to excommunicate Michael and then initiated measures to restore good relations. Peace between the Mamluks, the Byzantines and Berke's Mongols was restored. However, Michael was playing a double game. Adjacent to the lands of the Golden Horde and the *Ilkhanate* he did his best to stay on good terms with both, even sending an illegitimate daughter to marry Hūlegū (by the time she arrived, he was dead so she was married to his son and successor Abagha instead).

There was one further diplomatic event of note in Cairo at about this time. Charles of Anjou was about to attack the lands held by Manfred in Europe and could see how useful it would be to break the link between him and Baybars. Envoys were therefore sent to Egypt accompanied by gifts in order to see what they could do to divide the two. Diplomatic positioning was currently taking precedence over military action in the region as far as Christians and Mamluks were concerned, but this was shortly to change.

Baybars also had internal affairs to distract him. One issue was how to strengthen his legitimacy; he was after all both a regicide and a Mamluk usurper whose compatriots had overturned the legitimate dynasty. Soon after his accession, a new caliph, al-Mustansir, was recognised by Baybars who subsequently issued coins with the legend 'associate of the commander of the faithful' on them as a way of increasing his perceived legitimacy. This was further assisted when the caliph issued a formal decree recognising Baybars' right to be Sultan, a right that notably extended not just to Egypt but also to those lands held by 'Infidel' Franks and Mongols.[36] However, al-Mustansir's time in post was brief. He was sent with a tiny army to retake Baghdad. It was cut to pieces by a much larger Mongol force and the caliph disappeared without trace. He was replaced in 1262 by another, but Baybars paid little attention to him. He had got the recognition he wanted from the previous postholder and from this point on the Sultan only deferred to the caliph on ceremonial occasions when it cost him little to do so.

There were still dissentient Muslim elements in Syria for Baybars to deal with. Whilst some of the Bedouin supported him, not all did. One tribe, the Zubayd, who were to the south of Damascus, were thought to have been passing on useful information to the Franks on the coast, which led to Baybars launching a fierce raid against them in 1261.[37] Relations between the Bedouin and other Muslim powers were frequently strained. Sultan Aybeg had invited 3,000 Bedouin to a feast in Egypt in the 1250s. When they arrived he had them strung up by the road between Bilbeis and Cairo.[38] There were other irritatingly resistant factions too. The road between Cairo and Damascus was dominated by two formidable castles at Karak and Shawbak (known to the Crusaders as Montreal – the castles are both located in modern

Jordan). They were in the hands of the emir al-Mughīth who stubbornly refused to accept Baybars' rule. He was however increasingly isolated as Baybars' grip on Syria grew stronger. Eventually, in April 1263 he was lured out by a safe conduct issued by Baybars, but it was a trap. He was imprisoned and taken to Cairo where he was eventually murdered. As a result of the subduing of Karak and Shawbak Baybars' grip on the region grew yet tighter. Now that Syria was secure, Baybars could turn his attention to the Crusader states of Outremer. A day of reckoning for the Franks was now at hand.

6

Baybars the Annihilator

'The annihilator of Mongols and Franks'

The title awarded to Sultan Baybars

The Mamluks Flex Their Muscles

Following the great Mamluk victory at Ain Jalut, unity in Muslim Syria might have been hoped for but did not materialise. Having been freed, even if temporarily, from the Mongol threat, the Muslim cities in the region next sought to throw off the Mamluk yoke. There were rebellions against Qutuz in Damascus and Aleppo. The Mongols sent raiding parties into the north of the region to cause trouble and the Franks, too, sought to take advantage of the instability. A strong Mongol raid was met and defeated near Homs in 1261, a Muslim victory that was sealed with the timely arrival of Bedouin attacking the Mongol rear at the decisive point of the battle. Even though the numbers involved were relatively small, it was an important result as it confirmed that the victory at Ain Jalut was no fluke. Among those taken captive was a young Mongol warrior, Kitbughā. He was taken to Cairo and became a Mamluk. In an amazing role reversal, he would eventually rise through the ranks to become a Mamluk sultan.

It needed an inspirational leader to deal with the Mongol problem on a more permanent basis though, and Baybars was that man. The Mongol threat had not disappeared and he was able to prey on the insecurities of Muslim regimes in Syria to eventually unify the region as it had not been since the days of Saladin. One of Baybars' first steps as Sultan was to strengthen militarily. Some of the measures taken were defensive, such as the strengthening of key fortifications in Egypt at Alexandria, Rosetta and Damietta, or the rebuilding of those at Damascus. The fleet was also developed, the one remaining area in which the Franks retained supremacy. Administrative reform supported these improvements; the economy prospered and tax yields increased, thereby financing enhancements to the military machine. Baybars also radically overhauled the *barīd*, the postal system which had gone into steep decline in recent years. A mounted messenger service was reinstituted, possibly based on highly effective systems used by the Mongols, allowing news to travel between Cairo and Damascus within four days. Baybars played a key role in ensuring the effectiveness of the operation, arranging his day so that he could receive the post as soon as it arrived and answering it promptly – time was of the essence. He also ensured that the use of carrier pigeons and optical signalling stations, approaches which had gone into abeyance in recent years, was redeveloped, providing an integrated communications network across his territories.[1]

The need for military reform was pressing and there was a massive expansion in the size of the army during Baybars' rule, the number of cavalry for example expanding by 300–400 per cent.[2] Two hippodromes (*māydans*) were built in Cairo where training in horsemanship was given. So popular was this that time slots had to be allocated to those taking part in the training, with the lance and the bow especially popular weapons. The Mongol threat was potentially still substantial and no one could tell how events would play out in the future, which also helped to swell numbers as refugees from territories in danger of renewed attacks streamed into Egypt. Baybars also needed to keep a watch closer to home; a Mamluk ruler was as vulnerable to internal coup as he was to external attack. Military training was concentrated on those who were considered the most trustworthy by Baybars. In particular, his own Mamluk regiment the Zahiriyya – a name derived from his full regnal title, al-Malik al-Zahir Rukn al-Din Baybars al-Banduqdari al-Salihi – were beneficiaries. He increased their number from the standard size of around 1,000 warriors to 5,000.

Whilst the Western institution of knighthood is well known in Europe, contemporary Muslim attitudes to warfare are much less discussed. However, there is overwhelming evidence that the Muslim world saw the art of war in a similarly prestigious light, at least as far as its foremost exponents were concerned. A number of military manuals survive, the *Furusiyya* as they are collectively known. These developed over the course of many centuries though sometimes anachronisms remained in later versions regarding the use of weapons that had long been obsolete. The records we have of training techniques are extensive and revealing. Archery on horseback, for example, was developed only as a result of rigorous training. New recruits would start with the most basic of introductions such as how to pull back the bowstring without an arrow. When targets were then introduced, they were at first placed close to the apprentice archer. Only over time would they be moved further back so that the archer would develop his skills incrementally. Similarly, the draw required to pull back the bow would be gradually increased to build up strength.

Being able to launch an arrow accurately whilst on horseback was a particularly prized skill. Horsemanship was of course an integral part of this. Riding skills were honed through activities such as the playing of polo (analogous to the Mongol philosophy of combining enjoyment and training through the 'Great Hunt', albeit using different techniques). Physical development was not ignored either, with particular attention being paid to building up thigh muscles and upper-body strength. Sword drills were regularly held, monotonous exercises which required the slicing through of clay beds specially prepared for the purpose. The number of such beds would gradually be increased so that the strength of the swordsman was also progressively developed. Ultimately, they would have to slice through ten of these clay beds covered with a layer of felt. Several additional elements compounded the challenge. They would have to practise with both their right and their left arms. They could also not rely on brute strength alone; accuracy was important too. Ultimately when they were proficient in cutting through the maximum number of clay beds they would have to be able to do so without cutting into the fabric of a soft pillow that was placed underneath them, meaning that the sword cut must be powerful but controlled. All this was done within the construct of a strict code of loyalty known as *khushdashiyya*, emphasising that the Mamluk approach covered moral considerations as well as martial proficiency.[3]

There was always a danger that the Franks of Outremer would be unfortunate collateral victims of the military reforms promulgated by Baybars, but they did not help themselves. The years following

Ail Jalut and Baybars' rise to power were punctuated by raids and counter-raids. One Frankish foray against Turcomans in the Golan in 1261 met with disaster as the intended targets were apparently forewarned of the imminent attack and were ready for it when it came. 900 knights, 3,000 infantry and 1,500 Turcopoles were unable to score a success and many Franks were lost in what turned into a debacle. Mamluk raids were launched in response (even though the semi-nomadic Turcomans were hardly their devoted subjects) but a truce was agreed soon after. It certainly suited the Franks to have one and for the time being it also served Baybars' purpose. But not for long.

In 1263, Baybars launched a series of attacks in Palestine, with targets including the Church of the Annunciation in Nazareth, considered to be 'the most famous of the [Christians'] holy places'.[4] As one of the three main dominical sites in Outremer – the other two were the Holy Sepulchre in Jerusalem and the Church of the Nativity at Bethlehem – it was an especially sacred spot for the Franks. It was built on the site of the home of the Virgin Mary where the Archangel Gabriel had told her that she would give birth to Jesus. After an earthquake in 1170, the church had been greatly increased in size and magnificently decorated. The church was razed by the Mamluks, though some remains of the magnificent sculptural decoration of the portal were unearthed during digs in 1908–09 and the 1950s.[5] Its loss was an artistic tragedy as its style was very unusual, and possibly unique, in the region. It was 73 metres long with a nave of six bays, a choir and an apsidal east end.

Baybars then set up camp at Mount Tabor, where he ordered the demolition of the church and monastery there, which the Hospitallers, who had acquired the sites in 1255, intended to turn into a fortress.[6] These acts against churches were examples of iconoclasm in keeping with someone who wants to emphasise his credentials as a pious and faith-driven Muslim leader. Whilst engaged in this campaign, Baybars received a delegation from the Nizaris who sought to secure a peace with him, an arrangement that he was to find useful in the future. He was now not far from Acre and he moved on it during the night of 15 April 1263, arriving as dawn broke over the city. He launched an attack on a Templar mill at Duyuk, just outside the walls. It was surrounded and captured; a sally from the city was driven off. The sergeant of Acre, Geoffrey de Sergines, was wounded in the fighting whilst several other knights were killed, though Acre itself held firm.[7]

This was not an all-out attempt by Baybars to capture Acre. He had no heavy siege engines with him and the bulk of his army remained at Mount Tabor. It was more a combination of a reconnaissance mission and a way of reminding Acre of the power he could bring to bear should he choose.[8] Far worse than the loss of men that Acre suffered in this attack was the damage done to local food supplies. At the end of the year, the city was forced to sue for a truce so that devastated crops could be replanted. The food shortages were specifically mentioned in a letter from Pope Urban IV to Louis IX shortly afterwards. The raid generated significant alarm in Acre and a stream of letters appealing for help were sent from there to the west.[9] Baybars was given moral ammunition to attack Acre by the continued refusal of the Franks to exchange the prisoners they held in line with the agreement negotiated in 1261, as well as raids against his territories launched from there.

A truce was agreed between Acre and Baybars' local governors in December 1263. It did not survive a month. In a collaborative effort in January 1264, a combined Templar and Hospitaller force attacked al-Lajjun in the region of Megiddo. They returned with 300 prisoners and a good deal of booty. It was seemingly an easily won victory with the Muslims in the region perhaps lulled into a false sense of security by the recently agreed truce. In response, the Mamluks raided Ramla, where Gerard of Pinkeney, the castellan of Jaffa, was taken prisoner. This was followed by a Frankish raid on Ascalon; the raiders routed a force of 400 Mamluks who stood in their way, killing two emirs in the process. Baybars then ordered raids on Caesarea and Atlit. In response, the Franks of Acre assaulted Baysān, inspired to action by the arrival in the city of Oliver of Termes with fresh French forces. Oliver was a close confidant of Louis IX and a proven campaigner who breathed new life into the Frankish forces in the area.

Baybars Strikes

Tit-for-tat became the norm but the stakes were about to rise significantly. Baybars' opportunistic streak was well exemplified in 1265. At the end of the previous year Baybars had been out hunting in Egypt when he received disturbing news of an imminent Mongol attack on the important Mamluk fortress of al-Bīra on the Euphrates. This was on the edge of an area that had effectively become a no-man's-land after Ain Jalut and had recently been strengthened on the orders of Baybars and used as a launch pad for raids into Mongol-held neighbouring lands. Baybars sprang into action when he heard of the raid.[10] He hurried back to Cairo and assembled a force to deal with the threat. Light forces were sent at once whilst steps to put together a more substantial army were taken. Men were assembled both in Egypt and from further afield such as Aleppo and Hama. Bedouin from the north of Syria were also instructed to launch a diversionary raid across the desert.

It came to Baybars' attention that the Mongol attack was assisted by information sent to them by the Franks. According to Ibn 'Abd al-Zāhir, his private secretary, Baybars heard that the Franks had told the Mongols that Mamluk forces in the region were dispersed for winter feeding and that the time was therefore ripe for an attack.[11] In January 1265, Baybars moved up to Gaza, forcing the pace of the march with such ruthless determination that a number of the camels with his army died. The Mongol incursion still appeared to present a serious threat and there were suggestions that it was a precursor to a more sustained assault on Mamluk territory. Baybars received additional information that was also concerning, namely that the Mongols now had seventeen siege engines battering away against the walls of al-Bīra. The siege was fiercely prosecuted but strongly resisted by those inside, both men and women. When the Mongols filled the moat around al-Bīra with timber, the garrison managed to set it ablaze. Baybars stayed where he was, waiting to see how events unfolded. It was a prudent decision; when the garrison at al-Bīra put up a strong defence and the Mongols heard that Baybars had responded vigorously to the raid by raising a large army, they withdrew. As an advance force led by one of Baybars' generals, al-Mansur Mohammed, approached the town, the Mongols scurried away. Within four days, Baybars received the news, demonstrating how good the Mamluk communications network now was. Orders were despatched from Baybars that the fortifications at al-Bīra should be repaired where necessary and generous gifts were made to the garrison for their gallant and ultimately successful defence. Steps were also taken to ensure that it was provisioned with sufficient supplies to withstand a siege for ten years. A Mongol counter-attack which took place shortly afterwards was resisted, causing heavy losses among the raiders.

The recently released castellan of Jaffa, Gerard of Pinkeney, now rode into Baybars' camp bearing gifts including hunting falcons. He wished for peaceful interaction with Baybars, particularly now that the Sultan was on his doorstep with a large army. Baybars was having none of it, probably doubting the sincerity of the gesture. He berated the Franks for their ongoing raiding and general duplicity in cooperating with the Mongols. Gerard presumably went away with a flea in his ear and his political antennae nervously twitching. His nerves were not soothed by Baybars' next move. This was to ban the consumption of alcohol by his army, a measure that emphasised Baybars' piety. Such accentuations of religious conservatism often preceded a military campaign, particularly when it had the appearance of a *jihad,* a holy war. Saladin had gone out of his way to emphasise his piety before, during and after the Hattin campaign of 1187 when the Franks had been the target and their fortunes had been shattered as a result. Yet such pious measures should not be blown out of proportion; as a Mamluk war manual noted, 'an arrow from a warrior shot at an unbeliever counts more than the endless prayers said by a pious hermit'.[12]

Baybars had a large army with him and there was no immediate purpose for it now that the Mongols had retreated. He therefore decided to move on a different target, the Franks. He moved up to the region of Arsūf, site of Richard the Lionheart's great victory during the Third Crusade and close to Jaffa. The two main Frankish settlements here were Arsūf itself and Caesarea, first taken by them in 1101 shortly after conquering Jerusalem. Baybars was canny in his approach, making out that he was focused on nothing more threatening than a lion hunt. Whilst ostensibly engaged in this pursuit, he was in fact spying out the land. He then returned to his camp and ordered siege engines to be assembled. Skilled workers and stonemasons were brought in to help with the preparations for a major assault on Frankish territory and men were put to work in making scaling ladders. With little warning, he moved his substantial force up to Caesarea where he suddenly appeared on 27 February 1265. It had been much strengthened by Louis IX during his sojourn in the region and the walls had been reinforced in a way that made them impervious to mining. The town was encircled and a vigorous attack was launched by the Mamluks, who made impromptu siege ladders out of their bridles. The gates and walls of Caesarea were quickly overwhelmed and those of the defenders who managed to escape holed themselves up in the citadel. It was in a strong position, located on a promontory which could only be attacked from the land on one side; the other three sides were only open to attack from the sea and as Baybars did not have naval supremacy an assault from this direction was not a viable option.

Baybars moved up his siege towers. Artillery bombarded the citadel with stones whilst Greek fire rained down on it too, a nasty incendiary device that is almost impossible to put out once aflame. Arrows showered down on the defenders whilst men in siege towers attempted to approach the walls and jump across. Prominent amongst them was Baybars, extolling his men to make even greater efforts and leading by example; one account even has him firing arrows from a nearby church tower.[13] By 5 March it was over. Those defenders who could escape were taken off by ship and sailed to Acre where their news made for depressing listening. During the course of the siege of Caesarea, Baybars had despatched raiding parties to the very suburbs of Acre. These men, including Bedouin and Turcomans – highly mobile Turkic cavalry – kept Frankish forces in Acre occupied and therefore unable to assist Caesarea. In fact, so worried were they that they might be the next to be attacked that the citizens of the port demolished a mill and a monastery outside the walls so that they could not be used by Baybars in any siege.

Once Caesarea was taken, Baybars' strategy became clear. He had no intention of occupying it. Instead he demolished it, thereby denying it to the Franks in the future. This strategy, followed in a number of subsequent cases, denied coastal ports to the Franks from which they might otherwise launch attacks on Mamluk territory (though in contrast castles captured further inland were strengthened so that they could be used to resist Mongol incursions). This marked a turning point in Mamluk strategy. Whereas in the recent past a kind of accommodation, 'live and let live', had been acceptable, this was no longer the case. Baybars had decided that whatever trading opportunities the Franks might bring, they did not compensate for their propensity to cause trouble and act in consort with the Mongols. From this point on, the Franks were on the defensive and Baybars would take every opportunity to reduce their power on an incremental basis. It was a significant change of direction which should have sent alarm bells ringing in Acre and other Frankish cities in the region such as Antioch and Tripoli. But it apparently did not.

It has been suggested that this change of approach was encouraged by ongoing discussions between Mongols and Franks.[14] These discussions were soon to become a feature of wider international politics. Baybars may have been informally warned of a pending alliance between the Mongol *khanate* and Christian Europe by Manfred of Hohenstaufen, the ruler of Sicily. Baybars was certainly put out by the actions of local Franks in informing the Mongols of what was happening in the region. He said that 'These people [the local Franks] have committed many wrongs against me, such as their writing to the Mongols to attack my territories.'[15] He subsequently attacked several other Frankish strongholds in the region and even moved on the seemingly impregnable walls of Chastel Pèlerin ('Castle Pilgrim'), Atlit, though he did not ultimately attack it. Mamluk siege tactics were improving all the time, a necessary development as the manpower shortages suffered by the Franks had forced them to rely on the strength of their fortifications to compensate, meaning that they had become masters of the art of military construction as evidenced by examples like Crac des Chevaliers and Atlit.

From Caesarea Baybars moved to Arsūf, which he reached after a short march of two days. It was described as 'strongly fortified' by an eyewitness during Louis IX's time in the region.[16] On Baybars' arrival, he erected wooden shields to protect his siege works as well as revetments to strengthen the trenches constructed in front of the walls. He denuded the region of wood to do so. He then ordered that mines be constructed beneath the walls. This led to a sortie by the defenders who attempted to destroy these engineering works by setting them alight. The Mamluks succeeded in dousing the flames before they took hold. But the garrison was undaunted and dug a counter-mine beneath that of the Mamluks. They piled it up with wood, attached barrels of grease, set it ablaze and used bellows to fan the flames. Recent archaeological research has uncovered the remains of this counter-mine, which was successful, completely destroying the mines that had been dug by the Muslims before they could be brought into use.[17]

This setback persuaded Baybars to change strategy. He abandoned the mining operations and instead built trenches around Arsūf to launch a fierce assault on the walls of the city. In the meantime, the Mamluk artillery continued its fierce bombardment, using stones specially quarried and brought in from 10 miles away as ammunition. Baybars was again prominent during these operations, his energy and bravery once more inspiring his troops. Some of his siege engines were constructed locally from wood in the area but others were brought up from Damascus. There were various different types, including one that could simultaneously fire seven arrows, a primitive precursor of the Katyusha rocket launchers made famous by Russian forces during the Second World War. One of Baybars' commanders, Aybeg al-Afram, was singled out for particular praise for his work during this phase of the operation. This was, however, not just a military enterprise. Accompanying the army were various religious scholars and Sufis, Islamic mystics who emphasised the importance of spiritual closeness to Allah. They included one man known as 'the Crazy One' and another as 'the Weeper'. Whilst the fighting men were largely effectively professional soldiers – although there were volunteers also present, they seem to have only played a supplementary role in the attack – the operation was also seen as part of a *jihadi* movement, a form of holy war to parallel that which had been fought in the region by Crusaders for the past 170 years. The religious scholars played an important role in building morale amongst Baybars' men.

Some Frankish reinforcements now arrived at Acre. They were led by Hugh de Lusignan, the *bailli* of the Kingdom of Jerusalem.[18] The Lusignan name appears frequently in Crusader history as successive generations of the family involved themselves in the affairs of Outremer. They are one good example – the Montforts provide another – of how families from Western Europe developed family traditions of crusading and in some cases became integrally involved in Outremer on an ongoing basis. But useful though these reinforcements led by Hugh were, there were not enough of them to go to assist Arsūf. The artillery began to take its toll on the town. Details of the final attack are scant but on 26 April the Mamluks launched an assault in overwhelming force. Arsūf fell the same day, though the citadel remained untaken. Large concentrations of arrowheads found scattered around the citadel during recent digging suggest that archers poured down a rain of arrows on those inside. A scattering of trebuchet stones also intimates fierce bombardment, particularly focused on the gate to the citadel.

The citadel, in the hands of the Hospitallers who had purchased it from the Ibelins, was bombarded for three days, with the *bāshūrah*, or barbican, coming in for particularly heavy attention. The siege came to an end when the *bāshūrah* came crashing down. The garrison now knew that all they could hope to escape with was their lives. Baybars accordingly guaranteed the defenders their lives should they surrender. A Mamluk officer was hauled up into the citadel on a rope and the deal was struck. The garrison handed over their weapons and was led off into captivity, bringing forty days of campaigning to a conclusion. According to the Templar of Tyre, over 1,000 religious and secular knights and sergeants were taken prisoner, a loss of men that Outremer (and particularly the Hospitallers who were present at the siege in large numbers) could ill afford. The people of Acre suspected that something was awry when the tower of the Church of the Holy Cross in the city appeared to be hit by some kind of object, possibly some form of celestial debris.[19]

Historians have analysed the reasons for Baybars' success in this campaign and their conclusions provide a summary of the advantages that the Mamluks enjoyed over the Franks by this time. They had numerical superiority; the Mamluks had far greater access to manpower resources. Their success over the Mongols in recent years enabled them to focus increased attention on dealing with the Franks. The defenders conversely had limited prospects of being reinforced, particularly at Arsūf where the small harbour could be dominated from the land, meaning that help could not easily be brought in from the sea. The Mamluks also had access to sophisticated engineering skills, which enabled them to develop effective artillery. They had Baybars at their head, a ruthlessly talented leader. Last but not least, they had high levels of morale; nothing builds confidence like success and with each successive victory morale was strengthened.[20]

Baybars had pulled all of these ingredients together to create a potent cocktail. His tactics were repeated in later campaigns. Although the Franks did not yet know it, the events of 1265 launched the extended campaign that came to a triumphant conclusion at Acre in 1291. Again, rather than seek to occupy Arsūf, Baybars systematically destroyed it, giving those he had taken as captives the bitter task of destroying their own town. This task was not carried out as ruthlessly as Baybars might have hoped but well enough to make it difficult for the Franks to rebuild or use it as a launch pad for a renewed campaign. By destroying coastal cities, Baybars was denying their use to the Franks and negating their naval superiority. After the destruction of Caesarea and Arsūf, he ordered a castle, effectively a watchtower over the coastal plain, to be constructed at Qāqūn a few miles inland.

Prizes were handed out to the victors; thirty-seven captured villages were divided up between sixty-one senior officers. New 'sheriffs' were chosen for their overtly anti-Frankish attitudes. The loss of fertile land in the region was another challenge to the already overstretched food supplies available to the Franks and also hit them economically. Baybars sent news of his victory to Manfred in Sicily. Manfred in return responded with a congratulatory delegation bearing gifts; other ambassadors also arrived from Marseille and Genoa – ample evidence of the disunity of Christendom in the face of the threat presented by Baybars. A Byzantine embassy visited Cairo with the gift of a Muslim ship that had been captured by the Franks and then purchased on behalf of the emperor in Constantinople. Baybars enjoyed his latest victory and exploited its propaganda value to the full. He entered Cairo at the head of his victorious army on 29 May 1265. With them was a ragged collection of prisoners, broken crosses draped around their necks and their banners humiliatingly reversed. Baybars was awarded an ominous title as a result of his efforts, *mubid al-tatar wa-al-ifranj*, 'the annihilator of Mongols and Franks' – a worrying portent for the days ahead.[21]

Antioch and Armenia

Acre and Antioch as we have seen adopted different strategies towards Baybars than their fellow Christians in the region. The Franks of Acre generally sought to prevaricate, though some of their number raided Muslim territories. This was a dangerous approach as it pushed the patience of Baybars to the limit and eventually beyond it. The refusal of Acre to hand over captives in the agreed exchange of prisoners further irritated him and made eventual confrontation far more likely. Antioch was more openly opposed to Baybars, having showed its hand in the Mongol invasions of Syria. This would mark it out as a potential target for concerted Mamluk action.

Baybars gave early notice of his intention to hold Antioch to account. In 1262, he sent forces to the Euphrates but they deviated away from there towards the Mediterranean coast. St Symeon, located at the mouth of the Orontes River, was the port of Antioch. Earlier on in the century, it had done well as an *entrepot* for merchants to and from Aleppo to use. However, the Mongol invasions had brought chaos to the region and it was no longer a safe route. St Symeon suffered badly as a result. It was to suffer more violently when Baybars' army fell on it, causing significant damage. Antioch itself was also threatened, but the timely movement into the principality of a relieving force including Armenians and Mongols was sufficient to push the Muslim army away. This intervention demonstrated that at this stage the alliance between Antiochians, Armenians and Mongols was holding up and that it was capable of launching coordinated action against the Mamluks. It was a position, however, that would deteriorate alarmingly in the next few years. Shortly after, a retaliatory raid was launched into north Syria involving both Antiochians and Armenians but it was heavily defeated with many men captured and sent to Egypt as slaves. Although the desire to strike back against Baybars was in a human sense understandable, doing so was foolhardy as it effectively further stirred up a hornets' nest.

The stark reality was that Antioch was greatly threatened by Baybars' rise to power and so too was its Armenian ally. King Het'um, however, was slow to realise this. He had been at odds with the Seljuk Sultan of Rūm, Rukn al-Dīn, for a while but peace was brokered between the two by Hūlegū. Het'um took advantage of the breathing space to launch attacks into Muslim Syria. His first attempt, in coordination with Mongol troops, ended without much success due to the harsh winter conditions that faced his force. Frozen by snow and ice, and when the temperature rose slightly drenched by driving rain, they ran short of supplies and had no alternative but to retreat. When further raids against Syria were launched by Het'um in 1264, Baybars was confident enough to let his local generals deal with them rather than take control in person.

That said, he took meticulous care to ensure that the troops in Cairo that he sent to assist them were properly equipped. Each man was responsible for his own equipment. Whilst there were good practical reasons for each individual warrior to ensure that he was as well protected as possible, human nature being what it is inevitably some cut corners in order to limit the cost. Baybars guarded against this by insisting that each warrior be paraded in front of him, and all during the course of one day so that men could not deceive him by sharing equipment with others. This military parade took place in Cairo with all the men being marched in front of him in groups – and just to make sure of a good turnout these inspections were timed to coincide with pay parades. Following this initial inspection, extensive drilling took place to ensure that the men worked in proper coordination with each other. Baybars took these drills very seriously; on one occasion, five soldiers who were absent from an inspection in Homs were taken back to Cairo and hanged.[22]

Special instruction was given to his cavalry on how to use the lance effectively, a reminder that the men available to Baybars were not the same as would be found in a modern standing army in full-time professional training. Skills had to be refreshed from time to time and new tactics honed as necessary. One example in the latter category was the instruction of some of his cavalry in the gentle art of shooting Greek fire from horseback. This highly inflammable concoction needed in-depth instruction on how to use it; for a time, it seemed that the men shooting these arrows were, along with the horses they rode, in greater danger than the enemy. But it was another illustration of the modernisation of the army, a strategy that Baybars took very seriously.[23]

When Het'um launched another round of raids on Muslim Syria in 1264 he got rather more than he bargained for. Armenia remained an important entry point to the region with the port of Ayās doing steady business with Italian merchants from Genoa, Pisa and Venice and in return trading in spices and other important commodities from the interior. It was visited not long after by Marco Polo who wrote of Armenia in the following terms:

> The lord of Lesser Armenia is a king who maintains good and just government in his country under the suzerainty of the Tartars. It is a land of many villages and towns, amply stocked with the means of life. It also affords good sport with all sorts of wild game, both beast and fowl. The climate, however, is far from healthy; it is, in fact, extremely enervating. Hence, the nobility of the country, who used to be men of valour and stalwart soldiers, are now craven and mean-spirited and excel in nothing except drinking.[24]

Baybars ordered the local Bedouin not to travel to their summer hunting grounds as they normally did, so that they could employ their considerable skills in guerrilla warfare against Het'um. The Armenian army found itself under incessant attack and was forced once more to retreat having achieved next to nothing. It was a salutary reminder that the balance of military power in the region had radically shifted, though both Franks and Armenians were late in recognising the fact. Part of that power shift resulted from increasing dissension within the Mongol forces. Baybars' sensible alliance-building with Berke was paying dividends, as men flocked away from Hūlegū and sought sanctuary with Baybars. Increasingly large numbers of Mongol troops in Syria and Mesopotamia were deserting Hūlegū. At one stage, so many came over to Baybars that he was worried that it might be an act of Mongol subterfuge to undermine him from within. But such was not the case; it merely reflected the fact that Hūlegū was haemorrhaging support at a frightening rate.

Whilst the Mongol threat in Syria remained an issue, the swing in political and military equilibrium in the region freed Baybars up to concentrate on other priorities. Events were to further play into Baybars' hands. The death of Hūlegū in February 1265 unnerved King Het'um. Shortly afterwards he sent a delegation to Cairo to seek an accommodation with Baybars but it came to nothing. This rejection should have unnerved Het'um further, for it signified that Baybars had no interest in agreeing terms except ones that were enormously in his favour. Nor did a subsequent Armenian delegation to Cairo receive a warm reception. Mamluk retribution against Armenia was by now firmly on the agenda.

Betrayal at Safad

The capture of Caesarea and Arsūf merely whetted the appetite of Baybars. In 1266, he launched a campaign against the principality of Tripoli. Even the Hospitaller fortress of Crac des Chevaliers was threatened, though on this occasion it was not attacked. Other Frankish fortresses were not so fortunate. Close by Crac, the castle of Tuban proved less of an obstacle and fell in a day. The garrison at Alba were similarly lacking in resistance; as they fled from the castle, the rear of the retreating column was decimated and a number of the women fleeing in the group were captured. The garrison at 'Arqa, a Templar fortress, emulated their compatriots at Alba and also fled. Fortresses were picked off like ripe cherries from a tree and then almost invariably demolished to deny them to the Franks. They were seemingly powerless to strike back and when a small force on its way to reinforce Crac was sent, it was intercepted and fifty captured Franks were summarily beheaded.

Baybars again appeared with a force before Acre, staying there for a number of days before moving off. In the mountains about 50 km from Acre was the Templar fortress of Safad in Galilee. It was a large castle, with an ideal wartime complement of 2,200 men including 300 crossbowmen and 400 slaves. No fewer then 12,000 mule-loads of grain and barley were needed to feed the garrison annually whilst fresh fish were brought in daily from the Jordan and the Sea of Galilee. The man who allegedly inspired the building of this impressive fortress, Benedict of Alignan, Bishop of Marseille, when visiting it two decades later said of it that its 'exquisite and excellent construction seemed to be done not by man alone but rather through the omnipotence of God'.[25] The cost of building the reconstructed castle at Safad was enormous, some 1,100,000 Saracen bezants over and above the revenues accruing to the Templars from the surrounding region. To put this in perspective, it has been estimated that the Templars' total annual income at around this time was in the region of 3 million Saracen bezants.[26]

Safad served a dual purpose. It was in an intimidating defensive position, dominating the approaches to Acre and acting as part of the forward defences of Outremer. Due to its situation as a frontier post it was also the perfect spot from which to launch Frankish raids, *chevauchées,* into the Muslim-held lands beyond. Contemporary Muslim chroniclers vividly described it as 'a lump in Syria's throat and an obstacle to breathing in Islam's chest'.[27] Clearly, such an obstacle needed to be removed. As a result of its important strategic location, it had already been attacked by Baybars on three occasions, each time without success. He now determined on a different, subtler approach. The Templar element of the garrison at Safad was not large and relied heavily on the cooperation of the local Syrian population. Even if the latter were Christian, their beliefs and rituals were not of the Latin form but of the local Syriac variety.

Baybars resolved to conquer Safad and sent instructions to his emirs in Syria, ordering them to bring up reinforcements. Secrecy was to be scrupulously observed; the emirs were instructed not to open their detailed orders until their men were actually on the march. When the siege was put in place, various Frankish nobles sent delegations in an attempt to ensure that their own lands would escape Baybars' retribution. He rejected them all. Philip de Montfort sent a delegation from Tyre but it was rebuffed as Baybars accused him of breaching the terms of the treaty he had formerly made with him. The Lady of Beirut, Isabella of Ibelin, was castigated because some of her subjects had seized a Muslim ship. Templar envoys were sent away with a rebuke because the order had allowed mangonels to be erected on the walls of Jaffa, against the terms of the truce. Even a Nizari delegation received the cold shoulder as they had assisted the Franks in recent campaigns.

However, Baybars' initial attacks on Safad were no more successful than those made previously. Although he took the barbican around the castle, he lost many men doing so. He then ordered his heralds to deliver a proclamation to the defenders, stating that all the Syriacs inside the castle would be given safe conduct should they come out. By adopting this approach, he hoped to sow discord amongst those within. The strategy was not immediately successful and he was forced to continue the attack vigorously. Again, Baybars presented himself as the pious defender of Islam. Orders were given that his men were to abstain from alcohol, and any who ignored this command were to be hanged. But this was very much a carrot and stick approach; Baybars also offered 1,000 dirhams reward for each stone that his artillery managed to knock out of the walls. Nevertheless, the defenders continued their stubborn resistance and fifty of Baybars' senior commanders were incarcerated for not prosecuting the attack vigorously enough.

Despite this, the defenders began to lose heart. The Syriacs within were often perceived as second-class citizens in their own country.[28] However, the Templars inside the castle only numbered perhaps fifty knights and thirty sergeants. Further, the castle was surrounded and without realistic hope of being relieved. The garrison eventually sent out an envoy to negotiate terms. His name was Brother Leo, a Templar sergeant and a *casalier*, an estate administrator for the order. He spoke fluent Arabic (his name suggests he was of Armenian extraction) and he would therefore be able to communicate easily with Baybars. He was told by the Templars inside to agree the same terms with the Sultan that had already been offered to the Syriacs in the castle.

Publicly, Baybars agreed to this; privately, the Templar of Tyre suggests that he cut a nefarious deal with Leo (though unsurprisingly Muslim sources make no mention of this double-dealing). After giving Leo a cup of mare's milk – a sign of hospitality which was symbolically important as it gave notice of good intentions on his part – Baybars told Leo that he was livid at the stubborn resistance of the garrison and had no intention of letting them live. Tomorrow, he would arrange for a man who looked similar to himself to approach the walls and offer the garrison good terms. But when the garrison handed themselves over, they would be killed. Leo was to keep the secret to himself and he might then live; if he did not, then he would share the fate of his brethren. This was a vicious plan, even a dishonourable one, but Baybars had narrowly escaped injury or worse earlier in the siege when a missile fired from one of the engines inside the walls – the defenders apparently had 300 men manning the mangonels inside – just missed him.

Leo went along with the plan and all transpired as Baybars said it would. The lookalike was deployed; the garrison saw him approach the castle and were 'greatly reassured'. They trooped out of the castle with their goods loaded onto mules, expecting to make their way to Acre and freedom. But then the chronicler laconically noted 'They were betrayed and deceived.' Instead of their freedom, the garrison were presented with the dubious gift of martyrdom. They were led up a nearby hill and beheaded one by one – significantly, on the same spot where Templars had previously executed Muslim prisoners. Then their severed heads and decapitated bodies were enclosed within a circular wall, left scattered on the surface without the decency of a Christian burial so that they could still be seen years later. Leo lived on, dishonoured in the eyes of Christian commentators, particularly as he converted to Islam.[29] Only one other member of the garrison, receiving Baybars' conditional mercy so that he could return to Acre and tell the Franks there what had happened, was left alive.

These events gave Baybars control of Galilee. Following the capture of Safad, which he refortified and garrisoned, in August 1266 Baybars moved north towards Armenia; or to be more accurate his army did, this time led by his general al-Malik al-Mansūr. It made its way through the Amanus Gate, the path through the mountains that was the front door to Armenia from the south. Het'um was alarmed and sent envoys to negotiate but they were seized and imprisoned. Het'um made his way to the Mongols in Asia Minor in a vain attempt to enlist their help against the Mamluk attack. His two sons were, however, in the country. One, Thoros, was killed and the other, Leon,[30] was captured and taken to Egypt as the Mamluks pushed on through. As far as Safad was concerned, the Master of the Hospitallers, Hugh Revel, noted acerbically that the castle 'about which the Templars have talked so much' had barely lasted a fortnight.[31]

The fall of Safad left the door to Armenia wide open and the Mamluks duly entered it, leaving devastation in their wake. Adamodana, a great fortress held by the Teutonic Knights, was attacked. The garrison surrendered after receiving assurances for their safety but were promptly massacred. The women and children inside the castle were taken off as slaves. Sis was entered on 29 August and ransacked, though the citadel managed to hold out. The cathedral of the city was destroyed as possible retaliation for outrages against Muslim buildings in Damascus and elsewhere in the past. The Mamluk forces then split up with one element, led by the emir Qalāwūn, attacking Mamistra, Ayās and Tarsus among other places. The campaign was a triumph. So total was the success that the Mamluks returned south laden with such great booty that a prize ox was worth next to nothing, supply far exceeding demand. The army was greeted by Baybars on its return with great honour.

Having felt confident enough to let his subordinates lead the campaign in Armenia, Baybars turned to securing Syria itself. He heard that Christians near the village of Qara, on the road from Damascus to Homs, had mistreated their Muslim neighbours and sold some of them to the slave markets of Acre. Baybars visited brutal retribution upon them. A nearby monastery was attacked and demolished and its monks slaughtered. The church there was converted into a mosque. Women and children from the local population were taken off into slavery. This was exemplary justice at its least subtle.

Safad later became a favourite base for Baybars from where he could put pressure on Acre. This is a good example of his flexible strategy with regard to captured fortresses; those near the coast which could be used by the Franks for future expeditions if recaptured by them were demolished; those inland that were more useful to him were strengthened and reused. The Templar of Tyre records several raids on Acre soon after Safad was taken. In one, Baybars and his men managed to get close to the city by flying captured Templar and Hospitaller banners above them; too late, hundreds of defenceless peasants working the fields realised what was happening and were killed. Baybars supposedly had them scalped and displayed these gruesome trophies of war from the walls of Safad. When an Armenian delegation visited the castle soon after, seeking peace and hoping for the return of the captive prince Leon, the envoys were greeted by the disconcerting sight of decapitated heads stuck on poles around it; Baybars took pleasure in showing them off as a sign of his military prowess. He also adopted other measures to unsettle the Franks. For several years he had been offering land on the coast of the Mediterranean to Turcomans, reckoning that they would be in an ideal position to cause trouble for the Franks. It was a policy that enjoyed some success, adding further to the pressure on Acre.

The Franks sent out raiding parties in response to these events; life must have been harrowing for those unfortunate enough to be caught in the crossfire of this increasingly vicious conflict. The Franks continued to have the worst of it. When a raiding party including two renowned knights, Sir Robert Créseques and Oliver of Termes, was making its way back to Acre it rode straight into an ambush laid by Baybars. Initially, they managed to fight their way through, but in the pursuit that followed they were badly cut up. Whilst Oliver of Termes escaped, two of his nephews did not; they were captured and taken to Cairo where they later died. A party made its way out from Acre to inspect the damage; all they found were headless bodies. One survivor of the debacle, a Catalan knight called Cordate, had a remarkable escape. He was captured and incarcerated in a house in a village near Safad. He managed to climb out of a window and make a run for it. He kept to the fields, carefully avoiding the roads and finding his way by navigating using the stars. He made his way safely into Acre, where he told the Patriarch, William of Agen, of his adventure.[32]

Several more times Baybars moved on Acre, devastating the land round about. However, he did not yet feel ready to attack it. Cowed by his triumphs Tyre sent a delegation, along with money to compensate for the death of an important Mamluk who had been killed nearby. Satisfied with this gesture, Baybars agreed a ten-year truce with the port.

Baybars' success was also having an impact further afield. The Georgians sent negotiators to tell him that they would no longer side with the Mongols of Persia. Baybars' crushing successes against the Franks and Armenians were having a widespread effect, tipping the regional balance of power further in his favour, particularly when combined with the diminishment of the Mongol threat.

1. The citadel at Aleppo, which played a crucial part in the last decades of the Crusader Kingdom. (Author's collection)

2. Baku, which was attacked by the Mongols in the thirteenth century. (Author's collection)

3. The lion's head symbol of Sultan Baybars. (Author's collection)

4. Budapest, the modern capital of Hungary, which was decimated by Mongol attacks. (Author's collection)

5. The great mosque at Cairo, capital of the Mamluk dynasty. (Author's collection)

6. A modern replica of a medieval siege engine. (Author's collection)

Above: 7. Charles of Anjou who played a critical role in the demise of Outremer. (Author's collection)

Below: 8. Crac des Chevaliers, the mighty Hospitaller fortress. (Author's collection)

9. The refectory of the Hospitaller fortress Saint-Jean-d'Acre. (Courtesy of Lev Tsimbler under Creative Commons)

10. Franciscan friars. Men such as these sometimes journeyed as ambassadors to the Mongols. (Author's collection)

HIC. SITVS EST
ILLE MAGNI NOMINIS IMPERATOR ET REX SICILIAE
FRIDERICVS II OBIIT FLORENTINI IN APVLIA
IDIBVS DECEMBRIS ANNO MCCL

11. The tomb of Emperor Frederick II who introduced a dangerous new dynamic into the affairs of Outremer. (Author's collection)

Above: 12. Genghis Khan, one of the great figures of history who founded the Mongol dynasty. (Courtesy of A. Omer Karamollaoglu under Creative Commons)

Below: 13. The Great Wall of China which was unable to keep the Mongols out. (Author's collection)

14. The stupendous church of Hagia Sofia in the old city of Constantinople. (Author's collection)

15. The famous waterwheels of Hama which was uncomfortably placed in the line of the Mongol advance through Syria. (Author's collection)

16. The desert fortress of Karak. (Courtesy of Bernthold Werner under Creative Commons)

17. Medieval missiles from Syria used in siege engines. (Author's collection)

18. The crusader fortress of Montreal (Shobak). (Author's collection)

19. The old town of Acre, photographed in the nineteenth century. (Courtesy of New York Public Library)

Above: 20. Stunning medieval art from Palermo Cathedral in Sicily. (Author's collection)

Below: 21. The medieval town of Pisa, a great power during the time of the Crusades. (Author's collection)

22. Rome, home of the papacy which played such a prominent role in the crusading movement. (Author's collection)

Left: 23. Sultan Qutuz who helped lay the foundations of the Mamluk dynasty. (Author's collection)

Below: 24. The castle of Saone in Syria. (Author's collection)

25. The church of the Holy Sepulchre in Jerusalem, the spiritual heart of Christendom. (Courtesy of Bernthold Werner)

26. Medieval warriors from Saint Louis' church of St Chapelle in Paris. (Author's collection)

27. The tomb of Pope Innocent III in St John Lateran, Rome. (Author's collection)

28. St Mark's Square, Venice. The city played a crucial but not always honourable role in the last years of Outremer. (Author's collection)

7

Of Princes and Kings

'...if you had seen your churches destroyed, your crosses sawn
asunder ... you would have said "would to God that
I was transformed to dust."'

Baybars' letter to Prince Bohemond
after the fall of Antioch

The End of Antioch

Bohemond VI of Antioch was slow to realise the extent of the
danger presented by the rise of Baybars. Even as the latter's grip on
power tightened and his military resources were strengthened, raids
from Antioch against Muslim territory continued. One launched in
November 1265 was repulsed as it attempted to ford the Orontes
River and was chased back deep into Antiochian territory. Baybars
was only biding his time before returning to the issue of Antioch. In
1268, there were rumours of a Mongol attack on Syria but they came
to nothing. By now, there were just two places to the south of Acre
still in Frankish hands, the formidable Atlit and Jaffa. The death of
John of Ibelin, Count of the latter, in December 1266 gave Baybars
the opportunity to stake a claim there. On 11 March 1268, Baybars
and his army appeared before the walls of the port. It fell after half
a day's fighting though a missile launched from the mangonels inside
the walls narrowly missed Baybars and killed three of his men. Those
who survived the sack of the port locked themselves inside the citadel,
which had been strengthened by Louis IX. They eventually surrendered
and were allowed to make their way to Acre but according to the
Templar of Tyre many of the 'common people' were killed, holy relics

were burned and the head of St George was carried off in triumph.[1] The citadel was dismantled and some of the wood rescued during the demolition was shipped to Cairo to be used in the construction of a mosque that was being built there. The surrounding region was settled by Turcomans who would be useful in repelling any future Crusader incursion from the sea.

Baybars then moved on the Templar fortress of Beaufort. It had already been surrounded by Mamluk troops and signs of damage were apparent when Baybars arrived there. Now, twenty-six siege engines were put to work, launching their missiles at the walls, which soon started to show the strain. Ironically, they were launched from the outer walls of the fortress – the irony being that these had only recently been erected by the Templars to stop just such an artillery barrage from being inflicted on the garrison from outside. They gave the only convenient flat platform in the immediate area that was capable of holding artillery. Isolated and without hope of relief, the garrison surrendered. The women and children inside were escorted to safety by their Muslim conquerors but the soldiers were taken off into captivity. Like Safad, Baybars saw a future use for Beaufort – it was on a possible Mongol invasion route into the region – and installed a garrison there rather than demolishing it, though he did destroy the recently constructed outer walls that had proved to be so ineffective and indeed were actively counter-productive as far as the defence was concerned.

This was just the prelude to a much greater drama. Bohemond VI had profited greatly from his alliance with the Mongols. It is true that this had come at a cost. A Greek Orthodox patriarch had been foisted on Antioch – a position that had formerly been assumed by a Latin churchman since the arrival of the first Crusaders in the city – and a Mongol representative had also been installed there who was responsible for holding a census of the inhabitants and the collection of a tax of a dinar per person. As a result of his cooperation with the Mongols, Bohemond also found himself excommunicated. On the other hand, he had received generous grants of conquered territory in parts of Syria from the Mongols and with the help of the military orders had even managed to capture the important Mediterranean port of Latakia a few years before. In the process though, he inevitably incurred the enmity of Baybars. Resentment of the Mongols continued to fester with the Sultan. For his part, Abagha continued to demand Baybars' submission, an attitude neatly summed up in a message delivered to the Sultan in Damascus early in 1269 which asked the following question: 'You are a mamluk who was bought in Siwas. How do you rebel against the kings of the earth?' This was fully in keeping with the condescending views of a ruler whose coins carried legends such as 'lord of the world' and 'ruler of the necks of nations'. Mongol visions of manifest dynasty remained alive and well.[2]

A Mamluk army arrived outside of Tripoli, the other significant town in Bohemond's principality, on 30 April 1268 (the prince was currently inside). It had endured a difficult crossing of the mountains to get there; they were still topped with snow and some of the passes were blocked by Bohemond's troops. Appreciating the logistical problems of transporting them across the mountains, Baybars sent his siege engines back to Damascus. This was only going to be a raid in strength and no prolonged siege was planned. There were Templar strongholds nearby in Tortosa and Chastel Blanc (Safitā), the latter in a formidable position nearly 400 metres up in the hills, though it had suffered on at least two occasions from earthquake damage (in 1170 and 1202). The castle had a chequered history. It had been handed over to the Templars to garrison in around 1171 when it had suffered at the hands of the great Muslim leader of that time, Nur ad-Din. It had more recently benefitted from rebuilding works during Louis IX's time in Outremer. Dominated by its central tower or *donjon*, which still looms about the modern village that now surrounds it, it proved a hard nut to crack and Saladin avoided attacking it during his Hattin campaign. Even today, enough remains of its architecture to be able to envisage what life was like in its medieval heyday. The *donjon* has a chapel, still used as a church, at its lowest level whilst above it is a large hall, which was probably the dormitory of the Templar knights. There is a 'fineness and polish' about the interior finish of the walls which marks it out from the rather more functional examples in other castles of the period in the region.[3]

It was possible to see the Hospitaller super-fortress of Crac des Chevaliers from Safitā, which had a massive keep, so characteristic of military architecture of the period. Unnerved by the size of the raiding party, the garrison at Safitā sought an understanding with Baybars and released 300 Muslim prisoners to encourage him to leave them alone. Baybars had no desire for a fight with them; he had much bigger fish to fry. However, he would not agree to leave them in peace without payment and demanded that Jabala be handed over, a demand to which the Templars agreed, giving it up without a fight. Nothing could better epitomise how much the balance of power had swung towards the Mamluks in just a few years. These were developments of grave significance. Secular lords in Outremer were by now mostly incapable of holding on to fortresses outside the towns and the burden of doing so had as a result been largely passed on to the military orders. Evidence was now accumulating that they were also incapable of fulfilling this function.[4]

On 9 May Baybars moved up to Crac des Chevaliers, still in Hospitaller hands. Those inside were subject to a truce with Baybars but wisely refused to open the gates to him. He then moved on to Homs. Here he confirmed the prohibition on drinking alcohol and initiated plans to build a mosque. From Homs, Baybars moved his army to Hama after dividing it into three columns. One of his generals, Badr al-Din Bilik, was despatched with a force to St Symeon, the port of Antioch. A raid was also launched to the north of Antioch, a diversionary measure. The main body was to aim for Antioch itself, which was to be isolated from all sides. The city was surrounded by formidable walls that snaked up and down the mountains surrounding it, but their very extent was a burden to those inside because such a vast stretch of them needed to be defended.

The Antiochians knew what was coming. They sent out advance forces to intercept Baybars but these were insufficient to hold off the attack. In one skirmish, the constable of Antioch, Simon Mansel, was captured by a humble soldier who was allowed from that day on to bear Simon's heraldic device as a token of his personal triumph. Simon was a pragmatist and persuaded Baybars to let him return to Antioch as a negotiator. Baybars agreed to this plan, demanding from the city an annual tribute of 1 dinar for each citizen. This demand was rebuffed with the excuse that such a sum of money could not be raised (though it was the same as had been paid to the Mongols in the past). The stage was now set for an all-out assault on Antioch. As the battle lines were drawn for a potentially decisive confrontation, perhaps those inside the walls who knew their history reflected on the events of the summer of 1098 when Antioch had been stormed by the First Crusade. Then, against all odds, the city had been overwhelmed by the Crusaders led by the inspirational if self-obsessed Bohemond I. Even more remarkably, a huge relieving army led by Kerbogha, the Muslim Atabeg of Mosul, had been driven off by a vastly outnumbered Crusader force that had been on the verge of starvation. It was an outcome that was so remarkable that it was seen to be divinely inspired, a perception added to when a Crusader mystic, Peter Bartholomew, unearthed a piece of iron from the earth that was widely believed to be a relic of the spear that had pierced Christ's side on the Cross. A repeat of this miraculous deliverance was surely hoped for among those who had retained an element of their faith.

But there was to be no divine intervention now. From the outset, the siege that followed was a foregone conclusion. There were just a few thousand defenders to man those extended walls when on the morning of Friday 18 May 1268 Baybars' army laid siege to the city. The following day, the all-out attack came. It was launched with much vigour, though the Antiochians fought back stoically. Then some of Baybars' troops managed to breach the walls by Mount Silpius near the citadel. They filtered out from there and began to overrun the surrounding streets. The city effectively fell in one day in contrast to the eight months it had taken the First Crusade to capture it. Baybars took control of the city and gave an ominous order. All the gates were to be shut and guarded so that no one could escape. Nearly two centuries before, the triumphant Crusaders had unleashed an orgy of bloodletting in Antioch. That event was about to be brutally avenged. Fired up by their success, the Mamluk soldiers butchered thousands of those who fell into their hands, though many others were treated with dubious mercy and taken off into slavery.[5]

A fortunate minority of the population managed to make their way to the citadel, which was still in Antiochian hands. This was a temporary reprieve. There was insufficient food and water in the citadel to fight on for long. Those inside realised that all they could hope for was to escape with their lives. Terms were negotiated and those inside gave themselves up, in the main destined to live out their lives as slaves. Even common soldiers in the Mamluk army were given captives as part of their prize and local slave markets were so glutted that prices plummeted, particularly for girls.[6] Simon Mansel, though, was allowed his freedom and went to Armenia as he was of Armenian descent. The booty taken was immense and it took several days to apportion it among the victorious army. The citadel was set ablaze but it burned out of control and took some of the city with it. Antioch, the pride and joy of the Crusaders in Syria, was reduced to a ruin. It was a metaphor for the destruction of the Crusader dream. Isolated Frankish outposts in Syria were in the main indefensible now that the city was lost and were soon taken. The Templars in the region abandoned many of their castles without a fight. The remnant that remained in Frankish hands in Syria was now an irrelevance.

Baybars' determination was clear for all to see and Het'um, anxious to get his son Leon back from Cairo, offered to hand over some castles on the border between Armenia and Syria to tie up the deal. On 24 June, Leon was released on the border in return for a prominent Muslim captive, the emir Sunqur al-Ashqar, who had been captured when Aleppo was taken by the Mongols. Sunqur does not appear to have been badly treated during his captivity; he even had a Mongol wife and several children. The castles were also handed over. Het'um had been forced to give hostages in advance but they were safely returned once the fortresses were surrendered. Leon had been treated well by Baybars, who clearly appreciated the benefit of a valuable bargaining chip; the Armenian prince had even accompanied the Sultan on hunting expeditions. Baybars' actions reveal that he could be a statesman as well as a warrior in pursuit of his objectives. But the agreement put Het'um in a very difficult spot as regards his Mongol alliance, as his actions could be interpreted as marking a shift towards the Mamluks in his political positioning.

The news threatened to wake at least some West European leaders from their apathy. Antioch had a resonance in the West; the English King Henry III had an Antioch Chamber in his palace at Clarendon. Not only were these losses a blow politically, they also created significant economic pressure. William of Agen, the Patriarch of Jerusalem, appealed to the West for financial assistance, writing for example to Amaury de la Roche, commander of the Templars in Paris, asking for funds *inter alia* to finance some crossbowmen in Acre, to support the retention of fifty knights and to help pay off loans taken out by Geoffrey de Sergines.[7] Given subsequent efforts to launch another crusade, news of its loss probably rekindled the crusading spirit of Louis IX, who shortly afterwards put in train plans for a new expedition. Others, such as Prince Edward of England, also made arrangements to journey eastwards. Louis was not helped though when the commander of the French regiment in Acre, Geoffrey de Sergines, died in 1269. It would soon transpire that the sands of time, for both Louis and Outremer, were fast running out.

Charles of Anjou's Quest for Power

Baybars gloated over his great victory at Antioch. He wrote with undisguised pleasure to the defeated but absent Bohemond, taunting him with descriptions of the outrages that were committed there. If Bohemond had been present when the Muslim holy places in Damascus were desecrated a few years before, retribution must indeed have been sweet. Baybars wrote to Bohemond:

> ...if you had seen your churches destroyed, your crosses sawn asunder, the pages of the lying gospels exposed, if you had seen your enemy the Muslim trampling in the sanctuary, with the monk, the priest, the deacon sacrificed on the altar ... the Churches of Saint Paul and Saint Peter pulled down and destroyed, you would have said 'Would to God that I was transformed to dust or would to God that I had not received the letter that tells me of this sad catastrophe.'[8]

This was Holy War – bitter, vicious, unyielding, violent – as surely as any Christian crusade was.

With Antioch now lost, it was high time that the remaining territories in Outremer settled their differences and united against a common enemy. Instead, European politics was again about to intervene in the affairs of the Kingdom of Jerusalem, where the political landscape was to some extent an extension of Europe itself. Recent years had seen a struggle for dominance in Western Europe involving on the one hand the Angevin rulers, particularly Charles of Anjou, brother of Louis IX, and on the other a range of opponents including the Hohenstaufen dynasty and the rulers of Aragon on the Iberian peninsula. The Angevins claimed the right to provide the rulers of what was historically the Kingdom of Jerusalem – Fulk of Anjou had become king as long ago as 1131 – but this brought them into direct conflict with the Lusignan rulers of Cyprus who also staked a claim and who therefore had a distinct advantage, given their geographic proximity to the region that made up the rump of Outremer.

The Angevins had been particularly active in Italy and Sicily and in the latter, events were about to reach a grim climax. In 1265, Charles of Anjou was recognised as King of Sicily by Pope Clement IV in St Peters in opposition to the Hohenstaufen dynasty who held it. The papacy regarded Sicily (which it should be remembered included territories on mainland Italy as well as the island) as its personal fief to award to whichever man seemed to be the most appropriate. Given the disagreements in recent times between popes and emperors a transfer of power over Sicily to an Angevin who was largely supportive of the papacy seemed a desirable outcome to Clement. These moves were resisted and in February 1266 the Angevin and Hohenstaufen forces clashed at Benevento. On the eve of the battle, the Pope's official representative, the Bishop of Auxerre, had demanded that, in return for receiving absolution for their sins, the soldiers in Charles' army should strike the enemy 'with double their normal force'.[9] The Hohenstaufen prince, Manfred, half-brother of Conrad IV, led the army opposing Charles. He had been forewarned that he would die in a field that was festooned with flowers: he therefore knew he was doomed when he was told that the place he was about to fight on was called 'the Field of Flowers'. He was, as predicted, among the dead by the time that the battle ended. Opposition to Charles now collapsed, allowing him to assume in reality the throne he had already symbolically been granted; but the story of the Angevins in Sicily was far from completed.

Tensions between Italian city states remained a factor too. Matters came to a head in 1267, which was a time when the Christian forces in Outremer could least afford to be divided. A fleet of twenty-eight galleys set out from Genoa led by Admiral Luchetto Grimaldi. On 16 August, they descended on the harbour at Acre where they burned two Pisan ships (Pisa was an ally of Venice) and placed the Genoese standard over the Tower of Flies which stood on the harbour mole. Grimaldi then took half his fleet to Tyre, leaving the remainder in Acre under the command of Papano Mallone. The Venetians in the meantime had sent a flotilla of their own to Acre. When the reduced Genoese fleet saw they were coming they made their way quickly out of the harbour, wisely reasoning that if they were caught inside it, outnumbered and unable to manoeuvre, they would have little hope of escape. Five of the Genoese ships were taken but the rest of them made their way north, five to Tyre and three to Sidon. The Genoese armada eventually made its way back to Italy where a three-year truce was agreed between Venice and Genoa. It suited the purpose of the Genoese to have a temporary cessation of hostilities whilst they plotted their revenge.

The Hohenstaufens still claimed the Kingdom of Jerusalem through the bloodline of the remarkable Frederick II. Hugh II, King of Cyprus, died in 1267 and was replaced by his cousin, Hugh III, who claimed the regency of Acre in the ongoing absence of the locally recognised King, Conrad III (Conradin), Frederick's grandson. But events to the west were about to change the situation in Outremer dramatically.

Although Charles of Anjou had succeeded in taking Sicily, his rule was not universally popular and revolts broke out. Conradin was invited by the rebels to come from Germany and lead the fight. The armies of Charles of Anjou and Conradin met at Tagliacozzo, a hilly area in central Italy, on 23 August 1268. Conradin's men were at first successful and broke into Charles' camp. However, indiscipline then took over; the seemingly victorious troops began to pillage and the Angevin army launched a counter-attack. At the end of the battle, it was the Angevins who held the field, though Conradin managed to escape. But he was a marked man and was betrayed soon after. He was taken to Naples where he was tried for treason, found guilty and beheaded. It was a shocking conclusion as Conradin was barely sixteen years old. There was moral outrage against Charles' actions in some quarters. But the events that led to the fate of the young King had been fuelled by the vitriol of the papacy, which had labelled him 'the ward of slander and damnation'. These events wiped out the Hohenstaufen line. The right to be King of Jerusalem passed back to Conradin's grandmother's line in theory, but in practice this proved to be an extremely complicated situation. Three claimants to the throne emerged: Hugh of Brienne, Hugh III, King of Cyprus, and Maria of Antioch. Given all the threats that were facing Outremer, a disputed succession was the last thing that was needed.

The bitter legacy of the controversial Frederick II now came home to roost. His friendly relationships with Muslims had alienated hard-line Christians. Now the repercussions of that situation played themselves out. The response to news of Conradin's death in Acre was bonfires in the streets, lit in celebration of the demise of a dynasty that some of the populace saw as 'persecutors of Holy Church'.[10] On the other hand, it was probably not news that would be welcomed by Baybars. Not long before, Conradin had sent him a letter in an attempt to get his support, even from a distance, in his battle against the Angevins. Baybars had responded to this in friendly terms.

Baybars' recent campaign against the Frankish territories had caused alarm in Acre and the tangled web of inter-European rivalries made the situation worse. It was in this context that Hugh de Lusignan, who had in December 1267 become King Hugh III of Cyprus, journeyed to Acre in April 1268 even before the fall of Antioch. The catastrophe that the subsequent loss of that city represented made the case for some kind of accommodation with Baybars even more pressing. Negotiations took place in Damascus and given his dominant position Baybars demanded much. The Franks of Acre were to concede territory as the price of peace and Cyprus was also to be included in any peace deal, having the practical effect of preventing Cypriot intervention in the military affairs of the Frankish territories on the mainland. Hugh was not prepared to agree to these terms and the negotiations fizzled out. An accommodation was nevertheless reached between Baybars and Bohemond, now effectively Count of Tripoli only, who was in no place to offer meaningful resistance to any terms that the Sultan might demand as the price of peace, even given his recent humiliation at the Sultan's hands. In the meantime, Charles of Anjou had sent an embassy to Egypt to meet Baybars to further his own ambitions in Outremer. It was cordially received, a worrying development for Hugh III.

Outremer remained bitterly divided. It was also increasingly desperate as the European situation seemed to make any meaningful reinforcement from that direction unlikely. A Templar knight expressed his frustration in an unusual way by lamenting in a poem, *Ira et Dolor* ('anger and pain'), that the pope and the princes of Europe were too busy jostling for position in Europe to concern themselves with a new crusade. Even God had given up on them. He wrote that 'He is a fool who wishes to fight against the Turks [sic], since Jesus Christ does not contest them anymore.'[11] Acre itself was under huge pressure in the struggle to feed itself with raids on the land around it recorded in 1263, 1265, 1266, 1267 and 1269. The Kingdom seemed powerless to fight back and was struggling to sustain itself. Hugh Revel, Master of the Hospitallers, wrote to the prior of St Gilles in France in 1268 that Outremer had produced nothing for eight years and, just when help from Europe was most needed, it was drying up. Attacks on fertile Armenia, a friendly neighbour where the Hospitallers, Templars and Teutonic Knights all held lands, had also contributed to the growing logistical crisis. The Hospital was now in serious financial difficulties and was faced with the prospect of being forced to sell off many of its prize possessions to raise funds.[12]

On Conradin's death, the Cypriot King Hugh III journeyed to Tyre where he was proclaimed King of Jerusalem, the line of succession being passed back from the Hohenstaufens to the Cypriot Lusignans who had first acquired it through marriage in 1197. His right to do so was challenged by Maria de Lusignan who asserted that she had a better claim. The fact that she was an unmarried woman in her forties with no heir naturally counted against her, as did her inability to offer much in the way of resources to strengthen the defences of the kingdom. Her representative had nevertheless tried to interrupt Hugh's coronation ceremony.[13] The Templars and Hospitallers among others tried to arbitrate between them but without success. Maria eventually took her case before the Pope, Gregory X, at the Council of Lyons in 1274, but despite her efforts subsequent letters to Hugh of Lusignan (who was Maria's nephew and who also sent representatives to the Council) from the pontiff continued to refer to him as the King of Cyprus and Jerusalem. Maria was not prepared to give up her claim easily, but in 1277 in an unprecedented act she sold it off as if it was some mere trinket to be traded in a street bazaar to Charles of Anjou, with Pope Gregory now dead. It has often been contended that Gregory supported the claims of Charles of Anjou to be King of Jerusalem but recent research suggests that this was not the case and that the now deceased Pope on the contrary wished him to desist from pushing his case, given the impact that subsequent disputes would have on an already weak Outremer.[14] Charles had indeed been interested in affairs in Outremer for some time, even before the reign of Pope Gregory X. His support in providing supplies to Outremer for the best part of a decade before buying the throne had indeed been very important.[15] In return for an annual payment from his revenues, Charles had strategically strengthened his position in Outremer significantly, a move that was very much in keeping with the breathtaking sweep of his ambition. As well as Sicily, he had also taken lands in the Balkans and through judicious marriage alliances had even increased his influence into the kingdom of Hungary. Now Outremer, too, was on the menu.

Baybars had not finished with the Franks and was conveniently given an excuse to inflict yet more pain on them when a young Muslim woman was robbed and forced to convert to Christianity whilst journeying to Safad. The girl's mother complained to Baybars and he in turn demanded recompense. When none was forthcoming he launched a raid in the region of Tyre in which a number of prisoners were taken. This had a beneficial side effect for Baybars. Isabella of Ibelin, the Lady of Beirut, was alarmed by these events and sent a delegation to Baybars along with some Muslim prisoners who were released. Baybars responded favourably to these initiatives and a peace treaty was agreed between the two parties on 9 May 1269. Following on from the conquest of Antioch this was another boost to Muslim morale and a symbolic triumph that cemented Baybars' position still further. It was also a major strategic success as it secured the north Syrian frontier. One unambiguous phrase in the treaty in particular stood out: 'The lady shall not enable any of the Franks whomsoever to proceed against the Sultan's territory from the direction of Beirut and its territory. She shall restrain from that and repulse everyone seeking to gain access with evil intent.'[16] In other words, Beirut must stand meekly by should her Frankish neighbours need help.

So confident was he in his position that Baybars now felt able to undertake the *hajj* to Mecca. Although this was a once-in-a-lifetime requirement for devout Muslims, many – even among the ranks of the rich – did not always fulfil it. Even Saladin had not. Baybars' pilgrimage, along with other acts of piety such as the banning of alcohol and hashish and recent efforts to wipe out prostitution in Egypt, suggest a certain devoutness in this sometimes terrifying figure. He went in secret, travelling across the Jordanian desert via Shawbak and Karak and arriving in Medina on 26 July 1269. Once back in Syria, he toured the region. He paid a surprise visit to his governors in Aleppo and then visited Jerusalem. On 20 September 1269 he led his army out of Syria and back to Egypt, arriving in Cairo on 2 October. He had not been there for long when he heard news of a new crusading expedition making its way across the Mediterranean that had just arrived in Acre. Despite the disastrous outcomes that recent crusading expeditions had suffered, clearly there was still an appetite in some quarters in Europe to try yet again.

The 1260s were disastrous for Outremer. It is easy to be seduced into concentrating merely on the military and political reverses of these years, yet the economic effects were also potentially catastrophic. Secular barons found that they did not have the resources to maintain many of their castles and estates, which were therefore often sold off to the military orders. The latter consequently got deeper into debt and they were forced to seek greater contributions from their holdings in Europe, as well as enter into special pleading with popes and kings to obtain further funds. However, in many cases they then proved incapable of protecting their acquisitions against Mamluk raids. It was a classic 'double whammy'; expenditure rose whilst income from the properties purchased declined. From a modern economic perspective, the return on investment was awful, in many cases negative. Outremer had been fatally undermined; and so too for that matter had some at least of the military orders. One historian concluded that, despite large investments in Outremer, the Hospitallers were by the end of the 1260s almost entirely dependent on supplies from Europe.[17] By this stage, Outremer was in dire straits; and indeed its end might even now have been a foregone conclusion.

Louis IX's Last Crusade

At this time, the country we now call Spain did not exist. The Iberian peninsula was split into several states. In the south, there were still Muslim rulers in some parts – Granada, the last major city to fall, was not conquered by Christian forces until 1492, the year that Columbus 'discovered' the Americas. Further north, there were several competing Christian kingdoms such as Castile and Aragon. In the preceding two centuries, much of the peninsula had been overrun by Christian forces and taken from Muslim rulers whose ancestors had themselves conquered the region several hundred years before that. The process, known as the *Reconquista*, approximately coincided with the period during which crusading expeditions set out from Europe for the Levant, though in Iberia it started earlier and ended long after the last Crusaders left Outremer.

Aragon was particularly significant. Her present King, James I, had been given the nickname 'the Conqueror' on the back of victories he won over Muslim opponents in the West. In 1267, James was visited in Perpignan by a delegation from Abagha, the son and successor of Hūlegū, who now ruled the Mongol *Ilkhanate* in Persia. The Mongol civil war went on and Abagha continued to fight against forces from the Golden Horde in Russia who were on friendly terms with Baybars. Abagha sought out alliances with Christian powers who were opposed to the Sultan. His delegates also journeyed to Genoa. Unfortunately, they arrived at the same time as emissaries from Baybars. When the two embassies bumped into each other, there was a spontaneous and unseemly skirmish between the two in the city square, which the civic authorities had to break up. The Mongol embassy later visited Louis IX, who was planning another crusade, and his brother, Charles of Anjou.

The delegation to Aragon arrived at an opportune moment. James was at odds with the papacy and involvement in a crusade might help to improve relations. Clement IV was happy to offer papal sanction; an expedition to the Levant was timely given the recent successes of Baybars. James despatched a return delegation to Abagha and discussions between the Mongols and the Aragonese continued to go well. The leader of James' embassy, Jaime Alarich, returned after some time – it was a long and complicated journey – with confirmation of an alliance against Baybars. The crusade set sail from Barcelona on 4 September 1269. It immediately ran into trouble. Travelling the Mediterranean in the relatively flimsy craft of the day was a potentially hazardous process and the fleet was badly affected by violent squalls. Some were lost and others forced to divert to Aigues Mortes, the magnificent port close to Marseille constructed on the orders of Louis IX. This was far enough for James, who gave up on the expedition when it had hardly started. He decided to go no further, though two of his illegitimate sons, Fernando Sanchez and Pedro Fernandez, were deputed to lead the expedition eastwards in his absence. The armada duly arrived in Acre where it was joyfully received. The citizens were badly in need of a fillip given the battering they and their fellow Franks had received in recent years. They were also delighted at the provisions and horses that the Aragonese brought with them as they had been suffering a dearth of both. To further boost morale, Abagha kept his side of the bargain and Mongol forces raided the north of Syria. The coalition, it seemed, was working as planned.

However, the assumptions on which this effort was made proved to be erroneous. The alliance had not taken due account of the qualities of Baybars and the almost total dominance he had in the region now. So little was Baybars concerned by the threat posed by the Aragonese and the Mongols that he even sent half of his army home for the winter. His confidence proved to be well-founded. The force he sent to Syria was more than enough to drive the Mongols away without even a fight. At the same time, the Franks were seemingly unaware of the changed nature of political realities in the region. An expedition was sent out from Acre composed of local and Aragonese forces to raid in the region of Montfort, a fortress held by the Teutonic Order. Baybars was keeping a close watch on the city and sent men over the crossing of the upper Jordan at Jacob's Ford. These combined with local forces and met the Crusader army on 18 December. Oliver of Termes, who understood the local realities better than most, wanted to return to Acre without a fight. The Aragonese on the other hand were bristling for one; and it was they who won the argument.

And so the two forces clashed. It was another disaster for the Crusaders with most of the force wiped out. Christmas 1269 would not be a happy one for the people of Acre as they mourned the loss of not only their men but also of their fragile confidence. There was a Christian army outside Acre that was in theory close enough to intervene in the battle; but its leaders decided that such an action would only add to the losses without changing the result – following the wise military maxim, never reinforce failure – an action that was undoubtedly prudent but lacked vigour. It was some days before the Christian forces dared approach the battlefield to bury their dead. The Aragonese returned home the following spring. There was no further fighting and all they had achieved was to add yet more Crusader martyrs to the ever-growing roll call of the dead. It was a salutary lesson that such influxes of Crusaders from the West did not understand the realities of warfare in the Levant. Yet it was a lesson that would not be assimilated. To use words often attributed to Albert Einstein, this expedition followed the textbook definition of insanity: trying the same thing time and time again and expecting to get a different result.

In 1270 Louis IX, flagging through age and illness, decided that a final crusading act might help to secure his passport to Paradise. However it was not the Levant for which he set out but Tunis. The city was ruled by the emir Mustansir, who some hoped with unwarranted optimism was ripe for conversion to Christianity; one final push it was believed would do it. Unfortunately for the master strategists, things did not turn out as planned. The emir showed no desire to abandon his Muslim beliefs and resisted the attempts of the Crusaders to take his city. A siege loomed; this apple was not yet ready to drop into the lap of Crusader Europe. The Crusader army was poorly prepared to cope with the challenges of an African summer and disease – the scourge of so many medieval armies – soon started to decimate it. Men fell in their droves from the attacks of dysentery and other maladies. Worst of all, the health of King Louis, already on the decline, now gave out and he died on 25 August 1270, a few days after his son Tristan. There was a tragic symmetry about these events; Tristan had been born at Damietta during the catastrophic invasion of Egypt two decades previously.

The main beneficiary of Louis' demise in the immediate aftermath was his brother Charles of Anjou, who managed to negotiate a truce with Mustansir from which he did very well. In return for an annual tribute, Charles agreed to turn his attentions elsewhere. He was now free to return to his schemes in south-east Europe, which was where his own personal ambitions lay rather than in North Africa. But for the crusading movement Louis' death was a hammer blow. He had invested greatly in it, in terms of both his financial resources and his personal energies and commitment, and his untimely demise left a vacuum it would be hard to fill. A son, Philip III, became the new King of France. In the meantime, Philip's uncle, Charles of Anjou, was far too busy elsewhere to pick up the crusading mantle that Louis had laid down. Despite Louis' herculean efforts and the high cost of his campaigns, he had achieved very little. The move on Tunis was particularly hard to understand when there were greater priorities elsewhere. The Templar of Tyre claims to have direct insight into the mind of the Almighty who, he suggested, meted out terrible punishments to the Tunis expedition mainly because they should have been heading for the Holy Land.

Baybars had received word of Louis' crusade and clearly realised that the significant resources available to the King of France posed a threat, even if his previous expedition to Egypt had ended in abject disaster. He had therefore quickly returned to Cairo when he heard of it. His coastal cities were told to prepare for defensive action and bridges of boats were built across the Nile to allow the rapid movement of troops if necessary. However, the efforts that Baybars had made to strengthen his fleet were largely unsuccessful and the naval superiority that the Crusaders continued to enjoy remained a source of worry. Baybars' state of mind would not have been improved when enemy ships several times raided the harbour at Alexandria, causing significant damage in the process. He even took steps to render assistance to the emir of Tunis, but Louis' death and the subsequent abandonment of the crusade rendered such measures superfluous.

This did not stop Baybars from continuing to take a cautious stance just in case. The port of Ascalon was in a strategically crucial position on the border between the Frankish states and Egypt (though as a harbour it had its limitations). During the Third Crusade, Richard the Lionheart and Saladin had argued fiercely over its ownership as part of the final peace treaty agreed at the end of the campaign. Now Baybars visited

Ascalon and ensured that the fortifications there were demolished. Again, his strategy was to deny its use to the enemy rather than garrison it himself, which was the same approach that had been adopted by Saladin with regard to Ascalon. He also ordered that obstacles (tree trunks and rocks) be placed in the harbour there so that no Crusader ships could use it as a port of entry into the region. Clearly, the naval supremacy still enjoyed by the Franks continued to concern him.

Baybars and the Assassins

Baybars now decided to bring another troublesome group in the region into line. The Nizaris were a frequent source of irritation to Muslim rulers, who struggled to control them. The Nizaris were at the same time themselves vulnerable and thought it wisest to pay tribute to Baybars. They were now led by an ageing leader, Najm al-Din, who chose this inopportune moment to refuse to present himself to Baybars in a symbolic demonstration of subservience. Worse than this, his son – acting as his representative – now asked Baybars for a reduction in the annual tribute paid to the Sultan. It was a defiant but rash gesture which suggested that it was not only the Franks who had not fully understood the changes in the balance of power that had taken place in the region. Baybars' response was typically decisive and unambiguous; he declared that Najm al-Din was henceforth deposed.

His place was to be taken by another Nizari, Sārim al-Din al-Rida, who had sagaciously presented himself to Baybars bearing gifts. However, Baybars gave little without the need for the recipient to offer something back in return, and not mere baubles. The most formidable Nizari stronghold in the region was the mountaintop castle of Masyaf, crucially situated between Hama and Syria on one side and the lands that had once formed the bulk of the principality of Antioch on the other. Al-Rida was to hand it over as the price of his recognition as the new leader of the Nizaris. He agreed to do so, but when he duly took up his position, he then refused to comply. Al-Rida had also badly misjudged the Sultan. A Mamluk army seized Masyaf. Al-Rida escaped from the castle but was captured soon after. He was taken to Cairo where he was put in prison. Before long he was dead, probably as a result of being poisoned.[18] The position of the Nizaris may well have been weakened by the demise of Antioch, as the balance of power, which they had once helped to maintain, had now shifted irretrievably in favour of the Mamluks.

Najm al-Din had learned his lesson and submitted to Baybars. Perhaps in view of his advanced age, he was restored, though his son, Shams al-Din, was retained by the Sultan as a hostage for his good behaviour. The tribute was reimposed. However, the Nizaris were now living on borrowed time. Shams al-Din ultimately proved troublesome and the remaining Nizari fortresses in Syria were then picked off by the Mamluks one by one. The last of them, al-Kahf, was taken in 1273, bringing to an end the independent existence of the Nizaris as a political force. What his bitter enemies the Mongols had started in Persia, Baybars was finishing off in Syria. Yet the involvement of the Nizaris was still a factor, as was shown with the affair of Philip de Montfort. The Montfort family provide a good example of how the affairs of Outremer remained to some extent linked with those of Western Europe. Philip was first cousin to the famous Simon, who for a short time in the 1260s became the dominant figure in England when he held King Henry III captive and effectively treated him as a puppet ruler. Simon had earlier on in his career been on crusade to Outremer and was even suggested as a possible regent by local barons for the boy-Emperor Conrad, though this plan came to nothing. Simon's father (also named Simon) was a famous Crusader too, mainly known for his brutal crushing of heretic Cathars in the south of France, though he did spend a short time in the East where he refused point-blank to take part in the controversial diversion of the Fourth Crusade to Constantinople in 1204.

Philip had been in the region for some time, having been involved in Louis IX's disastrous crusade to Egypt. When Louis left he stayed on to play a key part in important events in Outremer, including the ejection of the Venetians from Tyre in the build-up to the War of St Sabas, though he still held lands around Toulouse.[19] He had been ejected from his lordship of Toron by Baybars in 1266 but even though he was now ageing, the Sultan apparently still felt threatened by him. Philip had been the ruler of Tyre, which formed part of the patrimony of the Kings of Cyprus and Jerusalem. The deal had later been sealed by an agreement between King Hugh III and the Montforts, which was secured when Hugh's sister, Margaret of Antioch, was married to Philip de Montfort's heir, John. Margaret was described by the Templar of Tyre as a fair woman, twenty-four years old. The writer says that he saw her 'all the time' and could vouch that she was at one time 'the most lovely of all maidens and ladies on this side of the sea'.

He was impressed particularly by her beautiful face and remarked that she was both good and wise and that her marriage was a happy one, with both parties to it having great affection for the other. However, he was less kind about her as the years went on, stating that she became unreasonably fat (as indeed he said her father had been) whilst her husband, John, was a martyr to gout and became virtually crippled by it in contrast to the vigour he had displayed in his younger days. It is a striking personal insight into the effect of the ageing process on two human beings, in contrast to the great events that usually engage the chronicler.[20]

Shortly afterwards two young men presented themselves at Tyre in the guise of men at arms for hire. They asked to be baptised to ingratiate themselves with Philip de Montfort and he was happy to oblige, not suspecting their motives. One took the Christian name of Philip and the other Julian, after the lord of Sidon who was his sponsor. Philip took them on as turcopoles – light cavalry – and came to trust them implicitly. However, they were not what they seemed. According to the Templar of Tyre they were Nizari assassins, determined to kill Philip and John de Montfort and Julian of Sidon. When a groom became suspicious of them, they became nervous that their plot would be discovered and that forced them into precipitate action.

What happened next is described in detail by the Templar of Tyre. On 17 March 1270, Philip de Montfort – 'The Old Lord' as the writer titles him – was outside his chapel talking to one of his bailiffs. One of the plotters approached him and Philip, thinking that he was about to attend Mass, commended him on his devotion and gave him some money to put into the offering; his son, John – 'The Young Lord' – was inside and a service was taking place. The plotter then entered and saw, to his satisfaction, that John was alone apart from one other man, a knight called William of Picquigny. The coast was therefore clear for him to execute his plan. The plotter went outside again. Philip was distracted, playing with a ring on his finger, and oblivious to the approaching nemesis. The attacker struck, plunging a dagger into his chest. Philip's hand was in the way, and the blade struck right through it, pinning it to his chest. The assassin then went back into the chapel, planning to bring down John too. However, the commotion outside alerted the two men inside to the threat. With imminent doom advancing down the aisle towards him, John took refuge behind a decorated altarpiece. The assassin struck at him but the altarpiece took the blow instead of the intended target. The dagger stuck tight in the wood and despite the assassin's frantic efforts refused to budge.

The tables were now turning. William of Picquigny grabbed the assassin from behind whilst John de Montfort came out from his place of sanctuary and caught hold of his would-be killer by his hair. In the meantime, Philip was still outside approaching a state of collapse. He made his way to a stone bench at the entrance to the chapel. Attendants came to help him but he told them to go and save his son. They rushed inside, striking down the assassin and thereby ensuring John's survival. But for Philip, it was too late; the wound was mortal. His body was taken away for an honourable burial in the church of the Holy Cross in Tyre. No such kindness was shown to the lifeless body of his killer; the corpse was taken away and hanged. The groom who knew of the plot but had said nothing, having been bought off by the assassins to stay silent, also suffered a terrible fate. He was seized and tortured and confessed to his part in the act. His tongue was ripped out, an appropriate if excruciating punishment for his silence, his hand was cut off, having been the guiltiest organ in the acceptance of a bribe, and he was dragged off and hanged. The other would-be assassin got wind of the fact that his comrade-in-arms had been caught in the act. Word had been sent post-haste to Julian of Sidon, who had moved on to Beirut, of what had happened in Tyre and he was therefore on his guard. Realising that his task was now hopeless, the surviving Nizari fled on horseback to safety. But the enterprise had been in part successful and a long-term opponent of Baybars had been removed for good.[21]

8

The End of Baybars

'...he ranged about and destroyed things and put everyone he
encountered to the sword.'

On Baybars' campaign to
Armenia in 1276

The Fall of Crac

Whilst the military orders still garrisoned some formidable fortresses in
the region, they were increasingly isolated. With the resources available
to him, Baybars could cherry-pick them off one by one. Time was no
longer of the essence; he appeared now to enjoy an insuperable and
irreversible advantage. Of course, he would welcome their elimination
but there was no desperate hurry to achieve this ambition; he could
prioritise his goals. The Hospitaller fortress of Margat/Marqab was
one such target. It lay close to the coast of the Mediterranean. He
made two attempts to attack it but on both occasions he was defeated
by particularly inclement weather including driving rain and snow.

The great fortress of Crac des Chevaliers was far more isolated than
Marqab, being well inside the Syrian hinterland near Homs. Its story
offered in some ways a typical example of how medieval castles, both
in Outremer and further afield, had evolved over time (a process that
in Crac's case did not end when it was eventually lost to the Franks).
First given to the Hospitallers in 1142, major repairs to it were made
when it was damaged by an earthquake in 1170 (as was the case at
other castles such as Safitā/Chastel Blanc). Another earthquake in
1202 caused a second, outer, ring of defences to be added to it. It
became the ultimate example of a concentric castle, with two lines

of defence, the inner overlooking the outer, allowing archers to fire from both at the same time, those on the inner walls firing over the heads of those on the outside. But Baybars' successes had made Crac's position increasingly vulnerable as it became ever more isolated. He led a small force from Hama against it in January 1270, but this was not a serious attempt to take it. He came close to the walls, as if taunting those inside to drive him off. They attempted to do so but were repulsed. Whilst Baybars did not have a sufficiently large force to take the castle, neither were those inside powerful enough to drive him away. The foray gave Baybars valuable information about the inherent weaknesses of Crac and its garrison that he could use in the future when returning in greater force.

When Baybars set out on campaign he took with him his son, al-Sa'id Baraka Khan, hoping to give him experience and also perhaps to cement his position as his eventual heir (a strategy that was unsuccessful as Baraka lacked his father's talent and political acumen). He led his army first to the region of Tripoli where his raids succeeded in killing a number of Christians and taking others captive. He then went to the Templar fortress of Chastel Blanc. The position of the hopelessly outnumbered garrison was serious but nevertheless they resolved to resist. However, orders came from the Templar commander at Tortosa who instructed them to negotiate favourable terms and, if they could do so, then surrender. This was duly done. Baybars clearly did not want to suffer unnecessary loss of life amongst his men and the terms were agreed. The castle was handed over and 700 men came out of it along with women and children and were allowed to make their way to safety. This time Baybars had employed a carrot rather than a stick; and the way in which the Templar hierarchy had capitulated suggested that it was a very successful strategy.

However, these operations were secondary compared to those against the primary target. From Chastel Blanc, Baybars made his way to the mighty Hospitaller fortress of Crac des Chevaliers again. Even today it looks the epitome of what a medieval castle should, in the imagination, look like. It was superbly constructed. If an enemy managed to break through the outer walls he would be faced with a moat between them and the inside walls. This space would effectively become a killing ground where crossbowmen on the inner walls could pick off opponents at will. If an enemy should break through the gates, he would be faced with a long passage with arrow slits on either side and 'murder holes' in the roof from which objects could be dropped. Most formidable of all was Crac's enormous donjon, the central tower, which dominated the site. It looked out imperiously over the Syrian plains that lay in its shadow. It was a style of fortification that would inspire emulation elsewhere, most notably by Edward I of England with his ring of castles in Wales. Nowadays, it is perhaps like an ageing film-star, its days of glory long past and fraying at the edges a little. But even after damage inflicted in the recent Syrian civil war, it remains an imposing and iconic site. Reminders of its glory days are never far away.

Crac dominates the strategically important Homs Gap. As such it was a site that Baybars would sooner or later have to eliminate if he wished to secure his control over all of Syria. It was increasingly isolated after his recent successes in the region but it remained an invasive growth which had to be removed from the body politic of the ruling regime in the country. The attack on it began in late February 1271. The outer walls were taken but the garrison continued to hold out in that mighty donjon. Baybars, wishing to avoid the heavy losses which must follow any attack on it, resorted to subterfuge. He forged a letter from the Hospitaller commander in Tripoli which instructed the garrison to surrender. Whether or not they were taken in by it is a moot point but surrender shortly followed and the castle was abandoned by the garrison, who were allowed to depart in peace. The reality was that Crac was now completely isolated, an oasis in a Crusader desert. Its loss was only a matter of time. It was also faced with major logistical challenges with much of the fertile land in the district, on which it relied for provisioning, either having been lost to the Mamluks or devastated by them.[1]

The fall of the famed 'Castle of the Knights', which had even survived Saladin's blitzkrieg of 1187 as well as all other attempts on it, must have come as a withering blow to the Franks when it came on 8 April 1271. Maybe its isolation meant that its strategic position was now less important but the symbolism of the handing over of the iconic fortress was a metaphor for the increasingly parlous state of Outremer. Taken alongside the surrender of Chastel Blanc, it did not augur well for the future, nor did it suggest that the fighting spirit of the military orders was in good health. Baybars took up occupation. He installed his famous lion emblem over the gates, a motif that remains in the castle today.[2] The connection with the lion would have resonated from a Christian perspective. The animal was regarded by them as being wild and uncontrollable; Templars were banned from hunting but an exception was made for the lion, given its fierce and deadly nature, a beast that 'goes around seeking who he can devour'.[3] There was no question of demolishing Crac; instead, Baybars put his engineers to work restoring it. He wrote a gloating letter to Hugh Revel, the Hospitaller Master, advising him to accept his fate and fall down before the feet of Baybars. Baybars had in fact enjoyed a narrow escape during the siege when two Nizari assassins sent to kill him were intercepted before they could launch their attack. Muslim accounts suggested that the understandably bitter Bohemond of Tripoli had put them up to it in collaboration with Najm al-Din.[4]

The Franks' position by now was weakening by the year. The Templars and Hospitallers both entered into peace treaties with Baybars, in return for which they were required to cede territory. It was like a death of a thousand cuts. On 12 May 1271, the fortress of Gibelacar (Akkar), close to Tripoli and about 20 miles from Crac, fell after a two-week siege and a nine-day bombardment. The castle was in the hands of a secular baron, Bohemond, rather than one of the military orders. The siege was not without its challenges for Baybars as Gibelacar's ridge-top position, surrounded as it was by wooded hills, was difficult for siege engines. One of Baybars' emirs was killed when praying outside his tent. But again, the end result was a triumph for Baybars, and once more the garrison was allowed to surrender and make its way to safety.[5] Another gloating letter to Bohemond followed, advising him to fly across the sea; otherwise, Baybars informed him, a set of chains had been especially prepared for him. But the chains could wait for now. Bohemond, increasingly powerless to resist, asked for a truce and this was agreed. It was to last for ten years and soon after delegates were sent to Tripoli with 3,000 *dirhams* to pay for the release of Muslim prisoners held there. Baybars then travelled to Gibelacar and Crac to inspect the work that had been undertaken to strengthen them. He had heard that there had been a new influx of troops into Acre. They were led by Edward, Prince of England, the great-nephew of the renowned Richard the Lionheart, who had his own aspirations for crusading glory. The loss of Crac was a blow to the security of Outremer and, according to some English observers, when the Prince landed after a stormy crossing of the Mediterranean even Acre was on the verge of being captured by Baybars.[6]

The Lord Edward

Very soon after Louis IX died in August 1270 and a truce was negotiated between the Crusaders and the emir of Tunis, Edward landed at Acre. He was the son and heir of King Henry III of England. He had already demonstrated in the civil wars between his father and Simon de Montfort that he was a ferocious warrior whilst possessing conventional piety; an ideal combination as far as a potential Crusader was concerned. He was disappointed when he arrived at Tunis to find that the fighting was at an end, but he determined to push on to Outremer to see if he could be of any use there. Edward would become famous as the *Malleus Scotorum*, 'Hammer of the Scots', King Edward I, for his ferocious but ultimately unsuccessful campaign against his northern neighbours. The great castles that ring the coast of North Wales like a scythe at the throat of the Principality are his eternal memorial. Their architecture betrays aspects of military design that have been borrowed from the East. The spectacular castle at Caernarfon, for example, has walls that look strikingly similar to those of the great city of Constantinople. Such similarities were entirely deliberate. Whilst the long-term impact of Edward on the Levant would be limited, the long-term impact of the Levant on him would be much more profound.

The Lord Edward, as he was known before he became King, had already honed his martial skills in the vicious civil war against Simon de Montfort, a conflict in which he effectively led the royalist forces to victory, a necessary task given the military inadequacies of his unmartial father. A suitable symbol for the ruthlessness of Edward towards his enemies, later to be infamously demonstrated in the hanging, drawing and quartering of the Scottish guerrilla leader William Wallace, was revealed when the body of Simon de Montfort was beheaded and his testicles cut off and stuffed in his mouth at the end of the decisive battle at Evesham in 1265: the dead man had been deliberately targeted by an assassination squad deputed to kill him. Evesham showed the dual sides of Edward; on the one hand, a formidable warrior, on the other someone who was capable of supreme ruthlessness even when judged by the standards of the time. He was certainly not a man to be crossed.[7]

Edward arrived in Acre on 9 May 1271 and was joined there by Hugh III of Cyprus; Edward's brother, Edmund of Lancaster, also arrived in September that year. Edward was accompanied by his wife,

Eleanor of Castile.[8] There were also others with him who would be inside Acre at the death two decades later: two Savoyards, Otho de Grandson and Jean de Grailly. This new influx of men did not however dissuade Baybars from visiting further havoc on the Franks and it was not a large force.[9] The most significant fortress held by the Teutonic Order was that at Montfort. Here they had set up their headquarters, not wishing to be in the shade of the Templars and Hospitallers in Acre. Montfort had already been attacked by Baybars in 1266 but on that occasion it managed to hold out. Baybars now returned accompanied by siege artillery, which quickly started to damage the walls. The castle had not originally been built primarily as a fortress and therefore was not as robust as some of the great military sites in the region; quite possibly the outer ward had never been completed. Baybars began to take the castle bit by bit and the defenders were forced to take up residence in the donjon as a place of last resort. Once more an honourable surrender was brokered and on 12 June the garrison walked out, though they were forced to leave their weapons and money behind them. This time, Baybars had no interest in hanging on to the castle and instead arranged for its total demolition. It was a bad start to Edward's mission and he was also shocked to find that Venetians in the city were trading food and military supplies freely with the 'Saracens'.[10]

Baybars then took his force to the walls of Acre, hoping to lure those inside into a rash foray where they could be ambushed. He did not however succeed in this objective. The defenders of Acre were primed to protect their city but were cowed by the size of the force outside the walls and did not contemplate offensive action. Baybars now came up with a far more ambitious plan. He put together a fleet to attack Cyprus, presumably hoping to force Hugh to return quickly from Acre to lead the defence of his island kingdom. Baybars' fleet was painted black to disguise them as Crusader ships and to complete the deception they were also to sail flying the sign of the cross. However, many of the ships ran aground on a reef and their crews were captured. Altogether about 1,800 men were taken prisoner. Some Muslim moralists ascribed this reverse to the blasphemous actions of the fleet when sailing under the sign of the cross. Hugh was buoyant when he received news of Baybars' failure and it was his turn this time to send the Sultan a gloating letter. Baybars responded with one of his own; castles were far more important to him, he said, and could not easily be replaced when lost, but it was easy to build new ships. As if to prove the point, he immediately issued orders for twenty new vessels to be constructed.

Later in the year there was a raid in the north of Syria launched by the Mongols with whom Edward had been communicating. As there was a simultaneous Frankish attack further south the suggestion was once more that the two parties were working in collaboration with each other. However, Abagha was half-hearted in the support he sent to complement Edward's raid and a rare opportunity to strike a major blow by the fledgling alliance was missed. Possibly he was more concerned with events elsewhere; Khurasan had been invaded by Chagatai Mongols in 1270 and Abagha had responded by sacking Bukhara in the following year. Convinced nevertheless of the Franks' duplicity, Baybars assembled a force to punish them but the winter weather put paid to his campaigning plans. The year ended on a diplomatic note. Baybars received a delegation from the emir of Tunis, which he felt paid him insufficient respect. He refused the gifts that they brought and chastised their master as a coward. He also received another delegation from Charles of Anjou, which then visited Acre.

The Franks of Acre, or more accurately Hugh III, were anxious by now for peace and negotiations were entered into with Baybars to bring this about. A *hudna* (truce) was finally agreed on 21 April 1272 and was to last for ten years, ten months, ten days and ten hours – such precise timescales reflecting Islamic law as this was the maximum allowable duration of a truce with 'infidels'. The Templars and Hospitallers were not directly party to the agreement and Baybars insisted that they should each take separate oaths to agree to the truce. He had seen too much of what he regarded as the duplicity of the military orders in the past to trust them without further assurances. The truce was marked in rather incongruous fashion with festivities at Acre during which Baybars took part in a jousting competition.

However, relations remained strained. A Mongol delegation was on its way to meet Baybars, travelling by ship, when it was captured by men from Marseille. With the delegation was a Muslim interpreter who had been sent by Baybars. Baybars demanded his release but the officials in Acre said that this could not be done as the captors were not their subjects but rather were answerable to Charles of Anjou; and as the capture had taken place at sea, and not in lands that formed part of the Kingdom of Jerusalem, they were powerless to intervene.

It was unwise to cross Baybars, who showed as much by threatening to close all his ports to traffic from Marseille. This predictably led to a climbdown as the trade that might otherwise be lost was a lucrative one.

For Baybars, Edward of England remained a potentially worrying opponent. Edward was energetic and strong-willed. From time to time he would take part in raids close to Acre but these created their own dangers. In one on the village of St George about 12 miles from the city, many Muslims were killed. However, it was a searing hot day and a number of the attacking force collapsed from exhaustion on the way back.[11] Like many Crusaders who had arrived from the West over the years, Edward was unhappy at the good relationships that were often maintained between Franks and Muslims in the region. This live-and-let-live attitude annoyed a man of his strong moral principles: he had come here to fight Muslims, not to trade with them. He on one occasion berated the Venetians for their business relationships with Muslims in Acre and sent a delegation to the *Ilkhan* Abagha, seeking an alliance with him against the Mamluks. The dream of a Christian-Mongol alliance continued to lure men on but there was not much substance behind such grand ideas.

Although his enthusiasm and military skills could not be doubted, Edward was more of an irritant than a threat to Baybars. He simply did not have enough men with him to tip the scales of power in the region. He led raids into the surrounding countryside that annoyed rather than worried the Sultan. These were not an unmitigated success. Many of Edward's men were cut down, not by Muslim swords but by disease. And the effects of an initially triumphant raid on Qāqūn, in which hundreds of Turcomans were killed and thousands of cattle captured, was immediately avenged when Edward's force, bloated by its spoils, was attacked by forces based at Ain Jalut whilst returning to Acre and badly cut up. Edward was not solely responsible for this attack. Hospitaller and Templar forces also took part and King Hugh was there with men from Acre and Cyprus. It was very much a case of one step forward and at least one back though.

Despite the limited success of Edward's efforts, Baybars was affronted that he had been so bold as to attack his territories. He decided that the prince must therefore be eliminated. To arrange for this outcome, he commissioned one of his officers, Ibn Shāwar, to hatch a plot. Ibn Shāwar sent a message to Edward saying that he and some of his men wished to convert to Christianity. Edward naively responded positively to the suggestion. Arrangements were therefore put in place for a group of Ibn Shāwar's men to journey to Acre so that suitable steps could be taken. Amongst their number was a Nizari assassin with a very specific target in mind.[12]

The assassin was taken on as Edward's attendant and, in true Nizari fashion, quickly earned the trust of his new master. In a repetition of tactics used by past assassins, to which intended targets should by now surely have become wise, he convinced Edward that he wished to be baptised. He also acted as a kind of double agent, passing on useful intelligence which Edward successfully utilised on occasion. As a result of this, Edward was seduced into dropping his guard. He gave orders that the attendant was to have open access to him at any time of the day or night. On 18 May 1272, Edward was relaxing in his apartment along with his wife. He lay on his bed, unwinding after the exertions of the day. He was casually dressed in just his undershirt and hose when the attendant sought admission along with an interpreter. Edward opened the door to him in person and the scene was transformed in an instant. Seeing that Edward was completely unprepared, the assassin charged at him with a knife, inflicting a deep gash to his hip. Edward however was in the prime of physical health and was a well-built, athletic figure (hence his nickname of 'Longshanks' – he was over 6 feet tall), well capable of looking after himself. He thumped the assassin on the temple, bringing him to the ground, temporarily stunned. Before he could recover himself, Edward had grabbed a knife of his own and killed him.

Nevertheless, Edward had been nicked by the knife and it was feared that the blade had been treated with poison. Legend has it that his life was saved only because his beautiful, dark-haired wife, Eleanor of Castile, attended him constantly and sucked out the poison from his wounds. It is a good story but much more likely the combination of Edward's physical robustness, his doctor's attentions and possibly the reality that the blade had not in fact been treated with poison at all enabled the stricken prince to survive.[13] Modern commentators tend to dismiss the tale of Eleanor's dramatic intervention (apart from anything else from a medical perspective it does not sound potentially very effective as a way of combating any poison). As one remarked, 'The reality of Edward's stay in the east was one of discomfort and frustration, not of romance.'[14] Baybars was quick to send a note to Edward, disclaiming all knowledge of the foul deed. Edward soon after returned home, with plenty of good stories to tell but little in the way of tangible long-term achievements to boast of. Men such as the Welsh prince, Llewelyn ap Gruffydd, or Scots like William Wallace and Robert Bruce, came to curse the day that Edward escaped from Baybars' assassin.

Edward returned west in October 1272 having achieved very little. A tower had been added to the defences of Acre that was sponsored by him and a small number of men that were left to form part of the garrison in the city were also paid for. It was whilst on his way back to England that Edward learned that his father, Henry III, had died. His country was not in a good place. Civil war had blighted England and the Welsh were threatening to prove troublesome. Edward's prize continental possessions were also at risk of attack from the French. Jerusalem remained important to the new king, but the Holy Land would have to wait before he could even start to think about leading a new crusade as he perhaps had intended to do when he sailed back home. He continued to offer moral support to Outremer and in the 1280s he would assume the role of senior statesman, pressurising the papacy and other warring parties in Italy to set aside their quarrels so that help to the Levant could be forthcoming, but he would never travel to the East again. There was though an interesting postscript to Edward's journey to Outremer. In his entourage in the East was supposedly a romantic writer called Rustichello of Pisa. In 1298, the same man was held as a prisoner in Genoa. He shared a cell with a Venetian who had clearly seen much of the world, far more indeed than any other Westerner alive. Fascinated, Rustichello offered to help his cellmate write up his notes; and so, by a happy quirk of fate, the adventures of Marco Polo were first committed to parchment.[15]

The Last Years of Baybars
With the fortunes of the Franks in terminal decline, Baybars could return to dealing with more dangerous opponents. A sizeable Mongol raid on the frontier fortress of al-Bīra on the Euphrates in December 1272 was driven back in a hard fight where Baybars' men had to swim their horses across the river before attacking. The Mongols had taken up a strong position behind palisades by a difficult ford. One of Baybars' lieutenants, Sayf al-Din Qalāwūn, again played an important part in winning the victory. The Mongols were thoroughly routed and their leader, Chinqar, killed – one account gives the credit

for his death to Kitbughā al-Mansuri, the former Mongol warrior and future Sultan. Al-Bīra was relieved and the Mongols fled, abandoning their siege engines in their hurry to escape. Baybars returned home in triumph. He gave lavish gifts to Qalāwūn to thank him for his part in the recent campaign. Qalāwūn had previously proved a loyal ally of Baybars, for example helping to defend him when plotters had tried to take his life; despite his formidable personality, Baybars – in common with most Mamluk Sultans – constantly had to be on his guard for potential conspirators. Fears of a renewed Crusader attack on Alexandria shortly after proved groundless, but Baybars now had an uprising in Nubia, to the south, to contend with. The Nubians were duly brought to book and a new ruler installed. The price of his throne was the ceding of a quarter of all Nubian territory to Egypt and payment of a crippling tribute thereafter. This proved much more difficult to deliver in practice than it was to agree to in theory.

In the meantime, the Mongols were still seeking an alliance with the West. The papal council which met at Lyons in 1274 received an unannounced visit from them. Some of the sixteen-strong Mongol delegation even underwent public baptism as a mark of their enthusiasm to embrace Christianity or, more likely, as a means of encouraging the West to embrace the Mongols as allies. With them was David of Ashby, formerly chaplain to Thomas Agni, one-time Bishop of Bethlehem and now Patriarch of Jerusalem. David had journeyed to Hūlegū in 1260 and spent much of the next fourteen years on and off with the Mongols and would have been an invaluable interlocutor for the delegation. He was said to have become a close confidant of the *Ilkhan;* the latter allegedly hinted to David that he was ripe for conversion to Christianity.[16]

During the last years of Baybars' life, that which remained of the Kingdom of Jerusalem was left in peace. What was left posed much less of a threat than it had once done, and the commercial advantages that Acre and the few other remaining Frankish possessions offered were worth the risk entailed in leaving them alone, even if the port had lost some of its commercial significance. In all probability, he continued to use spies he had in the Frankish camp to obtain useful information about the city, as he also did with regard to Armenia and the Mongols. There is sufficient evidence of Baybars' involvement in receiving news from what we might call his 'secret service' to suggest that it played a useful part in the development of his military strategy.

A network of informants inside enemy-occupied territory, variously called 'correspondents', 'possessors of information' or simply 'eyes', fed back information to the Sultan. A wide range of sources was available including Muslims who were living under the rule of the enemy, Bedouin, in the desert (although some of them proved of suspect reliability and could change sides from time to time), Mongol deserters and pilgrims passing through Syria to fulfil their *hajj* commitments.[17]

The reach of this spider's web of espionage was surprisingly extensive. It stretched for example to mainland Europe itself. Merchants travelling on Baybars' business were also enlisted to seek out useful items of information, invaluable given the complexities of European politics where competing power blocs sought out advantages over their rivals. Baybars turned this information to his advantage, skilfully playing off one party against another from a distance. Unsurprisingly, records of this spy network are limited but there are enough of them surviving to gain some insight into how it functioned. Information on who these secret agents were was strictly guarded and individual spies did not know the identity of their colleagues, which helped to ensure that they did not manipulate situations to their own personal advantage. When they reported back to Baybars, they were escorted into his presence hidden under a cloth to preserve their anonymity. To further ensure this, payments made to them were not listed in government accounting records.[18]

In addition to this spy network, Baybars also used various underhand methods to undermine his enemies. On several occasions he used what we might now call 'disinformation' or 'fake news' to destabilise them. One victim in the 1260s was a man called al-Zayn al-Hāfizi who had fled with the Mongols after Ain Jalut. Baybars had false rumours spread about him that were so successful that ultimately Hūlegū ordered the execution of him and his family. There are also accounts that Baybars repeated the trick in the 1270s, this time the victim being the Nestorian Catholicos in Baghdad, though the evidence for this is thin. Stories of suspected treachery by Muslims living in Mongol territory are frequent enough to raise the suspicion that disinformation was a widely used stratagem on the Sultan's part, though there is also enough to demonstrate that the Mongols used the same tactics as well. Baybars also sought to break the Georgians definitively away from the Mongol cause, though with limited success.

Baybars now had other distractions to occupy him rather than Acre. Het'um of Armenia was gone (tired and ageing, he had abdicated and entered a monastery to see out his remaining days, though he only survived for a year after doing so) and his successor, Leon II, had proved far from reliable in his obligations towards Baybars. The tribute that Het'um had paid was no longer forthcoming and caravans of Muslim traders were being attacked. Raids had been launched from Armenia into Syria for many years, further stirring up the hornets' nest. This was foolish behaviour of the most dangerous kind, especially as the Armenian port of Ayās was booming as the main *entrepot* to the region now that Antioch had been neutralised. War duly followed in 1275. Baybars led his army out from Egypt, adding more men to his forces when he arrived in Damascus. A diversionary attack was launched to keep the Mongols occupied so that they could not intervene on the part of the Armenians. Baybars then marched his men through the Taurus Mountains and up to the Armenian city of Sis, which was taken. The citadel there held out however, as Baybars had no heavy siege equipment with him. In fact, this was more of a punitive expedition against the Armenians for their misbehaviour rather than an all-out conquest. Leon, the Armenian king, was conspicuous by his absence and showed no desire to intervene.

The end of Ramadan was marked in the Armenian King's palace in Sis. The country round about was put to the sword and the torch. It was rather like Alexander the Great's sojourn at the Persian capital of Persepolis a millennium and a half previously; when Baybars departed from Sis to return south, he left a flaming wreck in his wake. The poorly advised Leon was incapable of making any meaningful intervention and had to watch from a safe distance whilst his kingdom was ransacked. As the Templar of Tyre remarked of Baybars' campaign, 'He ranged about and destroyed things and put everyone he encountered to the sword.'[19] On his way back to Egypt, Baybars gave the Franks a timely reminder that he had not forgotten them. The castle of Cursat remained in Frankish hands as part of an agreement that Baybars had made with the Patriarch of Antioch. It had been used as a bolthole for the Patriarch in times of trouble since it had first been acquired by his predecessors in the twelfth century. For this reason, it was sometimes called 'Castrum Patriarchae' – 'The Patriarch's Castle'. The castle survived the loss of Antioch in 1268, having been strengthened a decade or so earlier. Baybars had tried to take it at the time but was unsuccessful.

A deal had been struck whereby the castellan of Cursat was to share the revenues raised from the territories around it with the Muslims. Its strategic importance was anyway much diminished as it was now completely isolated from other Frankish territory. Baybars now accused its garrison of colluding with the Mongols and selling alcohol to his troops in defiance of his own pious prohibitions. After attempts to take Cursat by trickery failed, it was attacked and taken on 14 November 1275. Once more, the garrison surrendered and was allowed to leave unhindered. Whilst Baybars could be ruthless on occasion, as far as some of the Franks were concerned he also saw the merit in being lenient so that other garrisons might be encouraged to seek terms in the future when the opportunity arose.

With Armenia effectively neutralised, Baybars took the fight to the Seljuk Sultanate of Rüm in Asia Minor. This was in the pocket of the Mongols, who had conquered it and imposed a governor on the territory several decades earlier. Since the government of Hülegü, Mongol intervention in the Seljuk state was much more proactive than in earlier times and there was a marked increase in the numbers of their men there. Given Rüm's position adjacent to Syria, it posed an ongoing threat to Baybars' lands. By taking it, other advantages would also accrue to the Sultan. He would effectively isolate Armenia and would also be able to present himself as a protector of the Muslim Seljuk population. Baybars duly set out from Cairo with an army in February 1277, passing through Damascus and then picking up more troops elsewhere in Syria. By 13 April, his army was pushing through a pass in the Taurus Mountains known as the Aqcha Darband ('the Whitish Defile'). Two days later, his vanguard clashed with and defeated a Mongol contingent 3,000 strong, taking some prisoners and forcing the remainder to flee. Two days after this, the main body of Baybars' army had the full force of the enemy in its sights on the plain of Elbistan (also known as Abulustayn) in the south-eastern margins of Asia Minor.

There were eleven Mongol squadrons, each with about 1,000 men, and a Georgian contingent 3,000 strong: in other words, a total Mongol force of around 14,000 men. There were also Seljuk troops there with them but they played no part in the battle, possibly because the Mongol command did not trust them to fight against fellow Muslims. Initial reports suggested that not long before there had been 30,000 men in the Mongol army in Rüm, so either some of them were elsewhere and not on the battlefield or the original estimate of the army's size was wrong. Baybars probably enjoyed a significant numerical advantage over the Mongols in any event. Nor was this the only factor in his favour. It has been persuasively argued that the Mamluks also enjoyed superior firepower, their archers being able to outshoot their Mongol counterparts comfortably, and that the Mamluks were much better armoured than their opponents.[20]

A hard fight followed. At the start of the battle, the left wing of the Mongol army launched themselves at the centre of Baybars' force, which began to give way. Some of the Mamluk standard-bearers, the *sanjaqiyya*, were overwhelmed by this frenzied first charge. Inspired by this initial success, the Mongols surged onwards, seeking to push home their advantage. The right wing of Baybars' army then came under attack whilst the left was also engaged by the Mongols. The situation was now concerning for Baybars, but at this point his reserve, under the command of the Ayyubid prince of Hama, was called in. This started to swing the balance the other way and the Mongols were gradually forced back and finally overwhelmed. At the end of the battle, the Mamluks triumphed: 7,000 Mongol troops lay dead on the battlefield, having fought bravely and determinedly and finally in many cases resolving to die fighting rather than escape. Nevertheless, it was a crushing victory for Baybars; crushing but not decisive.[21]

The reality was that the Mongols and the Mamluks were now too finely balanced in the region for one side to overwhelm the other. The Mongols were for the time being safe in Asia Minor, as were the Mamluks in Syria. Baybars, with insufficient men and supplies to overwhelm Rüm, was back in Damascus on 10 June and there were rumours of an imminent counter-attack into Syria by Abagha, seeking vengeance for the reverse suffered at Elbistan. However, they came to nothing. Abagha instead went to Rüm to find out what had gone wrong there. He was joined by a deserter from Baybars, Aybeg al-Shaykhi. He briefed against the leading official in the region, the Pervaneh, and convinced Abagha that there were many more Mamluk troops in Syria than there probably were, thereby dissuading him from attacking. In fact, the information that he passed on seems to have benefitted Baybars more than it did Abagha, creating a very strong impression that he had been deliberately planted by the Sultan and that he was in reality not a deserter from his cause at all.

As a result of his briefing, and that of Mongol generals in Rüm too, the Pervaneh was duly suspected of being disloyal to the Mongol cause in the recent events, a suspicion that he ultimately paid for with his life.[22] The Pervaneh, who was a Persian by birth, had managed for a time to keep the Seljuks in line, but it had been a tricky task which at one stage involved the execution of their ruler, Rukn al-Din. He had indeed negotiated secretly with Baybars, fearing for his life at the hands of Abagha's younger brother and representative in Rüm, Ejei, but these discussions had petered out and the double game he had been playing ultimately had fatal consequences for him. When it came to the crunch, he had refused to support Baybars. Thousands of Seljuks were also put to death in the aftermath of Baybars' campaign as the Mongols exacted brutal retribution for what they saw as an act of rebellion. The Armenian historian known as Het'um (not be confused with kings of the same name) even suggested that the flesh of the Pervaneh was fed to some of the vengeful Mongol generals who indulged themselves in a macabre celebratory feast where he was the main course.

But no man is immortal, and the clock was ticking down for Baybars. On 17 June 1277, he helped himself to a generous portion of *koumiss*, fermented mare's milk, which was a personal favourite. The day after, he was unwell. He had a slight fever which an emetic failed to cure. The fever instead grew more serious. Attempts by his doctors to deal with his illness were unsuccessful and diarrhoea followed. Then Baybars started to haemorrhage and the fever now burned out of control. On 1 July, shortly after noon prayers, the Sultan expired. The scourge of the Franks – and a few others too – was no more. Stories developed to explain away his death. Poison was one suggestion, and it is by no means inconceivable that this was true. A Mamluk ruler's position was always an insecure one, even if he were a strongman like Baybars. Several accounts suggested that he accidentally drank from a cup in which poison had been administered at his command to al-Qahir 'Abd al-Malik, an Ayyubid prince whose loyalty he suspected. A more conventional explanation is that Baybars died of a form of dysentery. The Sultan, who was a great believer in astrology, had been concerned when early that year an astrologer had foretold that a great king was destined to die in the near future.[23]

There is one compelling statistic that could be quoted as a summary of Baybars' life. He was involved in nine campaigns against the Mongols, five against the Armenians, three against the Nizaris and twenty-one against the Franks.[24] He had been the latter's most implacable enemy, carrying on – consciously or not – the work started by Saladin. He was effectively the man who wrote Outremer's death warrant. No wonder he was awarded the title of Abu al-Futuh or 'Father of Conquest'. He was buried in the Az-Zahiriyah Library in Damascus that he himself had founded. Like Saladin, the basis of his power initially had been in Egypt but to both of them Damascus was the greatest prize and the most significant status symbol. Saladin, too, was buried in Damascus, in the magnificent Umayyad Mosque, which inspired some of the decoration of the library.

Baybars may have been ruthless, but his ruthlessness should be judged in the context of his time, not ours. Violence was the preserve of Franks and Mongols as well as Mamluks. Moral judgements on historical figures are anyway complicated but there can be no doubting his effectiveness. He succeeded in keeping Syria and Egypt as a united entity, although it threatened to fracture from time to time. In the process he laid the foundations for a Mamluk dynasty that would remain the predominant power in the region until the rise of the Ottomans. He also defended the borders of his territory in a way that kept the Mongols at bay; and by now, they were his main threat and not the Franks. This was recognised in an inscription carved on a curved sword he owned, now in the Khalili Collection in London: 'Glory to our Lord, the Sultan al-Malik, the Just, the Learned, the Defender of the Faith, the Warrior of the Frontiers ... al-Zahir Baybars, the Associate of the Commander of the Faithful, may God make his victories glorious'. He neutralised both the Armenians and the Franks and made them both largely an irrelevance to the long-term future of the region. The fate of the latter was now hanging in the balance. The Greek goddess Nemesis sometimes took generations to deliver retribution. Baybars did not live to see the final act of the drawn-out demise of Outremer, but he had certainly played a key role in the drama. By the time he departed, the tragic finale had in effect already been drafted.

9

The Civil War of Christendom

'If I forget thee o Jerusalem, let my right hand forget her cunning...'
Teobaldo Visconti in his last sermon in
Acre before becoming Pope Gregory X

Crusades to Outremer: More Frustrated Hopes
There was one significant event at Acre in 1271 which had a potentially invigorating impact on the crusading movement. Currently in the city was Teobaldo Visconti, who had been prominent in preaching the crusade in the 1240s at the instigation of Pope Innocent IV. He was a well-connected cleric who included among his associates the revered Thomas Aquinas. He had subsequently been made archdeacon of Liège and then journeyed to England on papal orders in 1265 where he was soon on good terms with Prince Edward. He journeyed out to Outremer in Edward's company on his crusade. Pope Clement IV died in 1268 and an extraordinarily extended papal election followed; in fact, it went on so long that it led to a change in the rules for such events. The hiatus was only ended in 1271 with the election of Visconti as the new pontiff. He took the papal name of Gregory X. When he preached his final sermon in Acre before leaving for Rome, he referred poignantly to the words of Psalm 137: 'If I forget thee o Jerusalem, let my right hand forget her cunning.'

Whilst still in Acre, Visconti played host to a delegation of merchants from Venice. They had first arrived there in 1269 but found that the omens were inauspicious for a mission further east. They had already spent time at the court of Kublai Khan a few years before and they had been instructed by him to later return with up to

100 Christian preachers; but as the papal throne was currently vacant Visconti suggested that they should wait until it was reoccupied. They therefore went back to Italy but returned to Acre in 1271. This time, the members of the mission felt that they could wait no longer – the new pope had at the time still not been elected – but they had not long left Acre when the news of Visconti's election meant that they went back to the city once more to seek out further instructions. As the new pope was actually still in Acre, on this occasion their timing could not have been better. They were told to set out again, now accompanied by two Dominican friars – though hugely short of the 100 demanded by Kublai Khan – who, as it proved, did not have the required stamina to stay with their expedition for long; in fact, they were in Armenia when Baybars ransacked it and were scared off going any further as a result. Nevertheless, the two brothers, Niccolò and Maffeo Polo, set out for their appointment with destiny without them. This time they were accompanied by a teenaged adventurer named Marco, the son of Niccolò and nephew of Maffeo. It would take three-and-a-half-years to reach Kublai's court. It would be well over two decades before Marco returned to the West and when he finally arrived back in Venice members of his own family did not recognise him.[1]

Gregory, as Visconti now officially became, was in no hurry to return to Europe from Acre but when he did so, he did what he could to rekindle the dying embers of the crusading fire. However, he was fighting in a lost cause. Crusades to the Levant were increasingly discredited; the last two major expeditions to Egypt had been fiascos. To make it worse, they had been very expensive fiascos in terms of human lives and money. If God had ordained that the First Crusade should succeed, then He had just as surely given up on the Crusader project now. It seemed to some that another expedition east would be throwing bad money after good. The concept of crusading to Outremer had lost its ability to move large crowds to respond to crusade recruitment initiatives so much that in around 1267 Humbert of Romans, a leading Dominican theologian, had written *De praedicatione crucis* ('Preaching the Cross'), which was essentially an instruction manual for how preachers should get their message across when faced with an apathetic audience. Hopes were raised that the Council of Lyons, held in 1274, would stoke the flames again but it was ultimately, in crusading terms, a damp squib. It also led to criticism of the papacy in some quarters as money that was ostensibly raised for a crusade in the Holy Land as a result of the Council's decisions was spent on Italian wars instead, though much of this happened after Gregory's death. There were other cases of funds raised for support to Outremer being spent for different purposes and several kings of England and France would at times protest at such monetary diversions.[2] A Dominican from Acre, William of Tripoli, had spoken at the Council urging that the Church should try to convert Muslims rather than defeat them, an insight into how perspectives might vary between East and West.[3] Despite hopes that the kings of Europe might settle their differences and unite in a new crusading enterprise, only one of them, the ageing James I of Aragon, presented himself. Much advice was given to Gregory about how to regain Outremer leading to a series of advisory comments from many quarters that became known as 'recovery treatises' and money was collected to fund such a crusade from Greece to Greenland; but these considerations led to no decisive action in practice.[4]

In the meantime, natural attrition was taking its toll on those in Outremer. Thomas Bérard, the long-serving Master of the Temple, died in 1273. His place was taken by William of Beaujeu. William was related to the king of France, which was enough on its own to suggest that his Order would remain supportive of the French crown. William would remain at the forefront of affairs until 1291 and the fall of Acre; indeed, his own end was intimately entwined with that of the city. He had great experience of Templar affairs in Western Europe, having been particularly active in France, England and Spain, and this made him a good candidate for the post of Master, as the support of the great West European powers was crucial to the survival of Outremer.

The Mongols were still hopeful of an alliance with the West. Another delegation visited Europe in 1276–77. It was headed by two brothers, James and John of Vassalli. They met Philip III of France and Edward I of England. They came with letters of support from Leon of Armenia, whose colours were still firmly nailed to the Mongol mast.[5] David of Ashby had already been to Edward's court in 1275. These approaches achieved little in practical terms. The Vassallis' delegation also journeyed to the papal court of John XXI, who was encouraged enough by requests for religious advisors to be sent to the Mongol court to despatch a Franciscan mission to China.

The papacy was at the time traversing stormy waters; 1276 had been a year of extraordinary goings-on when the position of pope appeared to be the deadliest of poisoned chalices. Gregory X, who wished so much to help Outremer, died, probably a disappointed man, on 10 January. He had tried his best to honour the sentiment of his farewell sermon in Acre but it was becoming an impossible job. Interest in Outremer was in decline and he was just one on a diminishing list of those who were seriously interested in another expensive and probably futile expedition to the Levant. Even though crusades there continued to be discussed for several decades more, other priorities always intervened. Gregory was soon followed to the grave by Innocent V – elected on 21 January, died 26 June – and Hadrian V – elected on 11 July and died on 18 August. John XXI would prove to be a man of comparative staying power, managing to survive until 12/14 May 1277 (accounts slightly differ) when, in a bizarre twist of fate, the room in which he was studying collapsed, burying him in rubble. He died about a week later. The highly unusual nature of his demise may have fuelled rumours that God was unhappy with him, for some said that he was a necromancer. To perfectly encapsulate the confusion of these bewildering times for the Holy See, John XXI was actually only the twentieth pope to bear that name.[6]

During his short pontificate John also tried to raise interest in another crusade to Outremer, though again not much came of it. He probably fell for a con trick on the part of the Mongol delegation who wished to ingratiate themselves with him and overemphasised the Mongols' ripeness for conversion as part of a well-conceived plan. When the delegation returned to Abagha soon after, it was in the company of representatives of Charles of Anjou who had just purchased a claim to the Kingdom of Jerusalem. Charles needed allies in the region and the Mongols seemed to fit the bill; but once again little came of these optimistic aspirations. The paramount reason for this was that Christendom was now so focused on its internal debates that the future of crusading to the Levant was a secondary matter. With many of the powers inside Europe essentially involved in plotting or even fighting against each other, Christendom set out on a kind of civil war at a moment when the hugely vulnerable Frankish territories in Outremer were faced with a greater threat than ever before.

Infighting in Tripoli

Whilst Tripoli and Antioch had initially been separate Crusader states in the Levant, the ruling line of the former had died out in 1187 and by 1219 the two had come under unified rule.[7]

The already much-reduced status of what was left of the principality of Antioch was further weakened in 1275 with the death of Bohemond VI and his replacement by his son, who became Count Bohemond VII (originality in naming their offspring was not a strong point of the rulers of Antioch). Bohemond VII was at the time under the protection of his uncle, King Leon of Armenia. The arrival of a young heir on the scene often presaged a period of instability in the medieval period and in this specific case it did nothing to improve the position of the principality, which was by now largely reduced to an area centred around Tripoli. Within a year, those risks had transformed into real issues. Young Bohemond's regent was his mother, Sibylla, and she brought in Bartholomew, Bishop of Tortosa, to govern the city on the count's behalf. He was deeply unpopular with the knightly class there and tensions quickly rose to boiling point.

It was a rather prosaic and grubby incident that brought matters to a head. The issue revolved around who should marry a rich heiress in the county of Tripoli, the daughter of a local noble, Hugh Saloman. It was initially agreed that she would marry John, the brother of Guy of Ibelin, the lord of Jubail (its Arabic name, known in antiquity as Byblos and to the Franks as Gibelet). Guy was descended from the Genoese Embriaco family. His marriage alliances suggest that he was an ambitious man, as he himself was married to Margaret, the daughter of the now dead Julian of Sidon. The Templar of Tyre describes Guy in some detail as 'an exceedingly handsome man with a great presence ... big and fair-limbed and blond and blue-eyed and of a lively colour, and valiant and hardy. But he was a bit on the stout side, and wilful.'[8]

That wilfulness was about to reveal itself. Guy requested permission from Bohemond, now back in Tripoli, for his brother John to marry the heiress and this was initially given. However, the Bishop of Tortosa had nephews and he intervened so that one of them could be given the great prize instead. Bohemond then changed his mind, but in Guy's opinion it was too late to do so. He proceeded with the plans for the marriage at once so that it was a *fait accompli*. Bohemond and the bishop were furious – but their fury prompted Guy to journey to Acre and strengthen his position by becoming a secular Templar knight, a *confrere,* buying him the powerful support of the order in any future dispute. He and William of Beaujeu were on good terms and Guy returned to Jubail confident of help, should it be needed. It was as well that he did so as open conflict now loomed.

Guy now took the heiress's land by force. Bohemond in response summoned him to Tripoli to explain himself. Instead, Guy went to Acre and came back with thirty Templar knights who proceeded to raid Bohemond's lands. Bohemond then ordered that the house of the Templars in Tripoli and a nearby estate of theirs should be destroyed. This led to a further escalation and William of Beaujeu came up to Tripoli with a sizeable force that laid siege to the city. This was unsuccessful as the defenders refused to be drawn out and stayed behind their protective walls, but several tit-for-tat actions followed. Eventually Bohemond counter-attacked against Jubail itself, which had a venerable old castle (one of the earliest Crusader castles in Outremer) with a strong stone keep and square corner towers in the Byzantine style. But in the end his force was defeated in battle. A number of important supporters of Bohemond were killed including Balian of Sidon, the late Julian's son and a cousin of the Prince, who suffocated whilst trying to remove his armour. Ultimately the conflict between Jubail and Tripoli petered out and a truce was agreed.[9] This would not stand the test of time.

Outremer continued to be a battleground by proxy for what was happening in Europe, and in Italy in particular. When he bought the claim to be King of Jerusalem from Maria of Antioch in 1277, Charles of Anjou sent Roger of San Severino east to be his *bailli* (his personal representative) in Acre. Charles now gloried in the grandiloquent title of King of Jerusalem, King of Sicily and Albania, Count of Anjou, Provence, Forcalquier and Maine, Regent of Achaea, Overlord of Tunis and Senator of Rome; those who know nothing else about Charles can identify his sense of bloated ambition by this unwieldy nomenclature alone. Roger arrived in Outremer in June with six galleys and a letter from the pope (by now Nicholas III, though it had been signed by John XXI before his untimely demise the month before).[10]

The High Court of the Kingdom of Jerusalem recognised Charles's claim to be king, as did Sidon and the Templars. Hugh of Cyprus, another claimant, had left the city over six months before, frustrated beyond measure at the inability of the various factions in Acre to work together. But Tyre and Beirut continued to recognise Hugh (who, potentially confusingly, was simultaneously Hugh I of Jerusalem and Hugh III of Cyprus). Tyre had been given to the Montfort family by the late King of Cyprus, Henry I. Hugh was no charismatic leader of men. He had been heavy-handed in his actions and alienated a number of would-be supporters as a result. When the somewhat tragic Bohemond VI died in 1275, Hugh sought to be made the legal guardian of his son and heir, Bohemond VII, though without success. He also adopted underhand tactics to acquire Tyre directly for himself, though when the chance eventually came to claim it in 1283 he did not have the funds to seal the deal.[11] The Templar of Tyre, who, given his connections to the French cause, may not be unbiased in his views, accuses Hugh of 'abandoning' Acre and going back to Cyprus, claiming that it was ungovernable because of the actions of the Templars and Hospitallers; but he then suggests that in reality it was the fact that Maria of Antioch had transferred her claim to Charles of Anjou that prompted him to leave, not wishing to be humiliated in Acre.

The cessation of hostilities between Tripoli and Guy of Ibelin and the Templars proved to be only temporary. When the truce expired in 1279, the Templars were soon on the warpath again. William of Beaujeu sent thirteen galleys to attack Tripoli, and there was a skirmish in which several men were killed. But though the Templars won this scrap their fleet was then scattered in a storm. Three ships ran aground, but the men onboard managed to escape. In retaliation, Bohemond raided Sidon. King Hugh also appeared at Tyre, hoping to push his claim to Acre but when he was rebuffed by the Templars he went back to Cyprus, destroying one of their properties in Limassol and confiscating their belongings in a fit of pique in response.

Qalāwūn Takes Control

Christian Outremer was not the only disunited polity in the region. On the death of Baybars in 1277, his initial replacement was Al-Sa'id Nasir al-Din Berke Khan (Baraka), his son. However, it was a situation that others were unhappy with. He ordered the advancement of his own Mamluks and potential opponents from the old regime were purged. One potential rival, Qalāwūn, was removed temporarily from the scene by despatching him with an army to attack Tarsus in Cilicia. The move backfired. Baraka made too many powerful internal enemies and they were soon plotting to replace him. He was removed from power in 1279 and sent to the grim fortress at Karak, on the edge of the Jordanian desert where it stood as a forbidding sentinel watching over the road between Damascus and Cairo. He died there in March 1280. Another son of Baybars, Sulamish, then took his place but as he was only seven years of age he was only ever likely to be a puppet ruler. The power now resided in others, especially Qalāwūn who became Sulamish's *Atabeg* (guardian). Soon after, all pretence was dropped and Sulamish too was deposed and also sent off to Karak. During his lifetime, Baybars had come to rely on the emir Qalāwūn. The highly experienced emir was now declared Sultan, taking the title of al-Malik al-Mansur. He was around sixty years of age, not young for such a role. He had been renowned when younger for his handsome looks. He had also generally managed to retain the trust of Baybars, no mean feat in itself.

The new Sultan did not have to look far for problems. There were internal opponents to deal with such as Sunqur al-Ashkar in Damascus, who rebelled against the new regime and even sought the support of the Mongols and for a time had the backing of other Muslim strongmen in Syria. The Bedouin in the desert were also proving truculent. Despite the internecine squabbles besetting Outremer, the Mongols still hoped to profit from an alliance with the Franks. Bohemond VII, Count of now just Tripoli rather than Antioch, was urged to cooperate with a raid in 1281, as was King Hugh III of Cyprus; but little was achieved in practice. Initially, the Mongols attacked the region of Aleppo, Hama and Homs, inflicting a good deal of damage there. The city of Aleppo was looted for several days and the great mosque there was torched. They were supported by men from Armenia. In response, Qalāwūn – whose spy network was working well and had given him advanced warning – led a large army up from Cairo to Homs. The Templar of Tyre describes it as a massive force with 80,000 cavalry and 100,000 infantry, and although this is surely an exaggeration it can nevertheless be assumed that this was a large army.

It was whilst he was near Acre that Qalāwūn got wind of a plot to eliminate him. He had negotiated a truce (*hudna*) for ten years and ten months with the Franks. This rolled forward an existing similar arrangement that had been made with Baybars for another decade and suited both parties' purposes at the time. This was despite the fact that just a year before Hospitallers from the city had worked in conjunction with a Mongol raid by attacking Marqab. Bohemond VII of Tripoli was also party to a similar *hudna*, though in his case it would later prove to be of limited use. Islam pragmatically allowed such temporary truces if the religion gained an advantage from it. But there were hostile opponents within Qalāwūn's own camp who wrote in secret to the Franks, urging them to reject the truce as the

Sultan was about to be overthrown. However, once more Qalāwūn's spy network was on top form and he soon received news from some of them inside Acre of the plans to depose him. He reacted vigorously. A bloodbath followed in which a number of those who had sought to betray him were executed, though a few managed to escape. Satisfied that the plot had been nipped in the bud, Qalāwūn moved on to Damascus to reinforce his rule over Syria.

The plot provided compelling evidence that all was not well in the Mamluk Sultanate. There were plenty of other items to support this general impression. Qalāwūn had after all usurped the throne from Baybars' son Baraka. Baraka had been exiled to the grim fortress of Karak where he soon after died, according to some accounts as a result of a convenient polo accident. Further, senior Mamluks loyal to Baybars had been purged and replaced by Qalāwūn's own cadre. In common with many new Sultans, Qalāwūn had his own preferred group of Mamluks, the *Burjiyya* – named after the citadel ('Burj') in Cairo – and wherever he could he replaced the old *Bahriyya* with men from this group of supporters. Such Stalinist-style manoeuvres inevitably compromised the fighting power of the Mamluk army, as a good deal of military experience was lost. There is also evidence that the amount of training provided to the Mamluks reduced significantly at around this time.

To compound the risk, the Mongols were still a powerful threat. They had recently sent a deputation to Acre, telling the authorities there of plans to attack Syria and urging the Franks to support them. Geoffrey, Bishop of Hebron, wrote a letter to Edward I of England dated 5 October 1280 telling of the expected arrival of a force of 50,000 cavalry plus additional infantry. Despite the approach, it appears that the Franks did not take advantage of the offer, perhaps remembering how they had been let down a decade before. The Mongols pushed on regardless, sending an army into Rūm. In August 1281, a Mongol reconnaissance party was attacked by a Mamluk patrol. It was driven off and one of the Mongol officers with it was captured and taken before Qalāwūn in Damascus on 1 September. When questioned he confirmed that a Mongol army around 80,000 strong was planning to attack Syria in October.

A major confrontation resulted. The Mongols were led by Mengü Temūr, brother of Abagha – for some unknown reason, Abagha was close by but remained on the other side of the Euphrates. Mengü Temūr was young, and contemporary sources suggest that his command was nominal and tactical decisions were left to more experienced generals accompanying him. A Mongol deserter reached the Sultan before the battle, revealing Mengū Temūr's battle plans and the size of the enemy's army.[12] Qalāwūn wanted to take up a defensive position around Damascus but some of his senior commanders argued that northern Syria must not be abandoned and that they should be more aggressive in their response. They won the argument – further suggesting that the Sultan was not yet secure in his position – and the Mamluk army duly advanced.

The Mongol army moved south from Hama over such a wide front – perhaps 24 km (15 miles) across – that it was difficult to maintain its cohesion; possibly the difficulty of obtaining suitable fodder for so many horses was again creating problems given the unhelpful local environment. Again, it contained Armenian and Georgian as well as Mongol elements. Battle was joined on the morning of Thursday 29 October 1281 close to Homs. It took place over such an extended area that it could be considered to be two battles that were only loosely connected. In the west, the Mongol right smashed into the Mamluk left and broke it apart. The Mongols chased it for miles, exuberant in victory. They eventually stopped, sated with their plunder and their killing, and waited for the rest of their army to join them. They rested by a lake, almost as if preparing themselves for a celebratory picnic. Some of the defeated Mamluks made it back to Damascus and a few even to Egypt with news of the reverse they had suffered.

Matters had gone rather differently elsewhere, however. The Mongol left fell on the Mamluk right and initially pushed it back. Many Muslim warriors fell in the initial stages of this part of the action. Despite this, the men there grimly held firm and the Mongol attacks started to lose their momentum. Surviving accounts suggest that the Bedouin under Īsā ibn Muhannā, who had only recently thrown in his lot with Qalāwūn, intervened at a decisive moment, possibly attacking the Mongol flank or alternatively the baggage. This created panic in the Mongol ranks. Then something happened to Mengū Temūr; in a number of accounts he was wounded, in others he panicked – it is probable that both things happened. This seems to have unnerved the Mongols. Some of them dismounted to fight to the death whilst others escorted their young leader from the field.

After a while, the Mongol right grew alarmed when the rest of the army did not join them. Returning to the battlefield they realised with horror the disastrous truth. They initially avoided the Mamluks without undue loss and indeed almost stumbled on a practically unguarded Qalāwūn, most of whose troops had rushed off in pursuit of their vanquished enemy. Fortunately for the Sultan, they did not see him and they moved on. As this still significant remnant of the Mongol army retreated, they fell prey to remorseless attacks. Even the local population, who had suffered badly at their hands in the past, joined in, exacting bloody retribution in retaliation for the outrages committed against them. So bad did things become that Georgian and Mongol elements in the army turned on each other. The nightmare continued when the Euphrates was reached. Many drowned attempting to get across whilst others were burned out of the reed beds where they had sought refuge and were slaughtered wholesale when they were flushed out. The King of Armenia was among the unhappy refugees; his forces were so badly cut up by Turcomans on their return that only thirty horsemen made it back home with him.[13]

The lust for revenge on the part of the local inhabitants was understandable. It is easy to forget how awful these years were for those caught up in the fighting that scarred the geopolitical landscape of the region. The Muslim chronicler Rashid al-Din wrote of how 'the entire population of some provinces, because they were frontier regions and were traversed by armies, was either killed or fled' and of how many lands and 'most of the cities on this and the other side of the Euphrates, were completely uncultivated and abandoned'.[14] These images of ghost towns make a deep impression; formerly bustling territories in Rüm and Syria were little more than cities of the dead. Many in Outremer would soon be joining them. Mongol attacks on Syria eventually ran out of steam and ended in failure. A variety of reasons have been suggested for their ultimate lack of success including the increasing strengthening of the Mamluk war machine, Baybars' dynamic leadership, which retained an influence even after his death, the morale of the Mamluks, which was buoyed by continuing success, dynastic wars between competing Mongol powers and the failure of the Mongols to build alliances with the West.[15]

Qalāwūn noted the involvement of the Franks in recent activities, though little was achieved, and marked them out for future retribution. Whilst on their own they may have been able to achieve little, their nuisance value, both as a launch pad for future crusades from the West and as potential Mongol allies in the region, still gave them an influential position. When Abagha died on 1 April 1282, his throne was taken by his brother, Tegüder. He converted to Islam, taking the name of Ahmad. He then wrote to Qalāwūn, seeking his submission. He argued that now he was a Muslim, there was no reason for Qalāwūn to resist him. This suggests that Tegüder/Ahmad's conversion was a matter of expediency rather than conviction, just as we should surely assume that Mongol delegations who opted to be baptised as Christians were also inspired by ulterior motives. Because the Mongols were not religious zealots, they had a flexibility of conscience which could be most useful on occasion. Whatever their reasons, they were taken out of the equation for the time being. They would not return to Syria in force for two decades, and when they eventually did so, Outremer would no longer exist.

The Franks of Outremer still seemed oblivious to the extent of the threat facing them from a resurgent Egypt and carried on their petty squabbling regardless. The matter of Tripoli was about to reach a violent conclusion. Guy of Ibelin, the lord of Jubail, had not given up in his efforts against Bohemond. On 12 January 1282, he made his way to the city with a force of about 500, including two of his brothers and a cousin, William Porcelet (which rather wonderfully translates as 'Piglet'). He planned to launch a surprise attack and to this end made his way to the headquarters of the Temple there. But the coup had been poorly planned and the commander in Tripoli, Brother Reddecouer (sometimes translated as Roderick), was absent.

Guy planned to attack the palace of Bohemond in Tripoli but news of this quickly leaked out. The alarm was raised and Guy went to the Hospital of St John where he locked himself up in a tower. The raid quickly disintegrated into a fiasco. Bohemond, roused from his sleep by warnings of an imminent attack, led up a force that laid siege to the tower. A deal was broached at the instigation of the Hospitallers by which Guy and his men would give themselves up. They were to be locked up for five years, after which time they would be released. The men duly surrendered but then Bohemond renaged on the deal. With Guy were a number of Genoese and other 'foreigners'; they were all blinded. Guy's fate was worse; with his brothers and several of his main supporters he was incarcerated at Nephin (Enfeh in Lebanon), where they were starved to death. Beirut shortly afterwards fell to Bohemond, whose position seemed to be greatly improved as a result. However, this was soon shown to be a hollow victory.

The disunited state of Outremer was perfectly summed up by the range of responses to the removal of Guy from the scene. Members of the Pisan faction in Acre were delighted and registered their joy in a time-honoured way recognised the world over: they threw a party. Trumpets rang out and other musical instruments joined them in cacophonous celebration. A man was dressed in a splendid robe with a belt of silver and a sword. He was put on a platform to act out the part of Bohemond who became, in this version of events, the hero of the piece. Another man was dressed in a cloak of squirrel fur to play the less desirable role of Guy. A satirical play was enacted, ending in the sentencing of Guy to death for his perceived treachery. Whilst this was happening, a visiting Genoese official, Tommaso Spinola, was in residence in the Hospital of St John in the city. He was livid when he witnessed the celebrations. He resolved to return to Genoa and seek vengeance for what he saw as an outrage; Guy sprang from the line of the Embriacos who came from the city. Relations between Pisa and Genoa were about to degenerate with repercussions in both Italy and the wider world. The intense rivalry between Genoa, Pisa and Venice had already blighted the Mediterranean landscape on more than one occasion and the situation showed no sign of improving any time soon.

Angevins and Lusignans

Wider European politics would soon have a significant impact on the affairs of Acre once more. The Mediterranean was becoming a battleground with on the one side the Angevins led by the immensely ambitious Charles of Anjou and on the other the Aragonese and their equally driven king, Peter III. Charles had taken advantage of the crusading privileges offered for services rendered against political opponents of the papacy, so much so that one contemporary commentator said that, although he wore the sign of the Cross, it was not that of Christ but of the unrepentant thief who was crucified next to him.[16] These were complex and uncertain times in Europe where the fortunes of the protagonists were built on shifting sand. 'The political and military situation in Italy was notoriously unstable, as the popes themselves complained. Allegiances were changed without moral qualms and apparently stable conditions dissolved and reformed with extraordinary rapidity.'[17] Whilst the papacy had to a significant extent been forced by events and its own vulnerable position into an alliance with the Angevins, this had not led to an improvement in the sustainability and stability of the institution. The knock-on effects of this would ripple eastwards across the Mediterranean to the shores of Outremer.

During Peter III's reign, Aragon, Valencia and Barcelona were united and he was on the lookout for further opportunities to expand his power base, though his rule was not universally popular at home and he was forced to deal with uprisings in the early years of his reign. Through his wife, Constance, he also had a claim to Sicily. Given its strategic position, it remained a great prize. The island was a honeypot attracting a range of unwelcome bears over the years. It had been abused during the rule of the Hohenstaufens, with Henry VI in particular acting harshly towards the Sicilians, though the late Frederick II had valued the island highly. With the seizure of the island by the Angevin dynasty, matters had deteriorated further. The French were seen as an occupying force and increasingly resented by the Sicilians. Their rule was generally efficient but only so that they could exploit the resources of the island, and indeed much of mainland Italy, to their own advantage. Tension grew and fed a burning desire to throw the occupiers out.

Peter had an ally in Michael VIII Palaeologus, the Byzantine emperor. Although the Latins had been ejected from Constantinople, they still held a rump of their short-lived empire in other parts of 'Greece'.[18] Charles of Anjou turned his acquisitive eyes on Constantinople for himself. Anything Michael could do to divert his attention elsewhere would help secure his own position, and he identified a suitable destabiliser in the shape of Peter of Aragon. The two men plotted together, hatching a plan by which Peter would assume control of Sicily. This would have the beneficial effect, as far as the emperor was concerned, of drawing Charles of Anjou's attention westwards. Peter got together a fleet of some thirty galleys and Michael sent an envoy, a Genoese burgess named Benedetto Zaccaria, toting a very acceptable monetary gift. Peter used this to help finance an expedition to Sicily.

The people of Sicily were encouraged to rebel against their Angevin overlords. These approaches from an alliance that involved the Byzantines, the Genoese and the Aragonese were not unwelcome to them. Charles distrusted the Sicilians and showed little interest in them except as a source of money. He had only visited their island when he stopped over on his way to his brother Louis' crusade to Tunis. The Angevin officials on the island acted like the alien masters that they were, making the Sicilians feel like cultural outsiders in their own home. Further, the Greek element of the population was opposed to the expedition against Constantinople that Charles planned and which some of them would no doubt be forced to support directly or indirectly. There was almost certainly a great deal of plotting going on, but in keeping with the affairs of an island which has become irrevocably associated with secret societies, very little has survived in the historical record.

An explosion was imminent and the spark that lit the fuse came on the day after Easter 1282. A relatively minor incident quickly assumed enormous proportions. Charles of Anjou had initially met with almost complete success in his early campaigning but as the years went on it became more difficult to maintain his grip on power on the island. That Easter, at a celebration held just outside Palermo, a party of French officials showed their faces. Their presence was not welcomed by the Sicilians in the crowd and their resentment was transformed to anger when the Frenchmen, who had apparently been helping themselves rather too freely to stocks of local wine, started to molest some of the women present. An insulted husband drew his dagger and plunged it into the body of an offending sergeant named Drouet who fell, dying, to the ground. The sergeant's friends, rushing to defend or avenge him, were soon overwhelmed. To a man they were killed.

Just then the bells rung for Vespers when evening prayers were offered up at the close of the day. To the Sicilians it appeared as if it was a call to arms. The streets of Palermo were soon alive with locals seeking out anybody who was French, striking them down where they stood. Sicilian women with French husbands were among those killed. The fury of the mob was unstoppable. Foreign friars were hauled out of their monastic establishments and made to speak the word 'ciciri' – 'chickpeas' – a word that it was difficult for Frenchmen to articulate properly. The word was for many the difference between life and death. Anyone that could not pronounce it properly was promptly butchered. By the next morning, 2,000 French men, women and children lay dead and Palermo was totally in Sicilian hands. The Angevin flags that had previously flown in the city had been torn down and replaced by the banners of the Hohenstaufens. The empire was back. The revolution launched by these events (which became known as 'the Sicilian Vespers') quickly spread. Everywhere the French were butchered with just a small number of exceptions where local officials had in the past acted benevolently and were consequently spared. Only Messina, where there was a strong Angevin garrison and a large Angevin fleet, stayed loyal to Charles. Even that situation was temporary, as the flames of revolt soon reached there too. These flames became real with the burning of the Angevin fleet in Messina harbour. Massacres followed there too, albeit on a smaller scale than in Palermo.

Charles reacted calmly, perhaps underestimating the scale of the threat. He eventually crossed over the straits with his army and laid siege to Messina. It proved a much harder nut to crack than anticipated. Resistance from the defenders was heroic and, try as he might, Charles was unable to break through. King Peter of Aragon still stood on the sidelines. The uprising had caught him by surprise. Although he was heavily involved in the plotting to change the regime in Sicily, he had always planned to descend on the island once Charles of Anjou had left it and launched his attack on Constantinople. The Sicilians realised that they could not win the war on their own. Several frantic delegations were sent to Peter (he was conveniently close by, leading a crusading expedition in North Africa). He took his time before responding. At last, he decided to show his hand. Early in September Charles received shattering news. Peter and his army had landed at Trapani in the west of Sicily. From here, he moved to Palermo where he was received with great enthusiasm. Messina was clearly next in his sights. Charles realised that his adversary was in a stronger position than he. He began to ferry his army back across the straits to the Italian mainland. Not everyone made it. Stragglers were slaughtered, though Charles managed to escape with most of his army. Soon after, the war followed them to the mainland. Desultory fighting followed. A decisive advantage proved elusive for either man. It was not so much that their respective strengths cancelled each other out, rather it was their respective weaknesses which did so. Neither Charles nor Peter had sufficiently strong allies to give one of them the edge. Further, both men were short of the financial resources necessary to fight a campaign to a triumphant conclusion.

The End of the Arch-schemer

These events impacted on Outremer extremely negatively. The great powers in the West were too busy fighting each other to involve themselves in another crusade to the Levant. Italy was the main arena for this infighting. As events played out against the Angevins and the papacy, they were sucked further into the war in an attempt to recover lost ground. Now the war in Italy turned into an extended slugging match that must have come to appear as being a fight without end. On the one side were the French in alliance with the papacy, on the other the Aragonese and the Hohenstaufens. Local forces, Guelfs and Ghibellines, allied themselves with the warring parties, the former with the Angevins, the latter with the Hohenstaufens. To compound the difficulties, a potentially ardent Crusader, King Edward of England, had far too many distractions in his own backyard (especially at the time in Wales, soon to be followed by Scotland) to involve himself in more expeditions across the Mediterranean. Pope Martin IV, a Frenchman who seems to have put national interests before those of Christendom, launched a crusade against first of all Sicily in 1283 and then another against Aragon in 1285, during the course of which the French King, Philip III, died whilst leading his army. Outremer was now a sideshow in which Western Europe generally retained little practical interest, however much hot air was exhaled discussing it.

Charles of Anjou still nurtured his claim to the Kingdom of Jerusalem up to this point. He had appointed Odo Poilechien as seneschal there. Another Frenchman, Jacques Vidal, was made marshal, an important post which involved the mustering and organisation of the military forces of the kingdom. The Templars had been strong supporters of him especially since William of Beaujeu had succeeded Thomas Bérard as Master; and in fairness, Charles probably offered access to more substantial resources that might come to the aid of Outremer than anyone else did. But Charles' position in the region was already under threat even before the Vespers. King Hugh III of Cyprus journeyed to Beirut in 1283 bringing with him an impressive array of men-at-arms. He then went to Tyre, which in contrast to Acre had remained loyal to him, where he flew his Lusignan banner over the walls. Ominously, it soon after fell down into the sea, which was inevitably seen as a sinister portent. There were other bad signs too. A Jewish doctor named Samuel was hit on the head when a cleric leading a religious procession carrying a cross accidentally dropped it on him. Hugh also suffered some losses when a party of his men outside the city were attacked by Muslim forces.

That same year, John de Montfort, who had survived the assassin's attempt on his life a few years before, died and was buried in Tyre.

He was Hugh's brother-in-law, having married his sister, Margaret. The Templar of Tyre, who wrote of these events, was present at his burial.[19] Tyre was given to John's brother Humphrey as his fief (the late John had no children). This was an unusual arrangement made according to the conditions that attached to the transaction. Under a deal made between the kings of Cyprus and the lords of Tyre in 1269 possession of Tyre would pass down only through the sons of the Montfort dynasty. Humphrey therefore did not qualify. It was agreed that he could retain possession of Tyre if he handed over 50,000 saracenate bezants by the following May.[20] If he failed to do so, then Tyre would revert to Hugh. In practice, the deal was overtaken by events when the unfortunate Humphrey died before the time for payment was reached and he was buried alongside his brother in Tyre. Hugh also suffered a personal loss when his son Bohemond developed an ugly tumour on his neck. Despite being bled – a common attempted remedy using the basic medical practices of the time – he died soon after. Premature death was an ever-present companion in those days. As one tragic example, Humphrey was father to five sons and a daughter; she and three of his sons died before their time.

Hugh III died in 1284. The Templar of Tyre deeply mourned his loss, describing him as a man of great intelligence and virtue. He was buried in three nested coffins – an unusual arrangement where one coffin fitted inside another – which were sealed in pitch. Then the King (who had died in Tyre) was shipped back to Cyprus for burial in the church of St Sophia in Nicosia. The new ruler was his eldest son, John, who died a year later. In the same year Charles of Anjou's son, Charles of Salerno, was taken prisoner when an Aragonese fleet attacked Naples and he had tried vainly to rebuff them. He was subsequently locked up in Catalonia for a time.[21]

Charles of Salerno was released several years later but by the time that he tasted freedom again the situation had changed markedly. On 7 January 1285, his father, Charles of Anjou, now in his late fifties, expired at Foggia in Italy. It marked the end of an eventful and controversial life during which he had attempted to achieve far more than he ultimately did. With the departure of the arch-schemer some men at least could probably breathe more easily. There had been no limit to his ambition, and his unquenchable thirst for power was to prove his undoing. He took no time to steal a breath before moving on to his next projected conquest and as a result those lands which he had already taken possession of, such as Sicily, refused to accept his rule. Not only was his excessive ambition to lead to his ultimate failure, it was also disastrous for Europe. The collateral damage suffered by Outremer as a result of these distractions was to prove very unfortunate for the Kingdom of Jerusalem. Attempts to recruit support for papal affairs in Italy meant resources which might have helped the East were kept back. The appeal by various popes for Crusaders 'to recover the lands of St Peter'[22] equated Rome with Jerusalem and Crusaders in Italy could now state with confidence: 'We do not need to go overseas to save our souls, for we can save them here.'[23] And it was not just men being diverted from the East either; it was money too. By the end of the thirteenth century, taxation that had initially been raised for crusades to Outremer was being increasingly used to support the ventures of secular allies of the papacy in Italy.[24] For a man of undoubted talent Charles of Anjou, who had been a key player in the events there, had caused considerable harm. Not even his death was to bring an end to the fallout.

10

Towards the Endgame

'You could not have found a single house standing.'
A description of Tripoli at the end of the siege

Acre: The Surrogate Battlefield

The frequent reverses suffered by the Crusaders in recent times were explained away in contemporary terms as a punishment from God for the sins committed by His people. There was even a term for this form of divine chastisement for the sins of humanity – *peccatis exigentibus hominum*.[1] Qalāwūn had not been idle and he started making preparations to attack the Franks, who were not protected by the existing truce. In 1285, he set out from Damascus to attack the formidable Hospitaller citadel at Marqab. The subsequent siege began on 17 April and lasted until 27 May. Marqab was in an imposing position atop a mountain and a mangonel from inside the walls rained down missiles on the besiegers, causing considerable destruction among Qalāwūn's ten siege engines. Despite this strong start, the Hospitallers inside, without hope of relief and having seen one of the key strongpoints, the Tower of Hope, collapse after being undermined, surrendered on good terms that were subsequently honoured. The defenders were given safe conduct to Tripoli and Tortosa and another important piece in the defensive bulwark around the reduced Frankish territories was lost. Given the strategic importance of Marqab, there was no thought this time of destroying the castle. The walls were repaired and a Muslim garrison of 1,500 men was installed. Islamic chroniclers exulted in the triumph: 'The Muslims went up to take

185

possession of the fort and from the heights of the citadel the call to prayer resounded with praise and thanks to God for having cast down the adorers of the Messiah and freed our land of them.'[2]

In Cyprus, the late King John's brother was crowned as Henry II at Nicosia in May 1285. The Grim Reaper though had not finished his work, removing both Philip III of France and Peter of Aragon in 1285, making this a veritable royal *annus horribilis*. The constable of France also expired, Louis of Beaujeu, the brother of William, Master of the Templars, meeting his end in Gerona. One of King Henry's first acts was to try to patch up relations with the Templars at Acre. He sent his envoy, Julien Le Jaune, to the city where he took up lodgings with the Hospitallers and his diplomatic skills were sufficient to lead to a treaty with the Templars. It served everyone's interests in the kingdom. With Qalāwūn seemingly on the warpath again, there was a need for unity to make the most of Outremer's much-reduced resources. The removal from the scene of Charles of Anjou probably made this a much easier outcome to achieve.

This thawing in relations was followed up by a royal visit by Henry II to Acre in June 1286. He came with an impressive entourage of knights and a well-equipped fleet. He was received with great honours and a splendid procession wended its way through the city streets to the Church of the Holy Cross. But not everybody was pleased to see him. Odo Poilechien remained loyal to his late master, Charles of Anjou, and his interests, and he and his men in the French Regiment in Acre barricaded themselves in the castle. They prepared their siege engines and readied themselves for a fight. This created tensions among other factions in the city too. The Masters of the Templars, the Hospitallers and the Teutonic Knights refused to meet Henry.

When open fighting broke out soon afterwards, however, with 'arrows and missiles ... fired here and there' and projectiles from the siege engines inside the castle catapulting through the air, the Masters were jointly shocked into action. They all presented themselves to King Henry in the Church of the Holy Cross and greeted him with 'great joy'. They then spoke to Odo Poilechien, convincing him to hand over the castle to the king a few days later. Henry was crowned as King of Jerusalem in Tyre on 15 August, Assumption Day. The new King of France, Philip IV, had refused Pope Honorius IV's offer to appoint him as the new custodian of the Kingdom of Jerusalem but had nevertheless sent payments to support the French Regiment in Acre. Abandoned by the Angevins' allies, especially the Templars, Odo was prevailed upon to surrender on the understanding that no reprisals would be exacted against him or his men. Bonnacorso of Gloria, the Archbishop of Tyre, performed the coronation ceremony. Henry afterwards returned to Acre where the subsequent celebrations in his honour lasted for over a fortnight. He took up residence in the Hospital of St John for the duration.[3]

The celebrations were memorable, the most impressive that anyone could remember. The emaciated Kingdom of Jerusalem had perhaps seen nothing like it for a century. Tableaux involving actors representing the Knights of the Round Table were played out in the city. Knights dressed as women acted out scenes from the mythical realm of the Queen of Feminie, a somewhat bizarre prospect to the modern mind. In this make-believe world nuns were dressed as monks and jousted together representing characters like Lancelot and Tristan among others. Yet, splendid though it was, it was also the perfect metaphor for what was left of Outremer, for this was not the real world, this was a realm of fantasy and illusion. Henry returned to Cyprus soon after leaving his uncle, Baldwin of Ibelin, as his *bailli* at Acre. Little did he know that he was the last man ever to be crowned King of Jerusalem in Outremer or that he would be back in Acre a few years later leading a fight for its very existence. His following years as the kingdom's ruler were those of a man presiding over an extended Last Supper.

The *Ilkhanate* in the meantime continued its struggle to find stability, reflecting tensions elsewhere in the wider Mongol *khanate*. Tegüder/ Ahmad did not survive for long and was killed, executed in a way that was specially reserved for rejected Mongol leaders by having his back broken (it avoided the shedding of the blood of a leader, which was anathema to Mongols). He was replaced by Abagha's son, Arghun. Arghun was quick to repudiate Tegüder/Ahmad's conversion and wrote to rulers in the West that he himself was a staunch supporter of Christendom, in stark contrast to the predecessor he had overthrown. Arghun ruled from 1284 to 1291 and in that time no fewer than four missions were despatched by him to Western Europe. He clung on to a desperate hope that an increasingly apathetic Christendom would reignite its interest in the affairs of the Middle East enough to intervene in them.

The first of these missions, in 1285, was accompanied by an envoy from the great *khagan*, Kublai Khan. It was his court that would host

Marco Polo for many years. Kublai had taken on all the trappings of a Chinese emperor and indeed his dynasty, the Yuan, was to rule in China for the next century. Kublai's messenger presented a letter in mangled Latin to Pope Honorius IV which offered to divide Egypt with the West if they jointly conquered it. Given these conditions, it would have been surprising if Qalāwūn in Egypt had not noted the nuisance value of the Franks once more. It is too much to say that these initiatives on their own sealed the fate of what was left of Outremer; Qalāwūn had been tightening the screw long before this. But they probably increased his determination to obliterate what was left of it.

Another Mongol delegation arrived at the papal court in 1287 during an interregnum as Pope Honorius IV had died and his successor had not yet been elected. This delegation was headed by a Nestorian monk, Rabban Sawma. Whilst in Naples, he witnessed a sea battle between the Aragonese and the Angevins, getting a first-hand insight into just how divided Christian Europe currently was. He also visited Philip III and then Edward I, who was in Bordeaux (Gascony at that time being part of English territory in France). Once more, he left with kind words and warm sentiments but no practical offers of meaningful support. This was also the case with yet another mission in 1289–90, which also visited the pope (Nicholas IV had by now been elected) and the French and English kings. A firm commitment was made for the Mongols to meet the French king outside Damascus in February 1291; but again, nothing concrete resulted. In fact, in all likelihood such a rendezvous would never have been viable given the huge logistical coordination and planning problems a major crusade involved by now and the length of time it would take to deal with them. Getting a crusade together in just over a year would have been an impossibility.

Rabban Sawma again tried to play the conversion card to Christian authorities as a way of encouraging them to enter into an alliance with the Mongols. He told Pope Nicholas that his master, the *Ilkhan* Arghun, wanted to be baptised but would only submit himself to the ceremony once Jerusalem had been retaken. Pope Nicholas was not falling for this. He told Rabban Sawma that Arghun should not put his immortal soul at risk by delaying; instead, he should be baptised immediately. Indeed, God might well look with greater favour on his endeavours to conquer Jerusalem if he submitted himself to the ceremony at once. This diplomatic wrangling predictably enough did not lead to Arghun's baptism or any other firm commitment to Christianity.

These initiatives were doomed to fail because some of the leading powers in Europe were more interested once more in fighting each other than a Muslim enemy. Acre was about to find itself a surrogate battlefield for factions from the Italian peninsula yet again. The spark that lit the conflagration occurred hundreds of miles to the west of Outremer on the rugged island of Corsica in the year 1286. The lord of the island, who had the grand title of the Judge of Cinarca (sometimes called Simoncello) was aligned with the interests of Genoa, but he wished to change his allegiance to the Pisan party. Unsurprisingly, the Genoese took a very dim view of this and they sent a messenger to Pisa, warning the authorities there of the consequences of accepting the approaches of the Judge of Cinarca. The Pisans politely but unequivocally rebuffed him.

The imminent stand-off was made worse when, with appalling timing, a ship arrived from Outremer with news that the Pisans had been abusing the Genoese in Acre just when tidings of the Pisan rebuff of the Genoese messenger was also received. There was now outrage in Genoa and protests rocked the streets demanding war with Pisa to bring their recalcitrant rivals back into line. The blood of the Genoese was up and Admiral Tommaso Spinola led a fleet of twenty galleys out to cause as much mischief as possible. The fleet attacked Elba, where the inhabitants promised to align themselves with Genoa and handed over hostages as security. Despite this, Elba soon changed sides and supported the Pisans. Whilst all this was going on, Spinola stayed on station off Elba. Shortly afterwards, two unsuspecting Pisan ships hove into view. When they spotted the Genoese galleys, the Pisans turned tail and tried to outrun them. Eagle-eyed lookouts on the Genoese vessels saw a cask thrown over the side of one of the Pisan ships which they soon retrieved. Inside were official letters informing them that ten Pisan ships were passing through the area carrying money.[4]

The Genoese won a further significant victory against the Pisans in the following year (1287). Pisa was on the back foot but she had a powerful ally, Venice. In Pisa at the time was an important Venetian official, Alberto Morisini. He loaded men onto Pisan galleys and moved on Genoa. In response the Genoese armed seventy ships. However, the Pisans were driven off station by bad weather. The Genoese chased after them and caught them up. They cleverly concealed some of their fleet, thereby luring the Pisans into an ambush. A fierce fight followed, lasting all day. It was a harshly hot day and the Pisans got by far the worst of the fight. The Genoese won a decisive victory and returned to their city with many captives in tow including Morisini himself. The Pisans were now beleaguered and their fleet was soon after blockaded. They had allegedly lost 22,000 men, 17,000 of them taken prisoner.[5] However, matters were soon evened up to some extent when the Pisans won a surprise victory at Piombino, on the mainland coast of Italy opposite Elba. The Genoese nobleman Niccolò de Mari was beheaded in sight of the galleys manned by his fellow citizens. In retaliation, 300 Pisan captives were similarly despatched. More Pisan raids followed leading to further Genoese attacks in response. The sphere of conflict widened and a chase off the coast of Tunisia followed.

The conflict moved even further afield, and Acre was soon dragged into it. What had been some vaguely interesting disturbance a long way from Outremer was about to appear on its front doorstep. The catalyst was the despatch of Tommaso Spinola to Outremer. He stopped en route at Paphos on Cyprus from where he went to Alexandria to present himself to Qalāwūn. Another senior Genoese official, Orlando Ascheri, went to Acre, arriving unexpectedly during the night. There were some Pisan ships in and around the harbour and Ascheri immediately went on the attack. Some were chased into the harbour itself where the fight continued right up to the inner harbour known as the Port of the Chain, which was effectively the harbour office of Acre. The next day, 1 June 1286, the fight continued. A Pisan *nef* – an ocean-going trading ship – was burned. The vessel belonged to Sir Raymond Napier and was loaded with valuable cargo including hazelnuts. A senior Templar, the commander Theobald Gaudin, intervened and arranged for the release of some of the captured Pisans, many of whom were fishermen of little value as hostages. In the meantime, the Templar Master, William of Beaujeu, was on his way to Acre. So, too, was a combined Pisan-Venetian fleet of eleven ships. These were well armed with a contingent of crossbowmen on board. The ships were strongly protected, reinforced by planking and surrounded by shields. They sailed under the banner of St Mark, with a Venetian admiral in command, determined to bring the Genoese aggressor to book.

William of Beaujeu was also very concerned at the threat posed by the arrival of the Genoese. The much-reduced Kingdom of Jerusalem could ill afford such distractions with an increasingly powerful Mamluk regime knocking at its gates. A number of Genoese vessels (eight in total, of different types) had anchored in the Quai of the Marquis, a small bay off Montmusard, the suburb of Acre. William approached their commander, Orlando Ascheri, asking him to take his force off to Tyre. The Genoese admiral agreed to do so provided that none of the enemy ships moved on him in the meantime. With impeccably bad timing, at that moment a flotilla of Pisan ships hove into view. It was a challenge that Ascheri was not prepared to overlook and he moved his fleet out in response. A fight between the Genoese and the Pisans followed in the port of Acre itself. A bombardment of lances, stones and crossbow bolts rained down, thudding into flesh and shattering bone. The Genoese slowly got the upper hand and the Pisan ships were forced back and ran out of space to manoeuvre. A Genoese grapnel locked itself onto a ship flying the Venetian standard and began to tow it off. Fortunately for the Venetians, the ship was so well anchored that the grapnel proved insufficient to move it far and the Genoese abandoned the attempt by cutting the cable. Ascheri blockaded Acre for three days before moving to Tyre.

In the meantime, Tommaso Spinola had completed his mission to Qalāwūn and now sailed to Tripoli where he intended to deliver a message to Bohemond. The latter however planned to seize and imprison Spinola when he returned, but the Genoese admiral had spies in Bohemond's camp who warned him of the plot. Forewarned, Spinola did not present himself again. He instead joined Ascheri and they re-laid the blockade of Acre so that the Pisans and their Venetian allies could not move out of port. Whilst there, they captured a Pisan ship making its way in from Damietta. It ran aground on the beach and the men onboard managed to make good their escape. After further talks with William of Beaujeu, Spinola left again for Tyre. Not long after, Ascheri was back with another blockading force and would not leave again until the enemy ships in the port had left.

The authorities in Acre were understandably furious at the ongoing crisis. They believed that the Genoese policy was 'an outrage to Christianity and dangerous, for the Saracens could follow their example'.[6] Two Franciscan friars were sent to Ascheri, who said he would leave if this was the wish of all the authorities in Acre. A document that arrived shortly after bearing the seals of the king, the Templars and the Hospitallers confirmed that this was indeed the case. This proved sufficient to persuade the Genoese to abandon their strategy; but the incident had sent a powerful message to Outremer's neighbours that the Christian states in the region were bitterly divided and subject to the whims of wider geopolitics. This made what was left of Outremer very vulnerable and those same neighbours now made plans to move in and pick the bones of the Kingdom of Jerusalem clean.

Latakia and the Threat to Tripoli

Of the ruined castles that have survived into modern times in the Middle East, that of Saone is in one of the most spectacular locations. The castle stands at the top of a high ridge and was reached in medieval times by a drawbridge that spanned a seemingly bottomless gorge in the rocky landscape. Now all that remains of this stunning entry to the castle is the spindly finger of rock that supported the drawbridge in the middle of the gorge, a thin granite needle pointing skyward. Whilst the remaining walls of the castle are somewhat battered, it is easy to appreciate its strong position. Despite this, it fell to Saladin during his 1187 campaign, proving that no castle is really impregnable if circumstances are against the defenders, no matter how intimidating it might look. Saone was now in the hands of a Muslim opponent of Qalāwūn, Sunqur al-Ashqar. The Sultan sent an army under Husam al-Din Turuntay to take it. Al-Ashqar was in a hopeless position. He had insufficient men with him to drive the besieging force away and if he stayed where he was he could simply be starved out. This presented Qalāwūn's army with a quick win and the castle's surrender soon followed. The army now had unexpected time on its hands. Just at that moment, fate played a card in their favour.

Nature itself now seemed to be conspiring against the Franks. On 22 March 1287, an earthquake created considerable damage to the defences of Frankish-held Latakia. Soon after, Turuntay's under-utilised army moved in to take possession. They were held up for a short time by a fort at the mouth of the harbour connected to the land by a narrow causeway. However, the Mamluks quickly got to work widening the causeway and there was no prospect of any relief for the defenders. On 20 April, the garrison surrendered. The port had a valuable commercial role, being a significant Mediterranean outlet for trade from Aleppo and it was another heavy loss to the Franks. It came at a generally inauspicious time for them anyway. In the same month that Latakia fell, the Genoese Admiral Orlando Ascheri attacked Pisan ships off the Syrian coast before sailing to Acre. Tommaso Spinola in the meantime made his way to Alexandria to negotiate the Mamluk Sultanate's neutrality in Genoa's conflict with Pisa.

The fall of Latakia was another blow to Outremer. Its vulnerability had increased since the loss of Antioch two decades before, as it had been the principality's port. However, worse was to follow. Bohemond VII, the nominal Prince of Antioch and the actual Count of Tripoli, died on 19 October 1287. He left no children behind him so the principality passed to a sister, Lucy, but it was not long before the Bishop of Tortosa, a destabilising influence on the city in the past, reappeared. A faction inside Tripoli led by the mayor, Bartholomew Embriaco, sent Pietro of Aubergamo to Genoa, asking the city state to send them a ruler. Genoa responded by despatching Benedetto Zaccaria with five galleys to Tripoli, where he was received with great joy. He was also met by a delegation including the Masters of the Temple, the Hospitallers and the Teutonic Knights along with representatives of the Venetians who sought to negotiate to avoid confrontation between Benedetto and the Lady Lucy.

Again, European politics was affecting the affairs of Outremer. Lucy was married to Narjot of Toucy, the French King's admiral in Apulia, Italy. When news reached them that Lucy had inherited Tripoli, her husband despatched her east to claim her prize, advising her to travel to Acre and seek the help of the Hospitallers to secure it. She sailed in February 1288. On her arrival in Acre, the Hospitallers agreed to support her and escorted her to the castle of Nephin, near Tripoli. Open conflict followed between the Hospitallers and the men of Tripoli in which lives were lost. Messages were sent to the Lady Lucy from Tripoli, telling her that the bad treatment of the principality by her brother and other members of her family had deprived her of her right to rule. A commune was formed to govern the city dedicated to the honour of God and Our Lady. Their aim was to defend the rights and privileges of the citizens. If Lucy was prepared to accept the commune, then they would receive her graciously; if not, then she would not be allowed in. Clearly, no resolution was reached as the delegation interceding on behalf of Lady Lucy soon after returned to Acre without having achieved anything.

A pact was now made between the commune of Tripoli and the Genoese, who were given a quarter in the city as part of the deal. However, though detail is scant it appears that the commune soon started to repent the deal. They sent letters to Lady Lucy saying that if she would accept the freedoms they had been granted as part of the agreement with Genoa they would come over to her side. Benedetto Zaccaria also realised that it was best to reach an accommodation with Lucy and began negotiations. He and Lady Lucy met in Tyre, neutral territory, with the Hospitaller Commander of the Holy Land, Boniface of Calamandrana, playing the part of honest broker. Agreement was reached and the parties journeyed to Tripoli with Lucy now recognised as the ruler of the city and the rights of the commune, and of Genoa within the city, confirmed.

These developments were in the nature of internal manoeuvring, but they were to have fatal consequences. There was one very dissatisfied party in Outremer – named by the Islamic writer Abu'l Mahasin as Bartholomew Embriaco, mayor of Tripoli – who had made his way to the court of Qalāwūn. The envoy, whoever he actually was, warned Qalāwūn of the increased risk posed by Tripoli now that the Genoese were installed there. The messenger emphasised the threat against Alexandria now that the Genoese, with their powerful navy, were present in Tripoli. He told the Sultan that they would 'rule the waves, and it will happen that those who will come to Alexandria will be at their mercy, whether they are coming or going or inside the port. This thing bodes very ill for the merchants who operate in your kingdom.'[7]

Qalāwūn took the warning to heart. He was officially at peace with Tripoli as there was a truce in place, but such niceties did not count for much. He also remembered that Bohemond VI, the late prince of Antioch, had entered in triumph into Damascus nearly thirty years before, an insult that possibly still rankled. Tripoli had continued to support the Mongols from time to time; in the build-up to the Homs campaign at the beginning of the decade Franks inside the city had dressed in Mongol helmets to mislead Mamluk spies into believing that a pincer movement was about to be launched. Qalāwūn consulted his council and they decided that they should assemble a force and lead it against Tripoli. There were those in Qalāwūn's court who did not wish for war and one of them, the emir Badr al-Din Bektash al-Fakhri, sent a secret message to William of Beaujeu, the Master of the Temple, warning him of the plans. From what we know, it was no moral imperative that drove the emir to this, rather it was the receipt of fine presents from the Temple on a regular basis. Then, as now, money talked.[8] Qalāwūn duly left Egypt with his army, headed for Syria.

William of Beaujeu sent a message to Tripoli about this unpalatable news. So unpalatable indeed was it that William, like a latter-day Cassandra, was not believed, possibly because his close alignment with the Angevin cause during his time as Master had led to him being perceived in some quarters as untrustworthy and partisan.[9] He was suspected of ulterior motives and ignored. When his initial warning was brushed aside, he sent the Spanish knight-brother, Reddecoeur, to Tripoli to repeat it. Reddecoeur was well-known to the people of Tripoli, having previously been the Templar commander there, and he was finally believed. But it was too late, as not long after the Sultan's armies appeared in front of the city.

The Attack on Tripoli

Qalāwūn had in fact been some time in arriving. The death of his designated heir, al-Malik al-Salih Ali, on 4 September 1288 had resulted in the Mamluk campaign against Tripoli being postponed. But it was only a temporary reprieve. On 9 March 1289, the Mamluk army arrived outside of Damascus and then marched through the Beqaa Valley to the outskirts of Tripoli. Alarm bells now started to ring loudly inside the city. News of the plight of Tripoli spread further afield and reinforcements started to arrive. They represented several different factions, often ones that had been at odds with each other in the recent past. The constable of Jerusalem, Amalric de Lusignan, the teenaged brother of King Henry II of Jerusalem and Cyprus, came with men-at-arms. A number of Templars arrived, including the Marshal, Geoffrey of Vendac, and a well-known knight, Peter of Moncada, as well as Reddecoeur. Hospitallers were despatched along with representatives of the French Regiment in Acre. Two Venetian galleys later made their way to Tripoli, as did men from Pisa. Genoa on the one side and Pisa and Venice on the other had been at each other's throats for a while and the Templar of Tyre suggests that the hostility continued even as the different factions stood alongside each other inside the besieged city. Even the Hospitallers had little time for the governing regime in Tripoli as they had recently been on opposite sides in the succession dispute involving the Lady Lucy.[10]

Lady Lucy was also present, as was 'the wife of the late prince' (possibly Sibylla of Armenia, widow of Bohemond VI, rather than Margaret of Brienne-Beaumont who had been married to Bohemond VII) and Margaret de Lusignan, the 'Lady of Tyre', first cousin to

Bohemond VI and widow of John de Montfort.[11] The city was packed with people seeking sanctuary from the terrifying army that had descended on the region. But the sanctuary that Tripoli offered was an illusion for all those inside except for those rich or well-connected enough to board a ship to safety when the siege turned against them. The defences of Tripoli were strong but the attacking forces were formidable. Qalāwūn had ample supplies of siege engines, such as trebuchets known as *carabohas* (in Arabic *manjaniq qarābughā*, 'the black camel'), a form of torsion siege engine which fired projectiles including blazing bolts ideal for setting defensive wooden fortifications aflame. Whilst trebuchets had been is use for several millennia, being first known of in China in the fourth and fifth centuries BC, the use of bolts rather than stones was relatively recent and was particularly developed by the Mamluks. The machine could also be quickly adapted by exchanging the bolt-firing mechanism for a sling for use as a stone-throwing device.[12] A total of nineteen siege engines including thirteen *carabohas* hammered away at the walls, which soon started to crack. Qalāwūn's forces were protected by *buches*, wooden revetments used to screen troops and siege engines from counter-bombardment from inside the besieged city. It would appear that Qalāwūn had a massive numerical advantage. So many Islamic archers were firing at the walls at a time that crossbowmen inside Tripoli dared not show their faces for they would instantly be hit. The attackers could therefore carry on the siege with virtual impunity.

Tripoli was an important part of Outremer, both symbolically and practically. It had been bypassed by the First Crusade en route to Jerusalem and was not attacked until 1102 and not finally taken until 1109. It then became part of the county, which was named after the city, one of the original four Frankish domains in Outremer along with the long-lost Edessa and the states of Antioch and Jerusalem. Although the port was in a very strong position, being surrounded by the sea on three sides, it was weak because of its very isolation, with little prospect of meaningful relief forces arriving. Mines were dug by the besieging forces on the landward side. Whether it was these or the constant thudding of projectiles into the walls that started to tell is unclear. But obvious signs of damage started to appear. Even the strongest fortifications usually have one spot that is weaker than others and it is the job of siege engineers to identify it so that an attacking force can concentrate its efforts there. Whether it was targeted deliberately (which was probably the case), or whether by unfortunate accident, the Bishop's Tower eventually started to fall apart. That it was indeed a weak spot was confirmed by the fact that it was so strongly defended as a compensatory measure. Then the newer and sturdier tower built recently by the Hospitallers started to go too. Gaps in it appeared that were so large that it was possible to walk a horse through them. It became increasingly obvious that Tripoli was living on borrowed time.

It was the Venetians who blinked first. Fearing the way that things were going, merchants made their way out on two Venetian galleys headed for Armenia. A disturbing domino effect followed. Benedetto Zaccaria followed the Venetians' example and the Genoese galleys also made good their escape. Those who could – that is those with access to ships and lots of money to make good their escape by paying exploitative ships' captains to take them to freedom – followed on. Tripoli, already badly damaged, became even less defensible as those who could sailed off. Perhaps it is unfairly judgmental and clichéd to talk of rats deserting a sinking ship – but some of the common folk who were stuck where they were must surely have seen it that way.

Remarkably, a highly summarised visual representation of these scenes can be found in a rare medieval manuscript, the Cocharelli Codex, a classic artistic production of the time (made in Genoa around 1330). It comes alive with vibrant colours, a healthy disrespect for perspective and a conflation of different events. In it can be seen Sibylla of Armenia attempting to place the Bishop of Tortosa in control whilst later events, such as the galleys off the coast, are added in alongside ominous scenes of bodies in the water. A man tumbles to his death from the walls of Tripoli, heads are hacked off and a fallen Frank is speared in the back by an Islamic horseman whilst another is butchered outside a church – powerful iconic imagery. It is an illustration that Hieronymus Bosch might have been proud of.

The besieging Muslims sensed the decreased vigour of the defence and gathered their forces together for a final assault. It came on 26 April 1289. It was short, sharp and decisive. Among those who had already made good their escape were the three royal ladies inside the walls and most of the great lords such as Amalric de Lusignan, the Marshal of the Temple and the Commander of the Hospital, Matthew of Clermont, along with Jean de Grailly, captain of the French Regiment and seneschal of the Kingdom of Jerusalem. Not everyone, even those amongst the upper echelons, was so lucky. Peter of Moncada lost his life, as did William of Cardona, another prominent Templar knight. Reddecoeur was taken prisoner along with other Templars when the city fell. A number of the Hospitallers were among the dead, as was Bartholomew Embriaco.

With the walls now pierced by gaping holes, the Muslim army poured through the panic-stricken streets of Tripoli and a bloodbath followed. Those inside the city who were not of any worth for ransom were either butchered or taken off into slavery. 1,200 were taken to assist with work on the Sultan's new arsenal at Alexandria. Some of the Franks managed to make their way to the nearby island of St Thomas, but this was also taken by the Mamluks on 29 April. A Muslim writer, Abu'l Fida, made his way over to it soon after but did not linger, being driven off by the stench of putrefying flesh. The Templar of Tyre described these events as a 'great calamity'. Qalāwūn determined to deny Tripoli to the Franks in the future and systematically demolished it 'so that you could not have found a single house standing'.[13] Among the booty taken were 4,000 weaver's looms; mundane items perhaps but they showed that despite the travails of recent times, Tripoli had remained a bustling hive of productive activity, especially with regard to textiles.[14] That was now no longer the case. Even the dead were not safe; the bones of Bohemond VII were dug up and thrown carelessly around the streets by the jubilant victors. The nearby towns of Botrun and Nephin were also taken though a Frankish lord, Peter of Gibelet, was able to keep his lands there for another decade by paying tribute to the Sultan.

Outremer was now slowly disintegrating. Edessa had been lost as far back as 1144 and the greatest loss of all, that of Jerusalem, had been suffered in 1187. Antioch had gone in 1268 and now so, too, had Tripoli. To make matters worse, the combined forces of the Temple, the Hospital, the Italian city states, the Kingdom of Jerusalem and the French Regiment had failed to resist the Mamluk juggernaut.

Henry II came over from Cyprus. He had not been in Outremer since 1286 and he was clearly deeply disturbed by the course of events, staying there from April to September 1289. Even though he had not been there for three years, he had closely followed events on the mainland and had regularly instructed his representatives to get involved. He had also sent men under his brother Amalric to assist in the defence of Tripoli. Now he ordered Jean de Grailly to depart post-haste for Europe to drum up support there. It was a sensible move; but even though Pope Nicholas IV responded positively, he still compromised the effectiveness of his good intentions by continuing to issue indulgences to those who planned to crusade in Sicily. A contemporary Sicilian chronicler, Bartholomew of Neocastro (who admittedly may not have been unbiased), reported that a Templar ambassador to Europe delivered the following rebuke to his audience: 'You could have saved the Holy Land [by using] the might of kings ... but instead you chose to attack a Christian king and the Christians of Sicily, arming kings against a king to recover the island.'[15] Cynicism about the idea of crusading generally was also fed by some of the rewards available to those who took the cross that were less than spiritual. The decision to go on crusade led to a moratorium on an individual's debt and even the Church recognised that some unscrupulous characters might take advantage of this; instructions were issued to the seneschal of Provence in 1270, for example, that he should look out for Crusader volunteers who took the cross 'with the aim of avoiding paying their debts to the Jews'.[16]

Even in more distant parts of Christian Europe the loss of Tripoli resonated: the writer of *The Lanercost Chronicle,* from a priory located on the borders of England and Scotland, blamed the sins of the Christians for its demise. He also told of the bravery of an English Minorite friar, originally from Oxford, who tried to rally the citizens by boldly marching towards the breach where the Muslims had broken in armed only with a cross. Whilst the story may have been true, it was not a very successful tactic. Few followed him and the enemy contemptuously chopped off the left arm in which he was carrying the cross. When he picked it up with his right arm, that was cut off too. Then he was trampled by horses and killed.[17] It was an apt metaphor for the helplessness of the Christian forces in Outremer when faced with a much larger Islamic force. Acre was now the capital of a failing state. And for her, too, time was running out.

11

The Pretext

'...he was most infuriated by it and raged against the people of Acre.'
Qalāwūn's response on hearing of the
massacre of Muslims at Acre

The Weakness of Outremer

With this stunning series of defeats the position of Outremer had
deteriorated alarmingly. Jerusalem, the greatest prize of all, had been
gone for half a century now. Antioch had been lost two decades before.
Most of the great castles in the region were in Muslim hands if they
had not been destroyed. Now Latakia and Tripoli had been taken. The
remainder was small and disjointed, with a few settlements surviving
such as Tyre and Sidon. Acre remained the most significant Frankish
possession but she, too, was in a parlous state. This was made clear
in a treaty between Acre and Qalāwūn brokered as long ago as 1283:

> The Franks shall not restore any wall, castle or tower or fortress,
> whether old or recent, outside the walls of Acre, Atlit and Sidon. If one
> of the Frankish maritime kings or others should move by sea with the
> intention of bringing harm to our lord the Sultan and his son in their
> territory to which this truce applies, the lords of the kingdom and the
> Masters in Acre are required to inform our Lord the Sultan and his
> son of their movement two months before their arrival in the Islamic
> territory covered by this truce... If an enemy comes from among the
> Mongols, or elsewhere, whichever of the two parties first learns of it
> must alert the other. If – may God forbid it! – such an enemy marches

against Syria and the troops of the Sultan withdraw before him, then the leaders of Acre and the masters there may protect themselves, their subjects and territories as best they can.[1]

That truce reveals several things. It tells us that the Mamluks still regarded Acre, emaciated as its power now was, as a threat and that there was still an element of anxiety concerning both new arrivals from Europe and a renewed Mongol invasion of Syria. But the fact that the authorities in Acre felt compelled to agree to such a one-sided treaty also shows just how weak Acre was, and how exposed it would be should Qalāwūn decide that it should be eliminated. The Franks were now only allowed to remain in Outremer on sufferance. Even in the West some realised this. Fidenzio of Padua, writing on the eve of the attack on Acre in 1291, considered that an assault on Egypt was now a waste of time and effort as the Mamluks were simply too strong.[2]

Qalāwūn noted that there had been representatives from all three major military orders (Templars, Hospitallers and Teutonic Knights) from Acre at Tripoli and protested to the authorities in the city about this. They pleaded that the truce that had been made a few years before was agreed between Qalāwūn and Acre, and that they were powerless to regulate the affairs of the order. This was true but it also suited the Sultan to bide his time, so he was happy enough to accept the excuse for the time being. He knew that Acre was the toughest nut of all to crack, especially as it was now effectively almost a place of last resort for the Franks of Outremer; should the city fall, there would be nowhere else to run. But he was already making covert preparations to attack it, for example he had by now secretly laid plans to construct the biggest mangonel yet seen in the Middle East. It was to be called *al-Manṣūra,* 'the Victorious'.

The fact that the authorities in Acre were compelled to justify themselves for their involvement (or in this case non-involvement) in the defence of a fellow Frankish settlement also epitomised their military emasculation. Their position was not helped by aggressive behaviour on the part of the Genoese, who launched frequent attacks against Egyptian shipping. The Sultan responded by closing the port of Alexandria to them. Hitting them in the pocket hurt and they sent a delegation to Cairo to try and rebuild diplomatic bridges. When they arrived there they found that they had to wait their turn behind a delegation from Constantinople and another from the Holy Roman

Empire. They even found themselves outdone by an embassy from Yemen; the Genoese had brought a huge dog with them as a gift, but the magnificence of this offering was overshadowed by the rhinoceros that accompanied the Yemenis. Trade routes had also shifted to Acre's disadvantage. As those Genoese visited Egypt, they might have seen traders from India and China there. Funds were pouring into Egypt and bypassing Acre. Therefore, arguments that it was commercially advantageous to keep a Frankish presence alive in the port were becoming less and less tenable to the Mamluks.

For those left inside Acre, the picture was increasingly bleak. Outremer had been going through a process of dismemberment piecemeal for several decades. It is a truism of most wars that they are rarely won by single decisive battles, no matter how spectacular they might be. To quote two near-contemporary battles, Bannockburn (1314) did not result in Scottish independence; that was over a decade longer in coming and even that did not bring an end to the Anglo-Scottish wars of the time. And Agincourt (1415) did not bring about the collapse of France; it only ushered in a further campaign in Normandy, and despite its ultimate success the English were permanently ejected from the country four decades later. The Hastings and Hattins of this world are few and far between. Rather, wars are usually won and lost by a process of attrition. It is sieges and skirmishes or raids on caravans and supply trains that win them, the gradual grinding down of the enemy bit by bit. That had certainly been the case in Outremer. Nor was it just the loss of towns that was an issue. The elimination of powerful fortresses like Crac des Chevaliers, Marqab, Safad and Montreal had also taken its toll. These were the outer defences of Outremer, like the shell of a turtle that had now been brutally removed leaving Acre increasingly vulnerable. It was dying from exhaustion and a general extinguishment of hope.

The loss of so much territory in Outremer had major practical repercussions. It caused serious damage to the economy; the time had long passed since the Kingdom of Jerusalem was widely held to be some kind of sacred totem and commerce as much as religion was now the spur for many, with the exception of the occasional influx of fanatical pilgrims from Europe. In addition, many fourth- or fifth-generation settlers now knew no other way of life and any feeling of spirituality that might have been present among those who were in the first wave of Crusaders nearly two centuries before had now for many been subsumed by the quotidian demands of existence.

These losses also denuded military resources. The kingdom had relied hugely on the military orders and they were inevitably feeling the strain of the progressive attrition they had suffered. For example, the Teutonic Knights were already showing signs that they were becoming more interested in the Baltic than the Mediterranean. Decades before, one of their most influential leaders, Hermann von Salza (Master from 1210–39), had become concerned that the East might be lost to Christendom and that a new theatre of operations might be needed; a very prescient piece of analysis as it turned out. He engaged in a number of initiatives to widen the sphere of influence of his Order including efforts in Armenia, the Peloponnese, Burzenland (the region around Brasov in modern Romania), and most successfully in the Baltic region.[3] The impact of all these losses on morale has to be taken into account too, an extremely significant consideration in times of war. If one party loses the will to fight, victory for the other is often a formality. It remained to be seen how much of that particular commodity remained inside the city of Acre, as the moment of reckoning was approaching.

New Arrivals

The years 1290 and 1291 were a time of massive importance for Outremer and the wider Middle East. Yet another Mongol mission made its way west in 1290 seeking an alliance. It remained there for a year, during which time the world was turned on its head. Arghun died whilst the delegation was away. Little help had come from the West, though there had been some peripheral assistance. 800 Genoese had arrived in Baghdad during the previous year and had been asked to help with building ships for use against Egyptian vessels in the southern approaches to the Red Sea. Although this marked a major change in policy by Genoa, possibly instigated by increasing Venetian influence in the Black Sea region, it did not last long. The Genoese government soon abandoned the scheme and re-cemented relations with the Mamluks. In an outbreak of uncontrolled brawling that was all too typical of the Italian city states at the time, the Genoese in Mesopotamia fell out with each other and split into factions. Much blood was shed between these competing groups in the coastal city of Basra.[4]

Despite the general apathy regarding the state of Outremer in the West, the fall of Tripoli still created a palpable sense of shock. A delegation including Jean de Grailly was sent from Outremer to Europe to drum up support. The new Pope (Nicholas IV, elected in 1288) persuaded Venice to send twenty galleys to Acre. They were under the command of Jacopo Tiepolo, son of the late Doge Lorenzo and grandson of another Jacopo. Genoa was unlikely to provide much help; the city had concluded a new commercial treaty with the Mamluks in May 1290. However, five galleys were sent by King James of Sicily to join the Venetian Crusader fleet on its way to Acre, reaching the port in early summer. Pope Nicholas was a Franciscan who had a strong interest in the crusading movement. A prominent landholder, Roux of Sully, was also involved in these expeditions. In addition, the Pope sent money to Acre but even he was far more interested in what was happening in Sicily rather than in Outremer, as was much of Europe. Edward I of England was one exception to this general rule, but only because he was so occupied in building his own empire in Britain that he had no time for wars elsewhere. He had actually taken the cross in 1287, that is, he had publicly committed himself to once more be a Crusader, but in keeping with precedents set by previous English monarchs such as Henry II and Henry III, making such a promise proved to be rather different than keeping it. The hopelessness of the position of Acre should a full-scale attack come is perhaps best evidenced by the arrival of the Master of the Teutonic Knights, Burchard von Schwanden, in Outremer in 1290. He came accompanied by forty knights and 400 other men-at-arms. This was a welcome addition to the resources available to the defenders, even if it was unlikely that on its own it would swing the balance in favour of the Crusaders. In any event, any initial elation was short-lived as soon after, Burchard announced that he was resigning and taking up a position in Europe instead. It was hardly a Churchillian statement of intent. Despite Nicholas's pleas for Crusader recruits, the most significant element would be a number of 'common people' from Italy, a combination of unemployed city dwellers and peasants who had been taken over by crusade fever. They took the cross and sailed enthusiastically to Acre. In a supreme irony it was these zealous but ill-disciplined Crusaders who would seal the ultimate fate of Outremer.

That said, regardless of the progressive emasculation of the Kingdom of Jerusalem, by some measures life appeared to go on and even in some respects thrive during the final years of its existence. Artistic production continued apace in Acre despite the loss of major Frankish centres such as Antioch and Tripoli. There is strong evidence of good-quality art continuing to be produced there, particularly in the forms of vividly illuminated manuscripts and icon painting in a distinctive Franco-Byzantine style. Some fine work was taken away from Acre by refugees when it eventually fell, examples that show that art not only continued to be produced but that creative development continued during the final years of the Kingdom of Jerusalem. This is a useful reminder that, whilst in retrospect it might appear that the loss of Acre was inevitable, it might not have seemed so at the time, as people went on with their everyday lives right up until the end.[5]

The art that survives also tells us something of the rather unique culture that had by now developed in Outremer. Whilst the manuscripts give clear indications of Western techniques, local inspirations are also very evident. For example, one illustration shows Frankish nobles playing chess; but they are sitting cross-legged on the ground, a pose often found in Persian portraits, instead of sitting on chairs or benches as they would be in the West. Amazons portrayed in the Brussels Codex are armed with bows and arrows, like Turcopoles, rather than carrying spears, swords and shields. Important figures in various manuscripts wear robes that appear to be influenced by Mongol costume. It may be coincidence in terms of those manuscripts which survived the destruction of Acre and those which did not, but all those that did escape the devastation are secular rather than ecclesiastical in nature and written in the vernacular. These works would likely have been of interest to the local aristocracy or well-off merchants. The artists would most likely have been laymen rather than clerics, as indeed is known to have been the case in Paris since about 1200.[6]

A truce had been in place between Acre and its Muslim neighbours since 1283 (it had recently been renewed) and it had been holding up to some extent as far as the city was concerned, though the attacks on Latakia and Tripoli showed that there was always a danger of an opportunistic breach of it by the Mamluks. However, life in Acre went on with a degree of peaceful co-existence. Peasants from the Muslim hinterlands were allowed to enter Acre freely and trade their wares including wheat and other goods. Apart from being in everyone's interests to have a period of peace, it was also plain common sense. Acre was not self-sufficient and goods needed to be brought in from the neighbouring territories to sustain the population. Local Muslim farmers were happy to oblige and make money. For most of those living in the region, be they Frank or Muslim, there was little interest in adopting entrenched moral positions fed by fanaticism. Throughout July 1290 traders from Syria moved in and out of Acre without a problem. Goods and money exchanged hands freely and all was generally well with the world.

But a storm cloud was coming in from the West. It would bring a hurricane in its wake. Crusading fervour back in Europe was fed by passionate oratory from preachers encouraging their listeners to make their way to the Holy Land and strike a blow for Christ. Anti-Semitic outrages perpetrated by Christian pilgrims had been all too common a feature of crusading missions ever since the movement first took form. Even more inevitably, Muslims were demonised. New arrivals in Outremer were often not Christian visitors prepared to turn the other cheek if they were attacked; rather they planned to get their blows in first. They were not acquainted with, and indeed probably not interested in, political realities on the ground in Outremer. They were not the first to struggle to cope with the degree of co-existence they found on arrival. Jacques de Vitry, Bishop of Acre from 1216 to 1225, lamented the lack of interest in converting local Muslims to Christianity that he found in Outremer. Modern historians postulate that this trend had been apparent from the second half of the twelfth century after the mass migration that was hoped for from the West did not happen and there was a need to rely on Muslim rural populations for the very pragmatic reason that the settlers needed to eat to live. There were also commercial opportunities arising from this. The widespread production of sugar cane in the hinterland meant that not only could it be used to feed Acre but also that surpluses could be shipped through there to Europe.

This sometimes created tensions within Christendom. The Church was on occasion extremely critical of secular Frankish society in the region, which often did not share its views on pressuring local Muslims to convert. As far back as 1199 Pope Innocent III had been complaining that the frequent use of truces by the Franks of Outremer diluted enthusiasm for crusades in Europe.[7] As we have already noted, the Muslim traveller Ibn Jubayr remarked on the generally tolerant way in which Islamic elements living among the Franks were treated. Muslims were allowed in some circumstances to own property in Frankish towns and also had their own law courts to deal with certain issues. Short-term arrivals from the West had previously noted the tolerance exhibited by the Frankish population to their Muslim neighbours. A German poet and Crusader called Freidank, who had been part of Frederick II's expedition to Outremer in 1228, was disconcerted to find that there was no real difference in the treatment of Christians and 'pagans' in the region. Regular peace agreements between men like Frederick and the Muslims only added to the sense of a need for co-existence if the Franks were to survive. Even the military orders got in on the act and there are records concerning some of the interpreters that they employed so that they could enter into dialogue with neighbouring Muslim powers.[8]

When this new influx of Italian Crusaders arrived in Acre and saw the degree of tolerance that was in place, they were at first confused and then enraged. They were expecting to be fighting Muslims, not trading with them. What they had been told back in Europe had not prepared them for the kind of *realpolitik* that they were witnessing. They simmered and seethed inwardly at such ungodly behaviour where Mammon was being put unashamedly before God. It would take only a stray ember to spark a conflagration. It duly came in August and the recently arrived Crusaders rushed through the streets and unleashed a frenzied orgy of killing. Anyone who looked alien seems to have been a target, not only bona fide Muslims whose only reason to be in Acre was to do business but also local Orthodox Syriac Christians. The latter were killed merely because it was their fashion to wear beards and this marked them out from Latin Christians who generally went clean-shaven. Rather than save the Holy Land for Christendom, this undisciplined rabble had sealed its fate. The authorities in Acre managed to restore order but much too late. In the current febrile environment, the actions of the out-of-control Italian Crusaders had been incendiary. The Mamluks had enjoyed years of almost unbroken triumph and held most of the trump cards. Outremer could ill afford to antagonise Qalāwūn, but now he was likely to be enraged. Various stories developed to explain the course of events. One version suggested that a Christian woman had been caught in adultery with a Muslim man and a jealous husband killed them both, after which a riot broke out. The truth of the matter was largely irrelevant; the Sultan would almost inevitably demand retribution.

As the Muslim holy day, Friday prayers have a particular importance for Muslims, a time when the Jumu'ah – the congregational prayer reserved for that day – is said. Paradoxically, given the significance of Fridays, a day which is especially respected by devout Muslims, it is also a popular day of protest when dissatisfaction may be expressed about the actions of the ruling elite. In 1111 for example, a party of Islamic scholars from Aleppo disrupted Friday prayers in Baghdad, protesting loudly at the inadequate response of the Islamic world to the Frankish invasions in the Levant which were, to them, an outrage. Even today, Fridays are often used as a time for protest by dissatisfied Muslims.

On Friday 30 August 1290 in Cairo a group of distressed men entered the Great Mosque. They carried with them the bloodstained clothes of their families and friends who had been murdered in Acre. They demanded retribution. The Templar of Tyre alleges that Qalāwūn was looking for an excuse to finish Acre off and this gave him the perfect justification to do so. This may be true, though quite how the Templar would know this is not clear. In any event, the fanatical actions of the new arrivals had made this really easy for Qalāwūn; the Templar is hardly overstating the case when he describes the murderous actions of the new arrivals as 'ill-done'. The Sultan was 'most infuriated by [these events] and raged against the people of Acre'.[9] He fired off a letter to the authorities there, demanding that the guilty parties be handed over for justice to be meted out.

This put the government of Acre in a quandary. To merely hand over the misguided Crusaders to Qalāwūn would put them in an invidious position with their own side. William of Beaujeu argued for expediency. He suggested that all those held for crimes in the royal prison and those of the Templars, Hospitallers, Pisans and Venetians who had been sentenced to death should be handed over to the Muslims for execution, even though they had nothing to do with the killings for which Qalāwūn sought justice. The Sultan would after all not know this and he might be satisfied with making an example of a group of prisoners who were destined to die anyway. Although some agreed with William, many others did not. They instead came up with a story that was almost certainly going to be unacceptable, namely that the killers were foreigners over whom they had no jurisdiction. This was a feeble response and unlikely to appease Qalāwūn; after all, the killings had taken place inside Acre's walls and the response from the authorities there was desperately weak.

There are hidden messages in these events which are easy to overlook. The first question to be asked is why the Sultan wrote to the Master of the Temple. Even though the Templars – and the other main orders – had a base in Acre, they did not apparently have a place on the ruling council of the city. It suggests that, even if the Temple did not have a legal role in the running of Acre, real power was seen to be in their hands more than those of anyone else. There is another clue to the state of Acre in the existence of at least five prisons in the city, all under different authorities. In short, Acre was a jurisdictional nightmare, a situation that was clearly highlighted in the response to Qalāwūn's demands. This was not some administrative breakdown of governance arrangements for the city; the lack of a coordinated response and a common purpose was about to come home to roost.

The Sultan waited for an answer, but it is probable that he was already thinking about his next move ahead of it being received. The response of the authorities at Acre notwithstanding, he was surely pondering over whether or not he wished to obliterate it altogether, as Antioch and more recently Latakia and Tripoli had been eliminated. But whatever action he eventually took, he was also keen to ensure that legally his actions were justified. The incident at Acre had occurred whilst there was a truce in force between the city and Qalāwūn. The Sultan had taken the most solemn oath to comply with the terms of the treaty when it was put in place and he wished to be justified in taking retribution should he choose to do so. His jurists considered the matter closely. Not all of them were convinced that the terms of the truce had been broken, as it was foreign visitors that had breached it and not citizens of Acre. But then one of them, by the name of Fath al-Din, advised him that the terms of the truce were flexible enough for the Sultan to decide for himself whether or not to attack Acre in retaliation; if he chose to do so, then in his opinion, he was legally justified. It was probably exactly the advice that Qalāwūn wanted to hear. Carte blanche was exactly what was required.

The Death of Qalāwūn

Acre's attempt to wash its hands of the killings in its streets led to a predictable response. The Templar of Tyre wrote that 'the Sultan took this answer badly'. He sent a demand to Acre for enormous compensation, which he knew would not be forthcoming. He then assembled a large army and got together a strong ensemble of siege engines, calling a general mobilisation of his forces in October 1290. Meticulous arrangements were made for the expedition. Way stations were set up in advance of his armies. Here the men could rest and pick up fresh provisions on their way to Acre. The emir Rukn ad-Din Taqsu al-Mansuri was also sent on ahead. He was to scour the area between Caesarea and Atlit for wood with which to make *buches* to protect troops in the trenches. In the event, Taqsu was to be there for four months undertaking his task. He told the locals that the intention was to take the timber he cut back to Cairo, but it is unlikely that anyone was fooled. Anyway, William of Beaujeu's spy in Cairo was still active and telling him what was really happening there. The gifts that the Templars had subscribed over the years were proving worthwhile – or at least they should have done, but once more, few believed the Master of the Templars when he passed his news on.

Qalāwūn duly set out from Cairo on 4 November 1290. There was a magnificent procession as he and his army headed towards Acre; though few knew it, this would also be his last farewell to the city. In an effort to throw the Franks off guard, he announced that his army was headed for Nubia. It was an entirely believable story. There had been trouble on Egypt's southern borders for some time. The issue had come to a head during the winter of 1289–90. King Shemamun of Makaria had retreated south and the Mamluks had installed a new king to take his place in Dongola. By March 1290, Shemamun was back. He retook Dongola and drove out the pro-Mamluk ruler, then himself accepted Mamluk suzerainty. It was certainly conceivable that the Mamluks might be unhappy at this regime change and would take steps to reverse it. The Sultan also made arrangements to send men to escort pilgrims making the *hajj* journey to Mecca so that they could complete it in safety. He may well have intended to make such a journey himself, but that plan had now been overtaken by events.

In Qalāwūn's entourage was the emir Husam al-Din Turuntay. He was a Turk, raised from an early age as a protégé of the Sultan. He had recently proved his worth in the campaigns against Tripoli. He had by now risen to a position of great prominence, but success, like the drug it can be, had gone to his head and he hoped for even more. Perhaps inspired by past coups against ruling Sultans like those against Turānshāh and Qutuz, he arranged for Qalāwūn to be assassinated. He poisoned the Sultan but was caught in the act, though not before Qalāwūn had swallowed a fatal dose. Qalāwūn realised that he was dying and summoned his eldest son, Khalil al-Ashraf, to his side to give him his last orders. It was a difficult encounter. Qalāwūn had wanted another son, al-Malik al-Salih Ali, to succeed but he had died in 1288. The dying Sultan did not apparently rate al-Ashraf's talents very highly. Qalāwūn's instructions to his heir were twofold. First of all, he must carry on with the expedition to take Acre and gain vengeance for the Muslims who had been killed there not long before. The second order was that Turuntay should be executed for his crime. After Qalāwūn was buried in an honourable fashion (he died on 10 November), justice was meted out to Turuntay on the very same day. The assassin was thrown on his back with his hands tied in front of Khalil al-Ashraf. The new Sultan (who was formally declared such on 12 November) tore out the beard of Turuntay as he lay prone and helpless before him, kneeling on his chest as he did so. It was an act of great humiliation and was followed by the assassin's death. His body was dismembered and left unburied.

That at least is the version given by the Templar of Tyre.[10] Muslim accounts tell quite a different story. They say that the Sultan had been ill for some time and that it was an ongoing malady that finally killed him. That may be true, but the execution of Turuntay leaves a lingering doubt in the mind. Pious Muslim commentators noted that, for all his great resources and his mighty army, Qalāwūn was as powerless as any other human being in the face of the greatest and most invincible enemy of all – death. The late Sultan's body was taken back to Cairo where he was buried with due reverence in an ornate mausoleum in January 1291.

Qalāwūn's army had not yet moved far from Cairo when these dramatic events intervened. The new Sultan, Khalil al-Ashraf, did not hurry to attack Acre and sent out orders that the campaign was to be postponed until the spring. This was wise. He had not yet secured his position in Cairo and Acre was not going anywhere soon. Further, the chances of those inside the city receiving meaningful reinforcements soon was small. So the work on the way stations was completed and the preparations for the men in his army were continued. It was clear that his force would anyway have a huge numerical superiority over the defenders of Acre. The Templar of Tyre says that al-Ashraf's army consisted of 70,000 horsemen and over 150,000 infantry. Inside Acre there were, at most, 40,000 people including women and children. There were only about 700 to 800 horsemen and 13,000 infantry available for the city's defence.

The news of Qalāwūn's death raised hopes inside Acre. Those inside her walls reasoned that there might now be a long delay before al-Ashraf was ready to attack the city. They hoped to ingratiate themselves with him by sending a delegation to Cairo replete with gifts. There were four envoys: Philip Mainebeuf, a knight in Acre who spoke good Arabic; a Templar named Bartholomew Pisan who originated in Cyprus; an unnamed Hospitaller knight; and a scribe. Al-Ashraf wished to make a strong first impression on both his own people and his enemies. He refused to accept the gifts or the letters sent and had the envoys thrown into prison. Al-Ashraf sent a response soon afterwards to Acre; we know this because the Templar of Tyre writes that he personally translated it into French from Arabic. The gloves were off. The missive was addressed to William of Beaujeu but was naturally shown by him to others, including the Patriarch and papal legate Nicholas of Hanapes, the Master of the Hospitallers and the Commander of the Teutonic Knights. The Teutonic Knights were in turmoil at the time as their Master, Burchard of Schwanden, had recently resigned and moved to Apulia in Italy. He would later join the Hospitallers and be replaced as Master by Conrad of Feuchtwangen. The Teutonic Order was on the verge of splitting over policy, namely whether to remain in the Holy Land or to concentrate instead on other areas, especially the Baltic, which was the ultimate decision that was made. Representatives of the Venetians and Pisans were also shown al-Ashraf's letter but seemed unconvinced that it represented a real threat.[11]

Al-Ashraf's letter was imperious in its tone and is worth quoting at length as it lays out clearly his position on the eve of the siege of Acre. It started with self-exulting declamations, which some might view as bluster (though such proud titles in the opening address were the normal way of doing things as far as Mamluk Sultans were concerned):

The Sultan of Sultans, King of Kings, Lord of Lords, al-Malik al-Ashraf, the Powerful, the Dreadful, the Scourge of Rebels, Hunter of Franks and Tartars and Armenians, Snatcher of Castles from the Hands of Miscreants, Lord of the Two Seas [the Red Sea and the Mediterranean – the latter was certainly not under Mamluk control], Guardian of the Two Pilgrim Sites, Khalil al-Salihi.

Al-Ashraf is setting out his credentials here. He is new to the role and has to do so. In the process he was exaggerating his track record but there was no doubt that his successors had certainly carried many of the credentials he now claimed for himself. However, this was a formulaic opening. It was what came next that carried the threat:

> To the noble master of the Temple [William of Beaujeu], the true and wise. Greetings and our goodwill! Because you have been a true man, so we send you advance notice of our intentions, and give you to understand that we are coming into your parts to right the wrongs that have been done. Therefore we do not want the community of Acre to send us any letters or presents for we will by no means receive them.[12]

Given the advantages he enjoyed and the weakness of Acre there was no need for al-Ashraf to retain the element of surprise. Instead, the tactic was now clearly to sew fear in advance of his attack, which would hopefully destroy the morale of those inside the city. It is again significant that the letter was sent to William of Beaujeu, who appears to have been playing the role of the moderating negotiator in recent times. It was a strategy that had clearly ultimately failed, perhaps because the mob behaviour of new arrivals had undermined it, perhaps because the new Sultan was determined to mark the start of his reign with a landmark triumph, or a combination of these and other factors. In any event, al-Ashraf's order that no delegations bearing gifts should journey to Cairo was ignored; and if the Templar of Tyre's account is correct, none of those involved in the subsequent hopeless peace missions to Cairo to try to prevent the inevitable ever came out of their prison cells there alive.[13]

12

Opening Exchanges

'There should be no abating of the amount of mangonel
fire in any hour of the day or night.'

The Islamic commentator al-Ansari on the
gentle arts of siege warfare

The Army Sets Out

An appeal for clemency was received from the authorities in Acre by al-Ashraf in early 1291. It fell on deaf ears, which was no surprise after the Sultan's unequivocal instructions to the city that they should send no more negotiators to waste his time. Passions were running high in the Muslim world after the massacre suffered by their co-religionists in the city and al-Ashraf, new to the role of Sultan as he was, could not afford to appear weak. Incumbent Sultans lived a life that was permanently in the public eye and there were too many precedents of ineffective, or even effective but blind-sided, predecessors being removed. What better way for the new man on the throne to start his reign than with a victory of historic proportions? Such would ensure his legacy even when his reign had barely begun.

During the winter, siege engines were constructed using timber from the Lebanese mountains. They were built in sections, making them easier to transport so that they could be pieced them together when in situ. On 6 March 1291, al-Ashraf and his army left Cairo. The flames of war were further fanned in Damascus where yet more passionate oratory flowed from Muslim preachers encouraging believers to commit themselves to *jihad*. The Egyptian Muslims were already onboard; now it was time to get the Syrians to follow suit. The preachers (*ghazis*) did their job exceedingly well. As in the build-up to the Hattin campaign, there was a huge rush of recruits, so much so that the number of untrained volunteers who offered their services outnumbered the professional soldiers in al-Ashraf's army. Even religious scholars – men more used to the pen than manual labour – offered to help push the mighty mangonels that had been constructed from Damascus to Acre. The main Syrian army set out for Acre on 25 March.

The weather was doing its best to make things difficult. Unusually heavy snow delayed the start of the contingent from Hama for Acre, whilst the huge mangonel known as al-Manşūra took a month to wheel up – a journey that would normally take just over a week. The rugged hills of Syria can experience marked extremes of temperature and such was clearly the case on this occasion. The mangonel was constructed at the castle of Hisn al-Akrad; a bitter irony this, as it was the former Hospitaller stronghold of Crac des Chevaliers. Overworked and exhausted oxen collapsed and died under the joint strain of their heavy burden and the debilitating wintry conditions as they lumbered through the snow and the cold. The cruel reality was that all these problems were irritating but not ultimately of decisive significance to subsequent events. The defenders of Acre were outmatched and with little hope of meaningful reinforcement. Some men might with luck come over from nearby Cyprus, but they were unlikely to be in sufficient numbers to make a difference. Any help from Europe was months away and in any event, recent precedents for assistance from that direction were not encouraging. The Muslim army had no such worries. By 28 March, the army of Hama was in Damascus and the siege and supply train was ready to set out.

There was just one area where the Franks still held an advantage. They yet retained dominance of the sea and this was to make some difference in the fight that lay ahead. It meant that provisions and also hopefully reinforcements could be shipped in. In addition there was still an escape route from the city, should it be needed. Despite the great challenge of holding firm in the face of the mighty army that was moving towards them, the defenders steeled themselves to put up a brave fight. All the available men from the military orders, Templars, Hospitallers, Teutonic Knights and others, were inside, alongside secular troops. They were determined to sell their city dearly. Most other Frankish garrisons in what remained of Outremer were denuded in an attempt to make the stronghold of Acre as formidable as possible; another echo of the Hattin campaign, though this time there was little prospect of the Franks taking the offensive as they had then. Circumstances had changed drastically over the course of the last century.

Acre housed major complexes for the military orders as well as for the secular authorities. The best surviving example is the Hospitaller fortress in the city. The Hospitallers had been present in Acre almost since the beginning, the first recorded granting of land to them (near the Church of the Holy Cross) being made as long ago as 1110. Later expansion of the cathedral caused them to rebuild their Acre headquarters in the north-west quarter where it remained in 1291. However, the residential quarters of the brothers (known as the *auberge*) were not here but in the suburb of Montmusard. Following the loss of Jerusalem after Hattin and the partial restoration of the kingdom, shortly after it was decided that the existing fortress was no longer fit for purpose and major building works started at the end of the twelfth century and continued into the thirteenth. It seems that the capacity of the existing Hospitaller buildings in Acre was simply insufficient, particularly when Chapter meetings were held involving visiting officials from Europe as well as Outremer.[1] Newer sites such as this would make formidable refuges of last resort, as subsequent events would prove. This was true of the Templars as well, whose *auberge* was also in Montmusard but who in addition had a very strong fortress in the Old City, right next to the harbour.

Whilst most discussions of the military orders at Acre in 1291 understandably focus on the three best-known examples, namely the Templars, the Hospitallers and the Teutonic Knights, there were others there. One of them was known as the Knights of St Thomas, composed of Englishmen. Formally entitled the Hospitallers of St Thomas of Canterbury at Acre, it had been founded exactly a century before by Richard the Lionheart during the previous great siege of the city. Once more, its initial function had been to care for the sick and the order had gained enough support to establish a church and hospital in Acre dedicated to St Thomas Becket, killed as a result of Richard's father, Henry II, losing his self-control. In common with many other orders, it soon became militarised as a result of the efforts of Peter des Roches, Bishop of Winchester, during the Fifth Crusade that had ended so disastrously in Egypt. They adopted the rule of the Teutonic Knights. In addition, there were secular troops there. A little-known source of information found in Lucca, Italy, only 100 years ago makes mention of men from France, Germany, Catalonia and Italy.[2] As we know that some men from other countries such as Otho de Grandson were present, this was truly a cosmopolitan force.

Acre was a strongly defended city. To the west it was protected by the sea, its rocky shoreline making it virtually unapproachable by an enemy fleet even if the Mamluks had possessed one that was powerful enough to achieve naval dominance. The harbour was to the south, effectively in the south-western corner of Acre. It was not particularly large and there was a narrow entrance into it, across which a chain could be raised and lowered. The main focus of the fortifications was inevitably on the landward side. Acre could simplistically be divided into two. The Old City was contained within a rectangle on the southern side. It was here that the Italian city states had their quarters abutting the harbour. The military orders also had substantial buildings here. To the north of the Old City, stretching about halfway along its northern walls, was the suburb of Montmusard.

The walls stretched for around a mile on the north and east side. There were two lines of walls all the way around Acre. As it was a commercial centre there were a number of gates built into these. The walls of Montmusard were interrupted by the Gate of Lazarus, close to the sea on the north-west side, the ominously named Gate of the Evil Step about halfway along, and right at the junction that abutted the walls of the Old City stood the St Anthony Gate. There was an entrance direct into the Old City from outside at the Gate of St Nicholas. The most vulnerable part of Acre's defences was between the St Anthony Gate and the Gate of St Nicholas and it was this sector that would be subject to the most relentless attention from the besieging forces. For obvious reasons, gateways were always a potential weak spot (the gatehouse of a medieval castle was often elaborately designed for defensive purposes to counteract this inherent vulnerability). There were a number of large towers liberally spread along the walls too, especially around the Old City. These were often named after those who were responsible for sponsoring their construction: the Tower of the Venetians, the Tower of the English, the King's Tower, the Tower of the Countess of Blois, the Tower of the Genoese, the Butcher's Tower.

Sections of these extended defences were allocated to different groups of troops. At the extreme north-west, where the suburb of Montmusard met the sea, the Templars under William of Beaujeu were given responsibility assisted by the Knights of St Lazarus. Then came the Hospitallers, supported by the English Knights of St Thomas, and next to them came the Teutonic Knights. They were responsible for the important section of the walls that led to St Anthony's Gate. The walls took a sharp right-angled turn by the King's Tower, the Accursed Tower and a barbican in front of it. This was a vulnerable section, protruding awkwardly and exposed to probably the strongest part of the enemy forces, who had identified it as a potential weakness. An enemy who managed to take the Accursed Tower would have direct access to the heart of the Old City and there would be little to stop him pushing on to the harbour, apart from the labyrinth of streets and houses. This key part of the defences was the responsibility of troops from Cyprus. The last section, running down the eastern side of old Acre to the port, was the responsibility of the French Regiment under Jean de Grailly and the small English contingent led by Otho de Grandson, who, although he was a Savoyard, had been in England since the 1250s. It was a fragmented command structure and to try and bring the various elements together a war council was arranged. Included on it were Amalric of Cyprus (the brother of King Henry II who was not yet present), Jean de Grailly, Otho de Grandson and the Patriarch of Jerusalem, Nicolas de Hanapes.[3]

The First Shots

Acre was now densely populated, especially the Old City, as dispossessed Franks who had lost their homes in the face of the Muslim advance in recent years had made their way there and attempted to rebuild their shattered lives. Because of this, the implacable economic rules of supply and demand had driven up prices. Merchants such as Albertino de Placa rented rather than purchased property, perhaps because of this.[4] To cope with the expansion of the city over the years, the suburb of Montmusard had grown up outside the walls, in a mostly ad hoc fashion. There are occasional historical glimpses of planned developments there; for example, a visiting pilgrim, Wilbrand of Oldenburg, who was in Acre in 1212, commented that the suburb had recently been fortified, possibly at the behest of the then King, John of Brienne. Further development followed and by 1291 the city was a formidable military obstacle.

The Muslim army came with an impressive array of siege artillery. These ranged from engines that could hurl massive balls of rock through the air to much smaller devices known as *arrada*. The *arrada* fired projectiles that travelled only about 120 metres but would still do immense damage to anybody unfortunate enough to get in the way. The Muslim version of Greek fire, *naft,* was particularly terrifying, a medieval equivalent of the notorious modern weapon napalm. Animal welfare advocates would not be impressed at its contents, which included dolphin fat and goats' kidneys.[5] It would cause immense damage when it took hold and of course it was indiscriminate in its targets. The concept of collateral damage did not generally exist in medieval warfare. There was no Geneva Convention and everybody was potentially a legitimate target. When not being used to shoot off incendiary missiles, the light artillery, which could be fired relatively quickly, could be employed as a very effective anti-personnel measure to keep the battlements clear of defenders. Thus medieval siege artillery had two primary objectives, destruction and neutralisation. Lighter engines could more easily be moved into positions from where they could be used to focus on new targets with less complications involved in shifting them. The larger ones of course were much less easy to manage and shifting them to new positions was much more of a challenge.

The heavy artillery would normally be the last to be called into use. The heavier machines no longer relied on brute force alone to operate them. More effective counterweight-based engines were a major technological advance that helped improve efficiency and effectiveness no end. There were fifteen heavy *bricolas* at Acre, capable of projecting rocks weighing 185 kg/400 lbs or more.[6] These are known in Arabic sources as the 'Frankish' trebuchet, emphasising how cross-fertilisation of ideas from West to East as well as East to West played a key role in the development of artillery; because of the shape of its firing mechanism it was also known as 'the two-testicle machine'.[7] Heavy machines often needed to be constructed on-site with raw materials brought in from further afield. Once they came into play the effect could be devastating. They would smash into walls with huge force, breaking masonry and sending fragments of shrapnel far and wide. Anyone unlucky enough to be in the way ran the risk of being crushed to a pulp or pierced through with sharp shards of stone. These machines were, however, cumbersome and slow to operate.

The missile bombardment launched by a besieging force would ideally be non-stop. To add to the cacophony hundreds of kettle drums would beat out an incessant rhythm, designed to both boost the morale of the attackers and shatter that of the defenders. The whole was designed to create an atmosphere of blind terror among those on the receiving end, hopefully forcing them to give up hope and abandon the fight. Miners would start chipping away at the foundations of fortifications, meaning that the defenders would need to look both up and down; a contingent from Aleppo would be particularly prominent in the siege of Acre.[8]

The Islamic commentator al-Ansari at the end of the fourteenth century wrote a military manual which makes clear that the psychological approach to waging war effectively was very well developed in the Islamic world:

> And when the armed attack takes place it is necessary that the men of the army fight with the most convenient of arms first then the next most convenient, delaying the use of the largest arms until last of those which they employ in attacking. In this manner it becomes apparent to the people in the fortress that each successive implement is a little more than the proceeding one... When the investment is under way there should be no pause in the discharging of the mangonels against them and there should be no abating of the amount of mangonel fire in any hour of the day or night. To desist in attack against them is among that which cools their fright and strengthens their heart.[9]

The huge assemblage of siege engines meant that a terrifying ordeal now loomed for the defenders of Acre. The sheer scale of such warfare had grown exponentially in the past century. When Saladin laid siege to Jerusalem in 1187, he had ten machines with him. The Muslim army outside Acre had as many as ninety.[10] The Franks inside Acre took what countermeasures they could to lessen the fearsome impact of these machines and their deadly projectiles. These included padding the walls with straw and cloth to absorb the blows of the enemy's missiles, hanging the 'palliasses' from wooden beams suspended about 1 metre out from the battlements.[11] In response to these countermeasures, the besieging forces used incendiary missiles in an attempt to set the straw and cloth alight; this is where the blazing-bolt-projecting *carabohas* came into play, projectiles from which were described by Baybars al-Mansuri as being like 'gleaming flashes of lightning'.

On 5 April, al-Ashraf established his headquarters on the hill of Tal al-Fukhar on the eastern side of Acre opposite the Legate's Tower, taking up residence in a red tent (*dihliz*) as the Mamluk forces started to get into position. His tent was pitched on the site of a Templar vineyard. It was positioned so that when he exited the porch of his tent Acre would be in full view and always therefore at the forefront of his mind, keeping him sharply focused on the task in hand. He may have mused that the end of an arduous journey was not now far off. It had been a lengthy path, trodden first by Baybars and then Qalāwūn. There had been many milestones along the way: Caesarea, Arsuf, Antioch, Safad, Crac, Montfort, Marqab, Latakia, Tripoli and many others. The terminus was Acre. There was also another symbolic element to the choice of this location; this was the very spot on which Guy of Lusignan had pitched his tent when first laying siege to Acre just over a century before.

The following day the siege formally began, although it was not until 11 April that a full-scale bombardment of the city started and indeed the artillery did not arrive outside Acre until 8 April, having made its way over from Syria. The build-up to the attack was slow and methodical, which in its own way would have ratcheted up the psychological pressure on those inside. There was little likelihood of help coming to Acre and time was therefore not of the essence. The Muslim army could take its time in encircling Acre like a constrictor sizing up and then moving in on its helpless prey. The Muslim line was quite far out at this stage, being some 2 kilometres from the city walls. The Muslims then gradually moved forwards closer to the perimeter of the city, setting up barricades and wicker screens (*buches*) as protection against counter-fire from inside the walls. But for the first eight days not much happened, almost a period of 'phoney war' punctuated by occasional skirmishes and a smattering of losses on either side. When at last the besieging army moved closer to the walls of Acre, it was accompanied by a tumultuous noise made by trumpets, cymbals, drums and the acclamation of thousands of voices. The roar of the siege engines was soon adding to the din. Commentators described them as bellowing like oxen, barking like dogs and roaring like lions. It was as if the machines had taken on an animate life of their own, assuming the character of monsters.[12] It added to the terror of the defenders no end that they could see their enemy meticulously preparing for the attack in full view of them. They were powerless to do very much about it.

As far as the land forces were concerned, the Mamluks certainly held the upper hand. They methodically laid their siege around the city, encircling it from the landward side. But Frankish naval forces still ruled the waves. One eyewitness from the army of Hama, Ismail Abu'l Fida, was on the right wing with his men next to the sea. They suddenly found themselves under attack from the water. Ships protected by timber vaulting with oxhides spread over them fired arrows down on his men. They had sailed out of the harbour and fallen on the extreme right of the Muslim army. One of the ships bore a Pisan mangonel on deck, which bombarded the men and the tents of their camp. It was able to do this with impunity and created alarm among those on the receiving end, who were unable to do much in response. However, a fierce storm on the night of 13/14 April tossed the ship about so much that the mangonel was broken and of no further use. It was an unsettling reverse for the Crusader cause. By this stage, even token moral victories were welcome and another grain of hope had now gone. It was a blow to the Pisans too. The part of the Italian city states in the last days of Acre was not generally a glorious one. The hearts of both Venice and Genoa were not in the fight; they had commercial rather than military motivations in mind. Pisa was an honourable and noteworthy exception to the rule and the siege engines that her men operated played a valuable if ultimately futile part in the defence. Probably operating from the garden of the monastery of St Romanus, one of the few open areas left in the Old City, the Pisan engineers played a gallant role in the defence.[13]

The wicker revetments erected by the besieging army soon began to prove their worth. These had been erected methodically by men operating in four shifts a day so that the work could be efficiently completed in as short a time as possible. The engineers were well-guarded by screening troops who would intervene should a counter-attack be launched from inside Acre. At night, Muslim soldiers would take advantage of the darkness to pile up further material at the front of their revetments, which reached to the edge of a ditch surrounding the city. When Frankish artillery tried to bring these down, the stones that they lobbed over bounced harmlessly off and into the ditch. The screw was being tightened.

The smaller anti-personnel machines such as the *carabohas* were said by the Templar of Tyre to have caused many losses among the defenders, more in fact than those caused by the larger engines. Few men dared to stick their heads over the parapet, giving the attackers more opportunity of carrying on with their work unhindered. Prominent in the attacks at this early stage was the emir Sanjar al-Shuja'i who would later be designated governor of Syria. The siege engines were defended so effectively by the outworks assembled in front of them that the Franks could make little impression. It soon became clear that purely defensive tactics were unlikely to prove successful in driving the Muslim army off and that more initiative needed to be shown to change the power balance between the competing armies. To take a more aggressive stance was a high-risk strategy; but it was becoming increasingly obvious that if it was not adopted then Acre was doomed.

Frankish Counter-attacks and Dashed Hopes

Those under siege now changed tack, taking their own steps to try and gain an advantage. As purely defensive tactics were having no impact in terms of stopping the inexorable Muslim assault, more active measures were now needed. A tactic sometimes employed in medieval sieges was for those inside the walls to launch surprise attacks, especially at night. This could yield good results but was also fraught with risk, as of course it was difficult for the attackers to make out where they were in the dark and total confusion could sometimes be the outcome. Such seems to have been the case on the night of 15/16 April when the besieged sallied out against the camp of the army of Hama on the north side of Acre by the sea. A number of prominent knights took part including Jean de Grailly and Otho de Grandson. Otho had been sent to Acre by Edward I along with a small force of sixty knights. He was accompanied east by the Hospitaller prior of England, William of Henley. They would have had no idea when they left England that they were about to walk right into the middle of a war zone. A Provencal knight was given specific instructions to set the defences around one of the great Mamluk siege engines ablaze and hopefully destroy it. 300 Templars rode out under the light of the all-seeing moon. They came armed with Greek fire, that terrifying weapon that could do great damage should it take hold.

Things started well and the Muslim sentries were driven back. However, the man who was ordered to use Greek fire and set the Muslim defences alight lost his nerve. His specific target was the great siege engine known as 'The Furious' but when he threw the Greek fire, it fell short and burned out harmlessly. A great moment of opportunity was therefore missed. Whilst the loss of one large mangonel would not swing the balance towards the defenders, it would be a big blow to

Muslim morale. Such engines cost a great deal of time and money to assemble and much effort even to get them to Acre in the first place. Then when the Franks got in among the tents of the enemy camp things deteriorated further. In the darkness, men began to stumble over guy-ropes and flounder about trying to find their way through. This seems to have inspired the Muslims to strike back and they began to cut down the Franks in significant numbers. One knight literally met a messy end when he fell into a latrine. The attack ended in failure with eighteen horsemen killed. Some minor trophies of war were seized but it was an inadequate prize when the cost was taken into account.

An attempted ambush launched by the men from Hama on the returning forces was however beaten off. The Muslim soldiers launched showers of javelins at the force that had sallied out, causing some losses. But they did not feel confident enough to come to close-quarters with the well-armed knights including members of the military orders who had a formidable and well-deserved reputation. All that the raiders returned with from their sortie were a few trophies as souvenirs of their night's work and some additional supplies. This was far from the decisive return that was hoped for and did very little to stop the Mamluk army from continuing to prosecute its attack as vigorously as they had been doing previously. This largely unsuccessful foray would have done little to improve morale inside the city, a situation not improved when on the following day the heads of some of the dead Franks were displayed on poles in full view of the defenders. In retaliation, shields captured by the garrison were hung from the walls in a crude psychological tit-for-tat.[14] Heads wins.

According to the Templar of Tyre, this foray was part of a planned series of assaults from the city over a wider area but in the other sectors the besieging force was ready and waiting, so little was achieved. Despite the limited returns from this attack, the tactic was repeated three nights later, this time against the siege lines to the south of Acre. However, the Muslim forces were ready for such a foray and again the attack was unsuccessful in its primary objective of destroying the Muslim artillery. This was to be expected; the besieging force would have anticipated such an attack on their engines as they were a crucial weapon in their assault. In the absence of any realistic prospect of significant reinforcements, trying to destroy these mighty beasts was one of the few tactics that the defenders could usefully employ. The night was dark; the moon was not prominent. The waiting Muslim forces lit up the darkness with torches. It is likely that they had informants inside the city who had got word of the planned foray and were ready and waiting. Certainly, there were stories that a convert to Islam inside Acre fired an arrow out with a message attached to it telling the Muslim army to expect an attack.[15]

As far as they were able, the defenders were still trying to stay on the front foot. Medieval fortifications often included small gates known as sally ports. These were not very large and were meant only for individuals or small groups to pass through easily. They were small enough not to allow the enemy to come flooding through and could be shut quickly if needed. Muslim writers tell how these small gates into Acre (and possibly even some of the main gates) were left virtually permanently open so that Frankish knights could sally forth for single combat. The Muslim siege was clearly as yet a reasonable distance from the walls, waiting until the artillery had softened up the defences. Given the disadvantages faced by the defenders of Acre, such counter-measures represented attempts to try and shift the balance in their favour; yet they also smack somewhat of desperation. The intention is clear enough – to create panic amongst the besieging forces and hope that as a result the siege would fall apart. There had been a few victories won against the odds in crusade history, especially during the First Crusade, at the Battle of Dorylaeum and also at Antioch and Jerusalem. They had been scarcer since, though Richard the Lionheart had won when heavily outnumbered at Jaffa. Perhaps men who were desperate understandably overlooked the procession of Crusader failures in more recent times since the epochal defeat of Hattin; the two crusades to Egypt and the disaster at La Forbie had also been major setbacks. They were in some cases very likely inspired by religious motives, seeing their actions as divinely sanctioned. If so, they possibly reasoned that what they needed was not an approach predicated on rationality; what they needed was a miracle.

The reality was that, with a defence that was almost inevitably a static one given the disparities between the two armies, all the cards lay in the favour of al-Ashraf. He had access to uninterrupted supply lines from the hinterland, he had by far the bigger numbers, he had his massive siege train and he also had men who saw themselves as agents of the Divine. They had something else that the Franks did not: genuine hopes of victory. And soon the siege engines started to do their work. The monotonous hammering of artillery stones against the walls started to take effect. In weaker places, masonry began to crumble and gaps began to appear. Such gaps soon became the focus of attention for both attackers and defenders. The siege engines would target them in an effort to make them larger and hopefully in the end to create a fatal breach. Those inside would place more men around the gap to compensate, though in the process such personnel would therefore be at greater risk of being the victims of the bombardment. The battle had in the main been a long-distance one so far, but it was soon to escalate into something far more visceral.

Something of the fight went out of the city after these setbacks. The writer of the *Chronicle of Lanercost* suggests that plans for renewed sorties were rejected by the Patriarch of Jerusalem who was, according to him, 'broken in spirit' and threatened that anyone who opened the gates of the city against his instruction would be punished with excommunication. The proponents of these plans suggested that prisoners of war should be marched out in front of the forces sallying out of the city to protect them and discourage their Muslim brothers from attacking, hardly a glorious tactic but one that had been used by others such as the Mongols in the recent past. But the idea anyway came to nothing. Whilst the chronicler was not present at the siege, he claimed to have spoken to an eyewitness who was, presumably, one of the English contingent who managed to escape the city.[16]

Then news reached the city which reignited hopes of a miraculous deliverance. Given the continued Frankish dominance of the waves, information could still reach Acre from beyond the shores of the Levant. News came in that the King, Henry II, was on his way from Cyprus with significant reinforcements. A scintilla of hope glimmered in some hearts. It was just a two-day sail from Cyprus in favourable weather. Those within hoped that they had experienced the darkest hour and the dawn was about to break. But in reality, the darkest hour was yet to come and its full horror was unimaginable.

On 4 May, spirits in Acre were dramatically raised for this was the day that King Henry II arrived, having sailed from Famagusta in Cyprus, with an army (a small one compared to what was hoped for it must be said, composed of 700 men) and forty ships. The Kingdoms of Cyprus and Jerusalem had been closely aligned ever since Aimery, King of the former, had married Isabella, Queen of the latter, in 1197. Cypriot troops had regularly participated in crusades ever since; and there were some, both secular nobles and clerical institutions, who had land interests in both Outremer and Cyprus.[17] However, a dispute had broken out between Hugh III and the Cypriot barons in 1271, the former barons arguing that their responsibility to provide men to the Crown was limited to service in Cyprus and not in Outremer. Hugh argued precedent and the final conclusion was that baronial service in the latter was limited to four months in any one year, and that only whilst the king or his son was present with them. Such dissension from among his own knights could hardly have encouraged the people of Acre that help would come from Cyprus if needed, but it had at least on this occasion arrived.[18] Whilst the Franks still controlled the sea routes in and out of the port, there was always a hope that reinforcements might arrive; and it was most likely that they would come from Cyprus with its adjacency and the fact that her king was also King of Jerusalem. In effect, all that was left of that latter kingdom now was Acre. Whilst the Franks still held other cities and fortresses in Outremer they would become largely non-viable should Acre fall. King Henry was therefore a man with much to lose. That said, given the numerical advantage enjoyed by the besieging force, there may have been disappointment inside the city that this new injection of men was not more substantial.

For the besieged, this could have been a classic case of 'cometh the hour, cometh the man'. But unfortunately for the Franks this was not to be the case here. There were several reasons for this. For one, Henry's claim to the Kingdom of Jerusalem had not been universally accepted. Decades of wrangling with the Angevins, the Templars and the papacy in particular had cast doubts in some quarters over his legitimacy and certainly his arrival did not act as a unifying influence. Another factor was that he was not blessed with outstanding martial leadership qualities. He was also in poor health, so the crisis could not have come at a worse time for him. It was also the case that the resources available to Henry were limited compared to the size of the challenge he faced. It is likely that 200 to 250 knights was the upper limit of what could be provided from Cyprus without dangerously denuding the garrisons there.[19] This was simply insufficient to swing the balance in favour of the defenders. Optimists inside Acre hoped that his arrival was a turning point for their fortunes and that a dramatic victory might yet be won. Instead, Henry's arrival was in some ways to seal the death warrant of Acre.

Henry quickly reviewed the situation. It did not take a military genius to conclude that it was dire. Yes, he had brought limited reinforcements over, but they were all that could realistically be expected. No further help was likely to be forthcoming from further afield and all his troops had done was make it possible for Acre to hold out for a little longer. They had not tipped the balance of power in favour of the defence. Further, he was King of two Kingdoms, not one. Whilst that of Jerusalem was hugely symbolically important, its viability was in grave doubt and he had anyway effectively been an absentee ruler. The seat of his power was Cyprus, which was fertile and sustainable; in the latter respect particularly it was quite a contrast to the Kingdom of Jerusalem. He needed those troops in Acre to protect Cyprus. Baybars had already attacked the island, with limited success it is true, but another Islamic attack on it was quite likely. Henry no doubt thought long and hard about such matters, but in the end his conclusion was something of a formality; Cyprus must come first.

The Cracks Appear

Despite their parlous plight, the Franks inside the city continued to remain defiant. They hung the armour and bucklers (small shields) of the enemy they had captured or killed over the walls, mocking the Muslim army and raising the temper of al-Ashraf to breaking point. So great was his anger that in the early days of May he berated his commanders for what he saw as their poor progress so far and even had some of them thrown into prison for their half-heartedness '*pour encourager les autres*'. This was a tactic that emulated Baybars, who had done the same when he was dissatisfied with the progress of a particular campaign. Ironically, this came at a time when the siege was about to turn decisively in favour of the Muslim army. Medieval fortifications were designed with the concept of 'strength in depth' at their heart. The idea was that there should be a series of obstacles that the attackers needed to overcome before they claimed the prize. Typically, these consisted first of all of outer defences, a ditch or water-filled moat with the main entrance protected by an outer fortress, the barbican. Then there would be the gatehouse, the most vulnerable part of the defences as it needed passageways large enough for carts as well as men to pass through. The challenge for the defenders was increased when, as was the case at Acre, we are talking about a city that needed more than one gate in order for trade traffic to pass in and out without undue difficulty. Because of the vulnerability of the entrance-ways there would often be extra lines of defence. Passages would be relatively confined and 'murder holes' would be gouged out of their ceilings so that defenders could pour burning hot oil or sand down on the heads of unwelcome visitors. The sides of the passages would be protected by arrow slits through which archers could unleash their missiles. There would normally be a portcullis too, a heavy iron grille that acted as an extra gate which needed to be broken through.

There were in fact two lines of gated walls at Acre as the suburb of Montmusard was also protected by walls that had been erected by Louis IX. Should the walls be broken through then there would be bastions (keeps or *donjons*) which could be used as places of last resort. In Acre there were several large buildings linked to the great military orders. The fact that there were several and not one is a salient reminder that here we are talking about a city, not a castle, and therefore the compact defences that might be expected in the latter were not necessarily present in the former. There were a number of weak points that might be identified and exploited by al-Ashraf's men and, once they had broken through, it would be difficult to stop the army from breaking in en masse.

If al-Ansari's tactics were followed at Acre, and the evidence is supportive of this conclusion, then by this stage of the siege the heavy artillery was in full swing. There would have been the harsh rhythm of harder rock crashing into weaker stone, sending showers of lethal shards up into the air and causing a great deal of damage to anyone unfortunate enough to be in the vicinity. The large balls of stone would progressively weaken the walls. Good siege engineers worth their salt would identify weaknesses in the defences and focus on these. Absolute accuracy was difficult to achieve but when cracks started to appear extra focus would be put on trying to widen them into breaches and hopefully in the end bring portions of the walls crashing down. Some of the larger siege engines used by the Mamluks were so terrifying that they almost took on a demonic personality of their own. 'The Furious' mentioned earlier was one such machine, which was set up opposite the section defended by the Templars. The fearsome 'al-Manṣūra' was deployed against the Pisans, whilst two other unnamed engines were set up opposite the section defended by the Hospitallers and the Accursed Tower respectively. The latter was the responsibility of the King and his men and was sited in a particularly vulnerable part of the walls.

By 8 May, the damage to the barbican ahead of the King's Tower was so serious that it was no longer tenable to mount a defence there, so it was abandoned. The attention of the Muslim siege engineers was then on the King's Tower itself, which was the next protective barrier on the outer walls in front of the critical Accursed Tower on the inner. The hypnotic pounding of the walls started to take effect there, too, and after a while the defences of the King's Tower started to crumble. This was not, however, the sole *schwerpunkt*. The English Tower, the neighbouring Tower of the Countess of Blois, the walls of St Anthony's Gate and those next to the Gate of St Nicholas were persistently attacked over the course of the next week. The Muslims were now in a position to dictate the course of events. The energy and vigour of the defenders was being drained out of them as the Muslim squeeze on the city tightened, slowly suffocating the life from Acre like a noose. The attack was on such a wide front that it was beyond the powers of the defenders to spread their resources effectively enough to fight them all off; they were simply too thinly deployed.

King Henry now felt that he had to put out peace feelers to al-Ashraf. A delegation made its way to the Sultan's camp. The precise timing is not clear from the Templar's account: he described it as taking place 'a few days' after the king's arrival and after the effects of mining had started to show themselves and the burning of the King's Tower, which stood in front of the Accursed Tower. The mere fact that the delegation made the journey at all was a form of admission of defeat, a recognition that the end could not long now be resisted. Perhaps precedents whirred around in al-Ashraf's mind: Qalāwūn's taking of Tripoli, or Baybars' triumph at Antioch. Even more resonant may have been the triumph of Saladin at Jerusalem in 1187 when a similar series of negotiations had taken place. Undoubtedly Jerusalem was in spiritual terms a greater prize than Acre; but his victory there had secured Saladin's place in history. Al-Ashraf – still it should be remembered a new Sultan with a point to prove – could establish his legacy in a similar way by driving the Franks once and for all out of Outremer. He knew now that he was on the brink of a spectacular triumph and he would hardly have been human if he passed up on the glorious chance to make a name for himself that had come his way.

Two negotiators were sent out, two Williams, of Villiers and Caffran respectively. They were faced with a mountainous challenge, namely to try and come to an agreement with the Sultan whereby those left inside could escape with their lives and their honour. Anything more than this would have been a bonus as the Mamluk army was now in an immensely strong position and clearly not far off launching one final decisive assault. They made their way towards the Sultan and knelt respectfully before him; this was no time for false bravado. Al-Ashraf was in a tent that had been set up opposite the Patriarch's Tower close to the sea on the south-eastern edge of Acre. Talks began with the Sultan enquiring whether they came with the keys to the city, to which they responded in the negative. The discussions as far as we know were civil but probably one-sided. There was no need for al-Ashraf to concede very much, though an easy surrender may have been marginally preferable to a last bloody assault, however relatively glorious that might be. He also knew that the Mamluks were honed for war and that losses of life in battle were unavoidable and, within reason, acceptable. A decisive triumph rather than a negotiated settlement may in some ways have strengthened his status as a warrior leader, welcome given his newness to the role of Sultan. There were also his soldiers to consider; a negotiated surrender would rob them of a rich haul of booty. Nevertheless, he offered terms that those inside could leave with safe passage but the city must be abandoned. Similar terms had been offered in the past by Baybars in his campaigns; they were sometimes subsequently honoured and sometimes not.

How these discussions would have ended we will never know – for whilst they were going on a stray shot from a Frankish mangonel inside Acre came flying through the air and narrowly missed the Sultan's tent. Whether this was an unfortunate accident or a deliberately aimed missile from some diehard 'no surrender' types inside the city is unclear, but al-Ashraf was understandably furious. In a dramatic gesture, the Sultan drew his sword part-way out of its scabbard and asked the negotiators why he should not cut off their heads there and then. At this, Sanjar al-Shuja'i intervened, advising him not to execute these 'pigs' as they were not directly responsible for the outrage. Al-Ashraf restrained himself, but the negotiators returned to the city with nothing achieved for their efforts. Soon after, the streaks of rocks flying through the sky to and from Acre could once more be seen soaring over the city. It did not take long for normal service to be resumed.

The advantage held by the attacking force was now approaching dominance. This meant that a variety of tactics could be employed with minimal risk of a response from those inside Acre who were becoming increasingly overstretched as they tried desperately to plug the holes in the defence that were starting to appear. There were simply not enough men to be in so many places at once and neither was there any respite from what had become an attritional siege. In contrast, the superior numbers of the Muslims meant that men could to some extent be rotated and taken out of the line for a rest. A good deal of the action was still at arms-length with a combination of missiles from the artillery and arrows from the archers sweeping the walls to try and keep them clear of the enemy. Beneath the ground, a much more silent but equally deadly weapon was being utilised. Sappers chipped away at the foundations, chiselling into them piece by piece in the hope that a combination of the constant hammering at the walls above ground and chipping away at them below would be sufficient to bring them down.

This was tedious and monotonous work, but it inevitably took its toll. Medieval sieges of this type (other types were less dramatic, such as those which attempted to starve an enemy out) were characterised by days of monotony and tedium (albeit of a potentially deadly nature) punctuated by sudden dramatic moments. One such took place on 15 May when the outer wall of the King's Tower collapsed. The destruction of the English Tower also left an inviting and potentially decisive breach in the outer walls. As the dust started to settle over the rubble, elated Mamluk warriors, inspired by the sight, came flooding through the outer walls through the gap which had opened up. There was a flurry of fighting as swords swung through the air, cutting into flesh and bone, before the defenders who had done their best to stop the unstoppable tide flowing towards them were swamped.

The Breakthrough

The Muslim army had now broken through the outer walls, but a significant challenge still faced them. Although the façade of the King's Tower had collapsed, the rear of it remained intact so that in a different context it might have been mistaken for a romantic ruin. But not here. Even though the tower was now clearly in a perilous situation, the defenders resolved to sell it dearly. Its position was crucial as it was the outer defence for the Accursed Tower and if the Muslim army took this then the city would almost inevitably fall soon after. The fallen rubble that now lay heaped up in untidy and irregular piles around the spots where once proud towers and walls had previously stood formed its own impromptu defence line. The gap between the outer and inner walls was dead ground and the breaches that had been made in certain parts of the outer line of defences meant that Muslim forces trying to follow up on their initial success were being funnelled into a fairly narrow area. The archers inside Acre of course well knew this and were focusing their efforts upon it. They poured down a murderous fire on the Muslim forces that were trying to cross the dead ground and attack the inner walls. It was in danger of becoming a killing ground that might soon be strewn with Muslim corpses. A *chat,* literally 'cat', a wooden siege work inside which the defenders could take shelter from the besieging Muslim forces whilst remaining in an advanced position, was also set up.

The Muslims responded with a simple but highly effective idea. It was allegedly the brainchild of Baybars al-Mansuri, the biographer of Qalāwūn and a veteran warrior himself, having fought in the Battle of Homs. On the night of 15/16 May, Mamluk engineers erected a screen made of felt during the hours of darkness. It was suspended between poles and was designed to act as a protective barrier that could be placed over the heads of men pushing their way forward across the dead ground. When archers atop the inner walls of Acre shot down on their enemy, their missiles would not breach the felt. It even provided protection against boulders thrown from the walls; there would be a tell-tale bulge in the fabric when the defenders dropped them down on the Muslims, but the felt did not break. This enabled the Mamluk sappers to construct an access path between the inner and outer walls of Acre and begin the arduous work of chipping away at what was left of Acre's defences. It also meant that the ditches that broke up the ground between the outer and inner walls could be filled in with rubble, allowing the Muslim army to push forward more cohesively when the time came.[20]

As the sun rose on the morning of Thursday 17 May over the increasingly fragmented walls of Acre, with some of its great towers reduced to little more than flinty stumps, Mamluk troops advanced under the cover of the screen. They were impervious to the arrows and rocks thrown down on them and pushed on to take the ruined King's Tower. There were now two main lines of attack being pursued. One of them was on St Anthony's Gate; if this fell the Mamluks would have a direct entry route towards the heart of the city. There was vicious fighting here, in which the Hospitallers and Templars were particularly prominent. In addition to the Gate, the Accursed Tower behind the lost King's Tower had also become a key defensive position. Already, those who had lost hope had made their way to the harbour, searching for a ship, on the night of 16 May. Just then, nature played a cruel trick as the sea became choppy. One of the strengths of Acre as a port is that it was south-facing on a shoreline where the prevailing wind was a westerly, but now the breeze was in an unhelpful direction. Despite the catastrophe unfolding in the city, the sailors felt they could not risk leaving the port. Some citizens who had spent the night aboard with the hope of sailing for safety in the morning were now put ashore again, sowing yet more terror in already troubled minds. Acre may have been one of the best harbours in the region, but it was still not very good. In addition, ships would now be in mangonel range if they stayed in port, so those that could stood offshore.

Al-Ashraf and his commanders now decided to try and extend their control along other parts of the outer wall. The idea was probably to overwhelm what was left of the defences by flooding over them in a number of different places. Acre was now like a ship that had been holed in several places where the water can come rushing in and eventually drag it down. Those inside Acre clearly knew this too. Even the metaphorical lifeboats which they had hoped would take them away from all this were stuck in the port and the end was drawing inexorably nearer.

13

The Last Stand

'He burned as if he had been a cauldron of pitch and died there.'
An eyewitness description of the fate of
one of those killed at Acre

The Denouement

Before the dawn, the Mamluk army was getting itself ready. Thousands of warriors took up position as silently as they could, though the Franks probably knew all too well what to expect. The Mamluk warriors, some of whom were veterans of many previous campaigns, acted like the professionals they were, checking equipment and armour. Fine margins would make the difference between life and death. It was these professionals who would bear the brunt of the fighting, though there were many irregulars there who, inspired by religious euphoria, the prospect of booty and adventure or probably a cocktail of motivations, were also eager to see battle, or at least profit from its aftermath. The more experienced among these men would have known that there was a chance that this might be their last day on earth.

Those inside the battered remains of Acre had nowhere to go. Some of them were professional warriors themselves, members of the military orders who many Mamluks may have hated but would certainly have a grudging respect for. Fighting in the streets, even in modern warfare, is something of a lottery; a stray arrow or a sword or spear from the blind side could end it all. For some this would be the most significant day in their life, for some their last.

The drums of war beat out at dawn, 300 camels carrying them as they hammered out their incessant, terrifying rhythms, like the drum beats accompanying a host of executioners marching their victims to the scaffold. The Templar of Tyre described it as 'a horrible and mighty voice'. It was 18 May 1291, a Friday – a holy day for Muslims. The Mamluk archers fired cloud upon cloud of their arrows down into the city, a deadly hail forcing the defenders under cover if they wished to enjoy a few short minutes longer of life. In concert with these arrow storms, a general attack was started across a wide front composed of infantry in their thousands. In the front rank were men carrying large shields followed by others bearing Greek fire. Then came soldiers carrying javelins and finally, the archers. It was an irresistible force faced by a far-from-immovable object and the Franks were quickly forced back from the advanced defensive positions that remained to them. The Muslims had still not yet penetrated the inner defences but they now pushed on in several directions, one contingent branching out towards the Accursed Tower, close to a section manned by the Pisans who had with them a great siege engine of their own, another pushing on to St Anthony's Gate.

This was the moment when the numerical superiority of the attacking forces was going to count. It was simply impossible for the undermanned defenders to be in more than one place at the same time. Daring not to raise their heads above the parapets because of the deadly deluge of arrows, javelins and rocks that was raining down on them, the defenders were now in a truly desperate position. It was a tried-and-tested tactic to try and overwhelm the walls of a besieged city by an assault on a wide front and there was little an outnumbered defence could do once their walls had been breached. Constantinople fell to such an assault in 1204 after nearly a millennium of resisting all attempts to pierce its massive walls by Arabs and barbarians. It would fall in the same way in 1453, though that later event would be accompanied by the sounds of cannon-fire and not just those of stone-throwing siege engines. It was first and foremost a numbers game; and the numbers were definitely on the side of the Mamluks at Acre in 1291.

William of Beaujeu was in the Templar *auberge* in the suburb of Montmusard, close to the section of walls that his Order was responsible for when he heard the driving rhythm of the war drums and correctly surmised that this was the signal for an all-out attack. He gathered together a small number of men, a dozen or so Templars and his own household guard, and headed for where he thought the bulk of the fighting would be. On his way, he was joined by some Hospitallers including their Master, as well as other local soldiers. The appropriately named Accursed Tower was a particular target for the fighting as if it had become the symbolic gateway to Acre and whoever held it would hold the city itself. Eventually, the Mamluk forces pushed their way in despite desperate attempts by the defenders to drive them back. St Anthony's Gate was also breached by the Muslim army and this was where the impromptu group of Templars, Hospitallers and others entered the battle. It was brutal fighting. The dreaded Greek fire was widely used by the Muslim forces, creating dense clouds of smoke. The Frankish counter-attack was brave but doomed. There were simply too many of the Muslim soldiers to fight off. In addition, the arrows of the Mamluk archers caused great damage to men and horses alike; a snippet of information that reveals that even inside the city the military orders preferred to act as cavalry.

Even more desperate counter-attacks were launched by the Templars, Hospitallers and others inside the city. These men, who had on occasion done all they could to score an advantage over the other, fought and died side by side. It is a pity that they had been unable to demonstrate the same unity in earlier times when Acre might still have been saved. But such musings should not detract from the fact that here beneath the shattered walls of Acre the military orders had in some respects their finest hour, selling their lives dearly and taking many of their opponents with them as they earned a martyr's death. It was heroic and inspiring; but ultimately it was also futile.

It was not the loss of the Accursed Tower alone that decided the battle once and for all. Another key moment came when the Mamluks slashed and hacked their way through to the inner entrance of St Anthony's Gate. Now the portals of this crucial entranceway were opened and the Mamluk army came pouring through. The position of the defenders was hopeless and it was a case of *sauve qui peut* – every man (or woman) for him or herself. A tide of euphoric Muslim soldiers came flooding in. Jean de Villiers, the Hospitaller Master who survived the fight, told of countless numbers pouring through the gate. He told his readers that on no fewer than three occasions the Muslim soldiers were pushed back but this was ultimately of no use.

The headquarters of the Teutonic Knights in Acre were close to the Accursed Tower (200 metres or so to the south-west of it on the eastern side of the city and close to St Nicholas' Gate). The Knights were in the front line of what was now a frantic close-quarters battle and many of them died in hand-to-hand fighting. Judging by the great loss of life they fought bravely before being overcome by the superior numbers of their foe. Those who fell included their leader, Heinrich von Bolanden, who had been summoned urgently from Sicily to organise the defence of Acre and who must have had a hard job trying to raise morale after the sudden, untimely departure of Burchard of Schwanden in the previous year in what must have felt like an act of desertion. They sold their lives dearly, in keeping with the best traditions of the military orders. Whilst on occasion one could criticise the orders' lack of discretion or political acumen, there were many instances of their members defiantly paying the ultimate price, for example after the defeat at Hattin a century before. Recent excavations have revealed the fragmentary remains of the building of the Teutonic Knights; an ash layer, presumably created when the building was destroyed, including a smattering of finds from the time such as a gold Hyperperon coin from the reign of the Byzantine Emperor John III Vatatzes, as well as more mundane items such as sugar jars and moulds.[1]

The Templars, too, were at the heart of the fray when they suffered a terrible blow which unnerved not just them but many of the other defenders. William of Beaujeu, despite being sixty years old, was in the thick of the fight when he was hit by a javelin. He was unprotected by a shield and only wore light armour such as would be put on in a hurry; he had seemingly been unprepared for this morning's attack. He dropped his weapon and started to take himself off to be treated. The Templar of Tyre says he was carrying a spear; the chronicler was probably nearby and may even have been one of the twelve hastily assembled Templar brethren who had accompanied the Master on this highly dangerous mission. Those around him were horrified at the sight of their Master exiting the battle and begged him to reconsider. Ashen-faced, he turned to them and said 'I'm not running away; I am dead. Here is the blow.' So saying, he lifted his arm to reveal a missile that had penetrated his armpit up to the depth of the palm of a hand (the armpit was always a potential weak spot in a suit of armour as there was a joint in it there). He was duly carried off on a shield and taken to a place of relative safety. The master of the Order of the Knights of St Thomas was also killed in the close-quarters melee, along with nine of his knights.

A further vignette from the Templar of Tyre tells us more of the horror of those moments. A group of Templars took their dying Master to the port where several barques were at work. When they saw this, the escort became more concerned for their own safety than that of William of Beaujeu. They threw themselves into the choppy waves but many of them drowned in their failed attempt to escape. The Master was then taken to the great fortress of the Templars, entering through a courtyard which was used for piling manure as it was too dangerous to open the main gate. He died later that day, having uttered barely a word since being mortally wounded.

The bloodshed was horrific. The writer of the *Excidium Acconis* wrote of it in vivid terms, of how there were

> ...many with heads severed from their necks and from their shoulder blades, hands from arms, others split up to the breastbones or run through with a spear or cut in two. Men were dying covered in blood or writhing in pain or with their eyes rolling in their heads, one with his head twisted back and another lying on his stomach, another with his tongue lolling dying in great pain, and others again, though mortally wounded, making feeble attempts to get up again and fight.[2]

Acre was now a charnel house. Mamluk banners now appeared on the battlements of the inner walls, in ones and twos at first and then by the score. They were signals that Acre was now theirs to do with as they willed. They were also symbolic of a horrific change in direction in the battle for Acre; the siege was now over and it was time for the sack. Even if the rules of medieval warfare as seen in the West had applied – and given the East-West/Muslim-Christian nature of the confrontation, this was certainly not the case – a city that held out against a summons to surrender could be dealt with in whatever way the victor saw fit. There were thousands of non-professional irregulars in the Muslim army. They had been whipped up into a religious frenzy by their preachers. They were taking part in *jihad* against an enemy that was obnoxious to them in both spiritual and secular terms. Further, this enemy had for centuries treated them with disdain. To add to these motivations, there was the more worldly attraction of substantial amounts of booty (both inanimate and human) to think about. Innocents had been slaughtered by the Franks in the aftermath of bitter sieges at Antioch and Jerusalem – and, of course, Acre in

1191. Saladin had shown mercy when he captured Jerusalem, though he did not have much choice if he wished to recapture intact the holy places of Islam inside the third holiest city in the Muslim world. No such mitigations applied here at Acre. There was only one way that the aftermath of the siege was likely to go from this moment on.

The Muslims unleashed more Greek fire on the defenders. Flames shot up in a Dantesque inferno and clouds of suffocating smoke hung like a pall over the shattered innards of Acre, making the air thick and acrid and virtually blinding those unfortunate enough to be caught up in it, as well as threatening to suffocate them. An eyewitness noted that one combatant was 'so badly hit by the Greek Fire that his surcoat burst into flames. There was no one to help him, and so his face was burned, and then his whole body, and he burned as if he had been a cauldron of pitch and died there.' We do not know the name of this poor soul but we do know something about him. We know that he originally fought on horseback for we are told that his horse was killed beneath him. We are also told he was English.[3]

Again, we are reminded of pictures of victims caught up in napalm blasts during the Vietnam War. However, such horrific images have been a potent symbol of violent death since time immemorial. Indeed, they are global in their application. A famous example can be found in the Mahabharata, an ancient Hindu epic whose exact dating is unclear but which is generally agreed to have been produced somewhen in the 1st Millennium BC:[4]

The animals scattered in all directions, screaming terrible screams.

Many were burning, others were burnt,

All were shattered and scattered mindlessly,

Their eyes bulging some hugged their sons, others their fathers and mothers

Unable to let them go. And so they died.

Others leapt up in their thousands, faces disfigured, and were consumed by the fire. Everywhere were bodies squirming on the ground, wings, eyes and paws all burning

They breathed their last as living torches.

These words are both hauntingly eloquent and deeply disturbing. They remind us that violence has been a part of the human condition ever since the dawn of history (and very probably before it; there is much archaeological evidence of violent and deliberate human death for the prehistoric period). There is nothing glorious in war; the concepts of both chivalry and crusading are ultimately best abandoned because they are based on totally hypocritical views of violence that seek to justify the unjustifiable. The victims of Acre (and of course of all those Muslim cities that had been sacked by the Franks or the Jewish communities that suffered as a result of the crusades) were just representatives of the forgotten dead of all times and all cultures. No heroic chivalric last stand or religiously inspired martyrdom for them.

The Muslim soldiers organised impromptu shield-walls to resist Frankish counter-attacks, almost like Vikings or Anglo-Saxons. They continued to throw their javelins and their Greek fire, fiercely resisting the efforts of the defenders to overcome them. The Templar of Tyre, who from the vividness of his account was nearby, informs us that the fighting went on until mid-morning. In fact, in the original untranslated account he is precise and mentions the hour of 'tierce', 9 o'clock in the morning. Given a likely time for dawn at this time of year of 5.30 a.m. the fighting had been going on for three-and-a-half hours. He goes on to give a detailed account of the last moments of Acre, or at least the last moments of all but a small portion of it, as we shall see. The defenders were demoralised by the death of William of Beaujeu and started to run. The Muslims poured after them, burning the great mangonel of the Pisans and sacking the convent of the Teutonic Knights. They broke into the Tower of the Legate that was on the sea by prising off a heavy metal grille forming part of its defences. Intense fighting went on here, involving among others Jean de Grailly, who was seriously wounded, Otho de Grandson, and the French Regiment that had been so proudly established by Louis IX. Jean nevertheless managed to escape to safety on a ship in the same way that he had extricated himself during the loss of Tripoli.

As the fighting started to slacken, so the raping and pillaging began. Organised defence disintegrated as the remaining pockets of defenders were overrun one by one. Muslim soldiers were now pouring in from all sides including along the seashore, which was only defended by an iron grille at the end of the land walls that could now easily be pulled out of the way. Now it was the turn of the civilians to be faced with the harsh realities of medieval warfare. Men were struck down indiscriminately in the streets including some Muslims who were unfortunate enough to have been trapped inside the city. Women and children were grabbed as slaves, with no doubt other outrages perpetrated upon them. Those citizens seized who appeared to be rich were tortured to reveal where they had hidden their treasures regardless of whether or not they actually had any. There were no rules in this brutal sack; many were slaughtered regardless of age or sex. Most of the Franciscan and Dominican friars in the city were among the dead. Even Dominican nuns were killed. There were accounts of last stands by small groups in streets and squares, some of which went on for hours; but these were all eventually overwhelmed. This was a bitter and bloody retribution.

The Flight of the Refugees

With the walls now breached and any last whiff of hope decisively snuffed out, it was time for those who could to escape the terrible moment of reckoning. A few Frankish vessels were moored in the harbour like lifeboats tied up alongside a sinking ship. Those who could (that is largely those who could afford to do so) scrambled aboard. Whilst the available ships were crammed with refugees trying to escape, and this limited the space available to move valuables to safety, it was probably possible to take smaller items like cash, bullion and precious jewels away. Apart from anything else, they were the wherewithal with which the ships' captains would be paid for their assistance in fleeing Acre. There are records of one Roger de Flor, a Templar, in his ship *The Falco* who charged large amounts for space on his sizeable vessel. Although he later handed over some of the proceeds to his Order, rumours abounded that he had kept much for himself. This suspicion must have appeared to be confirmed when he made his way to Marseille and left the Temple. He embarked on a second career as master of mercenaries in the Catalan Company. It was perhaps in keeping with his shadowy character that he was eventually murdered in 1305.[5]

As always in a war situation, there were profiteers who sought to, and did, take advantage of the misery of others, squeezing every last drop out of those who were in no position to bargain. That said, the way in which some of the refugees did so well in Cyprus after their escape suggests that they at least managed to take a good deal of moveable property with them.[6] Although all the three main military orders are known to have owned ships, it appears that this Templar vessel was the only one present at Acre, possibly reflecting a perception that no attack on the city had been expected until it was too late.

However, the presence of this one large ship was vitally important, as perhaps as many as 1,500 people were taken off in it. It made its way to safety, dropping most of its passengers off at Atlit. A Florentine family, the Peruzzi, did very well as they escaped with much of their wealth; and as some of their commercial partners were left behind and killed they did not have to repay their share of the capital.[7]

King Henry now decided to cut his losses and run. It was important for the people of Cyprus that he survived to look after their interests (or so he presumably reasoned). Having just spent a few brief days in Acre, Henry considered that he had done all that could reasonably be expected of him and sailed away to safety.[8] Back in Cyprus his troubles were far from over. His situation became increasingly unstable because of the volatile politics of the island. In 1303 he executed his brother, Guy, who had conspired against him. Then he was forced off the throne in 1306 by another brother, Amalric, in a coup supported by the Templars. The King, it was said, was ill (he was epileptic) and not up to the task, to which he responded that one of his ancestors (Baldwin IV of Jerusalem) was a leper and yet had ruled successfully. In 1310, Henry was returned to power in a further coup, this time supported by the Hospitallers. To the bitter end the military orders continued to work against each other. All this, though, was in the future, as Henry effectively washed his hands of Acre and sailed west.[9] The people of the city were now on their own again.

The King's escape is evidence that, although sea conditions were not ideal, it was still possible to get away. The 'great and the good' were more likely to escape with their lives than the *hoi polloi* as is almost invariably the case and most of those had already left days before, when conditions were better. Not all did though. William of Beaujeu, who had done everything in his power to prevent what was probably an unpreventable cataclysm, had paid for his devotion with his life. Jean de Villiers, Master of the Hospitallers, was able to extract himself even though he was seriously wounded. He and other surviving Hospitallers reached Cyprus, from where he wrote a letter resonant with grief and pain to the Grand Prior of the order in the south of France. This was one of the first messages to reach the West concerning the death of Crusader Acre and it must have created a great deal of heart-searching when its recipients took possession of it. Otho de Grandson was another man who escaped to Cyprus, where he seemed to be very short of money. He eventually returned to mainland Europe where he lived to the magnificent age for those times of ninety-one; his tomb can still be seen in Lausanne Cathedral, Switzerland. Those few Teutonic Knights who managed to survive also made their way to the island, although later a new headquarters for the order was established in Venice, a convenient bridging point between Germany in the north and the rest of Italy to the south. A few men from the much smaller Order of the Knights of St Thomas also made it to Cyprus. There was one painful reality that could not now be ignored: with Outremer lost, quite possibly forever, the military orders faced an uncertain future now that their primary *raison d'etre* had gone.

Some horrific word pictures were painted by the Templar of Tyre of these last moments; of women running through the streets with children in their arms, pleading to the sailors in the port to take them away, of them forced apart by the victorious Muslims and carried off into separate lives of slavery, of women being killed as men argued over who should carry them off, of babes-in-arms being thrown beneath the hooves of horses and killed, of pregnant women suffocated in the crush to escape. Wounded men were killed where they lay without pity. Whilst some of these scenes sound slightly formulaic and similar atrocities were attributed by Christian chroniclers to victorious Muslim armies on other occasions, in this case some of them at least were true.[10] Thadeus of Naples wrote in a similar vein, of virgins, young mothers and pregnant women being raped in the streets. There is disturbing evidence that these were not just standard motifs trotted out, but that, for example, young Jewish girls were subjected to awful assaults along such lines at Acre. There is more than a grain of truth in these horrific stories.[11]

Thadeus has precious little sympathy to dole out for the victims at Acre whose sinfulness had, in his view, brought about their end; but what there is is reserved for either individual warriors like William of Beaujeu who died in battle or, as a much larger category, the poor who had been abandoned in the city as they could not afford to buy their way out. Perhaps the worst of it was that humanitarian tendencies went out of the window at the end; fathers forgot sons, husbands their wives, brothers their siblings. It was as if thousands of people were frantically trying to make their way to safety on the last available lifeboat and did not care who they pushed out of their way in the rush.

There was one obvious place of last resort left: the Templar fortress by the sea. It had massive walls and the Templar of Tyre tells us that

10,000 people made their way there. This sounds a suspiciously large number and is probably shorthand for a lot of people, again many of them poor. By the time they got there, there were a number of ships offshore with refugees onboard. The Patriarch, Nicholas of Hanapes, was one of those trying to escape but the Templar of Tyre says that he slipped and fell into the water and drowned. An alternative end is given to him by Thadeus of Naples who says that he let too many people onboard the boat he was on and it capsized and sank. As he reached out his arms to fetch people aboard, with them extended in a parody of the crucifix, the boat sank and he died the death of a martyr. Either way, the Patriarch was no more. In contrast, the writer of the *Chronicle of Lanercost* was scathing in his comments, suggesting that the people of Acre deserved their punishment for their unprovoked attacks on peaceful Muslim traders. He also said unequivocally that 'the patriarch ... was the first to take flight with the other nobles and owners of great wealth; and it is said that those defended themselves longest who had no desire on earth but to have justice and poverty'.[12] It was a touching thought, though most of those embracing a life of poverty had no choice in the matter.

Those who could made their way to the harbour in a desperate race for life. The Inner Harbour was not large. It was protected by the chain across the narrow entrance, with sea walls enclosing it on the western and eastern sides; at the end of the latter was the Tower of Flies. It was not easy to access at the best of times; ships had to approach gingerly from the west negotiating their way past the Cape of Storms about 400 yards from the harbour entrance. Sudden changes in weather and wind direction could create problems. There were only a few ships available: six armed *leins* of the church,[13] some royal galleys and two Genoese vessels. The latter, under the command of a captain called Andrea Peleau (or Pellato), did sterling work ferrying refugees from the port to the offshore ships. Genoese and Venetians, often at loggerheads in the past, worked together to save lives. Peleau's actions in particular were seemingly motivated by nothing except human sympathy; he even cajoled the ships offshore to take away the poor he had rescued who could not meet the going rate for their passage. It was even more noteworthy as there was no longer a Genoese quarter in Acre since the War of St Sabas, though the city's merchants had at least been allowed to trade there in recent years. Eventually, there was nothing more to be done and the fleet set sail for Cyprus.

Some remarkable survival stories have come down to us. In 1328, a middle-aged stranger, Isaccho Venerio, turned up in Venice. He claimed that when he was a child he had been in Acre when it was stormed. He managed to escape to the 'lands beyond the Tartars' where he had spent the next thirty-seven years. Now he had returned home. *La Serenissima* considered his request that his Venetian citizenship should be confirmed and duly ratified it, a happy ending of sorts for at least one survivor of the apocalyptic end of Acre.[14]

Venice's role in the final days of Acre is not altogether a glorious one. A large number of Venetians escaped from the city long before the end. The genealogies of those who sat on the Great Council that was responsible for running the city in what was undoubtedly one of the most arcane governance structures ever seen included a long list of families whose ancestors had extricated themselves from Acre in good time before the end: Bondomier, Benedetti, Barisan, Boninsegna, Lion, Marmora, Polini, Alberti, Foscolo and Suriani.[15] Their escape reflected the entirely serendipitous arrival of Venetian ships at the beginning of May 1291 as part of the routine twice-yearly passage of ships from Venice to Acre. In contrast, there were no Pisan ships in port at the time and her citizens had to fend for themselves, though a number of richer ones did manage to get away.[16]

A number of refugees found their way to Famagusta and other parts of Cyprus. In 1318 Pope John XXII opined that their arrival had helped to invigorate a society and economy that was in danger of becoming moribund. Whilst Famagusta was the main beneficiary, other Cypriot towns also profited. A charter dated to 1294 mentions the presence of two women and a notary who had previously been in Acre who were now resident in Nicosia. The year after a Pisan refugee from Acre was also there. In 1300, one Martinus de Accon was living in Limassol. By the same time, about 100 refugees are identifiable as residents in Famagusta. Their point of origin is revealed by the use of names such as 'Accon', 'Acconensis' or 'Acconitanus' in their titles. This is likely to be a low estimate. We know of examples where former residents of Acre who had moved to Cyprus used their European point of origin as part of their title. For example, one Albertino de Placa, who made his will in 1294 in Famagusta, described himself as coming from the *sestiere* of Castello in Venice, but his name is on documents drafted in Acre in 1284 and his instructions mention a house in the city where he was living when it fell in 1291.[17]

There is, however, evidence that emigration from Acre to Cyprus long pre-dated the fall of the city. Pope Innocent IV referred in the 1240s to the assistance that had been given by Cyprus to refugees from the Kingdom of Jerusalem. In the aftermath of La Forbie and the Khwarazmian capture of Jerusalem, residents of Outremer had understandably sought to increase their security or carve out a new life for themselves. In another example of panic, a western chronicle records how many Italian settlers left Acre in 1267 after the emergent threat from Baybars. Agreements made in 1261 in Acre include contingencies about what should happen in the event of the loss of the city when the Mongol threat was seen to be at its peak. In 1283, the Hospitallers decided to transfer part of their archives from Acre to France. The monks of St Mary of the Valley of Jehoshaphat, who had left Jerusalem in 1244, sold their last possessions in Acre to the Hospitallers in 1289 and left for Sicily. These are examples that underline the fact that Acre had been living under threat of extermination for half a century and that, even before its apocalyptic end, others had reasoned that life in Outremer was now too dangerous for them.[18] This again suggests that Acre's loss had been long feared and even expected.

One particularly interesting will surviving from the time is that of Pietro Vassano, who had become very wealthy whilst living in Acre. His wealth was in the form of both movable and immovable possessions. He returned to Venice in 1284 and in his will of 1289 he instructed his son Andrea to sell all his property in Acre within a year of his death. Andrea remained for a time in Acre but sold up all his own property and emigrated from there in 1290, just in time. Others though did not. The Brizi family was prominent in Venice. Three siblings, the offspring of Pietro, managed to escape during the final days in 1291. Two brothers returned to Venice whilst a sister, Candelor, set up in Famagusta. Marco Zovene and his grandson were also escapees; Marco also initially settled in Famagusta before eventually returning to Venice. Another escapee, Theodorus de Tripoli de Accon, who managed to flee to Cyprus, had possibly experienced more than one narrow escape given the inclusion in his name of two places that had fallen to Muslim forces.[19]

Those who fled Acre may have escaped with their lives, but they suffered significantly in other ways. Aside from the chaos of their panicked departure if they left late on (though the consensus is that many of the wealthier element had already fled earlier on in the siege)[20] their problems were far from over when they reached safety. Their arrival in Cyprus forced prices of basic commodities up, as supply and demand economics kicked in. The situation was made worse by a series of poor harvests in Cyprus in the 1290s.[21] These were people who had already lost much of their wealth, left behind them in Acre. Some, such as Albertino de Placa, offered reduced payments to their creditors on the basis that much of their wealth had been left behind in the city. In his particular case, he may have been opportunistically using this as an excuse to get a good financial deal. A few years later, he is recorded as owning two houses in Famagusta, evidence of being quite well off. Given that most of his wealth in Acre was moveable, then presumably he had managed to get some if not all of it out with him.[22] Albertino had been very active whilst in Acre; he is recorded as transferring money (32 bezants) to Pietro Vendelin, a Venetian, in 1284 and in the same year he concluded a deal with a Greek, Vassili Cassellario, a cabinet and chest maker in Tripoli. Vassili ordered 1,000 pairs of thick wooden soles from Venice for making clogs, split equally between those for men and women.[23] Other escapees who are subsequently recorded in Cyprus included two blacksmiths, Domenico from Acre and Giorgio from Gibelet (Byblos) in Tripoli. In 1301, they started a short-term joint venture in Cyprus with Domenico investing cash and Giorgio inputting his skills, with the profits to be shared three-quarters to the former and a quarter to the latter.[24]

Viviano de Ginnebaldo was probably another escapee in 1291. He was in Acre in the 1270s and 1280s but was active in Famagusta in 1301, where his fluency in Arabic – presumably developed in Outremer, though he might possibly have picked it up from fellow refugees in Cyprus – proved valuable in negotiations between representatives of the Peruzzi banking firm from Florence and a Syrian camlet merchant.[25] Ginnebaldo was criticised for dealing in war materials with Egypt after the fall of Acre. Indeed, he was actually excommunicated for a time though his sentence was lifted by Boniface VIII in September 1300. Whilst this might superficially suggest a degree of repentance on his part, it is more likely that he made himself useful when a Mongol delegation from Ghazan arrived.

Whilst this trading between Ginnebaldo and Egypt demonstrates how flexible consciences were, even more so does the fact that he was probably involved in such transactions before Acre fell. Both Acre and Tyre were frequent transit points for such goods en route to

Egypt before the denouement of Outremer. They may have included timber, iron, pitch and weapons as well as slaves who would be trained and transformed into Mamluks. A papal embargo against trading with Egypt was nominally put in force in 1291 but ironically it helped men like Ginnebaldo who turned a blind eye to such niceties by reducing supply and pushing prices up. Venice, always quick to smell a commercial upside in every downside, also profited from the arms trade, especially when large concessions were granted to *La Serenissima* by the Sultan Al-Nasir Muhammad in 1302.

Ginnebaldo essentially acted as a middleman between East and West both before and after the fall of Acre. He continued to have access to significant wealth, as shown by his gift of 2,000 bezants as a dowry for his niece Agnese in Famagusta in 1302. He was also involved commercially in transactions with Armenia in 1296 and 1301. Armenia continued to play an important part in trade in the region, receiving corn from the West and in turn sending back cotton.[26] This is a salutary reminder that for some at least, life went on. Refugees of Venetian, Genoese and Pisan descent found a new life in Cyprus and in many cases prospered. They had been through an intensely traumatic experience in Acre but found a way to make a living in their new home. Perhaps many of them were already familiar with Cyprus before the torrid events of 1291 and that made the task easier. Their presence in the future would have two quite different side effects. Some would be involved in the political infighting that scarred Cyprus in the early decades of the fourteenth century; some would help to usher in and benefit from a period of economic growth on the island.

This information is derived from thorough research. However, it very likely represents the fortunes of only a small and relatively lucky element of the residents of Acre. For those of the non-merchant classes, the nobodies of Frankish society in Acre, their lot would have been much harder. If they were lucky enough to survive the slaughter in the city, for many a life of slavery and servitude beckoned. For the surviving indigenous population, whilst no doubt in some cases hardship also followed, for others this may have been just a change of authority to which taxes and dues should be paid. That said, there is also evidence that even some of those from the higher echelons of Acre society who survived did not always find it easy; records show that Charles II of Anjou was sending supplies to members of the nobility who had managed to get to Cyprus without presumably most of their wealth because they were finding things difficult there.[27]

Without going into detail, the Templar of Tyre does mention the fate of refugees to Cyprus. He refers to how poor those who escaped were, having been forced to leave much of their wealth behind. It is striking that he mentions that 'all their friends in Cyprus forgot about them and made no kindly mention of them'.[28] Indeed, Cyprus soon had internal problems of its own to cope with, including coups against the king and counter-coups in his favour. The involvement of men such as Philip of Ibelin (a family that was particularly prominent in Cypriot affairs), John of Jubail, Balian of Montgisard and James of Floury (a knight of Acre) – whose names betray their point of origin as being in the now lost Outremer – in these plots suggests that they may have brought some of the fractious infighting that characterised the latter days of the defunct Kingdom of Jerusalem with them. When a counter-coup was launched in 1310 and Henry II reclaimed his throne, a number of these men were shipped off to imprisonment in Armenia, which retained close relations with Cyprus until it was finally overwhelmed completely by the Mamluks in 1375. In the meantime, the scars inflicted by the loss of Acre lingered in Cyprus where as late as 1394 women dressed in black as a sign of mourning for it.[29]

During those apocalyptic final days of Acre, it was not just people who were taken to safety. The Templars were great collectors of relics and their most valued one was a cross made out of a bathtub in which Christ had supposedly bathed. It was credited with miraculous curative powers and for this reason was visited by pilgrims who were sick. It was also paraded when the region was suffering from drought. During the evacuation it was spirited away to Cyprus. So, too, were the human remains of St Euphemia, martyr and virgin, which were kept at Atlit and were also taken on the short crossing to the island. The Templar relic collection was later transferred to the Hospitallers after the Temple was disbanded in the early fourteenth century and pilgrims recalled seeing them in Rhodes half a century after the fall of Acre.[30] In contrast to the fate of the relics that were in the possession of the Templars in Acre, it appears that all those held by the Hospitallers there were lost in the sack of the city, possibly because of a shortage of transport to spirit them away to safety.[31]

The victims created, directly or indirectly, as a result of the capture of Acre were not just Christian. Rashid al-Din in his *History of the*

Franks (compiled 1305–6) claimed that the sacking of the Muslim enclave of Lucera in south-east Italy came about as retaliation for it. Many Muslims had chosen to settle here when Frederick II expelled them from Sicily in 1224 in response to uprisings there. The city did reasonably well thereafter and many of the citizens established themselves as farmers. During the confrontation between the papacy and Hohenstaufens in the 1260s the city worked in alliance with the latter and came in for severe criticism from the former as a result.[32] Manfred, the self-appointed ruler of Sicily at the time, was accused of 'plunging his savage hands into the bowels of the Church' and Pope Urban IV had commented then that 'the heathens have entered the inheritance of the Lord' (for this is how the papacy saw the papal states in Italy which were under threat as a result of the alliance) and that 'the followers of Mahomet [were] daring to invade and shake the Church, the bride of Christ, and the Catholic Faith, in their very foundations'.[33] But in 1300, Lucera was sacked by Charles II of Naples. Thousands were slaughtered and the survivors taken into slavery, though a few were exiled to Albania. The mosques were destroyed and churches erected in their place. Lucera was the last preserve of Islam in Italy. Whilst the general feeling is that Rashid al-Din was wrong in claiming that this was in part retribution for what had happened at Acre, it was an appropriate enough example of the grim spirit of the times.[34]

Last Rites

By nightfall on 18 May, all but four fortified buildings in the city were in Muslim hands; but as those that remained were all held by professional men-at-arms, they were likely to prove very difficult obstacles to overcome. They were held by the Templars, Hospitallers, Teutonic Knights and a group of warriors from Armenia respectively. Just two days later, the Hospitallers and Teutonic Knights who were besieged in their buildings asked al-Ashraf for an amnesty, which was granted. The Templars also requested the same but, although this was initially agreed to, the arrangement quickly began to unravel. The vast Templar fortress remained the main focal point for any resistance that was left. Inside were both men from the military orders and secular soldiers as well as non-combatants such as burgesses,[35] women and children.

As 400 mounted Mamluk soldiers entered the Templar fortress to take possession, some of them started to molest women and children inside.[36] Possibly they did not realise that these were inside the compound along with the knights and other men of the military orders when the surrender was arranged. No doubt they saw these as the prizes of war and the Templars were quickly roused to anger. They were a proud institution and to see non-combatants treated with such contempt as they meekly stood by and watched was anathema to them. Their tempers up, they lashed out and scores of Muslims were cut down on the spot. Nearly all of them trapped inside were killed and the banners – the equivalent of the white flags that modern negotiators might use as a way of marking their neutrality or at least their non-aggressive intentions – which had secured their egress to the tower were flung unceremoniously down from the walls.

It was a foolish act by the Mamluks who, blinded by their bloodlust, needlessly signed their own death warrants as well as those of some of their comrades who would now have to fight again to take this last defiant bastion. Some Muslims had already entered the fortress and jumped from it into the sea; some died as a result but a handful managed to survive to fight another day. The peace agreement had been decisively shattered and the gates were shut once more, though those Franks besieged in other places of last resort went through with their surrender nevertheless.

Brave as their actions were, the Templars were in a hopeless position. They were isolated and with no hope of rescue, as was recognised when some time on 25-26 May the order's treasury was evacuated to Cyprus with the new Master, Theobald Gaudin (the tower in which the treasure was stored was very wisely located right on the coast). The Franks still held the sea and this meant that the treasure and the recently appointed Templar Master were safe. The men who were left behind were not.

The great Templar fortress was in the south-west part of the city, overlooking the sea. Although the building has long since gone (a modern lighthouse now approximately marks its position), in 1994 tunnels some 150 metres long were discovered when a local resident was investigating problems with the sewers under his house. These had once led from the headquarters of the Templars to the port, passing underneath the Pisan quarter of Acre. They were invaluable during the siege and perhaps are the means by which the Templar treasure was shipped out. Contemporary accounts describe a powerful building guarded by two large towers and with walls 28 feet thick. Two smaller towers were also built, each topped by a gilded lion which would have added to their impressiveness. This formidable citadel was now the site of the last stand in Acre.

It is worth taking note of this detail concerning the Templar treasure. A story appeared in the press in 2019 announcing details concerning the discovery of a Templar tunnel in Acre. The unearthing of Crusader-era buildings in Acre is nothing new. Famously, in addition to the Templar tunnels found in 1994 some spectacular finds relating to the Hospitallers were found in the city, which are as yet not completely excavated. The destruction of buildings above ground may have been thorough during the final stages of the capture of Acre but may have been less so with respect to parts of the major buildings in the city that were subterranean. The detritus built up in subsequent centuries has only helped to conceal such sites further. The discovery of these new Templar tunnels in Acre does not mean that they are inevitably linked to lost treasure; similar features are found in many medieval fortresses without any proven link to such riches. Yet perhaps inevitably not long after the discovery of these tunnels such a link was postulated. One of the archaeologists involved in the investigation remarked that 'somewhere in the modern city of Acre lies their [the Templars] command centre, and possibly their treasure. It's the stuff of childhood dreams. I'm here to find them.' Given contemporary evidence that the treasure was successfully evacuated, there may be some treasure-seekers who will ultimately be very disappointed when these new discoveries are finally fully explored.[37]

By now, frustration was getting the better of al-Ashraf. He offered the Templars the same terms that had previously been on the table. He said he did not blame them for the killing of his men inside the citadel as they had acted incorrectly and those inside had been fully justified in their actions. The Templars, without any hope of escape or rescue, were tempted. On 28 May, a party was sent out from their fortress to finalise the deal. Things quickly began to go wrong again. The delegation was immediately seized and executed on the spot, possibly as a measure of revenge for the death of an emir killed earlier on. The Templar Commander Peter de Sevrey, who had led the delegation, was among those who were beheaded. The tit-for-tat killings went on, as five Islamic prisoners held inside by the Templars were thrown to their death from high windows in the tower. With nothing left to lose, a fight to the death was now inevitable.

It was clear that the Templars inside were determined to sell their lives dearly, making a frontal assault on their fortress highly costly.

Muslim sappers therefore got to work on undermining the tower in which the last Templars were holed up. There was no chance of any countermeasures being taken and the edifice finally came crashing down. The writer Bar Hebraeus tells of 2,000 Muslim warriors breaking into the tower as the end drew near – a suspiciously high number. The tower came crashing down in a deadly cloud of dust and rubble taking everyone inside, Christian and Muslim, with it. Muslim accounts tell of a much more prosaic end with the tower being evacuated and then demolished. Whatever the truth, the siege of Acre was over, though the killing was not quite at an end. An eyewitness, Abu'l Fida, noted:

> ...within the city were a number of well-fortified towers, and some Franks shut themselves inside and defended them. The Muslims killed vast numbers of people and gathered immense booty. The Sultan forced all those in the towers to surrender, and they submitted to the last man, and to the last man were decapitated outside the city walls.[38]

The brutal aftermath of Hattin was played out afresh. It is unsurprising that at least one Muslim commentator, Abu i-Mihasin, suggested that the slaughter was revenge for Richard the Lionheart's butchery of Muslim captives at Acre almost exactly a century before.[39]

It was nearly all over now. The dream that was Outremer was no more. Brutal, bloody reality had taken over. The Christian dead lay where they fell. Given the importance of a prompt burial with proper rites for Muslim dead, those of al-Ashraf's warriors who had paid the ultimate price would have been honoured with all due reverence and respect. It was an especially terrible scene for those survivors on the losing side. The cries of those being dragged off into a life of slavery mingled with the jubilant shouts of triumph of the victors in a jarring cacophony. The dust, the smoke and the flames climbed up into the Levantine sky, blown around in the hot breeze whilst weakened masonry tumbled to the ground with an earth-shaking crash. Out at sea, the last escapees were lost in their thoughts, wondering and fearing what the future held for them, in many cases with nowhere to go. Whilst they may have been relieved at their deliverance from death or captivity, it would have come at a terrible cost in lost wealth, lost families and lost dreams. For them, all that remained of Acre now was a distant smudge of smoke rapidly disappearing over the horizon and memories, some of which were nightmarish.

There was much going on in and around Acre at this moment, but it would soon become a ghost town. Al-Ashraf would be making sure that it could never again be used as a point of entry for the Franks into the Holy Land. The idea of the threat of the Franks still remained in Muslim consciousness for some time to come. Myths developed claiming that every time a new King of Cyprus came to the throne he visited the Holy Land in secret so that he could be properly consecrated in the land that by rights belonged to him. It was probably not true – the record shows that in future kings would be crowned at Nicosia for Cyprus and Famagusta for Jerusalem[40] – but it was believed to be true. It is though a fact that even in the late fifteenth century rulers of Cyprus would still call themselves the King of Jerusalem and that Cypriot coinage would proudly declaim the title.[41] That the Franks might yet one day return to try and rebuild Outremer continued to be an Islamic fear for some time to come.

The Reaction in the West

It was a Greek monk by the name of Arsenius who had witnessed the siege first-hand who came with news of Acre's loss to Pope Nicholas IV. He seemed to blame just about everyone for the loss: the Italians (including rather unfairly the Pisans who had fought bravely and whose consul in Acre had died in the slaughter there), King Henry who had fled, the military orders. Even the papacy came in for criticism because of its distractions elsewhere. He also warned that Cyprus was likely to be next on the Mamluk shopping list and indeed it was not long before al-Ashraf was preparing plans for just such an attack. Others blamed the sinful citizens of Acre. Jean de Joinville, Louis IX's chronicler, wrote up a probably apocryphal story in his biography of the king. When Louis was about to leave Outremer and return to France, Joinville had a meeting with the papal legate in the East. The legate told Joinville that 'No one knows as well as I do of all the mean and treacherous sins committed in Acre. That is why God will have to exact such vengeance for them that Acre shall be washed clean in the blood of its inhabitants and other people come to live there in their place.' As Joinville noted, Acre had indeed now been 'well washed' in their blood (he wrote in 1309, eighteen years after the fall of the city).[42] This *ex post* declaration of God declaring war on the people of Acre for their sins of course reads like revisionism, partly in defence of the king.

There was a tradition of Crusader responses being launched in the aftermath of the loss of great cities. The Second Crusade had followed on from news of the loss of Edessa in 1144 and the Third Crusade came in the wake of similar ill tidings of the conquest of Jerusalem by Saladin in 1187. It remained to be seen whether there would be an expedition from Europe in response to news of the loss of Acre. The nature and extent of that response, if any, would reveal much about European attitudes to the concept of crusading at this particular moment. Certainly, Pope Nicholas IV was quick to issue a document, *Dirum amaritudinis calicem*, on 13 August 1291 in which he announced the terrible tidings from Acre and also immediately called for a crusade to make good the losses suffered. Within days he issued instructions that provincial councils should be set up to consider how best to take practical steps to put these good intentions into action. This included the idea that the Hospitallers and the Templars might be combined, an ominous portent for the orders. An embargo against Western trade with the Mamluks was also put in place, it seems with limited effect, even though radical measures such as the right of sea captains to seize ships ignoring the ban on trade and keep all the goods taken were established.[43] There was a heavy flow of advice into the papal in-tray but much less in terms of practical support and no coherent focus for a new crusade came about. Not all of the suggestions envisaged a military reaction, with some advocating a large-scale evangelical effort to convert the Muslim East to Christianity.[44] The untimely death of Nicholas IV in 1292 and a two-year papal interregnum that followed took all the momentum out of these initiatives in any event.

When news of Acre's fall reached the West, two emotions were evident in some quarters at least: sadness and shame. Twenty galleys were sent to Cyprus at once, ten each from Ancona and Genoa. Wisely, it was deemed expedient to beef up the defences of the island in case a Mamluk attack followed. Although the Mamluks did not have a great naval tradition, in the time of Baybars attacks had been launched on Cyprus and it was possible that one might follow now. But none did and instead King Henry launched a raid on Alanya on the coast of Asia Minor, which was only partly successful. The fleet then made its way south to Alexandria but it does not appear to have achieved very much there. The response was in truth a rather meagre one, and reflects the fact that the sense of shock was greater in ecclesiastical circles than it was elsewhere, where the reaction was more one of a shrug of the shoulders from those who had become increasingly cynical about the utility or desirability of crusading in the Levant.[45]

In addition, the timing of the loss of Acre was particularly inauspicious. The most likely leader of any major crusading expedition at the time was Edward I of England. Just the year before, a seven-year-old princess sailed from Norway to Scotland to take up the throne of that country. This innocent abroad was next in line to be Scotland's ruler, although she would for the time being need to govern via a council of governors. After an arduous crossing, the 'Maid of Norway' died on Orkney, leaving the throne of Scotland vacant. Edward thought that it should pass to him and therefore at the very moment that news of Acre came in, his attentions were very much elsewhere.

A blame game started shortly after the fall of Acre. One writer, Thadeus of Naples, who lived in Syria for a time, was particularly critical of the role of some of the orders in the city. In a work entitled *Ystoria de desolatione et conculcatione civitatis Acconensis et totius Terre Sancte* ('History of the desolation and crushing of Acre and all the Holy Land'), Thadeus was generally scathing about what he suggests was the cowardice of the Templars and Hospitallers, though William of Beaujeu and Matthew of Clermont are exonerated for having the decency to die in battle. The Teutonic Knights, who suffered grievously, are also exempted from this criticism. Although he probably did not witness the shocking scenes in Acre first-hand, Thadeus was there not long before and as he wrote in Messina, Sicily, just a few months after the battle – the port was a major destination for travellers between the east and west Mediterranean – it is probable that he had spoken with people who were. His is an emotional text with less factual details than the Templar of Tyre but gives an insight into the deep reactions that the loss of Acre generated in some quarters.

Why, Thadeus wondered, had the Holy Land ejected the Christians, as if the region itself had physically thrown them out? It could only be because of the sinful nature of those living there, and so his condemnation extends beyond the orders to other Christians; another example of *peccatis exigentibus*. He made frequent use of references to the biblical prophet Jeremiah in his work, as indeed did other medieval chroniclers when something particularly disturbing happened. As an example of the 'Dies irae' approach he employed, quoting Jeremiah 9 he wrote: 'Thus says the Lord of hosts, the God of Israel: I am feeding this people with wormwood, and giving them poisonous water to drink.'[46] Other commentators employed similar themes though not necessarily trowelling it on quite as thickly as Thadeus does. Whilst not completely exonerating the orders, the anonymous writer of a work known as *De Excidio Urbis Acconis* saw the destruction of Acre as punishment for the wealthy sections of society there, more interested in luxury and worldly goods than the well-being of their souls.

A Dominican monk, Riccoldo de Monte Croce, a remarkable man who journeyed to the court of Arghun in Baghdad as a missionary – another example of the lure of the Mongols as potential converts to Christianity – also wrote of the loss of Acre:[47]

> I was saddened by the massacre and capture of the Christian people. I wept over the loss of Acre, seeing the Saracens joyous and prospering, the Christians squalid and consternated; little children, young girls, old people, whimpering, threatened to be led as captives and slaves into the remotest countries of the East, amongst barbarous nations. Suddenly in this sadness I began, stupefied, to ponder God's judgement concerning the government of the world, especially concerning the Saracens and the Christians. What could be the cause of such massacre and such degradation of the Christian people?

It was indeed a worrying question; as worrying was the fact that the monk could not find an answer however hard he searched for it.[48] He came to the conclusion that the age of crusading to the Levant was over as God clearly did not look on it with favour any more.

Over time, views evolved. Writing about fifty years after the fall of Acre, the pilgrim/writer Ludolph of Suchem unequivocally blamed the greed of the Italian city states for its loss. It is interesting that two centuries before, Bishop Jacques de Vitry had also castigated them for their focus on mercenary considerations ahead of the well-being of Outremer. Venice in particular came in for criticism. Indeed, not long after the capture of Constantinople in 1453 Venetian chroniclers were rewriting history in true Stalinist fashion to present her role in the final defence of Acre in a more positive light. Earlier Venetian chronicles made little mention of Venice's role in those events but suddenly her part was rewritten to present it as being something altogether glorious and heroic. The reasons for this were not hard to find; after Constantinople was taken, Venice quickly re-established trading relations with the victorious Ottoman Empire. The city suddenly found itself under critical attack from all parts of Christendom for putting money before morality. Therefore, her hitherto insignificant part in the loss of Acre was suddenly recast in an altogether more brilliant light in a typically Venetian attempt to present the city's history in a more favourable guise. It is reassuring to say that few outside of Venice were deceived by this gross distortion of history.

Pope Pius II (pontiff 1458–64) was one of the last important men to believe in the possibility of a crusade to the East. When he died, the crusade he had invested his hopes in was disintegrating even before it had left Italy. But even he was not deceived by Venice. He stated that 'everything is just to them if for the good of the state. It is legitimate if it increases their dominion'.[49] It had been true of *La Serenissima* for most of the 350 years she had been involved in the crusading movement, and indeed was true of most others too.

The loss of Acre was initially a source of inspiration to Islam. Some Muslim commentators noted the fact that the final fall of Acre came almost exactly a century after the Lionheart had slaughtered his prisoners outside the city, seeing it as an act of justified vengeance.[50] Soon after Acre's fall, Muslims from Morocco made the short crossing across the Straits of Gibraltar and attacked Christian Spain (or, to be more precise, the lands held at the time by King Sancho IV of Castile and Leon). Sancho enlisted the help of the Genoese admiral Benedetto Zaccaria. Initially he found that the Muslim ships were too quick for him so he devised a cunning plan to turn the tables. The Genoese ships were designed to give space for two oarsmen to a bench. He had them extended to allow an extra rower on each bench. When the Muslim ships next sailed, he told his men to row slowly to lull the enemy into a sense of complacency. Then when the moment seemed propitious he told his men to row at maximum speed. They soon started to catch the Muslim vessels, which frantically tried to escape. When they saw that they were being caught, a number of men jumped overboard and those who made it to land were killed by their own side, possibly trying to rob them. In the end, all twenty Muslim galleys were taken and the men onboard killed or captured. The Muslim army that had already crossed into Spain were stranded and the campaign came to nothing, with some of the Muslim soldiers allegedly converting to Christianity. Others were killed by Sancho's men, something we are told that the king was happy to do 'to assuage the heaviness of his heart on account of the loss of Acre and the destruction of the poor Christians of Syria'.[51]

14

The Reckoning

'God grant that they never set foot there again!'
The Muslim chronicler Abu'l Fida on the
ejection of the Franks from Acre

Mopping Up

Shortly after the fall of Acre, al-Ashraf and his men marched through the streets of Damascus in triumph. Behind them was a ragged trail of Crusader captives whilst the standards of the vanquished were carried upside-down in mock homage, some of them decorated with the scalps of dead Franks. It was an echo, intentional or otherwise, of the actions of Saladin after Hattin. There was shortly afterwards a repeat performance in Cairo. It was understandable that al-Ashraf was milking the moment for all it was worth. At this precise moment, he probably reasoned that life could not be any sweeter than this and that his place in history and as a ruler was secured. A few years later he was eliminated by an assassin. Such were the vagaries of life for a Mamluk Sultan.

The walls of Acre were demolished. Emulating Baybars' example, al-Ashraf was determined to deny the port to the Franks as the possible launch pad for a future crusade. Only a few selected fragments of the city survived as tokens of victory, such as the doorway from the church of Saint Andrew, earmarked to be taken to Cairo where it was to be incorporated into a mosque to mark al-Ashraf's victory. Acre was not the last place to be held by the Franks in Outremer but what remained to them in terms of territory was no longer viable. The Muslim mopping-up operation was eerily similar to that which followed the great victory of Saladin at Hattin in 1187, almost more of a procession than a military campaign. The other fortresses in Outremer had been denuded of troops to defend Acre and those that were left were too isolated in any event and could be picked off one by one. And so there was a terminal domino effect as the remaining Frankish possessions were taken: Sidon on 14 July 1291, Haifa on 30 July and Beirut on the following day. Tortosa in Syria was lost on 4 August and the mighty fortress of Atlit, impregnable to the last, was abandoned by the Franks on 14 August. Rather like the Maginot Line in the Second World War all that effort and money put into building it was ultimately ineffectual and it was given up without a fight. It was not captured by force but it did not need to be. It may have been impregnable but it was now also irrelevant.

An indication of just how much the fight had gone out of those left in Outremer is what happened at Tyre, first taken by the Franks in 1124. Undoubtedly, after Acre this was the most significant remaining Frankish possession. The stubborn defence of Tyre had been the catalyst that had kept Outremer alive after Hattin and played a significant part in extending its life for a further century. The Templar of Tyre described it as 'one of the strongest cities in the world'. It was under the command of the King's *bailli*, Adam of Caffran. As soon as he heard of the loss of Acre, he abandoned Tyre along with everyone else who could afford to buy their passage out. A greater contrast with what had happened after Hattin could not be imagined; Tyre was abandoned without the semblance of a fight. It was an apposite summation of the difference between Outremer in 1291 and the situation exactly a century earlier when the armies of Richard the Lionheart and Philip Augustus of France had been striving to rebuild the shattered kingdom. For the poorer inhabitants of Tyre who could not afford to buy their way out, only a life of slavery awaited, which followed when the Muslims took possession of the undefended city shortly after. For some though, there was not even that. Those who were of no value, the old and the very young for example, were just left to fend for themselves.

Sidon was another interesting example. The Commander of the Temple, Theobald Gaudin, had left Acre after the death of William of Beaujeu and made his way there. The people of Sidon made their way to an island just offshore where there was a mill. The city was abandoned and occupied by Sanjar al-Shuja'i, who had recently been at Acre. The offshore castle was within range of Muslim artillery from the shore and the Muslim engineers enthusiastically went about their task. Theobald told his Templars that he would go to Cyprus to get help, which he duly did. However, on arriving in Cyprus Theobald was so unenthusiastic in his efforts to drum up support that Sidon was effectively abandoned to its fate. Soon after, what was left of Sidon was evacuated by the remaining Frankish forces under cover of darkness. Some of the harbour was still under Templar control and the evacuation was very well-organised with the citizens as well as members of the order taken to safety. Sidon was then demolished by the Muslims and soon after so was Beirut, which was taken by the Sultan through subterfuge.

This was not quite the end of Frankish involvement in the Levant though. The Genoese Embriaco family were allowed to stay as Mamluk vassals at Jubail between Beirut and Tripoli for a few years. In addition, several castles held by the military orders remained in Armenia, close to Syria. Not until the close of the thirteenth century were the last two, Servantikar and Roche-Guillaume (in modern Turkey), taken by the Mamluks. Jacques de Molay, master of the Templars and his Hospitaller counterpart, William de Villaret, participated in the unsuccessful defence of these last vestiges of their presence on the mainland of the Levant. Both managed to escape with their lives. These were incidents that forewarned that Armenia itself was vulnerable to renewed threats from the Mamluks and was increasingly ill-prepared to face them. A force of sixteen galleys including Cypriot, Templar and Hospitaller troops did raid a number of Muslim coastal towns such as Alexandria, Tortosa and Acre in 1300 (though whether there was much left to raid at the latter is moot).[1]

The mention of these raids by the Templar of Tyre implies (from the small number of casualties suffered by the Muslims) that they were quite small-scale. They ended with an attack on Maraclea where it sounds as if the Frankish forces came off worst with twenty sergeants and a knight killed. The fleet then returned to Cyprus with little of significance achieved. At around the same time, there were also occasional Mamluk raids on Cyprus though they also achieved little and it was not until 1420 that they started to pose a greater threat to the island. It was just as well as Cyprus was vulnerable from other directions too. Not long after the fall of Acre there was a falling-out between Henry II and Genoa after he granted trading privileges to

Barcelona and Pisa, bitter commercial rivals of the Genoese. The Cypriots also took the part of the Venetians in the war that was about to break out anew between the two great Italian city states, which further infuriated the Genoese.[2]

An attempt was made to reoccupy Tortosa in November 1300 with a force led by Jacques de Molay and Amalric,[3] brother of King Henry who was, in theory at least, the Constable of the kingdom, even though it no longer in practice existed as far the Levantine mainland was concerned. It was not a very large force with about 600 men, half of them Cypriot soldiers and the other half made up of Templars and Hospitallers from the island. Though they raided Tortosa, they did not permanently occupy it and instead set up a base on the island of Ruad, about a mile offshore. They aimed to link up with Mongol forces but this did not lead to any concrete results. Ghazan's army did not show up and there was nothing more the Cypriot army could do, so most of them returned home in 1301.

Despite this apparently abortive effort, Jacques de Molay retained the hope that more reinforcements would arrive from the West and that another attack on the Muslim Levant might yet take place. He continued to appeal to Pope Boniface VIII for help and in November 1301 the outpost of Ruad was officially put into Templar hands. The garrison on the rocky outcrop was built up until it was about 1,000 strong with 120 knights, 500 archers and 400 servants in situ. Command of Ruad was given to Barthélemy de Quincy, Marshal of the Temple. From his nearby base on Cyprus, Jacques de Molay continued to appeal for help from the West as surviving examples of letters to Edward I of England as well as the King of Aragon demonstrate. Predictably enough, they did not lead to any meaningful response.

The Mamluks had now decided that this new threat needed to be eliminated once and for all. A fleet of sixteen ships was sent from Egypt to Tripoli, from where it moved on Ruad. They set up camp and preceded to besiege the garrison. Although the castle walls were strong and were not breached, thirst and hunger did the job instead. Whilst reinforcements had been assembled in Cyprus, they were too late in setting out and the garrison was left with little option but to capitulate. On 26 September 1302, an honourable surrender was agreed whereby the garrison would be allowed to leave for a safe Christian haven. Barely had they left the gates before the agreement was broken. A fight followed in which Barthélemy de Quincy was killed, along with most of his men. Not one of the Frankish bowmen there survived, although a few Templar knights were taken as captives to Cairo. They were allegedly put under pressure to convert to Islam but refused to do so. In the end they were starved to death.

The End of the Mongol Delusion

At one time, historians hopefully wrote of a *pax Mongolica,* an extensive region characterised by stability. In this blissful vision, cross-continental trade blossomed and traders from Europe and Asia freely moved to and fro, a kind of prototype internationalist trading zone. It is now by and large accepted that this situation was very short-lived, if it ever existed at all, and was no more than wishful thinking.[4] Any trading between East and West largely went through middlemen. The Polos and a few others of their ilk were the adventurous exception rather than the general rule. By the end of the thirteenth century, the Mongol *khanate* had fragmented on religious as well as political grounds: the east was in the main Buddhist, whilst further west the Mongols in Persia and those of the Golden Horde were substantially Muslim. The rulers of the West belatedly started to realise how little they had in common with people who at one time the more enthusiastic among them had regarded as being ripe for integration into the Latin church. The pipe dream of a Western-Mongol alliance was shown up to be the mirage it actually was.

Following the fall of Acre, diplomatic initiatives between the Mongols and the West became more fitful. Edward I sent an envoy, Geoffrey de Langley, to them in 1292 but there was no return visit. Arghun had died and been replaced by his brother Gaikhatu, who was then succeeded by Baidu in 1295. Neither of them sent missions westward. Only then did missions from the Mongols resume during the reign of Ghazan, who ironically was a Muslim. Henry II of Cyprus responded to his approaches and there were brief forays against Rosetta and Alexandria in Egypt and Acre, Tortosa and Maraclea on the Levantine coast, but they did not achieve very much.

The loss of all the Frankish ports in Outremer destroyed any hopes of Christian-Mongol cooperation in the region. All the major crusades since Frederick Barbarossa's disastrous crossing of Asia Minor in 1190 had come by sea. Now there was no point of entry to the region for such an expedition. It proved just how decisive a strategy the Mamluks had adopted in destroying major ports rather than trying to hold on to them, something even recognised by near-contemporary observers.[5] That said, even into the fourteenth century there was an occasional mooting of the idea of an attack launched from Europe on Egypt and even some raids, including a heavy attack on Alexandria in 1365 launched from Rhodes. But again, they had no long-term effect in terms of transforming the balance of power in the Eastern Mediterranean.

It was not necessarily for want of trying. Ghazan had not been idle despite the failure of his army to coordinate its actions with the small Cypriot force at the end of the thirteenth century. He inflicted a crushing defeat on Islamic forces at Wadi al-Khazandar near Homs on 22 December 1299. Although suggestions by the near-contemporary writer Peter of Duisburg that 200,000 Muslim warriors fell in battle against the Mongols at around this time are absurd; the Templar of Tyre suggests that 25,000 died in the battle but implies that a large number also perished in the retreat that followed it. A small party of Templars and Hospitallers from Armenia took part alongside the Mongol forces, experiencing a rare and presumably intoxicating moment of triumph in stark contrast to their ill-fortune in recent times. However the Mongols were late in contacting Christian forces on Cyprus and as a result an opportunity for greater collaboration was missed.[6] Nine days later, the Mongols moved back into Damascus. News of these events caused great excitement in the West and generated 'fake news' including that of the capture of the Sultan and the conquest of Egypt. It was certainly true that retreating Mamluk forces were chased as far as Gaza. There are even vague and inconclusive accounts that for a short time the Mongols took over Jerusalem. The exaggerated accounts fell on fertile ground as they arrived at the time of a Jubilee – an infrequent Catholic festival which was declared a 'holy period' and involved a large-scale pilgrimage – that was being held in Rome. It was therefore a time of heightened spiritual euphoria and it was easy to believe these joyous tidings in such a highly charged atmosphere. Pope Boniface VIII even announced the news to the whole of Christendom by means of a papal letter.

But the Mongols were only in Damascus for a couple of months before retreating. A further campaign against Aleppo in the following year found itself bogged down due to awful weather conditions. A third campaign to Syria in 1303 ended in a total Mongol defeat at the Battle of Marj al-Suffar, to the south of Damascus. The Mongols fled from the field in panic but many of them were cut down before they could reach safety. An Islamic writer wrote graphically of how Muslim warriors 'harvested their heads as men harvest barley with a sickle'.[7] The rout was completed when peasants vengefully flooded the fields through which the tattered remnants of the Mongol army were retreating. 5,000 Mongol survivors lost their horses and had to make the long journey back on foot. Ghazan died on 11 May 1304. He had been the most able Mongol leader to emerge for a while and had undertaken several positive acts in his reign. Militarily, steps had been taken to improve horses and armour and in a different field he also rebuilt the Persian economy but to little long-term effect. By this time, his letters to Henry II and Edward I of England showed barely concealed frustration at the inability of the West to provide meaningful help to supplement his own endeavours. Diplomatic initiatives from the Mongols fizzled out over the next two decades partly because, as often as not, they were too busy fighting each other to worry about further adventures in the cause of expanding their *khanate*. An embassy to Edward II, the ineffectual monarch who had succeeded Edward I in England in 1307, again came to nothing. In 1320, the Mongols at last made peace with the Mamluks. The threat posed to Syria by these predatory steppe warriors eventually dissipated away to nothing as the Mongol *khanate*, as all empires do, finally faded away.

The disappearance of the Mongol *khanate* was not an overnight event. The Golden Horde, for example, was an active power for several centuries to come after the fall of Acre. But in most cases they were gradually assimilated into the regions that they had previously conquered. They were not so much ejected as swallowed up. The great if violent warrior known as Tamerlane who was active at the end of the fourteenth century found their legacy useful. Quite cleverly, he did not try to claim he was of Genghis Khan's line and appoint himself as *khagan*. Instead he forged symbolic links with those who could claim to spring from this lineage. Rather as Baybars had treated the dispossessed caliphs of Baghdad as puppets on strings, so too did Tamerlane, with a good deal of success.

Western Christendom in the end failed to win over the Mongols. This failure to achieve anything much by way of diplomatic links between the two blocs was reflected in the efforts made to convert the Mongols to Catholicism. There were several initiatives launched to Asia during the fourteenth century but no mass conversions followed. There were several reasons for this disappointment. Some of them were very practical; there were too few missionaries and not enough interpreters, for example. The Nestorian Christians among the Mongols, rather than helping the Catholic missionaries, on the whole resisted them, finding their own position under threat (and probably not very impressed at the way that Western missionaries looked down their noses at them either). In contrast, the conversion of leading Mongols such as the *Ilkhan* Ghazan in 1295 to Islam meant that it was the Muslim religion that became dominant among the Mongols, especially those in Western Asia. Western Christendom lost not only the battle for the Levant but also that for Mongol hearts and minds. With its heavy-handed and hectoring approach and its failure to understand Mongol paradigms of the world and who should rule it, no other outcome was ever likely.

The Mamluk Dynasty

To the victor, the spoils. Although it was Baybars who laid the foundations of the Mamluk army that took Acre and Qalāwūn whose scheme it largely was to take the city, it was al-Ashraf who was eulogised for its capture. A panegyric written by the later Islamic commentator Ibn al-Furat towards the end of the fourteenth century extolled his virtues:

> Because of you no town is left in which unbelief can repair, no hope for the Christian religion!

> Through al-Ashraf the Lord Sultan we are delivered from the Trinity and Unity rejoices in the struggle!

> Praise be to God, the nation of the Cross has fallen, through the Turks the religion of the chosen Arab has triumphed![8]

The biographer Baybars al-Mansuri wrote glowingly of al-Ashraf's achievement. It was he said a great honour, by implication greater than anything achieved by Baybars or Qalāwūn. It was a sycophantic and unfair comment, ignoring the fact that the army that had achieved this victory was built on the foundations laid down by these illustrious predecessors. Al-Ashraf nevertheless initially built on his triumphs in Outremer. In May 1292 he led an army against the Armenian-held fortress of Qal'at al-Rūm, which fell after a short struggle, another victim of the massive siege artillery that had blasted through the walls of Acre. But fame is a fickle mistress. Al-Ashraf was surrounded by enemies within as well as without and his grandiose schemes for extending both his territories and his personal fortune inevitably brought him into conflict with some of his senior Mamluk commanders. On 13 December 1293, he was assassinated by senior officers who feared that the Sultan's ambitions endangered the Mamluk state and perhaps more pertinently their own interests. The first blow was struck by his uncle Baydara – his mother's brother – but only in a half-hearted fashion. Seeing this feeble attempt, another man, Lachin, berated him. This, he said, is how you kill a Sultan, unleashing a sword stroke so fierce that it allegedly cut al-Ashraf in half. It was a vicious blow that had been a long time in coming. Lachin had been with the Sultan at Acre where his loyalties were already suspected; in fact, he was arrested by al-Ashraf during the siege. The Sultan would have been well advised to have followed his instincts. He may have achieved something by the conquest of Acre that Baybars had not; but he had not developed the survival skills that his illustrious forebear had honed to a fine art.

A period of uncontrolled bloodletting, extraordinarily violent even by Mamluk standards, ended with a new Sultan, Kitbughā, coming to the throne. This event was also extraordinary in a different way, for he came originally of Mongol stock. His reign was short and marred by several assassination attempts before he was eventually forced out. His short period in office was punctuated by several awful events, including a very severe famine in 1295 and widespread outbreaks of disease in the country. His successor, Lachin, lasted from 1296 to 1299 when he was murdered in a mosque in Cairo by two Mamluks. The identity of the assassins was evidence of the increasing power of the personal armies of leading Mamluk officials. The rise of their armies was helped by a drop in the price of slaves shipped in from the Caucasus, a process from which the Genoese who shipped them over ironically benefitted greatly.

Subsequent years saw a gradual but undeniable decline in the Mamluk dynasty. There was a general dropping-off in standards and training, perhaps fuelled by a degree of complacency as the Mongol threat receded and Western European interest in the Levant largely disappeared, apart from the occasional flare-up which normally did not last for very long. The growing power of individual emirs led to a fatal concentration on internal affairs and a general decline in the fabric of the state as self-interest came ever more to the fore. Ruling Sultans were increasingly vulnerable; one of them, al-Nasir (active around 1340), reigned on no fewer than three occasions.

Almost unnoticed at first, a new power was emerging in Asia Minor. It would ultimately destroy both the Byzantine Empire and the Mamluk dynasty and would also pose a great threat to Western Christendom. It came in the shape of the Ottoman Turks who first began to emerge as a regional power in the 1340s. They were used as mercenaries by the Byzantines in 1369. This was perhaps one of the more extreme examples of the unforeseen consequences of inviting a cuckoo into the nest in recorded history. By 1389, the Ottoman Sultan Murad I had conquered Thrace (Bulgaria). The Battle of Kosovo followed soon after. Although Murad was killed, the Ottomans pushed deep into the Balkans. By 1402, most of the Byzantine Empire had gone and Constantinople itself was encircled. Only a few other scattered territories on the European mainland and in Asia Minor remained and the future looked desperate indeed.

Byzantium was saved for a time by the emergence of another great Central Asian power in the form of Tamerlane. He expanded his empire dramatically, sacking Delhi in India in one direction and pushing deep into Syria in the other. He attacked Sivas in Armenia; the garrison surrendered on condition that their blood would not be spilt, and true to his word he did not run them through with sword or spear or decapitate them; he buried them alive. Then he moved into Syria. The governor of Damascus cut his envoy in half when he demanded the city's surrender but, unlike the situation after Qutuz had done the same thing to Mongol envoys well over a century before, this time there would be no victory as at Ain Jalut. Aleppo was chosen as the focal point for the Syrian defence that followed, but foolishly the Mamluk forces inside allowed themselves to be lured out into a set-piece battle. This was a disaster in which Tamerlane's forces, including war elephants brought from India, created panic in the Mamluk ranks who soon broke and fled in terror.

Aleppo fell shortly after and an orgy of killing followed emulating any atrocity unleashed by the Mongols in the past. Heads were neatly arranged in piles outside the walls, some 20,000 of them. Homs and Hama fell soon after, as did those old Crusader haunts of Beirut and Sidon. Then it was on to Damascus, which surrendered in a negotiated settlement. However, some of the Mamluk forces inside the city broke the terms of the agreement and the events that followed in retribution were truly apocalyptic. Unmentionable tortures were perpetrated on many of the citizens and the Great Mosque was set ablaze when it had been packed with people. Damascus was turned into a death zone and Cairo looked as if it would be next. But Tamerlane was distracted as he needed to deal with the Ottomans in Anatolia. Before dealing with them, however, he moved on Baghdad where again the slaughter was indescribable; 120 piles of skulls were erected outside the city after it had been obliterated.

The decisive battle, or so at least it seemed, took place near Ankara on 28 July 1402. Here Tamerlane and the Ottomans led by Sultan Bayezid ('the Lightning') clashed. The outcome of the battle was decided when a mass defection of Tartar troops from the Ottomans to Tamerlane occurred and swung things decisively in his favour. The Ottoman army was obliterated and Bayezid was captured – he spent the rest of his life being towed around in a small cage as part of Tamerlane's entourage. However, things changed soon after when Tamerlane's ambition did for him. He decided to move east instead of west, on China no less, but died on the way. Despite the terrible setback it had suffered, the Ottoman Empire found a new lease of life after his death.

In 1453, the Ottomans moved in on the greatest prize of all, the city of Constantinople, which had outlived its prestigious ancestor, Ancient Rome, by a thousand years. It had been slowly strangled to death in a meticulous and relentless process overseen by Sultan Mehmet II ('the Conqueror') which included the building of a castle where the straits between Europe and Asia reached their narrowest point. The castle, Rumelihisari, gloried in the name of 'the Throat Cutter'. Mehmet's cannon blasted the walls of the city to rubble and the outnumbered defenders were overwhelmed. The last Byzantine Emperor Constantine XI Palaeologus died fighting in the streets alongside his soldiers. It was a heroic contrast to the actions of Henry II, the last holder of the title of King of Jerusalem who could meaningfully claim it, who had abandoned the city of Acre rather than fight. The loss of Constantinople was a terminal blow to the Byzantine Empire and the last rites of that ancient institution were played out over the next few years as the last bits and pieces of it were gobbled up by the rapacious Ottomans with a seemingly insatiable appetite. It was also a terrible blow for Western Christendom; the Ottomans pushed deeper into

Europe and were not stopped until they were turned back at the gates of Vienna two centuries later.

For the Mamluks too, the rise of this new Turkish power was fatal. The Mamluk dynasty lived on into the sixteenth century when it came up against the formidable though still young power of the Ottomans. Ironically, the Turks now had their own slave soldiers, the Janissaries. The proud but dated Mamluk forces were no match for the new professional army now facing them. The last Mamluk Sultan, al-Malik al-Ashraf Tumanbay, was forced to surrender to the Ottoman Selim. In the ultimate humiliation, he was subsequently publicly hanged. The extermination of the Mamluks continued during the reign of Selim's son, the renowned Suleiman the Magnificent. A few of them survived as a quaint reminder of a glorious but now fading past. They were kept mainly for their novelty and ceremonial value rather than their prowess as warriors.

The postscript to the Mamluk story provides a remarkable finale. In 1798, a French army arrived in the Middle East under the leadership of Napoleon Bonaparte. He tried but failed to take Acre. Then he moved on to Egypt. In the shadow of the pyramids he annihilated the Egyptian army – including Mamluk soldiers – in the military equivalent of *un clin d'oeil*. However, he was also seduced by the Mamluk legend and recruited a party of them into his army. They returned to Europe with him and served him loyally for the next decade. Their last hurrah, as was Napoleon's, was during the Waterloo campaign of 1815, a fitting conclusion to the story of an extraordinary military dynasty. The Mamluks and Bonaparte exited military history together.

The Military Orders

With the fall of Acre, the status of the military orders was under grave threat as a big part of their *raison d'être* had been removed. They were already the subject of much criticism, and even more dangerously their wealth encouraged envy, especially as the fundamental justification for their existence had now been removed. The Teutonic Knights at least carved out a new, meaningful role for themselves by engaging in wars against pagans in Prussia and the Baltic, something which they had already been doing for half a century previously. They were now able to give this their full-time attention, in contrast to the previous situation where they had been dividing their interests there with what was happening in Outremer. They briefly set up their headquarters in

Venice before moving to Marienburg in Prussia in 1309.[9] This was an extremely wise move, given what was happening to the Templars elsewhere at the time. It was well away from the heart of European affairs where the order was less likely to attract criticism or at least avoid decisive action being taken against it. This was certainly a case of out of sight being out of mind.

The future of the Teutonic Knights lay in the Baltic, but the painful memory of the loss of Acre lived on in their societal memory. In 1326 Peter von Duisburg wrote of it in a piece that began with the haunting words, *querimonia desolacionis terre sancte* – 'lament the desolation of the Holy Land'. Not only did Peter mention the devastation of that loss and help to ensure that it remained a powerful emotional element for the Teutonic brethren, he also wrote of subsequent events involving the Mamluks and the Mongols in Syria, though not, it must be said, in particularly accurate terms. Peter was a distant observer when he wrote, far removed from events in the Levant, and inspired perhaps more by sentiment than realism. Though his observations were full of poignancy and pathos, the truth was that they did nothing to change the reality that crusading as far as the Teutonic Knights were concerned was now decisively and irrevocably focused on the Baltic.

The orders more widely came under close, often negative, scrutiny following the fall of Acre and their ejection from the Levant. There was already resentment in some quarters before this for their lack of accountability to any secular authority; even the relatively young Teutonic Knights had fallen out with those they were supposed to be helping, such as in Burzenland where they were ultimately expelled after initially being invited in earlier in the thirteenth century.[10] Critics wondered why such vast resources as those enjoyed by the orders had not led to more success. The Templars had access to 9,000 manors and the Hospitallers 19,000, each supposed to furnish one knight for Outremer, giving access to a theoretically vast Crusader army. Yet though the resources tied up were indeed enormous, so were the costs. Many Templars were non-combatant 'support staff'. Costs had also rocketed. The price of a horse (each Templar knight was entitled to three) tripled between 1140 and 1180 and then doubled again by 1220.[11] This required expenditure on a massive scale and critics now started to ask what benefits were being achieved in return for the investment. For a time there was talk of merging the Hospitallers and the Templars, although the Templar Master Jacques de Molay argued, not altogether convincingly, that the two orders performed complimentary strategic roles. The idea of such a merger was by no means new (it had been discussed as an option at the Council of Lyons in 1274) but a series of events led to something even more dramatic happening.

The Hospitallers and the Templars initially relocated to Cyprus. They both continued to involve themselves in forays in the Levant. However, it was the Hospitallers who achieved greater levels of success. William de Villaret died and was replaced, unusually, by his nephew Fulk in 1305. Close to Cyprus and handily placed adjacent to the mainland of the Levant was the island of Rhodes. It was also close to shipping routes to Egypt and lumber, iron and slaves regularly passed along these. It was in addition used as a base by pirates: attacks had been launched from here on Cyprus in 1302, which resulted in the seizing of Guy of Ibelin from his castle near Limassol and the payment of a heavy ransom of 45,000 silver pieces. The island was under Byzantine control and Fulk decided to conquer it. Rhodes was betrayed to the Hospitallers by a local man, 'a Greek sergeant', who had been beaten by the castellan. He gained revenge by opening the gates of the city of Rhodes at night and admitting a force of Hospitallers who were waiting outside. The city was taken and 300 'Turkish Saracens' found inside were killed, whilst the women and children there took refuge from the slaughter in local churches. The castle held out for two years before it, too, was taken. The Hospitallers then strengthened the defences and as a result the trade with Egypt that had flowed through the island previously was stopped. They were able to exert pressure on adjacent Turkish towns on the mainland of Asia Minor. Whilst this did not compensate for the loss of Outremer, it was a valuable and strategic addition to Frankish territories in the region.[12]

It was perhaps as well for the Hospitallers that they could boast success in their battle for Rhodes, as the orders were under even greater pressure from their critics. They now had a state of sorts to call their own, as did the Teutonic Knights in the Baltic. The Templars had lost their chance after their brief and unsuccessful time in control of Cyprus before it was sold to the Lusignans in the time of Richard the Lionheart; it is an interesting 'what if' scenario to ask what might have happened to them if they still had a territory to call their own. Famously, it was the Templars who were to suffer the most spectacular fall. In 1307, Jacques de Molay was summoned to France. Despite the fact that the anonymous Templar of Tyre was closely connected to his order, the chronicler described de Molay as being 'miserly beyond all reason'. Apparently suspecting nothing when he journeyed to France, de Molay found himself being grilled as to the full extent of the Templar treasure on his arrival in Paris. The exact reasons for what happened next are subject to some debate, but the outcome was clear enough. The Temple soon found itself liquidated, its brethren accused of all sorts of demonic crimes and deviant practices and its treasure seized (though some suggestions have been made that it was in fact shipped out before it was grabbed).[13] They were accused of extreme avarice, despite strong evidence that the Temple took its charitable responsibilities seriously, both in the last years of Frankish Acre and subsequently in Cyprus.[14]

The timing of this strike against the Templars was significant. Not long before, Edward I of England had died. He was considered to be 'the senior statesman and Crusader in Europe, retaining to the end a primacy of respect'.[15] The role of 'senior statesman' therefore fell vacant and Philip IV, King of France, sought to step into the breach. With a French pope in exile in the pocket of the French king, an unholy alliance between the two was formed. Philip was under huge financial strain and the prospect of asset-stripping the Templars was irresistible. It was at this moment in particular that the close financial relationship between the Temple and the French crown, potentially of great benefit to the order in the past, now turned out to be a curse. Intimidation and torture were used to extort confessions out of the Templars who were seized in France (and there were other brethren imprisoned in other states with varying degrees of enthusiasm from one place to another); fifty-four were executed. De Molay confessed to his 'crimes' but later recanted. He was burned alive on an island in the Seine in Paris along with three other Templars. His end was wrapped in legend. In one account, he allegedly defiantly shouted at the last that both King Philip and Pope Clement V (who was in the king's pocket and had been formally responsible for the dissolution of the order)[16] should meet before God to answer for their own crimes within the year. He was executed on 18 March 1314, King Philip died on 29 November 1314 and the pope on 20 April 1314. These deaths may have been timely for the Hospitallers, as in 1312 moves had been launched against them with a view to their 'reform' too.[17] These moves now faded.

There is an intriguing late reference by the Templar of Tyre in his chronicle to the end of the Temple. Despite his suggestions of 'miserliness' concerning Jacques de Molay, he was clearly in a dilemma as to what to say about the death of the order with which he had been so closely associated. On the one hand, if he condemned the decision to dissolve the order, his own position may have been under threat; on the other, if he did not, then he may have felt himself to be morally compromised. In the end, he did what many might have done in such a situation – he equivocated, though in a way that makes clear enough what his true opinion was. Rather than summarise what he said, in this case a full rendition of his own words is more compelling:

> So they took him and cast him [de Molay] into the fire, and he was burnt. And if Almighty God, who knows and understands hidden things, knows that he and the others who were burned were innocent of those deeds of which they were accused, then they are martyrs before God; and if they received what they deserved, they have been punished – but I may truly say that, to all appearances, I knew them for good Christians and devout in their masses and in their lives, and especially my lord the master, Brother William of Beaujeu, who gave great and generous alms to many good people, both privately and openly, as anyone who cares to find out knows.[18]

There was one remarkable survival story concerning some of the Templars. Half a century after the fall of Acre, Ludolph of Suchem was on pilgrimage to the Holy Land when he met two elderly men on the shores of the Dead Sea. Something about them must have attracted his attention, for they fell into conversation. It transpired that the two old men had formerly been Templars and had fought at Acre. Since then they had made their home in the region, marrying local women and having families. They had decided to return to Europe to see out their twilight years, which they did, and they were received honourably despite the fall of the Temple.[19] Somewhere in this story is a Hollywood movie waiting to be made.

In the aftermath of the spectacular fall from grace of the Templars, other military orders benefitted from acquiring a portion of their wealth. The Hospitallers were particular beneficiaries.[20] But some of the smaller orders had been in trouble even before the fall of Acre. The Knights of St Thomas had been short of resources for a while;

Pope Alexander IV commented on this as far back as 1257. They had been forced to appeal for funds to Edward I in 1279 and there had even been talk of them merging with the Templars; talk which, fortunately for them, came to nothing. Although they managed to avoid being taken over, there was no escape from harsh economic reality. By 1330 their buildings in London were on the brink of ruin and the last Master known was recorded as being in Nicosia in 1360. Eventually, they became a charitable institution, adopting the rule of the Augustinians. The Order of the Knights, in its new monastic guise, was dissolved in 1538 as part of Henry VIII's great land grab, the Dissolution of the Monasteries.

The Last Ripples over the Sea

If a stone is tossed into the water, it will create ripples. However, the further away from the initial point of impact the ripple is, the less obvious it becomes until eventually it is imperceptible. History too has its 'ripple effects', of which crusading is a good example. The First Crusade was the initial point of impact, leading to strong follow-up expeditions in its immediate aftermath. The successful outcome had a powerful motivational effect and others were inspired to follow suit. By the thirteenth century, the ripples emanating from the initial success of the movement were becoming weaker in terms of motivating fresh groups of Crusaders, although Louis IX, a Crusader par excellence, was an exception in this respect. With each successive crusading failure, the motivational pull of Jerusalem and the Holy Land diminished. After the loss of Outremer, the ripples became much weaker, though they did not even then dissipate altogether. Papal appeals to launch new crusades to the east were launched in 1291, 1311–12 and 1333, but no major expedition followed.

There were several reasons for this. Pope Innocent III introduced a new and in some ways dangerous concept when he launched his *Ad Liberandam* principle at the Fourth Lateran Council of 1215. This preached the need to protect the Church from both internal and external enemies. It was a significant development in the evolution of crusading. It has been cogently argued that Innocent did not evolve new concepts through this pronouncement; rather, he codified principles that had already been enunciated in the previous century. However, it gave a legitimacy to a wider scope of crusading than had previously been the case, demonstrating a degree of political pragmatism that gives the papal name of 'Innocent' a rather ironic ring. Although the *Ad Liberandam* title (approximately translated as 'to free the Holy Land') might suggest that its main focus was on crusades to the Levant, in the margins discussions were ongoing to widen the concept of crusading. Innocent's successors, particularly Urban IV, took the principles expounded to new levels in what have been simplistically labelled 'political crusades' against secular enemies of the Papacy.[21] Actions spoke louder than words and the increasing diversion of crusades to areas outside the Holy Land led to an inevitable dilution of the importance of expeditions specifically to the Levant. This widening in scope meant that spiritual rewards previously only available in Outremer and a few other selected destinations such as Spain now became accessible much closer to home. Why then take the long and dangerous journey across the Mediterranean when the same benefits could be found with less effort, time and cost involved?[22]

It also devalued the principle of crusading and had negative motivational effects. The crusades against the Cathars in the south of France were brutal and understandably created a huge amount of resentment among those who suffered from them. The crusades launched against the Hohenstaufens were even less defensible as they were fought against fellow Catholics, albeit ones who stubbornly refused to accept papal pronouncements. The diversion of the Fourth Crusade to Constantinople in 1204, initially condemned by the papacy but soon after accepted and eventually embraced by it, was yet another example of an expedition launched against a non-Muslim enemy. At least those launched in the Baltic were largely against pagans; by the time of Pope Honorius III (1216–27) spiritual rewards for taking part in a crusade there were given equal status to those available for going to the Levant and during the fourteenth century crusades there became much more prominent than any discussions about launching a new expedition to the Eastern Mediterranean. The ever-widening scope of Crusader targets, accompanied by the increasingly *laissez faire* issuance of indulgences, fed a rising sense of disillusionment with respect to the crusading ideal, certainly as far as Outremer was concerned.

There were in addition underlying fissures within Christendom that the crusading movement could not ignore, or at least could not overcome. Whether the Genoese and Venetians were inspired by empathy to work together and rescue their fellow Christians from Acre, or whether instead it was the opportunity to turn a profit that motivated them, is debatable. Within a year of the fall of Acre the two city states were fighting each other again. The Templar of Tyre, who survived the catastrophe at Acre and continued to chronicle the course of events from his new base in Cyprus, regales us with tales of several clashes between the two. In one skirmish, a Templar onboard a Venetian ship, Brother William de la Tour, was killed by a crossbow bolt. A Venetian fleet raided the Genoese quarter in Limassol. Famagusta was abandoned by the Genoese and the Venetians then attacked the port of Ayas in Armenia, which had become more important with the loss of Acre. At Ayas they captured and ransomed a Genoese ship and caused considerable damage, forcing many of the Genoese there to hurriedly evacuate. In response, a Genoese fleet attacked and defeated the Venetians who had occupied Ayas.[23] When a unified response was needed, the city states continued their infighting as if nothing had happened. It appears that Christendom had learned nothing from the events that led up to the loss of Outremer, or perhaps more accurately it did not care to learn. As the German philosopher Georg Wilhelm Friedrich Hegel (1770–1831) famously wrote, 'We learn from history that we do not learn from history.'[24]

Such divisions were deplored by the papacy. Pope Celestine V, elected in July 1294 after a papal interregnum of two years, took the highly unusual step of abdicating five months and eight days later. Whilst he stated that he felt he was unsuited to the role and wished for a humbler life, he also listed as one of his reasons for abdicating 'the perverseness of the people'. There were occasional discussions concerning another crusade to Outremer that emerged from time to time thereafter. Pope Clement V discussed plans for such a scheme in 1305 and several years later received Mongol envoys who, it was hoped, would be able to bring about that long-awaited alliance between the two blocs. These optimistic pretensions came to nothing. Then in 1306 Clement held discussions with Jacques de Molay of the Templars and William de Villaret of the Hospitallers to come up with proposals of how a new crusade might be planned and executed. These again led to very little. With hindsight, it seems almost ridiculous that Charles II, the latest Angevin ruler, continued to insist that he was the rightful King of Jerusalem; and even more so that he subsequently negotiated with the rulers of Aragon to hand over his claim to them. It was as if the right to rule the most sacred realm in Christendom was a mere trinket to be handed over on a whim; a trinket which was no longer in

Christendom's hands. In the meantime, the Lusignan Kings continued to appoint Cypriot nobles to honorific posts concerning the Kingdom of Jerusalem even though their roles were now entirely symbolic.[25]

The reality was that Western Europe and its rulers were far too occupied with their own internal affairs to seriously consider another crusade. Edward I of England, a possible candidate as a leader for such an expedition, was often at odds with Philip IV of France (war broke out between them in 1298) and then was involved in what threatened to become a war seemingly without end in Scotland. Apart from anything else, Edward's campaigns in France, Wales and Scotland had not only tied up military resources, they were also crippling his overstretched treasury. It has been acutely observed of Edward that 'the crusade was always the next task but one, pushed into the future by domestic crises, but not forgotten'.[26] Philip was also caught up in a war with the Flemings (who were allied to the English) and his forces suffered a heavy defeat at Courtrai in 1302. Given these ongoing tensions in the West, a major expedition to the Levant was always a long shot. But this did not mean that the idea went away completely. There was a so-called 'Crusade of the Poor' in 1309 and many people also took the cross in France in 1313. Clearly, hopes of a new crusade did not die but they did not ultimately lead to any significant new expedition to the lost lands of Outremer.

In 1306, Antony Bek, Bishop of Durham, was given the by now ceremonial title of Patriarch of Jerusalem, the only Englishman ever to receive the honour. Just a year later, his King, Edward I, died. Edward always felt an attachment to the Holy Land and in one account it was even stated that after his death his heart should be cut out and sent to the East accompanied by eighty knights.[27] Yet Edward never got close to journeying back east. And despite the fact that crusades continued to be called, money to be raised and Crusaders to take the cross, no monarch from Western Europe stepped forward to take on the key leadership role. The political landscape was simply not right. So there would be no major expedition launched to try and retake Outremer, no heroic plans executed to recreate the lost Kingdom of Jerusalem. During the fourteenth century, there was often fairly easy access to Jerusalem for Christian pilgrims anyway, which also helped to take the heat out of the situation. Dominicans and Franciscans were allowed to set themselves up again in Palestine and the Muslim authorities gave them limited rights to oversee the Holy Sepulchre in Jerusalem.

The ongoing distractions in Italy were the priority for the papacy, and whilst this was a cause for complaint to some, particularly Franks and their Armenian allies living in the Levant, a string of popes found themselves faced with what they genuinely believed was a fight for political survival on the Italian peninsula. It was understandable from their perspective that what were their homelands would come first. Confronting huge challenges in Italy and also in what they could do in terms of sending practical help to the Levant, they could not meet both objectives. And despite many decades of trying to improve its position in Italy, by 1330 the policies employed by the papacy had resulted in failure. It may be true as some have suggested that the institution genuinely believed it could bring the fighting on the peninsula quickly to a successful conclusion and then focus all its attention on the Holy Land, but if it was so, this optimism was a deluded fantasy. Meanwhile, the papacy's opponents in Italy, such as the Ghibellines and Imperialists, were quick to use the news of serious losses in the Levant as propaganda sticks to beat several popes with. No less a figure than Dante, a man with Ghibelline affiliations, used the formidable weapon that was his quill to criticise various pontiffs for their inaction over Levantine crusades.[28]

This does not mean that all interventions from the West in Levantine affairs stopped after the fall of Acre, but they were irregular and often motivated by quite different non-crusading considerations. A good example was the capture of Smyrna (now Izmir) on the coast of the west of Turkey. This was taken by a combination of Venetian, Cypriot and papal troops in 1344. But despite the involvement of the latter, the main reason for the attack was commercial. Smyrna had become a thorn in the flesh as a base for Turkish pirates and the main reason for attacking it was to deny it to them and protect shipping.

The last attempt to mount a major crusading expedition to the Levant took place in 1336, but the fleet raised by Philip VI of France never left port. Political complications again got in the way; Edward III of England was warring with Philip over Gascony and the French king felt that he could not leave until a truce had been agreed. The expedition ended in farce when the ships put to sea and staged a mock battle in which sailors threw oranges at each other.[29] It was not just the papacy that was torn by competing priorities.

There were, it is true, occasional revivals of crusading interest concerning the Muslim Levant, but they did not often end in any meaningful action, and certainly not in any long-term sustainable results. It was not that there were no opportunities to generate a counter-attack, rather that for potential Crusader recruits spiritual benefits that had motivated them in the past, certainly those focused on peregrinations to Jerusalem, no longer had the same allure. In October 1365, Peter I, King of Cyprus, launched a raid on Alexandria. This was an example of a phenomenon which had become more popularly known as a *passagium particulare,* an expedition with limited objectives, as opposed to a *passagium generale,* a wider crusading expedition. Such a raid had always been a possibility, certainly since the Knights Hospitaller were established in a new military base on Rhodes in 1308. Peter had been actively drumming up support in Western Europe since 1362 and, although not all of it subsequently materialised (partly due to the rather protracted distraction of the Hundred Years War between England and France), a substantial force still made its way to Rhodes consisting of 165 ships, 10,000 men and 1,400 horses, more than enough to make a significant impact.

A very good example of 'fake news' worked wonderfully well. It was leaked that the fleet would be heading for Tripoli, an unofficial news bulletin that was entirely believed. When the fleet arrived off Alexandria it was completely unexpected and misidentified as a flotilla of merchant ships. Peter's plan was to capture the port and then exchange it for Jerusalem. The expedition got off to a spectacularly good start. Alexandria harbour was split into two sections, with the western one set aside for Muslim ships. The Crusader fleet moved into this and too late the Alexandrians realised to their horror what was happening. The defence was a shambles; the governor was away and his deputy had insufficient personnel to fight back. The Crusaders then launched an attack from the east as well. The defences were overwhelmed and although some street fighting was still needed, within forty-eight hours Alexandria was in Western hands. So far, so good.

But things soon began to go wrong. So thorough was the pillaging of Alexandria that most of the force wanted nothing more than to return home to spend their ill-gotten gains. Fires took hold of the city and key parts of its defences such as the gates were destroyed. Peter also realised that a relief army from Cairo was bound to be sent in urgent response to these events and his force was in a rapidly disintegrating position to fight it off. The relief army was soon nearby. This was the signal for many English and French participants in the attack to set sail with their booty. The remainder of the army was insufficient to resist the imminent counter-attack and therefore also had to leave. After an occupation of just six days, all the Crusaders had gone and all the Mamluk relieving force had to do was move in and retake possession. A glorious opportunity had been lost. It had been more a large-scale pirate raid than a crusade.

From time to time there would be a resurgence, albeit briefly, of Crusader interest in the East, but now the target location had moved closer to Europe. The seemingly unstoppable rise to power of the Ottomans touched a nerve and, when the West was not distracted elsewhere, led to a response. One notable example of this was when an expedition was sent to Bulgaria in 1396. As well as local forces, it included the flower of French chivalry. This substantial force met the Ottomans at Nicopolis. The Ottomans were methodical and well-coordinated, an eerie reminder of how the Mamluks had once been. The French fought as if they were taking part in some kind of giant tournament with the rules of chivalry paramount in their minds. The predictable result was utter carnage. In an action that was in some ways strangely resonant of Agincourt nineteen years later, the Crusader force was annihilated in part by Turkish archers firing from behind a line of stakes. Another expedition to Varna in Bulgaria in 1444 met with similarly disastrous results. There were also other enemies closer to home, such as the heretic Hussites who were the subject of Crusader expeditions in the fifteenth century. The papacy would soon find itself facing the greatest threat of all to the survival of Christendom, at least in its Roman Catholic form, but this time from within: the rise of Protestantism and the Reformation.

The idea of crusading to, and holding lands in, the Levant ultimately became an anachronism in the West. Where people did continue to refer back to those rapidly receding times it was in a semi-imaginary way in terms of a symbolic rather than a real connection with the past. Ripples of this nostalgic yearning for a lost legacy appear in some surprising ways. For example, in one of Venice's lesser-known churches (to non-Venetians at least), that of San Salvador near the Rialto, is the tomb of a Venetian queen. Venice did not have a monarch – the Doge was more like an elected-for-life president with limited powers and he was invariably male – but Caterina Cornaro/Corner was Queen of Cyprus. A Venetian by birth, she married into the Lusignan family on Cyprus. She soon found herself a widow but, very unusually for those days, then became queen regnant until forced to abdicate, ironically by her own state, Venice, in 1489. She lived the rest of her life back home in Venice and the surrounding Veneto region on the mainland. She died in 1510 and had a magnificent state funeral, though her sepulchre was not erected for another seventy years. There, shaded by a regal canopy beneath an enormous monument, lies her simple grave slab. On it is carved a memorial to Caterina Cornaro, Queen of Cyprus, Jerusalem and Armenia. In late sixteenth-century Venice, it was still deemed worthwhile to keep the flimsy pretence alive that both Jerusalem and Armenia mattered in a symbolic sense, even if they were by now phantom kingdoms. It was irrelevant that the rulers of Cyprus had not ruled in Jerusalem for three centuries or in Armenia for almost as long. Armenia had finally been overrun by the Mamluks in 1374, an event accompanied by horrific atrocities. Monks were ruthlessly slaughtered in their monasteries and though the bishops were allowed to live, their tongues were cut out so that they could no longer preach. It was difficult to argue with the conclusion that 'the kingdom had never fully recovered from the punishment inflicted on it by Baybars in 1266'. There had been a series of attacks on Armenia throughout the fourteenth century and it was a painful, drawn-out death. Its ultimate demise was made yet more certain by regular infighting within Armenia itself in a manner that eerily echoed what had happened in Outremer. Even as the kingdom wearily staggered towards the edge of an abyss, the papacy continued to insist that the Armenian church recognise Latin papal authority as the price for any help.[30] The last chance of a successful intervention from the West was therefore missed.

Outremer – Doomed to Fail?

As well as military tactics and grand strategy and the materiel of the parties, one of the decisive factors in war is often unity; unity of vision and of action. During the two centuries of crusading to the Levant, there were decisive alterations in this factor. At the outset, the First Crusade descended on the Muslim Levant at a time when it was preoccupied with its own factional infighting where local warlords sought to gain personal advantage over their opponents. There was at this stage no *jihad* spirit to cement the various factions in the Islamic East together. In contrast, whilst the Crusaders also had their own warlords striving for self-aggrandisement, there was enough of a common purpose often (but not always) to overcome the problems that this might otherwise have caused – thus the ultimate, seemingly miraculous, capture of the Holy City was assisted significantly by the fissures in the Muslim world. The 'unity factor' was at this time working in favour of the Crusaders.

Over time, there was a swing in the other direction. Gradually, the Muslim Levant started to reunite. This is not to say that no tensions remained, for they assuredly did. But several charismatic leaders, notably Nur ad-Din and Saladin, managed to provide a common vision which was strong enough to lead to a certain degree of coherence in strategy. In contrast, crusading went the other way. Following the success of the First Crusade, subsequent major missions to Outremer were almost invariably characterised by disunity and dissent. This is certainly true of the so-called Second, Third, Fourth and Fifth Crusades. It was only under the leadership of Louis IX that a sense of unity under a common leader re-emerged and that particular expedition went awry for other reasons.

In later years, Muslims powers showed a degree of unity and single-mindedness in their campaigns against Outremer that the West could not match. This is not to say that Islam was consistently united; on many occasions that sense of unity was stretched to breaking point and beyond. However, the rules of the game changed with Baybars. Not only was he militarily outstanding; he was also politically astute and able to take advantage of antipathy towards the Christian Franks to whip up religious fervour against them. Even he had to deal with the occasional attempted coup and assassination plot, and indeed in his case in the end he may have succumbed to one, but on the whole he managed to maintain a degree of unity that was generally sufficient for the task in hand. None of his successors were of comparable stature and competence, but his legacy was strong enough for them to finish the job that he had started.

In stark contrast, the Christian response to the emerging Islamic threat against Outremer was erratic. Occasional major expeditions punctured periods of inactivity and distraction elsewhere closer to home. There were far too many tensions in Europe to focus minds on the Levant. Western naval supremacy continued but it was not used to significantly affect the war in the Levant. A blockade against Egyptian ports, for example, could have created massive disruption to the Mamluks, but such Nelsonian tactics were anathema to commercial city states like Pisa, Genoa and Venice who were more worried about the bottom line.

Nor was it only political distractions in Europe that impeded any persistent sense of momentum in crusading to the Levant. Crusades were enormously costly. Both Richard I of England and Louis IX of France had spent vast sums of money on such expeditions; and other less-remembered forays had also been very expensive. As the thirteenth century progressed, there were definite signs of diminishing returns for the exorbitant financial resources committed to such expeditions. Ironically the only major thirteenth-century expedition to the East that could in any way be termed a 'success' was the Fourth Crusade, which resulted in the conquest of Constantinople and which never got close to fighting a non-Christian enemy. The two major crusades to Egypt had both ended in abject catastrophe. According to very straightforward cost-benefit analyses, further expeditions would present far too high a degree of risk to be considered attractive propositions. As economists would say, the risk-reward ratio of such large-scale initiatives no longer made sense. Particularly after the failure of Louis IX's crusades the odds against achieving a successful – and even more importantly a sustainable – outcome in terms of strengthening the diminished Frankish territories in Outremer had simply become too great. This initially concerned those who were at the top of the feudal ladder, the kings, who would have to raise large amounts of finance from the countries that they ruled; much of this would be raised through compulsory taxes that could create political difficulties for the monarchs levying them. And the cost of taxation plus additional voluntary personal contributions also put a strain on those lower down the scale for whom crusading was a major expense at an individual level. As a general rule, few crusade participants became richer rather than poorer as a result of their involvement.[31] It is little wonder that the passionate enthusiasm that had characterised earlier crusades was turning irrevocably into apathy and cynicism as far as the Levant was concerned. Even the Italian maritime city states, who certainly profited from their involvement in shipping Crusaders to the Levant, were by now more worried that such expeditions would interfere negatively with their lucrative trade with Muslim powers in the region.

By the end, Acre and Outremer were largely anachronisms. It is arguable that it might have been better if the whole façade had come crashing down after the Hattin campaign of 1187. In the event, it was only the disunity of Islam after the death of Saladin that bought the Kingdom of Jerusalem breathing space. However, once Baybars had managed to reunite Egypt and Syria more or less successfully, Outremer was clearly living on borrowed time. Once the Muslim world made a coherent, coordinated effort against Acre the end was a formality. With little prospect of meaningful reinforcements to take up the largely tarnished crusading cause then there was no hope of Outremer surviving. Given the short supply lines of the Mamluk armies and their access to much larger pools of manpower, the moment for salvation had long passed.

There was however a brief interlude when there was some cause for optimism. In 1229 Frederick II, that much-maligned figure, negotiated the return of Jerusalem, albeit with caveats attached to the deal that left the city largely unprotected and to some extent shared with the Muslims who held on to some key religious sites there. By the end of the following decade further lands had been restored. It was the Mongol incursions that disturbed the delicate equilibrium. Their intervention ultimately threw everything out of balance. They disrupted Frankish politics and created internal divisions in Outremer. Their apocalyptic threat inadvertently built a powerful Mamluk dynasty in Cairo that forged a degree of unity in the Muslim Levant that had been absent for decades. They also created false hopes of alliance in Western minds that were never likely to reach fruition. These factors together combined to bring about the end of Outremer.

Yet despite this sense of inevitability, the despair over the loss of Acre is clear in the words of the Templar of Tyre, who took to poetry to express his feelings, of which the following extract from what is a rather long threnody gives a flavour:

When Acre was despoiled and all Syria laid waste,
The world longed for some good thing in the midst of great evils.
Men who were already evil now became even more vile,
And in my view, no one cared about anyone else.
For rancour, discord and hatred have put down roots between men;
Love has fled from them and Envy is sown amongst them.

He saw the loss of Acre, and Outremer generally, as a watershed moment. He lamented the loss of morality and human feeling that he witnessed so often now; perhaps this is an early example of a man suffering from what we would call 'survivor guilt'. Men were more interested in getting drunk and offering false words of flattery rather than sincere advice to their fellows. Arrogance was misconstrued for valour and socially inferior men were considered superior. The 'Lord Money', Mammon, now ruled supreme over all things; when God comes to judge the world, he opines that 'shit will be more useful than money'. These read like the despairing words of a bitter man, lamenting the passing of a Golden Age that had never actually existed. He bemoans the passing of the social order of the nobility, always a highly suspect concept, in a way that suggests that the changing of the social guard is more important to him than the loss of Outremer. With such dated and aloof paradigms, perhaps it is little wonder that the Templars met such a spectacularly destructive end, unloved, envied and resented by many. Whilst we should be grateful for the work of the unnamed chronicler whose words illuminate the fall of Acre and the events that led up to it so eloquently, he does sometimes come across as being an anachronism, a defender of old and misguided values in a rapidly changing world.[32]

The concluding words on the end of Outremer and the fall of Acre should perhaps go to a man who was on the winning side, Abu'l Fida:

> With these conquests all the lands of the coast were fully restored to the Muslims, a result undreamed of. Thus were the *Franj*, who had once nearly conquered Damascus, Egypt and many other lands expelled from all Syria and the coastal zones. God grant that they never set foot there again!

These were assuredly words from the heart, but the Muslim triumph also came at a great cost. The devastation wrought to the littoral of the Levant put economic development back for centuries. Psychologically, the region went into its shell as if trying to hide itself from the outside world. As is the case with many wars, in the end there were few ultimate winners. The fear that one day the Franks might come back continued to haunt Muslim nightmares; indeed, in recent times such an idea has been rekindled (or at least recycled) by prominent figures such as Osama bin Laden. The ghosts of the Crusaders lived on in the Levant; in some ways they still do.

Notes

1 In the Beginning

1. In Folda 18
2. Blaides and Paik 2
3. See France 1
4. See Edgington in France 21. It should be noted that not only the participation of the Pisans is unclear: other accounts mention forty or ninety rather than seventy ships.
5. 'Franks' was the generic name for the settlers who set up home in the Crusader states: once vows had been fulfilled in reaching Jerusalem they were no longer strictly speaking Crusaders. The term 'Crusader' in any event did not come into widespread use until the late twelfth century.
6. Barber 64
7. Ibid 115
8. Jones 192
9. The term 'Latin' is often used as an alternative name for the Franks.
10. One is reminded of the famous quote of the eighteenth-century philosopher Voltaire that the Holy Roman Empire was neither Holy, nor Roman, nor an Empire. Whilst the imperial element of his quote was not appropriate in the twelfth century, the other elements had great relevance even then.
11. Bronstein 19-20
12. In Barber 130
13. Tyerman, *God's War*, 739
14. E.g. Runciman *Crusades* 161. The historian admits to his brilliance but also says that 'of all the great Crusaders the Emperor Frederick II is the most disappointing'.
15. How *de facto* this was varied to an extent over time. A twelfth-century Queen of Jerusalem, Melisende (1105-1161), for some of her reign acted effectively as a co-ruler with her husband Fulk of Anjou whereas in other cases the Queen seems to have had less actual power.
16. Rothelin Continuation 37
17. The Ibelins went back a number of generations in Outremer and were a good

example of how settlers could put down long-term roots in the kingdom. The founder of what effectively became an Outremer dynasty of Ibelins, Barisan, is known to have been Consta–le of Jaffa in 1115.

18. Jones 260. The Templars had strong traditional links with France and during the course of the thirteenth century these would become even more pronounced.
19. Barber 134-135. Some Muslim chroniclers also wrote that the Templars were involved in such a nefarious plot.
20. Ibid 142. Barber suggests that this was part of a wider internal dispute that did not just involve the two major military orders.

2 A New Equilibrium

1. See Waterson 38
2. In Thorau 17
3. Waterson 42
4. Thorau 27
5. Morgan 18
6. Thorau 28
7. Daud, the emir of Karak, had attacked Jerusalem in 1239, allegedly because steps had been taken by the Franks to start rebuilding the walls there in contravention of the truce terms. See Folda 97.
8. The Hospitaller Gerald of Newcastle quoted by the contemporary chronicler Matthew Paris: see Jones 278.
9. Folda 65
10. In Hillenbrand 306
11. Barber 147
12. Joinville 299-300
13. Jotischky 231
14. Bronstein 24
15. Mayer 260
16. Ibid 262
17. In Maalouf 237
18. Ibid 238–40
19. Barber 148
20. Mayer 263
21. In Gabrieli p285
22. The term 'victory disease' has been used to describe the hubris that followed on from initial Japanese successes in the Second World War and subsequently led to the Japanese army overextending itself in the Pacific. As Louis' actions centuries earlier show, this was by no means a new phenomenon.
23. Thorau 39
24. Joinville 265
25. Ibid 265
26. In Folda 103
27. Barber 186
28. Joinville 306
29. Jackson *Mongols* 98-99

30. Mayer 262. The cost of the whole crusade to Louis' treasury came to 1.3 million *livres tournois,* five years' revenue.
31. Runciman *Sicilian Vespers* 16
32. Housley 92
33. Ibid 128
34. Mayer 272

3 Rising Powers
1. Mayer 268
2. Juvaini 21
3. Jackson *Mongols*, 41, argues that by 1241 the Mongols were actually outnumbered by Turkic elements who had been absorbed into their expanded kingdom. The name of one group, the Tatars, a broad-brush designation given in the West to tribesmen on the Russian steppes, eventually became virtually interchangeable with that of 'Mongol'.
4. Not everyone is convinced that Ogadai's death was the reason for the halt in the Mongol advance. Other suggestions include the not unreasonable one that the Mongol invasion only had limited aims to start with, which had by then been achieved. See Jackson 74.
5. Strictly speaking, this should be called Lesser Armenia, a kingdom which was based around the borders of modern south-east Turkey. It is also sometimes referred to as Cilicia, the name of a Roman province in the region. 'Armenia' will be used hereafter as a convenient abbreviation. The kingdom had only been in existence since the eleventh century though a predecessor, Greater Armenia, had existed in the east of modern Turkey, around Lake Van and Mount Ararat (where Noah's Ark came to rest after the Flood), for several millennia. See Ghazarian 32.
6. Jackson *Mongols* 315
7. Juvaini 26
8. Jackson *Mongols* 175. See also Stewart, 2018
9. Amitai-Preiss 20
10. In Maalouf 235
11. Abu'l-Faraj in Lewis p81
12. Carpini 108 also reports seeing ambassadors from the caliph at the court of his predecessor Güyüg.
13. For the numbers, see Amitai-Preiss 15
14. William of Rubruck 89-90
15. Juvaini 621
16. Ibid 724
17. *Marco Polo* 71-73
18. In Waterson 67
19. Thorau 62
20. *Marco Polo* 53. Joinville, 310, Louis IX's chronicler, says that the King received word of the fall of Baghdad whilst he was in Sidon. He is plainly incorrect as Louis had returned to France in 1254. Joinville however tells a similar story concerning the end of the caliph: as his work came after that of Marco Polo, it is possible that there is some plagiarism going on here. The

Templar of Tyre, *TT* 149, has a variation on this theme, saying that molten gold was poured down the caliph's gullet.

21. Jackson EHR 481
22. Lewis p84
23. Stewart, 2018
24. Jackson *Mongols* 21
25. More recent historians have also sometimes been seduced by the idea. René goes so far as to call Hūlegū's expedition 'a Nestorian campaign'. See Jackson EHR 482
26. William of Rubruck 38
27. Joinville 283
28. Stewart, 2018. Several modern commentators have tentatively identified him as the Mongol general Kitbughā and the other two figures as Bohemond VI of Antioch and King Het'um of Armenia – see Folda 121. The many caveats in the main body of the text allude to a good deal of uncertainty concerning its origin.
29. Mayer 267
30. William of Rubruck 56, 74
31. Jackson *Mongols* 60
32. *Marco Polo* 96
33. Jackson *Mongols* 92
34. Carpini 34
35. Ibid 69
36. Jackson *Mongols* 314
37. Ibid *Mongols* 256
38. William of Rubruck 46
39. Jackson *Mongols* 70, William of Rubruck 66 and 90. The latter tells us that Guillame and the bishop's nephew were probably taken captive in Belgrade, which was at the time held by the Hungarians. There is some debate about whether this occupation of the city ever took place but if it did it was probably in 1241–2.
40. Jackson *Mongols* 274-278
41. Jones 301
42. Jackson *Mongols* 60
43. Ibid 114
44. Joinville 288
45. See Bronstein 31. He may well have heard the news personally from the Master of the Order of St Thomas on a visit to St Albans, Matthew's home.
46. Jackson *Mongols* 104-105
47. Latham in the Introduction to *Marco Polo* 11
48. Jackson EHR 488, quoting the contemporary work of Matthew Paris
49. Ibid 494

4 The Turning of the Tide

1. Runciman *Crusades...* 255
2. TT 34
3. In a closing reference in his chronicle, he refers to William as 'my lord the master'. TT 181

4. *Marco Polo* 49
5. Jackson EHR 490
6. Jackson *Mongols* 178. Not everyone is convinced by the explanation of insufficient pasture for the Mongols' horses as a reason for retreating. See Amitai-Preiss 28-29
7. Thorau 67
8. TT 35. Some modern scholars are sceptical of these accounts as they are not mentioned by Muslim chroniclers who, one assumes, would have made much of them if they had actually happened. See Stewart, 2018.
9. Jackson EHR 490
10. Amitai-Preiss 36
11. Thorau 69
12. Stewart, 2018
13. Jackson EHR 492. Amitai-Preiss suggests a figure of only around 10,000 to 12,000 men.
14. Amitai-Preiss 41
15. This is one version of Kitbughā's end as given by Rashid al-Din. However, some feel that this is a drama manufactured by chroniclers and that it was more likely that Kitbughā was killed in the fighting. See Jackson 118 and Amitai-Preiss 41.
16. Again, there is not unanimity on this, showing how confused and potentially confusing accounts on the battle are. Amitai-Preiss 43 suggests that there was no second battle at Baysān.
17. Thorau 78
18. Amitai-Preiss 205
19. *Marco Polo* 97
20. The title *Ilkhan* is believed to mean 'subordinate khan'. See Jackson *Mongols* 127. However, an alternative suggestion which has recently gained some traction is that it may be based on the Turkic *elkhan* which merely means 'ruler' – see Amitai-Preiss 14
21. Thorau 123
22. Jackson EHR 482 suggests that the Mamluk triumphs in 1260 led to 'a far greater threat to the Frankish enclaves on the coast'.
23. Thorau 80
24. Ibid 81-82
25. Jackson EHR 508
26. Waterson 93
27. See Stewart, 2018. Whilst not every historian accepts the presence of Bohemond at Damascus, there are a number that do, based on the available evidence. I think it is likely that he was indeed there.
28. Bohemond was Het'um's son-in-law, reflecting currently good relations between two states that had in the past had their differences. See Stewart, 2018. Whilst by now Antioch and Armenia were on good terms, at the turn of the twelfth century there was often tension between them.
29. Joinville 303
30. Jackson EHR 506
31. TT 36
32. Ibid 57

33. Jackson *Mongols* 123
34. Thorau 143, Edbury *John of Ibelin...* 97
35. Amitai 66

5 Acre and the Crusader States in the Mid-thirteenth Century

1. Jones 195
2. Jotischky 190-191
3. Favreau-Lilie 222
4. Joinville 291
5. In Folda 26
6. Rubin in France 90
7. Edbury *Kingdom of Cyprus...* 84
8. Jotischky 151-152
9. Jacoby *Everyday Life ...* 95
10. Folda 112
11. Jotischky 149
12. Ibid 153-154
13. Jackson *Mongols* 22
14. Riley-Smith *Hospitallers...* 22
15. Ibid 25
16. Jones 35
17. Barber 3
18. Precise datings are unclear. William of Tyre says they were founded in 1118 but Barber 9 prefers a date between January and September 1120.
19. Barber 13
20. Jones 53
21. Ibid 54
22. Ibid 56
23. Ibid 63
24. An interesting survival from the time are some of the floor tiles from their hospital at Burton Lazars, Leicestershire, England which are on display in the British Museum.
25. This numbering system moves straight from the Third Crusade (1189–92) to the Fourth Crusade, which conquered Constantinople in 1204.
26. Barber 70
27. Ibid 60
28. Ibid 2
29. Jones 226
30. Amitai-Preiss 108
31. Jackson *Mongols* 165
32. Amitai-Preiss 107
33. Jackson *Mongols* 182. See also Juvaini 39
34. Jackson *Mongols* 176
35. Ibid 186
36. Amitai-Preiss 56
37. Ibid 66
38. Waterson 86

6 Baybars the Annihilator

1. Thorau 103-105
2. Amitai-Preiss 71, Waterson 113-114
3. For a detailed and very interesting exposition with more detail than the summary included here see Waterson Chapter 6.
4. In Thorau 147
5. See Folda 61-62. The remains are powerful evidence of a multicultural artistic approach with a mixture of elements that owe something to Romanesque French influences but also to Levantine, even Islamic, traits.
6. Bronstein 35
7. TT 40
8. Thorau 148
9. Bronstein 37
10. Al-Bīra and al-Rahba were the two most significant fortresses tasked with protecting this strategically crucial frontier. They guarded fords, acted as forward-warning stations and were responsible for absorbing the first shock of Mongol attacks. Connected up to the carrier-pigeon network and the *bārid* they were perfectly integrated into the Mamluk defensive barrier and some regarded them as 'the lock of Syria'. See Amitai-Preiss 202.
11. Amitai, 62
12. In Waterson 81
13. Thorau 160
14. Amitai 67
15. Ibid 68
16. Joinville 306
17. Amitai 71
18. A *bailli* was a royal official with significant judicial, financial and military powers. The modern English word bailiff has its origins in *bailli*.
19. TT 44. Footnote 4 has an interesting discussion on the many comets that appear to have been visible in the 1260s.
20. Amitai 76
21. Ibid 78
22. Amitai-Preiss 73-74
23. Thorau 151
24. *Marco Polo* 46
25. Barber 165
26. Bronstein 22
27. See Thorau 168
28. Jackson *Mongols* 94
29. TT 51
30. The Latinised version of his Armenian name, Levon.
31. Barber 168
32. TT 55

7 Of Princes and Kings

1. TT 59
2. Amitai-Preiss 231

3. Kennedy 138-141
4. See e.g. Mayer 278
5. TT, 59, suggests that 17,000 were killed and 100,000 captured. Such figures should be treated with caution but suggest that the killing, whilst undoubtedly on a terrible scale, was not totally uncontrolled.
6. Thorau 192
7. Barber 266-267
8. In Waterson 126
9. Housley 133
10. TT 59
11. In Bronstein 40
12. Ibid 42
13. Edbury *Kingdom of Cyprus...* 93
14. See Baldwin
15. Ibid
16. Waterson 138
17. Bronstein 144
18. Thorau 202
19. Baldwin 6
20. TT 62
21. Ibid 63-66

8 The End of Baybars

1. Bronstein 43
2. A number of these lion symbols survive in various places. Some of them show the lion Baybars crushing a rat beneath its paws, such as that on the bridge at Jindas in Israel.
3. In Barber 205
4. Thorau 205
5. Kennedy 67-68
6. Prestwich 75
7. The aftermath of Evesham continued to reverberate for years across Europe. Two surviving sons of Simon de Montfort, Gui and Simon, murdered a supporter of Edward's, Henry of Almain, in a church in Viterbo, Italy. Edward despatched several missions to the Continent for the next decade in an attempt to bring the men to justice. The incident caused men to shudder, including Dante who referred to Gui in his *Inferno* as standing outside the seventh circle of Hell, up to his neck in blood. Gui served in the ranks of those supporting Charles of Anjou and as the Montforts had a long history of involvement and influence in Outremer, they also play a part in our story. See Ambler 332-333.
8. Edward was devastated at news of her death in 1290. Twelve memorial crosses were erected at each overnight stop where her bier paused on its journey back to London from Nottinghamshire where she died. Probably the most famous of them is Charing Cross in the city, though the monument that now stands there is not original.
9. Prestwich 71 argues that it was unlikely that it was as many as the 1,000 men that the chronicler Walter of Guisborough suggested.

10. Prestwich 76
11. TT 68
12. Though not everybody concurs that this was a Nizari assassin in action; he may for example have been sent by the emir of Ramlah. See Prestwich 78.
13. Stories of Eleanor's actions do not appear in contemporary accounts but were added to the story much later on. See Thorau, 244, footnote 13. Eleanor gave birth to a daughter, Joan, whilst she was in Acre.
14. Prestwich 66
15. Latham in the Introduction to *Marco Polo* 16-17
16. Jackson *Mongols* 175
17. See Amitai-Preiss Chapter 9 in particular
18. Waterson 102-103
19. TT 70
20. Waterson 167
21. For more detail on the Elbistan campaign see Amitai-Preiss 168-178. The contemporary commentator Bar Hebraeus wrote of 5,000 Mongols and 2,000 of their Georgian allies dead, whilst other accounts say that Baybars subsequently ordered a body count which numbered the enemy dead at 6,770.
22. The Pervaneh's full name was Mu'in al-Din Sulayman ibn Muhadhdhab al-Din Ali al-Daylami.
23. Thorau 240-243
24. Mayer 284

9 *The Civil War of Christendom*
1. At least, according to the account of Giambattista Ramussio in a printed edition of Polo's book in 1553. See Latham in the Introduction to *Marco Polo* 16
2. Housley 107
3. Tyerman *God's War* 815
4. See Jotischky 244-245
5. Further letters from Armenia to Edward followed on five occasions between 1291 and 1307. By then Outremer had fallen and Armenia was in the front line of the Mamluk advance. See Jackson 174.
6. Maxwell-Stuart 119
7. Thorau 4
8. TT 71-72
9. Ibid 72-73. Balian's death was bizarre. His head was caught in his cuirass when he tried to remove his armour to escape more rapidly. His nose was bleeding at the time and it is possible that he drowned in his own blood – an unpleasant and strange demise.
10. In fact, the Pope never sanctioned the transfer of claim. The papacy never recognised the legitimacy of Maria's claim in the first place, so there was in its eyes none to transfer. See footnote 7, TT 74.
11. Mayer 284
12. This was probably an exaggeration. Amitai-Preiss 194 suggests a figure of around half this number. It is of course not impossible that the 'deserter' had been planted to pass on 'fake news'.

13. TT 78. The battle of Homs and the campaign that led up to it is expertly covered in Amitai-Preiss Chapter 8. See also Waterson 179-181.
14. In Amitai-Preiss 202
15. Ibid 233
16. Jotischky 197
17. Housley 31
18. The term 'Greece' was applied to the Byzantine territories in Europe and was not just restricted to the modern boundaries of the country we now know by that name.
19. TT 82
20. Ibid 83. Edbury *Kingdom of Cyprus...* 98 however quotes a figure of 150,000 bezants. A saracenate bezant was a gold coin issued in Tyre, closely resembling a Muslim coin of the time.
21. Housley 21
22. Ibid 164
23. Ibid 167
24. Ibid 174

10 Towards the Endgame

1. Siberry 1985 gives useful background to this.
2. In Gabrieli p337
3. TT 86
4. Ibid 88. The text in the Templar's chronicle stops abruptly here and possibly some of it has been lost. However, the writer's statement that the Pisans suffered great hurt from the disclosure of this information gives a very strong impression that the Genoese used it to intercept their convoy and deprive it of its valuable cargo.
5. Ibid 91
6. ibid 94
7. Ibid 98
8. Ibid 99
9. Barber 176
10. TT 99
11. Ibid 99, footnote 8
12. See Chevedden which discusses extensively the mechanics of such siege engines.
13. TT 101
14. Folda 142
15. In Jotischky 247
16. Housley 134
17. *Chronicle of Lanercost* 61-62

11 The Pretext

1. In Waterson 182-183
2. Jotischky 257
3. Though this should not be overplayed. It has been argued that the Holy Land continued to provide the primary focus for the Order even in the latter

days of Outremer. See paper by Shlomo Lotan ...*Burzenland*... See also France 71

4. Jackson *Mongols* 169-170
5. Folda 143
6. Ibid 143-144
7. Barber 124
8. Lotan *The 'Other'*...
9. TT 102
10. Ibid 103
11. Ibid 104 and footnote 3 especially. There are divergent opinions on Burchard's ultimate destination with suggestions that he might actually have taken a position with the Hospitallers in Switzerland.
12. Ibid 105
13. It has been pointed out that the Templar's account appears to be in error here as some of those incarcerated were released several decades later. See Crowley 110.

12 Opening Exchanges

1. See Bronstein 13-14
2. Favreau-Lilie in France 170. It is unfortunate that only extracts of what sounds like a valuable document have as yet been published.
3. Crowley 129
4. Jacoby *Refugees...* 59
5. Waterson 106
6. Chevedden 252
7. Ibid 271, Fig. 6
8. Crowley 146
9. In Waterson 107
10. Ibid 108. This claim is probably on the high side. It has been suggested that Arabic sources claiming there were ninety-two machines may result from a common transcription error where 'nine' is mis-transcribed for 'seven' and therefore the accurate number is probably 72. It was still the highest number ever deployed by the Mamluk army. See Chevedden 257.
11. Ibid 248
12. Crowley 144
13. Jacoby *Everyday Life...* 79. This is an excellent and detailed paper on the evolution of Acre in the thirteenth century.
14. Crowley 153
15. Ibid 154
16. *Chronicle of Lanercost* 79-80
17. For more detail, see Edbury *Kingdom of Cyprus ...* Chapter 5
18. Ibid ... 93
19. Ibid... 99
20. Waterson 194

13 *The Last Stand*

1. See Boas and Melloni, Chapter 4 in France, for details of the excavations.
2. *Excidium Acconis* 88-89
3. TT 111
4. These words have been set to music by the modern composer Karl Jenkins in his *Armed Man – A Mass for Peace.*
5. Barber 241
6. Jacoby *Refugees...*61
7. Favreau-Lilie 211. There is evidence that some larger contemporary vessels could take as many as 2,000 passengers.
8. Accounts are contradictory on when Henry left Acre; some have him leaving several days earlier.
9. The Genoese subsequently claimed that he escaped on one of their ships. This is widely considered to be wishful thinking on their part. In any event, this myth (such as it probably was) did not emerge until several centuries later. See Favreau-Lilie in France 168.
10. TT 114
11. Shagrir in France 162, Footnote 63
12. *Chronicle of Lanercost* 80
13. The term 'lein' is rather vague but is generally applied to a small ship, sometimes but not always a galley.
14. Jackson *Mongols* 315
15. See Favreau-Lilie in France 176
16. Ibid 215
17. Jacoby *Refugees...*55
18. Ibid 57
19. Ibid 58
20. Favreau-Lilie 212
21. Edbury *Kingdom of Cyprus...*101
22. Jacoby *Refugees...*60
23. Ibid 61
24. Ibid
25. Camlet was a woven fabric, possibly originally made from camel hair but later from silk or other fine materials.
26. Jacoby *Refugees...*64
27. Favreau-Lilie 225
28. TT 119
29. Edbury *Kingdom of Cyprus...*109
30. Barber 199-200
31. Riley-Smith *Hospitallers...*55
32. Housley 19
33. Ibid 45
34. Jackson *Mongols* 330
35. The term 'burgess' broadly refers to someone of importance inside the city but not a member of the nobility. This was someone of a reasonably high social

class, as evidenced by links between the word and 'bourgeois'. Maybe 'affluent middle class' would be a suitable simplified description.

36. The Templar of Tyre mentions just women whilst the *Excidio Urbis Acconis* mentions both women and boys, as do a number of Muslim sources. See *TT* 117, F/N 1. It is unusual to find such unanimity among potentially contradictory sources, so perhaps the latter details are more likely than not to be accurate.
37. See *Independent* 29 October 2019: 'Knights Templar secret tunnels "leading to treasure trove" discovered in Israel'.
38. Gabrieli 346
39. Bartlett *Richard the Lionheart* 194
40. France 9. The Kings of Cyprus continued to be crowned as Kings of Jerusalem even though it was no longer in their possession.
41. Hurlburt 73
42. Joinville 318
43. Edbury *Kingdom of Cyprus…*103
44. See Connell in France 143
45. Ibid 142-143
46. See Shagrir, Chapter 9 in France. As an earlier example of the use of Jeremiah as a role model when writing up commentaries on great disasters to hit the Christian world, chroniclers had turned to him when referring to Viking attacks. Jeremiah 1-14. 'From the north an evil will spread out upon all the inhabitants of the land' – fitted the bill perfectly.
47. When the Mongols in Persia converted to Islam in 1295, his position became a dangerous one. He left Baghdad disguised as a camel-driver. It is good to note that he survived this ordeal and arrived back in Florence in around 1300, where he lived on until around 1320.
48. *Letters on the Fall of Acre* in Tolan xiii
49. Hurlburt 212
50. Crowley 204
51. TT 130 and F/N 1: until the fourteenth century two oarsmen per bench was the norm. Zaccaria's innovative use of three per bench, *treseul* as it was known, therefore gave him an unexpected advantage and caught the Muslim fleet off guard.

14 The Reckoning

1. Acre remained in a ruinous state until the seventeenth century; see France 4. That said, in the mid-fourteenth century Ludolph of Suchem stated that whilst the place was undoubtedly wrecked, the ruins were still substantial; see France 72-73.
2. Edbury *Kingdom of Cyprus…*110
3. The name 'Amalric' is sometimes shown as 'Amaury'.
4. Jackson *Mongols* 310 discusses a number of cases where diversions were needed because of internecine warfare between competing Mongol factions.
5. Ibid 181
6. Edbury *Kingdom of Cyprus…*104-105
7. Waterson 212

8. Ibid 192
9. Now called Malbork in Poland, and allegedly the largest castle by area in the world according to Wikipedia.
10. See Lotan *Burzenland...*
11. Barber 230-231
12. TT 171-172
13. Most famously referred to in Dan Brown's *Da Vinci Code* (published in 2003) but some of the underlying ideas were written of long before that in *The Holy Blood and the Holy Grail,* Lincoln, Baigent and Leigh, first published 1982.
14. See Favreau-Lilie 227
15. Tyerman *England and the Crusades* 240
16. The Order was officially dissolved at the Council of Vienne on 22 March 1312.
17. Barber 309
18. TT 181. This is in the last few pages of his chronicle that have survived, though sadly there were clearly other pages after it which have now been lost.
19. Barber 1
20. In Cyprus for example, where most Templar property was transferred to them. See Edbury *Kingdom of Cyprus...*78.
21. One of the bases of Housley's excellent *Italian Crusades* is that the phrase is actively misleading as popes of the era did not distinguish between political and spiritual aims but saw them as being part of one and the same.
22. For the crusading innovations of Innocent see Jotischky 170-181.
23. Venice, Genoa and Pisa had all forged links with Ayas in the thirteenth century. See Ghazarian 126.
24. The latter pages of *The Templar of Tyre* record in some detail a string of confrontations between the Genoese and the Venetians in the latter years of the thirteenth century.
25. Edbury *Kingdom of Cyprus...* 108
26. Tyerman *England and the Crusades* 231. Edward's foremost modern biographer, Michael Prestwich, states that '[his] reign ended with the financial system in a state of near collapse.' (535). Funds for crusading were therefore in short supply.
27. Prestwich 333. Edward's resilient rival, Robert I (Robert Bruce) of Scotland, gave similar instructions and his heart was in fact despatched with that intention, though it did not arrive in the East as its escort was attacked and defeated in Spain. The heart was returned to Scotland.
28. The issues around the papacy's challenge in coping with these two rival priorities at the same time are explored in depth in Housley Chapter 4.
29. Jotischky 253
30. See Ghazarian 64 and 157-159
31. See Blaydes and Paik for a more detailed discussion of crusade finance.
32. For the poem, see TT 123-129

Maps

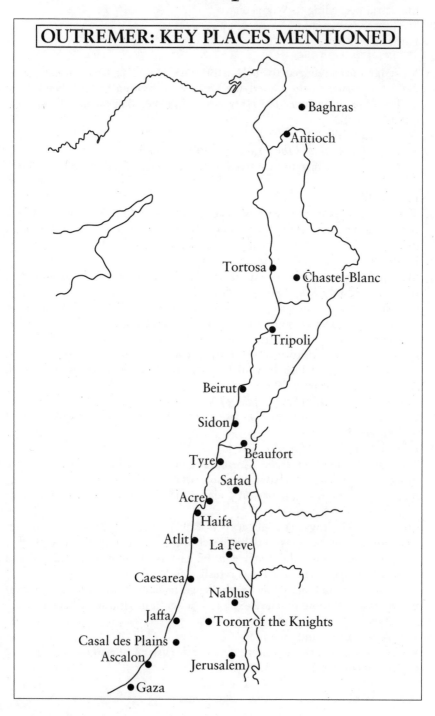

OUTREMER: KEY PLACES MENTIONED

Baghras

Antioch

Tortosa

Chastel-Blanc

Tripoli

Beirut

Sidon

Béaufort

Tyre

Safad

Acre

Haifa

Atlit

La Feve

Caesarea

Nablus

Jaffa

Toron of the Knights

Casal des Plains

Ascalon

Jerusalem

Gaza

THE LITTORAL OF OUTREMER

- Sis
- Ayas
- Antioch
- St. Simeon
- *R. Orontes*
- Latakia
- CYPRUS
- Famagusta
- Tortosa
- Chastel-Blanc
- Hama
- Tripoli
- Crac des Chevaliers
- Homs
- MEDITERRANEAN
- Beirut
- Sidon
- Damascus
- Tyre
- Acre
- THE SEA OF GALILEE
- Haifa
- Caesarea
- R. Jordan
- Jaffa
- Arsuf
- Ascalon
- Gaza
- THE DEAD SEA

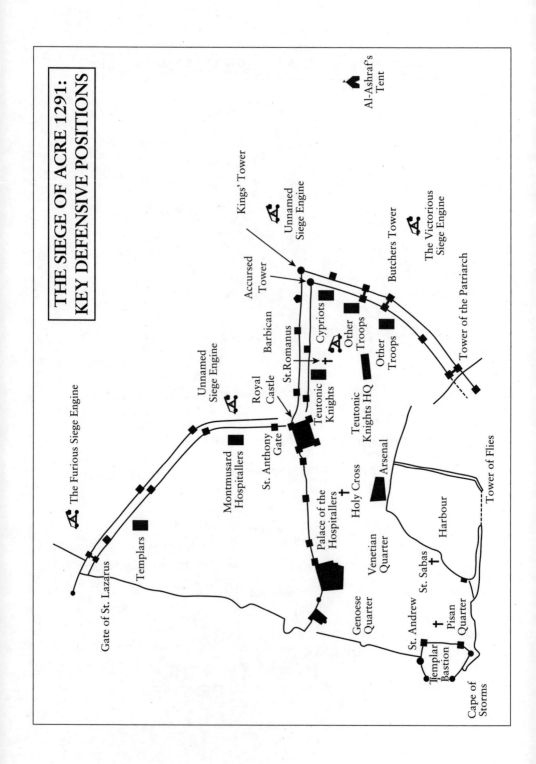

THE SIEGE OF ACRE 1291:
KEY DEFENSIVE POSITIONS

Al-Ashraf's Tent

Kings' Tower

Unnamed Siege Engine

Butchers Tower

The Victorious Siege Engine

Accursed Tower

Barbican

St. Romanus

Cypriots

Other Troops

Other Troops

Tower of the Patriarch

Unnamed Siege Engine

Royal Castle

Teutonic Knights

Teutonic Knights HQ

The Furious Siege Engine

Montmusard Hospitallers

St. Anthony Gate

Arsenal

Holy Cross

Palace of the Hospitallers

Tower of Flies

Templars

Venetian Quarter

Harbour

Gate of St. Lazarus

Genoese Quarter

St. Sabas

St. Andrew

Pisan Quarter

Templar Bastion

Cape of Storms

Bibliography

Primary Sources

Boyle, J. A.: *Genghis Khan – The History of the World Conqueror by Ata-Malik Juvaini,* Manchester University Press, 1997

Crawford, Paul F (translated): *The Templar of Tyre* [TT], Farnham, 2003

Fink, Harold S (edited): *A History of the Expedition to Jerusalem, 1095-1127 by Fulcher of Chartres,* University of Tennessee, 1973 edition

Gabrieli, Francesco: *Arab Historians of the Crusades,* Berkeley and Los Angeles, 1984 printing

Herbert, Sir Maxwell (translated): *The Chronicle of Lanercost,* Glasgow, 1913

Hildinger, Erik (translated); *The Story of the Mongols whom we Call the Tartars by Friar Giovanni Di Plano Carpini,* Brandon Publishing Company, Boston, 1996

Huygens, R. B.C.: *The Fall of Acre 1291* (incl. *Excidium Acconis),* Brepols, 2004

Latham, R. E: *Marco Polo – The Travels,* Penguin, London etc., 1958

Rockhill, William Woodville: *William of Rubruck's Account of the Mongols,* reprinted in Maryland, USA by Rana Sand, 2005 [originally published 1900]

Shaw, M. R. B. (translated): *Villehardouin and de Joinville – Chronicles of the Crusades,* Penguin, London etc., 1963

Shirley, Janet (translated): *Crusader Syria in the thirteenth Century – The Rothelin Continuation of the History of William of Tyre with part of the Eracles or Acre Text* [Rothelin Continuation], Farnham and Burlington, 1999

Stewart, Aubrey (translated): *Jacques de Vitry – A History of Jerusalem,* Palestine Pilgrims' Society, 1896

Secondary Sources

Ambler, Sophie Thérèse: *The Song of Simon de Montfort – England's First Revolutionary and the Death of Chivalry,* London, 2019

Amitai, Reuven: 'The Conquest of Arsūf by Baybars: Political and Military Aspects', in *Mamluk Studies Review,* 2005

Amitai-Preiss, Reuven: *Mongols and Mamluks – The Mamluk-Ilkhanid War 1260-1281,* Cambridge University Press, 2004

Asbridge, Thomas: *The Crusades – The War for the Holy Land,* London and Sydney, 2010

Baldwin, Philip B: 'Charles of Anjou, Pope Gregory X and the crown of Jerusalem', *Journal of Medieval History,* 2012

Barber, Malcolm: *The New Knighthood – A History of the Order of the Temple,* Cambridge University Press, 1998 edition

Bartlett, W. B.: *Islam's War Against the Crusaders,* Stroud, Gloucestershire, 2008

Bartlett, W. B.: *The Last Crusade – The Seventh Crusade & the Final Battle for the Holy Land,* Stroud, Gloucestershire, 2007

Bartlett, W. B.: *The Road to Armageddon – The Last Years of the Crusader Kingdom of Jerusalem,* Stroud, Gloucestershire, 2007

Bartlett, W. B.: *Richard the Lionheart – The Crusader King of England,* Stroud, Gloucestershire, 2019

Blaydes, Lisa and Paik, Christopher: *The Impact of Holy Land Crusades on State Formation: War Mobilization, Trade Development and Political Development in Medieval Europe,* July 2015

Boase, T. S. R: *Kingdoms and Strongholds of The Crusaders,* London, 1971

Bronstein, Judith: *The Hospitallers and the Holy Land – Financing the Latin East, 1187-1274,* Suffolk, 2005

Burman, Edward: *Supremely Abominable Crimes – The Trial of the Knights Templar,* London, 1994

Chambers, James: *The Devil's Horsemen – The Mongol Invasion of Europe,* London, 1988

Chevedden, Paul E.: 'Black Camels and Blazing Bolts – The Bolt-Projecting Trebuchet in the Mamluk Army', *Mamluk Studies Review,* 2004

Crowley, Roger: *Accursed Tower – The Crusaders' Last Battle for the Holy Land,* Yale University Press, 2019

Edbury, Peter W.: *John of Ibelin and the Kingdom of Jerusalem,* Woodbridge and Rochester NY, 1997

Edbury, Peter W.: *The Kingdom of Cyprus and the Crusades 1191-1374,* Cambridge University Press, 1991

Eychenne, Mathieu: *The Citadel of Cairo,* Farid Atiya Press, Giza, 2010

Favreau-Lilie, Marie-Luise: *The Military Orders and the escape of the Christian population from the Holy Land in 1291,* Journal of Medieval History, 19:3, 201-227

Folda, Jaroslav: *Crusader Art – The Art of the Crusaders in the Holy Land,* Aldershot and Burlington, 2008

France, John (edited): *Acre and Its Falls – Studies in the History of a Crusader City,* Leiden/Boston, 2018

Ghazarian, Jacob G.: *The Armenian Kingdom in Cilicia During the Crusades – The Integration of Cilician Armenians with the Latins 1080-1393,* London and New York, 2000

Hanska, Jussi: *Strategies of Sanity and Survival: Religious Responses to Natural Disasters in the Middle Ages,* SF Folkloristika, 2002

Harari, Yuval Noah: *Special Operations in the Age of Chivalry, 1100-1550,* Suffolk, 2007

Hillenbrand, Carole: *The Crusades – Islamic Perspectives*, Edinburgh, 2006

Holt, P. M.: *The Age of the Crusades – The Near East from the Eleventh Century to 1517*, London and New York, 2013

Housley, Norman: *The Italian Crusades – The Papal-Angevin Alliance and the Crusades Against Christian Lay Powers, 1254-1343*, Oxford, 1999 edition

Hurlburt, Holly S.: *Daughter of Venice – Caterina Corner, Queen of Cyprus and Women of the Renaissance*, Yale University Press, 2015

Irwin, Robert: *The Middle East in the Middle Ages: The Early Mamluk Sultanate, 1250-1382*, Kent, 1986

Jackson, Peter: 'The Crisis in the Holy Land in 1260', *English Historical Review* [EHR], No. CCCLXXVI, July 1980

Jackson, Peter: *The Mongols and the West*, Harlow, 2005

Jacoby, David: *Everyday Life in Frankish Acre*, www.academia.edu

Jacoby, David: *Refugees from Acre in Famagusta Around 1300*, www.academia.edu

Jones, Dan: *The Templars*, London, 2017

Jones, Terry and Ereira, Alan: *Crusades*, Penguin, 1996

Jotischky, Andrew: *Crusading and the Crusader States*, London etc., 2004

Kennedy, Hugh: *Crusader Castles*, Cambridge University Press, 1994

Lewis, Bernard: *Islam from the Prophet Mohammad to the Capture of Constantinople*, New York etc., 1974

Lotan, Shlomo: 'Between the Latin Kingdom of Jerusalem and Burzenland in Medieval Hungary – The Teutonic Military Order Status and Rule in the Poles of Christianity', *The Middle Ages and the Crusades*, January–June 2010

Lotan, Shlomo: 'Querimonia desolacionis terre sancte – The Fall of Acre and the Holy Land in 1291 as an emotional element in the Tradition of the Teutonic Order', *Mirabilia* 15 (2012/2)

Lotan, Shlomo: *The 'Other' in the Latin Kingdom of Jerusalem. The Crusaders and their Varying Images of the Muslims in the Eastern Mediterranean Basin*, www.academia.edu

Maalouf, Amin: *The Crusades through Arab Eyes*, London, 2006 edition

Marshall, Christopher: *Warfare in the Latin East, 1192-1291*, Cambridge University Press, 1996

Maxwell-Stuart, P.G: *Chronicles of the Popes*, London, 1997

Mayer, Hans Eberhard: *The Crusades*, Oxford University Press, 1990

Morton, Nicholas: *The Teutonic Knights in the Holy Land, 1190-1291*, Suffolk, 2017

Nicolle, David: *Acre 1291 – Bloody sunset of the Crusader states*, Oxford and New York, 2005

Nicolle, David: *Crusader Warfare*, London and New York, 2007 (2 volumes)

Nicolle, David: *Teutonic Knight – 1190-1561*, Oxford, 2007

Oldenbourg, Zoe: *The Crusades*, New York, 1966

Prawer, Joshua: *Crusader Institutions*, Oxford, 1998

Prawer, Joshua: *The Crusaders' Kingdom – European Colonialism in the Middle Ages*, London, 2001 edition

Prestwich, Michael: *Edward I,* Yale University Press, 1997

Richard, Jean: *The Crusades – c1071-c1291,* Cambridge University Press, 2001

Riley-Smith: *Hospitallers – The History of the Order of St John,* London and Rio Grande, 1999

Riley-Smith: *The Crusades – A Short History,* London and New York, 1987

Runciman, Steven: *A History of the Crusades Volume III: The Kingdom of Acre,* Penguin Books, UK, 2016 edition

Runciman, Steven: *The Sicilian Vespers – A History of the Mediterranean World in the Later Thirteenth Century,* Cambridge University Press, 1998 edition

Shagrir, Iris: 'The Fall of Acre as a Spiritual Crisis: The Letters of Riccoldo of Monte Croce', in *Revue Belge de Philologie et d'Histoire,* 2012

Siberry, E.: *Criticism of Crusading 1095-1274,* Oxford, 1985

Stewart, Angus: *Reframing the Mongols in 1260: The Armenians, the Mongols and the Magi,* Journal of the Royal Asiatic Society, Volume 28, Issue 1, January 2018

Thorau, Peter (translated by P. M. Holt): *The Lion of Egypt – Sultan Baybars I and the Near East in the thirteenth Century,* London and New York, 1992

Tolan, John V.: *Saracens: Islam in the European Imagination,* New York, 2002

Tyerman, Christopher: *England and the Crusades 1095-1588,* University of Chicago Press, 1988

Tyerman, Christopher: *God's War,* Penguin, 2006

Urban, William: *The Teutonic Knights – A Military History,* Barnsley, 2003

Waterson, James: *The Knights of Islam – The Wars of the Mamluks,* Greenhill, London, 2007

Index